Exam Ref AZ-30 Microsoft Azure Architect Design Certification and Beyond

Design secure and reliable solutions for the real world in Microsoft Azure

Brett Hargreaves

BIRMINGHAM—MUMBAI

Exam Ref AZ-304 Microsoft Azure Architect Design Certification and Beyond

Group Product Manager: Wilson D'souza

Publishing Product Manager: Rahul Nair

Senior Editor: Shazeen Iqbal

Content Development Editor: Romy Dias

Technical Editor: Nithik Cheruvakodan

Copy Editor: Safis Editing

Project Coordinator: Shagun Saini

Proofreader: Safis Editing

Indexer: Manju Arasan

Production Designer: Shankar Kalbhor

First published: June 2021
Production reference: 1230621

Published by Packt Publishing Ltd.
Livery Place
35 Livery Street
Birmingham
B3 2PB, UK.
ISBN 978-1-80056-693-4

www.packt.com

To the doctors, nurses, public health officials, and first responders who are protecting us from COVID-19.

Contributors

About the author

Based in the UK, **Brett Hargreaves** is a lead Azure consultant who has worked for some of the world's biggest companies for over 25 years, helping them design and build cutting-edge solutions. With a career spanning infrastructure, development, consulting, and architecture, he has been involved in projects covering the entire solution stack, including hardware, virtualization, databases, storage, software development, and the cloud.

He loves passing on his knowledge to others through books, blogging, and his online training courses, which have over 20,000 students (and counting!).

I want to thank my amazing wife, Cathy, for giving me the space and support I've needed to write this book, even while the COVID-19 global pandemic was raging around us. I'd also like to thank the many experienced professionals who I work with daily and who continually provide exciting challenges that help deepen my knowledge. Finally, I would like to thank the Packt team for giving me this opportunity to put my knowledge down on paper.

About the reviewers

Sandeep Soni is an Azure Solutions Architect with expertise in designing, developing, and architecting Azure solutions. He has had experience with all the services offered on the Azure cloud, including PaaS, IaaS, storage, virtual networking, and so on. He offers expertise across the whole spectrum of software technology. As a Microsoft Certified Trainer with 25 years of IT experience, he is adept at technology training, including corporate training, live training, and online webinars. He has trained over 100,000 individuals all over the world and delivered over 200 corporate training events across India and abroad in Microsoft Azure, covering development, infrastructure, security, architecture, Azure DevOps, orchestration microservices using Kubernetes and Azure Service Fabric, C#, .NET Core, ASP.NET, and ASP.NET Core, to name a few.

> *I would like to thank my family for their continued support and encouragement in everything that I do, and the team of Deccansoft, who manage background work while I am delivering training, earning certifications, and making other contributions to the world of IT.*

Ricardo Cabral is a licensed computer engineer with several Microsoft certifications, and is also a **Microsoft Certified Trainer (MCT)**. Having worked in both administration and development roles, with several years' experience in IT management, development, and projects, he now works as an IT consultant and trainer. In his spare time, he actively participates in, volunteers, and speaks at technical community meetings.

Table of Contents

Section 2:
Identity and Security

3

Understanding User Authentication

4
Managing User Authorization

5
Ensuring Platform Governance

6
Building Application Security

Section 3:
Infrastructure and Storage Components

7

Designing Compute Solutions

8

Network Connectivity and Security

9
Exploring Storage Solutions

10
Migrating Workloads to Azure

Section 4: Applications and Databases

11

Comparing Application Components

12

Creating Scalable and Secure Databases

13
Options for Data Integration

14
High Availability and Redundancy Concepts

Section 5:
Operations and Monitoring

15
Designing for Logging and Monitoring

16
Developing Business Continuity

17
Scripted Deployments and DevOps Automation

Section 6:
Beyond the Exam

18
Engaging with Real-World Customers

19
Enterprise Design Considerations

Preface

Exam AZ-304 tests an architect's ability to design scalable, reliable, and secure solutions in Azure based on customer requirements. *Exam Ref AZ-304 Microsoft Azure Architect Design Certification and Beyond* offers complete, up-to-date coverage of Exam AZ-304 so you can take it with confidence, pass the first time, and prepare for real-world challenges.

A common question that is asked about the Azure architecture exams is what is the difference between Exam AZ-303 and Exam AZ-304? AZ-303 tests your ability to create and configure resources in Azure, whereas AZ-304 is about choosing and recommending the correct service for your needs.

This means much of the exam is scenario-based and you are expected to select the correct component for a given use case.

This book will help you investigate the need for good architectural practices and how they address common concerns in cloud-based solutions. You will work through the cloud stack from identity and access, through to Infrastructure as a Service (IaaS), data, applications, and serverless (PaaS). You will then look at operations including monitoring, resilience, scalability, and disaster recovery. Finally, we look at how these fit into the real world, with full scenario-based examples throughout the book.

By the end of this book, you'll have covered everything you need to pass the AZ-304 certification exams and have a handy, on-the-job desktop reference guide.

Who this book is for

This book is for Azure Solution Architects who advise stakeholders and help translate business requirements into secure, scalable, and reliable solutions. Junior architects wanting to advance their skills in the cloud will also benefit from this book. Experience of the Azure platform in general is expected and a general understanding of development patterns would be advantageous.

What this book covers

Chapter 1, Architecture for the Cloud, explores what architecture means in the cloud and how it has evolved over the years.

Chapter 2, Principles of Modern Architecture, offers a high-level view of the areas we need to consider when architecting solutions, including security, resilience, performance, and operations.

Chapter 3, Understanding User Authentication, explores the differences between authentication and authorization, followed by an architectural view of Active Directory and using Conditional Access.

Chapter 4, Managing User Authorization, teaches you how to control user authorization using management groups, roles, privileged identity management, and identity protection.

Chapter 5, Ensuring Platform Governance, helps you to keep platforms compliant with corporate and legal policies through the use of tagging, Azure Blueprints, and Azure Policy.

Chapter 6, Building Application Security, shows you how to enhance system security using Azure Key Vault, security principles, and managed identities.

Chapter 7, Designing Compute Solutions, covers the different types of compute in Azure, how to automate VM management, and a look at containerization and Kubernetes.

Chapter 8, Network Connectivity and Security, explores the options for networking in Azure, including IP addressing, DNS, connecting networks, traffic routing, and securing resources with network and application security groups.

Chapter 9, Exploring Storage Solutions, teaches you about the different storage options in Azure, when to use each one, and how to secure them.

Chapter 10, Migrating Workloads to Azure, shows how to assess your on-premises infrastructure, and the options for migrating VMs and databases.

Chapter 11, Comparing Application Components, explores the architectural considerations of using native application components such as Web Apps, Event Grid, Event Hubs, Storage Queues, Service Bus, and API Gateway.

Chapter 12, Creating Scalable and Secure Databases, looks at different database platforms including Azure SQL and Azure Cosmos DB, comparing the use cases for each.

Chapter 13, Options for Data Integration, helps us understand why we use dataflows, and the different technologies available to build data analytics pipelines, including Data Lake Storage, Data Factory, Synapse Analytics, and Data Bricks.

Chapter 14, High Availability and Redundancy Concepts, teaches you how to architect redundancy into your solutions, looking at VM availability options, storage replication, Azure SQL and Cosmos DB.

Chapter 15, Designing for Logging and Monitoring, looks at how to ensure your solutions have adequate and usable monitoring in place for operations, security, compliance, cost management, and reporting.

Chapter 16, Developing Business Continuity, shows you how to design solutions that can accommodate complete regional failures using Azure Backup and recovery solutions.

Chapter 17, Scripted Deployments and DevOps Automation, explores the different options for deploying solutions in an automated and scripted manner using ARM templates, Azure PowerShell, the Azure CLI, and Azure DevOps.

Chapter 18, Engaging with Real-World Customers, offers an exploration of design considerations that goes beyond Exam AZ-304, including how we can best work with customers to help gather and map requirements and respond to feedback.

Chapter 19, Enterprise Design Considerations, continues the beyond-the-exam theme, looking at some example requirements different organizations may have and how best to address them.

To get the most out of this book

An Azure subscription and an Azure DevOps account are required to complete this book, along with the following software/tools:

Software/hardware covered in the book	OS requirements
PowerShell	Windows, macOS, and Linux (any)
Azure CLI	Windows (note that although there is a version that runs on macOS, the examples in this book will not work on it)
Visual Studio	Windows, macOS, and Linux (any)
Visual Studio Code	Windows, macOS, and Linux (any)

If you are using the digital version of this book, we advise you to type the code yourself or access the code via the GitHub repository (link available in the next section). Doing so will help you avoid any potential errors related to the copying and pasting of code.

Download the example code files

You can download the example code files for this book from GitHub at `https://github.com/PacktPublishing/Exam-Ref-AZ-304-Microsoft-Azure-Architect-Design-Certification-and-Beyond`. In case there's an update to the code, it will be updated on the existing GitHub repository.

We also have other code bundles from our rich catalog of books and videos available at `https://github.com/PacktPublishing/`. Check them out!

Download the color images

We also provide a PDF file that has color images of the screenshots/diagrams used in this book. You can download it here: `http://www.packtpub.com/sites/default/files/downloads/9781800566934_ColorImages.pdf`.

Conventions used

There are a number of text conventions used throughout this book.

`Code in text`: Indicates code words in text, database table names, folder names, filenames, file extensions, pathnames, dummy URLs, user input, and Twitter handles. Here is an example: "If you wish to merge tags using an update command, you can use `Update-AzTag -Operation Merge`."

A block of code is set as follows:

```
{
    "$schema": "https://schema.management.azure.com/
schemas/2019-04-01/deploymentTemplate.json#",
    "contentVersion": "1.0.0.0",
    "resources": [
        {
```

When we wish to draw your attention to a particular part of a code block, the relevant lines or items are set in bold:

```
        "location": "eastus",
    "tags": {
                "Dept": "Finance",
                "CostCenter": "001"
            },
        "sku": {
```

Any command-line input or output is written as follows:

```
$resource = Get-AzResource -Name 'packtstoragewithtags'
-ResourceGroup 'packtstorageresourcegroup'
```

Bold: Indicates a new term, an important word, or words that you see onscreen. For example, words in menus or dialog boxes appear in the text like this. Here is an example: "If you need to modify or add additional tags to an existing resource, this can be performed by clicking on the **change** option next to **Tags**."

> **Tips or important notes**
> Appear like this.

Get in touch

Feedback from our readers is always welcome.

General feedback: If you have questions about any aspect of this book, mention the book title in the subject of your message and email us at customercare@packtpub.com.

Errata: Although we have taken every care to ensure the accuracy of our content, mistakes do happen. If you have found a mistake in this book, we would be grateful if you would report this to us. Please visit www.packtpub.com/support/errata, selecting your book, clicking on the Errata Submission Form link, and entering the details.

Piracy: If you come across any illegal copies of our works in any form on the Internet, we would be grateful if you would provide us with the location address or website name. Please contact us at copyright@packt.com with a link to the material.

If you are interested in becoming an author: If there is a topic that you have expertise in and you are interested in either writing or contributing to a book, please visit authors.packtpub.com.

Reviews

Please leave a review. Once you have read and used this book, why not leave a review on the site that you purchased it from? Potential readers can then see and use your unbiased opinion to make purchase decisions, we at Packt can understand what you think about our products, and our authors can see your feedback on their book. Thank you!

For more information about Packt, please visit `packt.com`.

Section 1: Exploring Modern Architecture

Aspiring architects can often misunderstand what architecture is. This section discusses how the advent of the cloud has forced architecture to evolve and sets the context for why we must learn what is covered in this book.

The following chapters will be covered under this section:

- *Chapter 1, Architecture for the Cloud*
- *Chapter 2, Principles of Modern Architecture*

1
Architecture for the Cloud

Before we examine the detailed knowledge that the **AZ-304 exam** tests, this chapter discusses some general principles of **solution architecture** and how the advent of **cloud computing** has changed the role of the architect. As applications have moved toward ever more sophisticated constructs, the role of the architect has, in turn, become more critical to ensure security, reliability, and scalability.

It is useful to agree on what architecture means today, how we arrived here, and what we need to achieve when documenting requirements and producing designs.

In this chapter, we're going to cover the following main topics:

- Introducing architecture
- Exploring the transition from monolithic to microservices
- Migrating to the cloud from on-premises
- Understanding infrastructure and platform services
- Moving from waterfall to Agile projects

Introducing architecture

It may seem a strange question to ask in a book about solution architecture—after all, it could be assumed that if you are reading this book, then you already know the answer to that question.

In my experience, many architects I have worked with all have a very different view of what architecture is or, to be more precise, what falls into the realms of architecture and what falls into other workstreams such as engineering or operational support.

These differing views usually depend on an architect's background. Infrastructure engineers concern themselves with the more physical aspects such as servers, networking, and storage. Software developers see solutions in terms of communication layers, interactions, and lower-level data schemas. Finally, former business analysts are naturally more focused on operations, processes, and support tiers.

For me, as someone involved across disciplines, architecture is about all these aspects, and we need to realize that a solution's components aren't just technical—they also cover business, operations, and security.

Some would argue that actually, these would typically be broken down into infrastructure, application, or business architecture, with **enterprise architecture** sitting over the top of all three, providing strategic direction. In a more traditional, on-premises world, this indeed makes sense; however, as business has embraced and adopted cloud, how software is designed, built, and deployed has changed radically.

Where once there was a clear line between all these fields, today they are all treated the same. Every part of a solution's components, from servers to code, must be created and implemented as part of a single set of tasks.

Software is no longer shaped by hardware; quite the opposite—the supporting systems that run code are now smaller, more agile, and more dynamic.

With so much change, cloud architects must now comprehend the entire stack, from storage to networking, code patterns to project management, and everything in between.

Let's now look at how systems are transitioned from monolithic to microservices.

Exploring the transition from monolithic to microservices

I've often felt that it helps to understand what has led us to where we are in terms of what we're trying to achieve—that is, well-designed solutions that provide business value and meet all technical and non-technical requirements.

When we architect a system, we must consider many aspects—security, resilience, performance, and more. But why do we need to think of these? At some point, something will go wrong, and therefore we must accommodate that eventuality in our designs.

For this reason, I want to go through a brief history of how technology has changed over the years, how it has affected system design, what new issues have arisen, and—most importantly—how it has changed the role of an IT architect.

We will start in the 1960s when big businesses began to leverage computers to bring efficiencies to their operating models.

Mainframe computing

Older IT systems were monolithic. The first business systems consisted of a large mainframe computer that users interacted with through dumb terminals—simple screens and keyboards with no processing power of their own.

The software that ran on them was often built similarly—they were often unwieldy chunks of code. There is a particularly famous photograph of the **National Aeronautics and Space Administration (NASA)** computer scientist Margaret Hamilton standing by a stack of printed code that is as tall as she is—this was the code that ran the **Apollo Guidance Computer (AGC)**.

In these systems, the biggest concern was computing resources, and therefore architecture was about managing these resources efficiently. Security was primarily performed by a single user database contained within this monolithic system. While the internet did exist in a primitive way, external communications and, therefore, the security around them didn't come into play. In other words, as the entire solution was essentially one big computer, there was a natural security boundary.

If we examine the following diagram, we can see that in many ways, the role of an architect dealt with fewer moving parts than today, and many of today's complexities, such as security, didn't exist because so much was intrinsic to the mainframe itself:

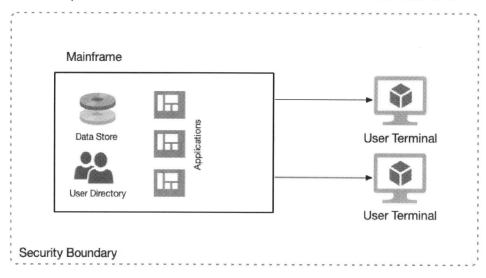

Figure 1.1 – Mainframe computing

Mainframe computing slowly gave way to personal computing, so next, we will look at how the PC revolution changed systems, and therefore design requirements.

Personal computing

The PC era brought about a business computing model in which you had lower-powered servers that delivered one or two duties—for example, a file server, a print server, or an internal email server.

PCs now connected to these servers over a local network and performed much of the processing themselves.

Early on, each of these servers might have had a user database to control access. However, this was very quickly addressed. The notion of a directory server quickly became the norm so that now we still have a single user database, as in the days of the mainframe; however, the information in that database must control access to services running on other servers.

Security had now become more complex as the resources were distributed, but there was still a naturally secure boundary—that of the local network.

Software also started to become more modular in that individual programs were written to run on single servers that performed discrete tasks; however, these servers and programs might have needed to communicate with each other.

The following diagram shows a typical server-based system whereby individual servers provide discrete services, but all within a corporate network:

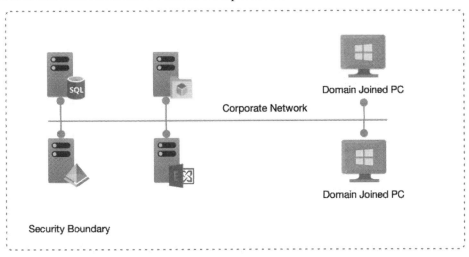

Figure 1.2 – The personal computing era

Decentralizing applications into individual components running on their own servers enabled a new type of software architecture to emerge—that of **N-tier architecture**. N-tier architecture is a paradigm whereby the first tier would be the user interface, and the second tier the database. Each was run on a separate server and was responsible for providing those specific services.

As systems developed, additional tiers were added—for example, in a three-tier application the database moved to the third tier, and the middle tier encapsulated business logic—for example, performing calculations, or providing a façade over the database layer, which in turn made the software easier to update and expand.

As PCs effectively brought about a divergence in hardware and software design, so too did the role of an architect also split. It now became more common to see architects who specialized in hardware and networking, with responsibilities for communication protocols and role-based security, and software architects who were more concerned with development patterns, data models, and user interfaces.

The lower-cost entry for PCs also vastly expanded their use; now, smaller businesses could start to leverage technologies. Greater adoption led to greater innovation—and one such advancement was to make more efficient use of hardware—through the use of virtualization.

Virtualization

As the software that ran on servers started to become more complex and take on more diverse tasks, it began to become clear that having a server that ran internal emails during the day but was unused in the evening and at the weekend was not very efficient.

Conversely, a backup or report-building server might only be used in the evening and not during the day.

One solution to this problem was virtualization, whereby multiple servers—even those with a different underlying operating system—could be run on the same physical hardware. The key was that physical resources such as **random-access memory** (**RAM**) and compute could be dynamically reassigned to the virtual servers running on them.

So, in the preceding example, more resources would be given to the email server during core hours, but would then be reduced and given to backup and reporting servers outside of core hours.

Virtualization also enabled better resilience as the software was no longer tied to hardware. It could move across physical servers in response to an underlying problem such as a power cut or a hardware failure. However, to truly leverage this, the software needed to accommodate it and automatically recover if a move caused a momentary communications failure.

From an architectural perspective, the usual issues remained the same—we still used a single user database directory; virtual servers needed to be able to communicate; and we still had the physically secure boundary of a network.

Virtualization technologies presented different capabilities to design around—centrally shared disks rather than dedicated disks communicating over an internal data bus; faster and more efficient communications between physical servers; the ability to detect and respond to a physical server failing, and moving its resources to another physical server that has capacity.

In the following diagram, we see that discrete servers such as databases, file services, and email servers run as separate virtual services, but now they share hardware. However, from a networking point of view, and arguably a software and security point of view, nothing has changed. A large role of the virtualization layer is to abstract away the underlying complexity so that the operating systems and applications they run are entirely unaware:

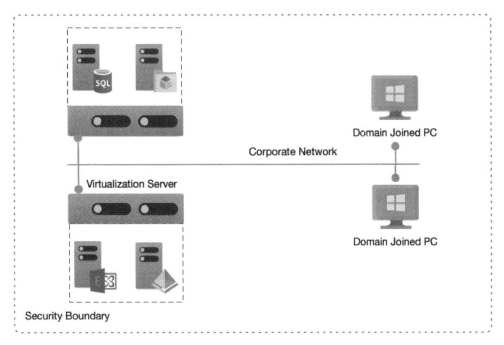

Figure 1.3 – Virtualization of servers

We will now look at web apps, mobile apps, and **application programming interfaces (APIs)**.

Web apps, mobile apps, and APIs

At around the same time, virtualization was starting to grow, and the internet began to mature beyond an academic and military tool. Static, informational websites built purely in HTML gave way to database-driven dynamic content that enabled small start-ups to sell on a worldwide platform with minimal infrastructure.

Websites started to become ever more complex, and slowly the developer community began to realize that full-blown applications could be run as **web apps** within a browser window, rather than having to control and deploy software directly to a user's PC.

Processing requirements now moved to the backend server—dynamic web pages were generated on the fly by the web server, with the user's PC only rendering the HTML.

With all this reliance on the backend, those designing applications had to take into account how to react to failures automatically. The virtualization layer, and the software running on top, had to be able to respond to issues in a way that made the user completely unaware of them.

Architects had to design solutions to be able to cope with an unknown number of users that may vary over time, coming from different countries. Web farms helped spread the load across multiple servers, but this in itself meant a new way of maintaining state or remembering what a user was doing from one page request to the next, keeping in mind that they might be running on a different server from one request to the next.

As the mobile world exploded, more and more mobile apps needed a way of using a centralized data store—one that could be accessed over the internet. Thus, a new type of web app, the API app, started serving raw data as RESTful services (where **REST** stands for **REpresentational State Transfer**) using formats such as **Extensible Markup Language (XML)** or **JavaScript Object Notation (JSON)**.

Information

A **RESTful service** is an architectural pattern that uses web services to expose data that other systems can then consume. **REST** allows systems to interchange data in a pre-defined way. As opposed to an application that communicates directly with a database using database-specific commands and connection types, RESTful services use HTTP/HTTPS with standard methods (GET, POST, DELETE, and so on). This allows the underlying data source to be independent of the actual implementation—in other words, the consuming application does not need to know what the source database is, and in fact could be changed without the need to update the consumer.

Eventually, hosted web sites also started using these APIs, with JavaScript-based frameworks to provide a more fluid experience to users. Ironically, this moved the compute requirements back to the user's PC.

Now, architects have to consider both the capabilities of a backend server and the potential power of a user's device—be it a phone, tablet, laptop, or desktop.

Security now starts to become increasingly problematic for many different reasons.

The first-generation apps mainly used form-based authentication backed by the same database running the app, which worked well for applications such as shopping sites. But as web applications started to serve businesses, users had to remember multiple logins and passwords for all the different systems they use.

As web applications became more popular—being used by corporates, small businesses, and retail customers—ensuring security became equally more difficult. There was no longer a natural internal barrier—systems needed to be accessible from anywhere. As apps themselves needed to be able to communicate to their respective backend APIs, or even APIs from other businesses providing complementary services, it was no longer just users we had to secure, but additional services too.

Having multiple user databases will no longer do the job, and therefore new security mechanisms must be designed and built. **OpenID**, **OAuth2.0**, **SAML** (which stands for **Security Assertion Markup Language**), and others have been created to address these needs; however, each has its own nuances, and each needs to be considered when architecting solutions. The wrong decision no longer means it won't work; it could mean a user's data being exposed, which in turn leads to massive reputational and financial risk.

From an architectural point of view, solutions are more complex, and as the following diagram shows, the number of components required also increases to accommodate this:

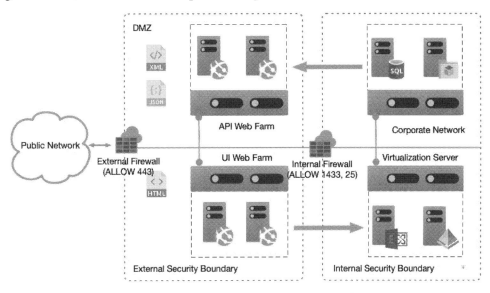

Figure 1.4 – Web apps and APIs increase complexity

Advancements in hardware to support this new era and provide ever more stable and robust systems meant networking, storage, and compute required roles focused on these niche, but highly complex components.

In many ways, this complexity of the underlying hosting platforms led to businesses struggling to cope with or afford the necessary systems and skills. This, in turn, led to our next and final step—cloud computing.

Cloud computing

Cloud platforms such as Azure sought to remove the difficulty and cost of maintaining the underlying hardware by providing pure compute and storage services on a pay-as-you-go or **operational expenditure** (**OpEx**) model rather than a **capital expenditure** (**CapEx**) model.

So, instead of providing hardware hosting, they offered **Infrastructure as a Service (IaaS)** components such as VMs, networking and storage, and **Platform as a Service (PaaS)** components such as Azure Web Apps and Azure SQL Databases. The latter is the most interesting. Azure Web Apps and Azure SQL Databases were the first PaaS offerings. The key difference is that they are services that are fully managed by Microsoft.

Under the hood, these services run on VMs; however, whereas with VMs you are responsible for the maintenance and management of them—patching, backups, resilience—with PaaS, the vendor takes over these tasks and just offers the basic service you want to consume.

Over time, Microsoft has developed and enhanced its service offerings and built many new ones as well. But as an architect, it is vital that you understand the differences and how each type of service has its own configurations, and what impact these have.

Many see Azure as "easy to use", and to a certain extent, one of the marketing points around Microsoft's service is just that—it's easy. Billions of dollars are spent on securing the platform, and a central feature is that the vendor takes responsibility for ensuring the security of its services.

A common mistake made by many engineers, developers, system administrators, and architects is that this means you can just start up a service, such as Azure Web Apps or Azure SQL Databases, and that it is inherently secure "out of the box".

While to a certain extent this may be true, by the very nature of cloud, many services are open to the internet. Every component has its own configuration options, and some of these revolve around securing communications and how they interact with other Azure services.

Now, more than ever, with security taking center stage, an architect must be vigilant of all these aspects and ensure they are taken into consideration. So, whereas the requirement to design underlying hardware is no longer an issue, the correct configuration of higher-level services is critical.

As we can see in the following diagram, the designs of our solutions to a certain extent become more complex in that we must now consider how services communicate between our corporate and cloud networks. However, the need to worry about VMs and hardware disappears—at least when purely using PaaS:

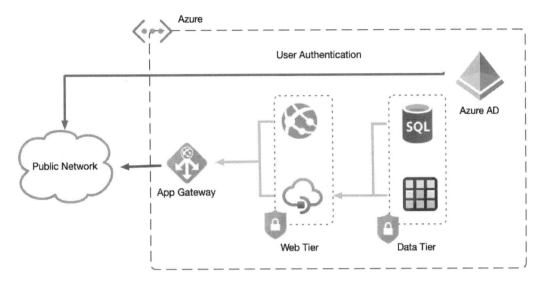

Figure 1.5 – Cloud integration

As we have moved from confined systems such as mainframes to distributed systems with the cloud provider taking on more responsibility, our role as an architect has evolved. Certain aspects may no longer be required, such as hardware design, which has become extremely specialized. However, a cloud architect must simultaneously broaden their range of skills to handle software, security, resilience, and scalability.

For many enterprises, the move to the cloud provides a massive opportunity, but due to existing assets, moving to a provider such as Azure will not necessarily be straightforward. Therefore, let's consider which additional challenges may face an architect when considering migration.

Migrating to the cloud from on-premises

A new company starting up today can build its IT services as *cloud native* from day one. These *born-in-the-cloud* enterprises arguably have a much simpler route.

For existing businesses, especially larger ones, they must consider how any cloud-based service operates with existing applications currently running within their infrastructure.

Even when a corporation chooses to migrate to the cloud, this is rarely performed in a single big-bang approach. Tools exist to perform a lift-and-shift copy of existing servers to VMs, but even this takes time and lots of planning.

For such companies, consideration at each step of the way is crucial. Individual services don't always run on a single piece of hardware—even websites are generally split into at least two tiers: a frontend user interface running on an **Internet Information Services (IIS)**, with a backend database running on a separate SQL server.

Other services may also communicate with each other—a payroll system will most likely need to interface with an HR database. At the very least, many systems share a standard user directory such as Microsoft **Active Directory (AD)** for user authentication and authorization.

An architect must decide which servers and systems should be migrated together to ensure these communication lines aren't impacted by adverse latency and can move independently with adequate cloud-to-on-premises network links. Should we use dedicated connectivity such as ExpressRoute, or will a **virtual private network (VPN)** channel running over the internet suffice?

As already discussed, as we move to the cloud, we change from an inherently secure platform whereby services are firewalled off by default, to an open one whereby connectivity is exposed to the internet by default. Any new communication channels from the cloud to your on-premises network, required to support a potentially long drawn-out migration, effectively provide an entry point from the internet back into your corporate system.

To alleviate business concerns, a strong governance and monitoring model must be in place, and this needs to be well designed from the outset. Will additional teams be required to support this? Will these tasks be added to existing teams' responsibilities? What tooling is used? Will it be your current compliance monitoring and reporting software, or will you have a different set for the cloud?

There are many different ways to achieve this, all depending on the answers to these specific questions. However, for those who wish to embrace a cloud-first solution, this may involve the following technologies:

- Azure Policy and Azure Blueprints for build control
- Azure Recovery Services
- Azure Update Management for VM patching
- Azure Security Center for alerting and compliance reporting
- Azure Monitor Agent installed on VMs
- Azure Monitor
- Azure Log Analytics and Azure Monitor Workbooks

Although these are Azure solutions, they can, however, also be integrated with on-premises infrastructure as well. The following diagram shows an example of this:

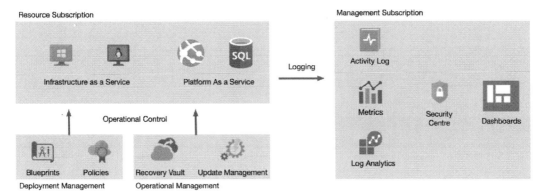

Figure 1.6 – Cloud compliance and monitoring tooling

As you can see, having a well-architected framework in place is crucial for ensuring the health and safety of your platform, and this in turn feeds into your strategies and overall solution design when considering a migration into the cloud.

Once we have decided how our integration with an on-premises system might look, we can then start to consider whether we perform a simple "lift and shift" or take the opportunity to re-platform. Before making these choices, we need to understand the main differences between IaaS and PaaS, and when one might be better than the other.

Understanding infrastructure and platform services

One of the big differences between IaaS and PaaS is about how the responsibility of components shifts.

The simplest examples of this are with websites and **Structured Query Language** (**SQL**) databases. Before we look at IaaS, let's consider an on-premise implementation.

When hosted in your own data center, you might have a server running IIS, upon which your website is hosted, and a database server running SQL. In this traditional scenario, you own full responsibility for the hardware, **Basic Input/Output System** (**BIOS**) updates, **operating system** (**OS**) patching, security updates, resilience, inbound and outbound traffic—often via a centralized firewall—and all physical security.

IaaS

The first step in migrating to cloud might be via a lift-and-shift approach using **virtual networks** (**VNETs**) and VMs—again, running IIS and SQL. Because you are running in Microsoft's data centers, you no longer need to worry about the physical aspects of the underlying hardware.

Microsoft ensures their data centers have all the necessary physical security systems, including personnel, monitoring, and access processes. They also worry about hardware maintenance and BIOS updates, as well as the resilience of the underlying hypervisor layer that all the VMs run on.

You must still, however, maintain the software and operating systems of those VMs. You need to ensure they are patched regularly with the latest security and improvement updates. You must architect your solution to provide application-level resilience, perhaps by building your SQL database as a failover cluster over multiple VMs; similarly, your web application may be load-balanced across a farm of IIS servers.

Microsoft maintains network access in general, through its networking and firewall hardware. However, you are still responsible for configuring certain aspects to ensure only the correct ports are open to valid sources and destinations.

A typical example of this split in responsibility is around access to an application. Microsoft ensures protection around the general Azure infrastructure, but it provides the relevant tools and options to allow you to set which ports are exposed from your platform. Through the use of **network security groups** (**NSGs**) and firewall appliances, you define source and destination firewall rules just as you would with a physical firewall device in your data center. If you misconfigure a rule, you're still open to attack—and that's your responsibility.

PaaS

As we move toward PaaS, accountability shifts again. With Azure SQL databases and Azure web apps, Microsoft takes full responsibility for ensuring all OS-level patches are applied; it ensures the platforms that run Azure SQL databases and Azure web apps are resilient against hardware failure.

Your focus now moves toward the configuration of these appliances. Again, for many services, this includes setting the appropriate firewalls. However, depending on your corporate governance rules, this needs to be well planned.

By default, communications from a web app to a backend Azure SQL database are over the public network. Although it is, of course, contained within Microsoft's network, it is technically open. To provide more secure connectivity, Azure provides the option to use service connections—direct communication over its internal backbone—but this needs specifically configuring at the web app, the SQL service, and the VNET level.

As the methods of those who wish to circumvent these systems become increasingly sophisticated, further controls are required. For web applications, the use of **Web Application Firewall (WAF)** is an essential part of this—as the architect, you must ensure they are included in your designs and configured correctly; they are not included by default.

> **Important note**
>
> Even though Microsoft spends billions of dollars a year on securing the Azure platform, unless you carefully architect your solutions, you are still vulnerable to attack. Making an incorrect assumption about where your responsibility lies leads to designing systems that are exposed—remember, many cloud platforms' networking is open by default; it has to be, and you need to ensure you fully understand where the lines are drawn.

Throughout this chapter, we have covered how changing technologies have significantly impacted how we design and build solutions; however, so far, the discussion has been around the technical implementation.

As software and infrastructure become closely aligned, teams implementing solutions have started to utilize the same tools as developers, which has changed the way projects are managed.

This doesn't just affect the day-to-day life of an architect; it has yet another impact on the way we design those solutions as well.

Moving from Waterfall to Agile projects

As we move into the cloud, other new terms around working practices come to the fore. **DevOps**, **DevSecOps**, and **Agile** are becoming ingrained in those responsible for building software and infrastructure.

If you come from a software or a DevOps background, there is a good chance you already understand these concepts, but if not, it helps to understand them.

Waterfall

Traditional waterfall project delivery has distinct phases to manage and control the build. In the past, it has often been considered crucial that much effort goes into planning and designing a solution before any engineering or building work commences.

A typical example is that of building a house. Before a single brick is laid, a complete architectural blueprint is produced. Next, foundations must be put in place, followed by the walls, roof, and interiors. The idea is that should you change your mind halfway through, it would be challenging to change anything. If you decide a house needs to be larger after the roof is built, you would need to tear everything down and start again.

With a waterfall approach, every step must be well planned and agreed at the outset. The software industry developed a bad reputation for delivering projects late and over budget. Businesses soon realized that this was not necessarily because of mismanagement but because it is difficult to articulate a vision for something that does not yet exist and, in many cases, has never existed before.

If we take the building metaphor, houses can be built as they are because, in many cases, they are merely copying elements of another house. Each house has a lot in common—walls, floors, and a roof, and there are set ways of building each of these.

The following diagram shows a typical setup of a waterfall project, with well-defined steps completed in turn:

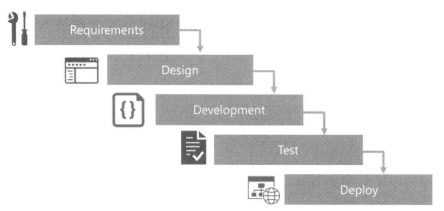

Figure 1.7 – Typical waterfall process

With software, this is not always the case. We often build new applications to address a need that has never been considered or addressed before. Trying to follow a waterfall approach has led to many failed projects, mainly because it's impossible to design or even articulate the requirements upfront fully.

Agile

Thus, Agile was born. The concept is to break down a big project into lots of smaller projects that each deliver a particular facet of the entire solution. Each mini-project is called a sprint, and each sprint runs through a complete project life cycle—design, plan, build, test, and review.

The following diagram shows that in many ways, Agile is lots of mini-waterfall projects:

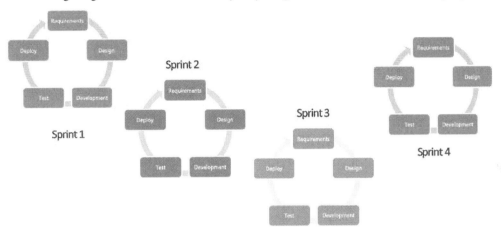

Figure 1.8 – Agile process

Sprints are also short-lived, usually 1 or 2 weeks, but at the end of each one, something is delivered. A waterfall project may last months or years before anything is provided to a customer—thus, there is a high margin for error. A small misunderstanding of a single element along the way results in an end state that does not meet requirements.

A particular tenet of Agile is "fail fast"—it is better to know something is wrong and correct it as soon as possible than have that problem exacerbate over time.

This sprint-led delivery mechanism can only be achieved if solutions are built in a particular manner. The application must be modular, and those modules designed in such a way that they can be easily swapped out or modified in response to changing requirements. An application architect must consider this when designing systems.

At this point, you may be wondering how this relates to the cloud. Agile suits software delivery because solutions can be built in small increments, creating lots of small modules combined into an entire solution. To support this, DevOps tooling provides automated mechanisms that deploy code in a repeatable, consistent manner.

As infrastructure in the cloud is virtualized, deployments can now be scripted and therefore automated—this is known as **Infrastructure as Code (IaC)**.

IaC

In Azure, components can be created either in the portal using the **graphical user interface (GUI)** with PowerShell or by using JSON templates. In other words, you can deploy infrastructure in Azure purely with code.

IaC provides many benefits, such as the ability to define VMs, storage, databases, or any Azure component in a way that promotes reusability, automation, and testing.

Tools such as Azure DevOps provide a central repository for all your code that can be controlled and built upon in an iterative process by multiple engineers. DevOps also builds, tests, and releases your infrastructure using automated pipelines—again, in the same way that modern software is deployed.

The DevOps name embodies the fact that operational infrastructure can now be built using development methodologies and can follow the same Agile principles.

DevSecOps takes this even further and includes codifying security components into release pipelines. Security must be designed and built hand in hand with infrastructure and security at every level, as opposed to merely being a perimeter or gateway device.

Cloud architects must, therefore, be fully conversant with the taxonomy, principles, and benefits of Agile, DevOps, and DevSecOps, incorporating them into working practices and designs.

Microsoft provides a range of tools and components to support your role and provides best-in-class solutions that are reliable, resilient, scalable, and—of course—secure.

As we have seen, architecture in the cloud involves many more areas than you might traditionally have gotten involved in. Hopefully, you will appreciate the reasons why these changes have occurred.

From changes in technology to new ways of working, your role has changed in different ways—although challenging, this can also be very exciting as you become involved across various disciplines and work closely with business users.

Summary

During this chapter, we have defined what we mean by architecture in the context of the AZ-304 exam, which is an important starting point to ensure we agree on what the role entails and precisely what is expected for the Azure certification.

We have walked through a brief history of business computing and how this has changed architecture over the years, from monolithic systems through to the era of personal computing, virtualization, the web, and ultimately to the cloud. We examined how each period changed the responsibilities and design requirements for the solutions built on top.

Finally, we had a brief introduction to modern working practices with IaC and project management methodologies, moving from waterfall to Agile, and how this has also changed how we as architects must think about systems.

In the next chapter, we will explore specific areas of architectural principles, specifically those aligned to the Microsoft Azure Well-Architected Framework.

2
Principles of Modern Architecture

In the previous chapter, we looked at why architecture is important, what it seeks to achieve, and how it has changed over time. Understanding how we got to where we are today helps us in our role and provides a solid framework for our designs.

This chapter will look at how we architect systems in general to understand the high-level requirements and potential methods. Split into *pillars*, we will examine different aspects of each; however, as we will see, they are all interlinked and have some element of dependency on each other.

We will start by looking at security, perhaps one of the essential aspects of architecture, and understand how access to systems is gained and how we prevent it.

Next, we'll investigate resilience, which is closely related to performance. By understanding the principles of these subjects, we can ensure our designs produce stable and performant applications.

Deployment mechanisms have become far more sophisticated in recent years, and we'll learn how our decisions around how we build platforms have become entwined with the systems themselves.

Finally, we will see how a well-designed solution must include a suite of monitoring, alerting, and analytics to support the other pillars.

With this in mind, throughout this chapter, we will cover the following topics:

- Architecting for security
- Architecting for resilience and business continuity
- Architecting for performance
- Architecting for deployment
- Architecting for monitoring and operations

Architecting for security

As technology has advanced, the solutions we build have become more powerful, flexible, and complex. Our applications' flexibility and dynamic nature enable a business to leverage data and intelligence at a level previously unknown. The cloud is often touted by many vendors as having near unlimited capacity and processing power that is accessible by *anyone*.

But power comes at a cost, because it's not just businesses who wish to leverage the potential of the cloud—hackers also have access to that tooling. Therefore, the architect of any system must keep security at the core of any design they produce.

Knowing the enemy

The first step in ensuring security is to understand the hacker mindset or, at the very least, to think about what they wish to accomplish—why do hackers hack?

Of course, there are lots of reasons, but we'll state the obvious one—because they can! Some people see hacking a system as a challenge. Because of this, their attack vector could be any security hole they can exploit, even if this didn't result in any valuable benefit.

The most dangerous attackers are the ones who wish to profit or cause damage from their actions, either directly by selling/releasing private data or by holding their victim to ransom by encrypting data and demanding money to release it.

Some wish to simply disrupt by bringing a system down—depending on the nature of the solution in question, the damage this causes can be reputational or financial.

All of these scenarios highlight some interesting points. The first is that when designing, you need to consider all areas of your solutions that might be vulnerable—authorization, data, application access points, network traffic, and so on.

The second is that, depending on your solution, you can prioritize the areas that would cause you the most damage. For example, if you are a high-volume internet retailer, uptime may be your primary concern, and you might therefore concentrate on preventing attacks that could overload your system. If data is your most valuable asset, then you should think about ways to ensure it cannot be accessed, either by preventing an intrusion in the first place or protecting information if it is accessed via encryption or obfuscation.

Once we have the *why*, we need to think about the *how*.

How do they hack?

There are, of course, many ways hackers can gain access to your systems, but once you have identified the reason why an attacker may want to hack you, you can at least narrow down the potential methods. The following are some of the more common ones:

- **Researching login credentials**: Although the simplest method, this is perhaps one of the most common. If an attacker can get your login details, they can do a lot of damage very quickly. Details can be captured either by researching a user's social and public profiles, to guess the password or find answers to your security questions.

- **Phishing**: Another way of capturing your credentials; you may receive an email notifying you that your account has been locked, with a link to a fake website. The website looks like what you are expecting, and when you enter your details, it merely captures them.

- **Email**: Rather than capturing login details, some emails may contain malicious code in the form of an attachment or a link to a compromised site. The purpose is to infect your computer with a virus, Trojan, or similar. The payload could be a keylogger to capture keystrokes (that is, login details) or spread and use more sophisticated attacks to access other systems.

- **Website vulnerabilities**: Poorly written code can lead to all sorts of entry points. **SQL injection attacks** whereby **Transact-SQL (T-SQL)** statements are posted within a form can update, add, or delete data if the backend is not written to protect against this type of attack. **Cross-site** scripts that run on the hacker's website but access the backend on yours can override form posts, and so on.

- **Distributed Denial of Service (DDoS)**: A DDoS attack seeks to overwhelm your servers and endpoints by flooding them with requests—this can either bring down your applications or potentially trigger other exploits that grant complete access.

- **Vulnerability exploits**: Third-party applications and operating systems can also have vulnerable code that hackers seek to exploit in many different ways, from triggering remote execution scripts to taking complete control of the affected system.

Of course, there are many more, but understanding the main reasons why and how hackers hack is the first step in your defense. With this knowledge, we can start to define and plan our strategy.

Defining your strategy

Once we have identified what we need to protect, including any prioritization based on your platform's characteristics, we can start to define a set of rules that set out how we protect ourselves.

Based on your requirements, which may be solution- and business-led, the strategy will state which elements need protecting, and how. For example, you may have a rule that states all data must be encrypted at rest, or that all logging is monitored and captured.

There are several industry compliance standards, such as **ISO27001**, **National Institute of Standards and Technology** (**NIST**), and the **Payment Card Industry Data Security Standard** (**PCI DSS**). These can either form the basis of your internal policies or be used as a reference; however, depending on your business's nature, you may be required to align with one or more of them.

> Information
>
> ISO is the acronym for International Organization for Standardization, which is an international standard-setting body with representatives from multiple other standards organizations.

We can now consider which technologies we will use to implement the various policies; next, we will look at some of the more common ones.

Networking and firewalls

Preventing access to systems from non-authorized networks is, of course, a great way to control access. In an on-premises environment this is generally by default, but for cloud environments, many services are open by default—at least from a networking perspective.

If your application is an internal system, consider controls that would force access along internal routes and block access to external routes.

If systems do need to be external-facing, consider network segregation by breaking up the individual components into their networks or subnets. In this scenario, your solution would have externally facing user interfaces in a public subnet, a middle tier managing business rules in another subnet, and your backend database on another subnet.

Using firewalls, you would only allow public access to the public subnet. The other subnets would only allow access on specific ports on the adjacent subnet. In this way, the user interface would have no direct access to the databases; it would only be allowed access to the business layer that then facilitates that access.

Azure provides firewall appliances and **network security groups** (**NSGs**) that deny and allow access between source and destination services, and using a combination of the two together provides even greater control.

Finally, creating a **virtual private network** (**VPN**) from an on-premises network into a cloud environment ensures only corporate users can access your systems, as though they were accessing them on-premises.

Network-level controls help control both perimeter and internal routes, but once a user has access, we need to confirm that the user is who they claim to be.

Identity management

Managing user access is sometimes considered the first line of defense, especially for cloud solutions that need to support mobile workforces.

Therefore, you must have a well-thought-out plan for managing access. **Identity management** is split into two distinct areas: **authentication** and **authorization**.

Authentication is the act of a user proving they are who they say they are. Typically, this would be a username/password combination; however, as discussed in the hacking techniques section *How do they hack?*, somebody could compromise these.

Therefore, you need to consider options for preventing these types of attacks, as either guessing or capturing a user's password is a common exploit. You could use alternatives such as **Multi-Factor Authentication** (**MFA**) or monitoring for suspicious login attributes, such as from *where* a user is logging on.

Once a user is authenticated, the act of authorization determines *what* they can access. Following principles such as **least privilege** or **Just Enough Access** (**JEA**) ensures users should only access what they require to perform their role. **Just-in-Time** (**JIT**) processes provide elevated access only when a user needs it and remove it after a set period.

Continual monitoring with automated alerting and threat management tools helps ensure that any compromised accounts are flagged and shut down quickly.

Using a combination of authorization and authentication management and good user education around the danger of phishing emails should help prevent the worst attacks. Still, you also need to protect against attacks that bypass the identity layer.

Patching

When working with virtual machines (VMs), you are responsible for managing the operating system that runs on them, and attackers can seek to exploit known vulnerabilities in that code.

Regular and timely patching and security updates with anti-virus and anti-malware agents are the best line of defense against this. Therefore, your solution design needs to include processes and tools for checking, testing, and applying updates.

Of course, it is not just third-party code operating systems that are susceptible; your application code is vulnerable too.

Application code

Most cloud services run custom code, in the form of web apps or backend **application programming interface (API)** services. Hackers often look for programming errors that can open holes in the application. As with other forms of protection, multiple options can be included in your architecture, and some are listed here:

- **Coding techniques**: Breaking code into smaller, individually deployed components and employing good development practices such as **Test-Driven Design (TDD)**, paired programming, or code reviews can help ensure code is cleaner and error-free.

- **Code scanners**: Code can be scanned before deployment to check for known security problems, either accidental or malicious, as part of a deployment pipeline.

- **Web application firewalls (WAFs)**: Unlike layer 3 or 4 firewalls that block access based on **Internet Protocol (IP)** or protocol, WAFs inspect network packet contents, looking for arbitrary code or common exploits such as SQL injection attacks.

Application-level security controls help protect you against code-level exploits; however, new vulnerabilities are uncovered daily, so you still need to prepare for the eventuality of a hacker gaining data access.

Data encryption

If the data you hold is sensitive or valuable, you should plan for the eventuality that your security controls are bypassed by making that data impossible to read. Encryption will achieve this; however, there are multiple levels you can apply. Each level makes your information more secure, but at the cost of performance.

Encryption strategies should be planned carefully—standard encryption at rest is lightweight but provides a basic protection level and should be used for all data as standard.

For more sensitive data such as credit card numbers, personal details, passwords, and so on, additional levels can be applied. Examples of how and where we can apply controls are given here:

- **Databases**: Many databases now support **Transparent Data Encryption** (TDE), whereby the data is encrypted. Applied by the database engine itself, consuming applications are unaware and therefore do not need to be modified.

- **Database fields**: Some databases provide field-level encryption that can be applied by the database engine itself or via client software. Again, this can be transparent from a code point of view but may involve additional client software.

- **Applications**: Applications themselves can be built to encrypt and decrypt data before it is even sent to the database. Thus, the database is unaware of the encryption, but the client must be built specifically to perform this.

- **Transport**: Data can be encrypted when transferring between application components. **HyperText Transfer Protocol Secure** (**HTTPS**) using **Secure Sockets Layer** (**SSL**) certificates is the most commonly known for end-user websites, but communications between elements such as APIs should also be protected. Other transport layer encryption is also available—for example, SQL database connections or file shares.

Data can be encrypted using either string keys or, preferably, certificates. When using certificates, many cloud vendors, including Azure, offer either managed or customer-supplied keys. With managed keys, the cloud vendors generate, store, and rotate the certificates for you, whereas with customer-supplied keys, you are responsible for obtaining and managing them.

Keys, secrets, and certificates should always be stored in a suitably secure container such as a **key vault**, with access explicitly granted to the users or services that need them, and access being logged.

As with other security concerns, the variability and ranges of choices mean that you must carefully plan your encryption techniques.

On their own, each control can provide some protection; however, to give your solution the best defense, you need to implement multiple tactics.

Defense-in-Depth

Modern solutions, especially those built in the cloud using **microservice** patterns, will be made from many components. Although these provide excellent power and flexibility, they also offer numerous attack points.

Therefore, when considering our security controls, we need to consider multiple layers of defense. Always assume that your primary measures will fail, and ensure you have backup controls in place as well.

Known as **Defense-In-Depth** (**DID**), an example would be data protection in a database that serves an e-commerce website. Enforcing an authentication mechanism on a database might be your primary control, but you need to consider how to protect your application if those credentials are compromised. An example of a multilayer implementation might include (but not be limited to) the following:

- Network segregation between the database and web app

- Firewalls to only allow access from the web app

- TDE on the database

- Field-level encryption on sensitive data (for example, credit card numbers; passwords)

- A WAF

The following diagram shows an example of a multilayer implementation:

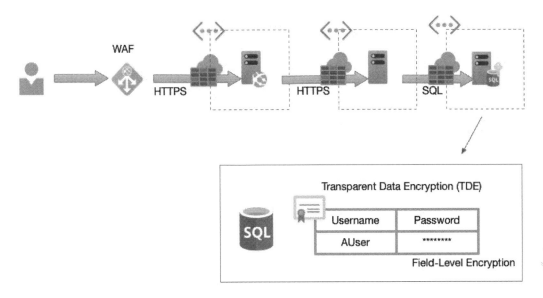

Figure 2.1 – Multiple-layer protection example

We have covered many different technical layers that we can use to protect our services, but it is equally important to consider the human element, as this is often the first point of entry for hacks.

User education

Many attacks originate from either a phishing/email attack or social data harvesting.

With this and an excellent technical defense in mind, a solid education plan is also an invaluable way to prevent attacks at the beginning.

Training users in acceptable online practices that help prevent them from leaking important information, and therefore any plan, should include the following:

- **Social media data harvesting**: Social media platforms are a gold mine for hackers; users rarely consider the information they routinely supply could be used to access password-protected systems. Birth dates, geographical locations, even pet names and relationship information are routinely supplied and advertised—all of which are often used as security questions when confirming your identity through security questions, and so on.

   Some platforms present quizzes and games that again ask questions that answer common security challenges.

- **Phishing emails**: A typical exploit is to send an email stating that an account has been suspended or a new payment has been made. A link will direct the user to a fake website that looks identical to an official site, so they enter their login details, which are then logged by the hacker. These details can not only be used to access the targeted site in question but can also obtain additional information such as an address, contact information, and, as stated previously, answers to common security questions.

- **Password policies**: Many people reuse the same password. If one system is successfully hacked, that same password can then be used across other sites. Educating users in password managers or the dangers of password reuse can protect your platform against such exploits.

This section has looked at the importance of design security throughout our solutions, from understanding how and why we may be attacked, to common defenses across different layers. Perhaps the critical point is that good design should include multiple layers of protection across your applications.

Next, we will look at how we can protect our systems against failure—this could be hardware, software, or network failure, or even an attack.

Architecting for resilience and business continuity

Keeping your applications running can be important for different reasons. Depending on your solution's nature, downtime can range from a loss of productivity to direct financial loss. Building systems that can withstand some form of failure has always been a critical aspect of architecture, and with the cloud, there are more options available to us.

Building resilient solutions comes at a cost; therefore, you need to balance the cost of an outage against the cost of preventing it.

High Availability (HA) is the traditional option and essentially involves doubling up on components so that if one fails, the other automatically takes over. An example might be a database server—building two or more nodes in a cluster with data replication between them protects against one of those servers failing as traffic would be redirected to the secondary replica in the event of a failure, as per the example in the following diagram:

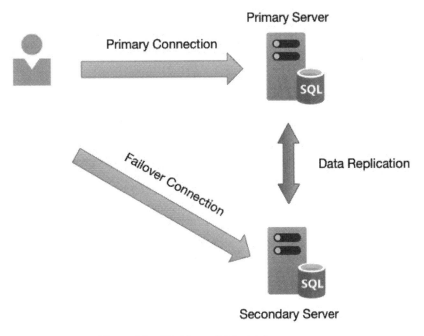

Figure 2.2 – Highly available database servers

However, multiple servers are always powered on, which in turn means increased cost. Quite often, the additional hardware is not used except in the event of a failure.

For some applications, this additional cost is less than the cost of a potential failure, but it may be more cost-effective for less critical systems to have them unavailable for a short time. In such cases, our design must attempt to reduce how long it takes to recover.

The purpose of HA is to reduce the **Mean Time Between Failures** (**MTBF**). In contrast, the alternative is to reduce the **Mean Time To Recovery** (**MTTR**)—in other words, rather than concentrating on *preventing* outages, spend resources on *reducing the impact* and *speeding up recovery* from an outage. Ultimately, it is the business who must decide which of these is the most important, and therefore the first step is to define their requirements.

Defining requirements

When working with a business to understand their needs for a particular solution, you need to consider many aspects of how this might impact your design.

Identifying individual workloads is the first step—what are the individual tasks that are performed, and where do they happen? How does data flow around your system?

For each of these components, look for what failure would mean to them—would it cause the system as a whole to fail or merely disrupt a non-essential task? The act of calculating costs during a transactional process is critical, whereas sending a confirmation email could withstand a delay or even complete failure in some cases.

Understand the usage patterns. For example, a global e-commerce site will be used 24/7, whereas a tax calculation service would be used most at particular times of the year or at the month-end.

The business will need to advise on two important metrics—the **Recovery Time Objective (RTO)** and the **Recovery Point Objective (RPO)**. The RTO dictates an acceptable amount of time a system can be offline, whereas the RPO determines the acceptable amount of data loss. For example, a daily backup might mean you lose up to a day's worth of data; if this is not acceptable, more frequent backups are required.

Non-functional requirements such as these will help define our solution's design, which we can use to build our architecture with industry best practices.

Using architectural best practices

Through years of research and experience, vendors such as Microsoft have collected a set of best practices that provide a solid framework for good architecture when followed.

With the business requirements in mind, we can perform a **Failure Model Analysis (FMA)**. An FMA is a process for identifying common types of failures and where they might appear in our application.

From the FMA, we can then start to create a redundancy and scalability plan; designing with scalability in mind helps build a resilient solution and a performant one, as technologies that allow us to scale also protect us from failure.

A load balancer is a powerful tool for achieving scale and resilience. This allows us to build multiple service copies and then distribute the load between them, with unhealthy nodes being automatically removed.

Consider the cost implications of any choices. As mentioned previously, we need to balance the cost of downtime versus the cost of providing protection. This, in turn, may impact decisions between the use of **Infrastructure-as-a-Service (IaaS)** components such as VMs or **Platform-as-a-Service (PaaS)** technologies such as web apps, functions, and containers. Using VMs in our solution means we must build out load balancing farms manually, which are challenging to scale, and demand that components such as load balancers be explicitly included. Opting for managed services such as Azure Web Apps or Azure Functions can be cheaper and far more dynamic, with load-balancing and auto-scaling technologies built in.

Data needs to be managed effectively, and there are multiple options for providing resilience and backup. Replication strategies involving geographically dispersed copies provide the best RPO as the data is always consistent, but this comes at a financial cost.

For less critical data or information that does not change often, daily backup tools that are cheaper may suffice, but these require manual intervention in the event of a failure.

A well-defined set of requirements and adherence to best practices will help design a robust solution, but regular testing should also be performed to ensure the correct choices have been made.

Testing and disaster recovery plans

A good architecture defines a blueprint for your solution, but it is only theory until it is built; therefore, solutions need to be tested to validate our design choices.

Work through the identified areas of concern and then forcefully attempt to break them. Document and run through simulations that trigger the danger points we are trying to protect.

Perform failover and failback tests to ensure that the application behaves as it should, and that data loss is within allowable tolerances.

Build test probes and monitoring systems to continually check for possible issues and to alert you to failed components so that these can be further investigated.

Always prepare for the worst—create a disaster recovery plan to detail how you would recover from complete system failure or loss, and then regularly run through that plan to ensure its integrity.

We have seen how a well-architected solution, combined with robust testing and detailed recovery plans, will prepare you for the worst outcomes. Next, we will look at a closely related aspect of design—performance.

Architecting for performance

As we have already seen, resilience can be closely linked to performance. If a system is overloaded, it will either impact the user experience or, in the worst case, fail altogether.

Ensuring a performant solution is more than just increasing resources; how our system is built can directly impact the options available and how efficient they are.

Breaking applications down into smaller discrete components not only makes our solution more manageable but also allows us to increase resources just where they are needed. If we wish to scale in a monolithic, single-server environment, our only option is to add more **random-access memory** (**RAM**) and CPU to the entire system. As we decompose our applications and head toward a microservices pattern whereby individual services are hosted independently, we can apportion additional resources where needed, thus increasing performance efficiently.

When we need to scale components, we have two options: the first is to *scale up*—add more CPU and RAM; the second option is to *scale out*—deploy additional instances of our services behind a load balancer, as per the example in the following diagram:

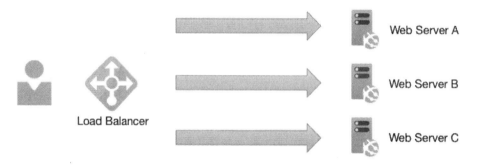

Figure 2.3 – Scale-out: identical web servers behind a load balancer

Again, our choice of the underlying technology is important here—virtual servers can be scaled up or out relatively quickly, and with scale, sets can be dynamic. However, virtual servers are slower to scale since a new machine must be imaged, loaded, and added to the load balancer. With containers and PaaS options such as Azure Web Apps, this is much more lightweight and far easier to set up; containers are exceptionally efficient from a resource usage perspective.

We can also decide what triggers a scaling event; services can be set to scale in response to demand—as more requests come in, we can increase resources as required and remove them again when idle. Alternatively, we may wish to scale to a schedule—this helps control costs but requires us to already know the periods when we need more power.

An important design aspect to understand is that it is generally more efficient to scale out than up; however, to take advantage of such technologies, our applications need to avoid client affinity.

Client affinity is a scenario whereby the service processing a request is tied to the client; that is, it needs to remember state information for that client from one request to another. In a system built from multiple backend hosts, the actual host performing the work may change between requests.

Particular types of functions can often cause bottlenecks—for example, processing large volumes of data for a report, or actions that must contact external systems such as sending emails. Instead of building these tasks as synchronous activities, consider using queuing mechanisms instead. As in the example in the following diagram, requests by the **User** are placed in a **Job Queue** and control is released back to the **User**. A separate service processes the job that was placed in the **Job Queue** and updates the **User** once complete:

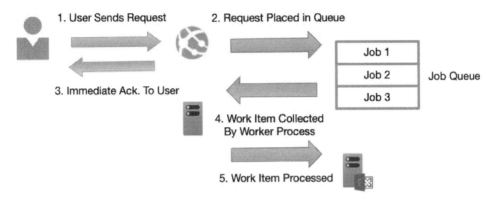

Figure 2.4 – Messaging/queueing architectures

Decoupling services in this fashion gives the perception of a more responsive system and reduces the number of resources to service the request. Scaling patterns can now be based on the number of items in a queue rather than an immediate load, which is more efficient.

By thinking about systems as individual components and how those components respond—either directly or indirectly—your solution can be built to not just scale, but to scale in the most efficient manner, thereby saving costs without sacrificing the user experience.

In this section, we have examined how the right architecture can impact our solution's ability to scale and perform in response to demand. Next, we will look at how we ensure these design considerations are carried through into the deployment phase.

Architecting for deployment

One area of IT solutions in which the cloud has had a dramatic impact is around deployment. Traditional system builds, certainly at the infrastructure level, were mostly manual in their process. Engineers would run through a series of instructions then build and configure the underlying hosting platform, followed by another set of instructions for deploying the software on top.

Manual methods are error-prone because instructions can be misunderstood or implemented wrongly. Validating a deployment is also a complicated process as it would involve walking back through an installation guide, cross-checking the various configurations.

Software deployments led the way on this with automated mechanisms that are scripted, which means they can be repeated time and time again consistently—in other words, we remove the human element.

We can define our infrastructure in code within Azure, too, using either **Azure Resource Manager** (**ARM**) templates or other third-party tools; the entire platform can be codified and deployed by automated systems.

The ability to consistently deploy and re-deploy in a consistent manner gives rise to some additional opportunities. **Infrastructure as Code** (**IaC**) enables another paradigm—**immutable infrastructure**.

Traditionally, when modifications are required to the server's configuration, the process would be to manually make the configuration on the server and record the change in the build documentation. With immutable infrastructure, any modifications are made to the deployment code, and then the server is re-deployed. In other words, the server never changes; it is immutable. Instead, it is destroyed and recreated with the new configuration.

IaC and immutable infrastructure have an impact on our designs. PaaS components are more straightforward to automate than IaaS ones. That is not to say you can't automate IaaS components; however, PaaS's management does tend to be simpler. Although not a reason to use PaaS in its own right, it does provide yet one more reason to use technologies such as web apps over VMs running **Internet Information Services** (**IIS**).

You also need to consider which deployment tooling you will use. Again, Microsoft has its own native solution in the form of **Azure DevOps**; however, there are other third-party options. Whichever you choose will have some impact around connectivity and any additional agents and tools you use.

For example, most DevOps rules require some form of deployment agent to pull your code from a repository. Connectivity between the repository, the agent, and the Azure platform is required and must be established in a secure and resilient manner.

Because IaC and DevOps make deployments quicker and more consistent, it is easier to build different environments—development, testing, staging, and production. Solution changes progress through each environment and can be checked and signed off by various parties, thus creating a quality culture—as per the example in the following diagram:

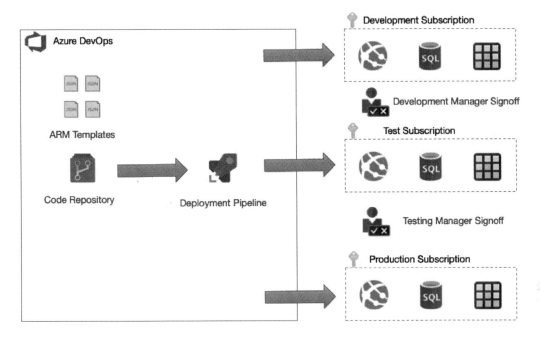

Figure 2.5 – Example DevOps flow

The ability to codify and deploy complete solutions at the click of a button broadens the scope of your solution. An entire application environment can be encapsulated and deployed multiple times; this, in turn, provides the opportunity to create various single-tenant solutions instead of a one-off multi-tenant solution. This aspect is becoming increasingly valuable to organizations as it allows for better separation of data between customers.

In this section, we have introduced how deployment mechanisms can change what our end-state solution looks like, which impacts the architecture. Next, we will look in more detail at how monitoring and operations help keep our system healthy and secure.

Architecting for monitoring and operations

For the topics we have covered in this chapter to be effective, we must continually monitor all aspects of our system. From security to resilience and performance, we must know what is happening at all times.

Monitoring for security

Maintaining the security of a solution requires a monitoring solution that can detect, respond, and ultimately recover from incidents. When an attack happens, the speed at which we respond will determine how much damage is incurred.

However, a monitoring solution needs to be intelligent enough to prioritize and filter false positives.

Azure provides several different monitoring mechanisms in general and, specifically, in terms of security, and can be configured according to your organization's capabilities. Therefore, when designing a monitoring solution, you must align with your company's existing teams to effectively direct and alert appropriately, and send pertinent information as required.

Monitoring requirements cover more than just alerts; the policies that define business requirements around configuration settings such as encryption, passwords, and allowed resources must be checked to confirm they are being adhered to. The Azure risk and compliance reports will highlight any items that deviate so that the necessary team can investigate and remediate.

Other tools, such as Azure Security Center, will continually monitor your risk profile and suggest advice on improving your security posture.

Finally, security patching reports also need regular reviews to ensure VMs are being patched so that insecure hosts can be investigated and brought in line.

Monitoring for resilience

Monitoring your solution is not just about being alerted to any issues; the ideal scenario is to detect and remediate problems *before* they occur—in other words, we can use it as an early warning system.

Applications should include in their designs the ability to output relevant logs and errors; this then enables health alerts to be set up that, when combined with resource thresholds, provide details of the running processes.

Next, a set of baselines can be created that identify what a healthy system looks like. When anomalies occur, such as long-running processes or specific error logs, they are spotted earlier.

As well as defined alerts that will proactively contact administrators when possible issues are detected, visualization dashboards and reporting can also help responsible teams see potential problems or irregular readings as part of their daily checks.

Monitoring for performance

The same CPU, RAM, and **input/output (I/O)** thresholds used for early warning signs of errors also help identify performance issues. By monitoring response times and resource usage over time, you can understand usage patterns and predict when more power is required.

Performance statistics can either manually set scaling events through the use of schedules or set automated scaling rules more accurately.

Keeping track of scaling events throughout the life cycle of an application is useful. If an application is continually scaling up and down or not scaling at all, it could indicate that thresholds are set incorrectly.

Again, creating and updating baseline metrics will help alert you to potential issues. If resources for a particular service are steadily increasing over time, this information can predict future bottlenecks.

Network monitoring

CPU and RAM utilization are not the only source of problems; problems can also arise from misconfigured firewalls and routing, or misbehaving services causing too much traffic.

Traffic analytics tools will provide an overview of the networks in the solution and help identify sources that generate high traffic levels. Network performance managers offer tools that allow you to create specific tests between two endpoints to investigate particular issues.

For hybrid environments, VPN meters specifically monitor your direct connection links to your on-premises networks.

Monitoring for DevOps and applications

For solutions with well-integrated DevOps code libraries and deployment pipelines, additional metrics and alerts will notify you of failed builds and deployments. Information, support tickets, or work tasks can be automatically raised and linked to the affected build.

Additional application-specific monitoring tools allow for an in-depth analysis of your application's overall health, and again will help with troubleshooting problems.

Application maps, **artificial intelligence (AI)**-driven smart detection, usage analytics, and component communications can all be included in your designs to help drive operational efficiencies and warn of future problems.

We can see that for every aspect of your solution design—security, resilience, performance, and deployments—an effective monitoring and alerting regime is vital to ensure the platform's ongoing health. With proper forethought, issues can be prevented before they happen. Forecasting and planning can be based on intelligent extrapolation rather than guesswork, and responding to failure events becomes a science instead of an art.

Summary

In this chapter, we looked at a high-level view of the architecture and the types of decisions that must be considered, agreed upon, and documented.

By thinking about how we might design for security, resilience, performance, and deployment and monitor all our systems, we get a greater understanding of our solution as a whole.

The last point is important—although a system design must contain the individual components, they must all work together as a single, seamless solution.

In the next chapter, we will look at the different tools and patterns we can use in Azure to build great applications that align with best-practice principles.

Further reading

You can check out the following link for more information about Microsoft's Well-Architected Framework:

`https://docs.microsoft.com/en-us/azure/architecture/framework/`

Section 2: Identity and Security

From authentication to governance, in this section we delve into the core aspects of security in Azure and how to create security in depth by continually managing, monitoring, and reporting on user access.

The following chapters will be covered under this section:

3

Understanding User Authentication

User security is perhaps one of the most critical aspects of a system and, therefore, its architecture. Security has, of course, always been important to protect sensitive information within an organization. However, as we move our applications online and widen our audience, the need to ensure only the correct people gain access to their data has become crucial.

In this chapter, we explore the key differences between **authentication** and **authorization**, what tooling we have available within **Azure** to ensure the safety of *user accounts*, and how we *design solutions* according to different business needs.

In this chapter, we will examine the following topics:

- Differentiating authentication from authorization
- Introducing **Active Directory (AD)**
- Integrating AD
- Understanding **Conditional Access (CA)**, **Multi-Factor Authentication (MFA)**, and security defaults
- Using external identities

Differentiating authentication from authorization

A significant and essential role of any platform is that of authentication and authorization. These two terms are often confused and combined as a single entity. When understanding security on platforms such as Azure, it's vital to know how the different technologies are used.

Authentication is the act of proving who you are, often performed with a username/password combination. If you can provide the correct details, a system authenticates you.

Authentication does *not* give you access to anything; it merely proves *who* you are.

Once a system knows the *who*, it then checks to see *what* you have access to—this is termed **authorization**.

In Azure, authorization is the act of checking whether you have access to a particular resource such as a storage account, and what actions you can perform, such as creating, deleting, modifying, or even reading the data in the storage account.

Because of the number of different services and their associated actions that are available to a user in Azure, and the importance of ensuring the validity of a user, the ensuing mechanisms that control all this can become quite complicated.

Luckily, Azure provides a range of services, broken down into authentication and authorization services, that enable you to strictly control how users authenticate and what they can then access, in a very granular way.

Traditionally, authentication has been via simple username/password combinations; however, this is ineffective on its own, and therefore you need to consider many factors and strategies when designing an *authentication mechanism*. For example, the following scenarios may apply:

- A user may choose too simple a password, increasing the chances of it being compromised.

- Complex passwords or regular changes mean users are more likely to forget their password.

- There may be delays in the authentication process if a user needs to call a helpdesk to request a password reset.

- A *username/password* combination itself is open to phishing attacks.

- Password databases can be compromised.

> **Important note**
>
> A **phishing attack** is an action whereby a malicious person will attempt to steal your password by sending you to a *dummy* website that looks like the one you want to access but is, in fact, their site. You enter your details, thinking it is the correct site, and now they have your personal information and can then use this to log in to the real site.

When systems are hosted on a physically isolated network, some of these issues are mitigated as you first need physical access to a building or at least a device set up with a **virtual private network** (**VPN**) connection that, in turn, would require a certificate.

However, in cloud scenarios, and especially *hybrid systems*, whereby you need external authentication mechanisms that must also map or sync to internal systems, this physical *firewall* cannot always be achieved.

With these scenarios in mind, we need to consider how we might address the following:

- Managing and enforcing password complexity rules

- Providing additional layers over and above a password

- How to securely store and protect passwords

Now that we understand some of the issues we face with authentication systems, especially those that rely on username/password combinations, we can investigate what options are available to mitigate them. First, we will examine Microsoft's established security platform, AD.

Introducing Azure AD

Azure AD is a cloud-based mechanism that provides the tools to address our security needs. Backed by **Microsoft AD**, an *industry-standard* and, importantly, *proven secure authentication and authorization system*, it gives both cloud-first (that is, stored and managed entirely in the cloud) and hybrid (a mix of cloud and on-premises) solutions.

Some of these tools are included by default when you create an Azure AD tenant. Others require a *Premium add-on*, which we will cover later.

These tools include the following:

- **Self-service password resets**: Allowing your users to reset their passwords themselves (through the provision of additional security measures) without needing to call the helpdesk.

- **MFA**: MFA enforces a second form of identification during the authentication process—a code is generated and sent to the user, and this is entered along with the password. The code is typically sent to a user's device as either a text message or an MFA authentication app on their mobile device.

- You can also use biometric devices such as fingerprint or face scanners.

- **Hybrid integration with password writebacks**: When Azure AD is synchronized to an on-premises AD with AD Connect, changes to the user's password in Azure AD is sent back to the on-premises AD to ensure the directories remain in sync.

- **Password protection policies**: Policies in Azure can be set to enforce complex passwords or the period between password changes. These policies can be integrated with on-premises directories to ensure consistency.

- **Passwordless authentication**: For many organizations, the desire to remove the need for passwords altogether in favor of alternative methods is seen as the ultimate solution to many authentication issues. Credentials are provided through the use of biometrics or a **FIDO2** security key. These cannot be easily duplicated, and this removes the need for remembering complex passwords.

- **Single sign-on (SSO)**: With SSO, users only need to authenticate once to access all their applications—regardless of whether they sign on through their on-premises directory or Azure AD, the single authentication process should identify the user across different environments.

- **CA**: To further tighten security, CA policies can provide further restrictions to user sign-in, or when different rules may apply. For example, MFA can be set not to be required when signing in from specific **Internet Protocol** (**IP**) ranges, such as a corporate network range.

Why AD?

Let's take a step back and consider a straightforward scenario: that of an online e-commerce website. Before you can order something, you need to register with that website and provide some basic details—a *sign-in name*, an *email*, a *password*, and so on.

A typical website such as the one shown in the following diagram may simply store your details in a database and, at its simplest, this may just be a user record in a table:

Username	Password
AUser	P@ssw0rd

Figure 3.1 – Simple username and password authentication

For more advanced scenarios that may require different users to have different levels of access—for example, in the preceding e-commerce website—the user databases may need to accommodate administrative users as well as customers. Administrative users will want to log in and process orders and, of course, we need to ensure the end customers don't get this level of access.

So, now, we must also record who has access to what, and ensure users are granted access accordingly, as in the example shown in the following diagram:

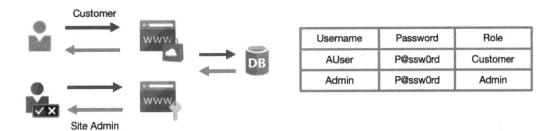

Figure 3.2 – Role-based authorization

The same would also be valid for a corporate user database. For example, the company you work for must provide access to various internal systems—payroll, marketing, sales, file shares, email, and so on. Each application will have its own set of security requirements, and users may need access across multiple systems.

For corporate users, Microsoft introduced **Active Directory Domain Services (AD DS)**, which is a dedicated identity management system that allows businesses to manage user databases in a secure and well-organized way. Users in an AD are granted access to other systems (provided they support it) from a single user database. Microsoft AD DS takes care of the complexity and security of user management. See the example shown in the following diagram:

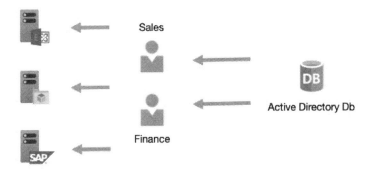

Figure 3.3 – AD

From a single account, IT administrators can provide access to file shares, email systems, and even web applications—provided those systems are integrated with AD. Typically, this would be achieved by domain-joining the device that hosts the application—be it an email server, web server, or file server; that is, the hosting device becomes part of the network, and AD manages not only the user accounts but the computer accounts as well.

In this way, the identity mechanism is a closed system—that is, only internal computers and users have access. Although external access mechanisms have been developed over time to provide remote access, these are still about securely connecting users by essentially extending that "internal" network.

Microsoft AD DS uses specific networking protocols to manage the security of devices and users—that is, the way devices communicate with each other—known as **Integrated Windows Authentication (IWA)**; they are **New Technology LAN Manager (NTLM)** and **Kerberos**.

Microsoft AD DS is a common standard today for many organizations. Still, as discussed, it is built around the concept of a closed system—that is, the components are all tightly integrated by enforcing the requirement for them to be "joined."

Azure AD versus AD DS

Azure AD is the next evolution. It takes identity to the next level by building upon **AD DS** and provides an **Identity as a Service (IDaaS)** to provide this same level of security and access management to the *cloud*.

Just as with AD DS, Azure AD is a database of users that can be used to grant access to all your systems. It's important to understand that it is an entirely separate database— one that is stored within Azure—and therefore the underlying hardware and software that powers it is wholly managed by Azure—hence IDaaS.

In a traditional on-premises world, you would be responsible for building directory servers to host and manage AD DS. As an IT administrator or architect, you need to consider how many servers you require and what specifications they need to be to support your user load and resilience, to ensure the system is always available. If your identity system failed due to hardware failure, access to all your systems would be blocked.

Azure AD is a managed service, and Microsoft ensures the integrity, security, and resilience of the platform for you.

Whereas AD DS secures domain-joined devices, Azure AD secures cloud-based systems such as web apps. With Azure Web Apps, for example, they are not domain-joined to an internal network. Users may authenticate over the internet—that is, over public networks, as opposed to internal networks. As such, the protocols used must also be different—NTLM and Kerberos used in AD DS would not be suitable and, instead, traditional web protocols must be used—that is, **HyperText Transfer Protocol Secure (HTTPS)**, as depicted in the following diagram:

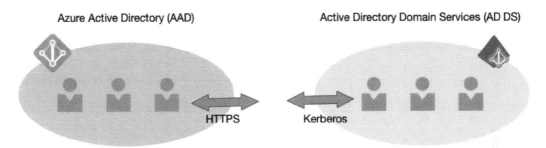

Figure 3.4 – Azure AD versus AD DS protocols

Azure AD also integrates with other Microsoft online services such as *Office 365*. If you sign up for *Microsoft Office 365*, an Azure AD tenant will be created for you to manage your users. This same "tenant" can also be used to manage your Azure subscriptions and the apps you build within them.

Azure AD is distinctly separate from AD DS—that is, they are entirely different databases. However, you can link or synchronize Azure AD and your on-premises AD DS, effectively extending your internal directory into the cloud. We will cover this in more detail later, but for now, understand that although different, AD DS and cloud-based Azure AD can be connected.

> **Important note**
> Azure AD, even with synchronization, does not support domain-joining virtual machines (VMs). For domain-joined VMs in Azure, either allow AD DS traffic back to on-premises, build domain controllers within the Azure network or use Azure AD DS, which is a fully managed AD DS solution.

The following table shows some of the common differences between the two services:

Aspect	Azure AD-joined	AD DS/Azure AD DS
Device controlled by	Azure AD	Azure AD DS managed domain
Representation in directory	Device objects in the Azure AD	Computer objects in the Azure AD DS managed domain
Authentication	OAuth/OpenID Connect protocols	Kerberos and NTML
Management	**Mobile Device Management** (MDM)	Group policy
Networking	Internet/External	**Virtual network** (VNET)/ Peered/Internal network
Great for	Mobile or desktop	Servers deployed in Azure

An *instance* of Azure AD is called an **Azure tenant**. Think of a tenant as the user database. In the next section, we will look at tenants in more detail.

Azure tenants

Each tenant has its *own set of users*; therefore, if you have more than one tenant, you would have distinctly separate user databases.

A tenant, therefore, defines your administrative boundaries, and Azure subscriptions can only belong to one *single tenant*, although a single tenant can contain *multiple subscriptions*, as we can see in the following diagram:

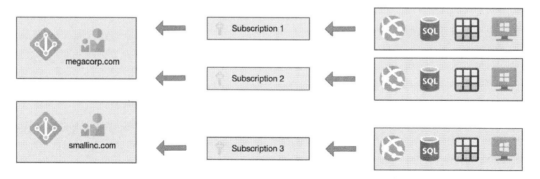

Figure 3.5 – Azure AD tenants

A single tenant is generally sufficient for corporate systems whereby only *internal* people require access. However, there are scenarios whereby you may want to build applications that support users from *different* companies.

Software-as-a-Service (SaaS) products such as **Microsoft Dynamics CRM** are a classic example. This is built as a single saleable system; however, it is multi-tenant in that because it is made for external users and not just Microsoft employees, it must be able to support sign-on from other organizations.

Another scenario to consider is whether you want to separate your users into development and production tenants. For some, a single tenant that houses the same user accounts for development and production systems is acceptable. In such cases, production and development may instead be covered in separate subscriptions, or even just different resource groups within a subscription.

However, having a single tenant makes it harder to test new identity policies, for example, and therefore a separate tenant may be required. While it is possible to move Azure subscriptions between tenants, because each tenant has a unique user database, doing so essentially resets any roles and permissions you have set.

As you can see, it is essential to define your tenant strategy early on to prevent problems later.

Azure AD editions

Azure AD provides a range of management tools; however, each user must be licensed, and depending on the type of license, this will determine which tools are available.

Out of the box, Azure provides a free *tier* known as **Azure AD Free**.

The free tier provides user and group management, on-premises synchronization, basic reports, and self-service password change facilities for cloud users. In other words, it gives you the absolute basics you need to provide your *cloud-based* access.

For more advanced scenarios, you can purchase **AD Premium P1** licenses. Over and above the free tier, P1 lets your hybrid users—those with synchronized accounts between on-premises and cloud—to access both on-premises and cloud resources seamlessly.

It also provides more advanced administration tooling and reporting, such as dynamic groups, self-service group management, **Microsoft Identity Manager** (**MIM**), and *cloud writebacks* for password changes; that is, if a user changes their password through the cloud-based self-service tool, this change will write back to the on-premises account as well.

AD Premium P2 gives everything in basic and P1 licenses but adds on **Azure AD Identity Protection** and **Privileged Identity Management** (**PIM**). We will cover each of these in detail later, but for now, it's essential for the exam to understand you'll need a P2 license to use these advanced features.

Finally, you can also get additional **Pay As You Go** licenses for Azure AD **Business-to-Consumer** (**B2C**) services. These can help you provide identity and access management solutions for customer-facing apps.

In this section, we have looked at how AD and Azure AD differ, how we can provide services for external users, and what the different editions provide. Next, we will consider how we integrate an existing on-premises directory with the cloud.

Integrating AD

One of the first steps is to understand how your organization wishes to authenticate its users and from where. A cloud-native approach may be sufficient for some, but some form of integration with an on-premises directory will be required for others. We will look at what they are in the following sections.

Cloud native

The simplest scenario is cloud native; we only need to set up user accounts within Azure AD. Authentication is performed via the web using HTTPS, and access is only required into Azure or other services that integrate with Azure AD—such as a web application using token-based authentication, as we can see in the following diagram:

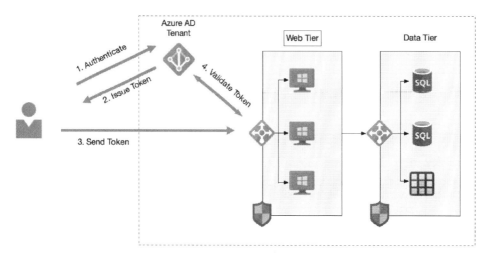

Figure 3.6 – Cloud-native authentication

Cloud native is mostly used by new organizations or those without an existing directory service. For companies that already have an AD database, it is common to integrate with it, and for this we can use **Azure AD Connect**.

Azure AD Connect

Azure AD Connect provides the most straightforward option when you need to provide integration with AD.

AD Connect is a *synchronization* tool that you install on an on-premises server and that essentially copies objects between your on-premises network and your Azure AD.

This scenario is excellent for providing access to Azure resources for existing users and has self-service capabilities such as a password reset, although this requires the Azure AD Premium add-on.

In a typical use case, you may have a web application deployed in Azure that you need to provide remote access to for your users. In other words, users may be connecting to the web app over the *public* internet, but still need to be challenged for authentication. The following diagram depicts such a scenario:

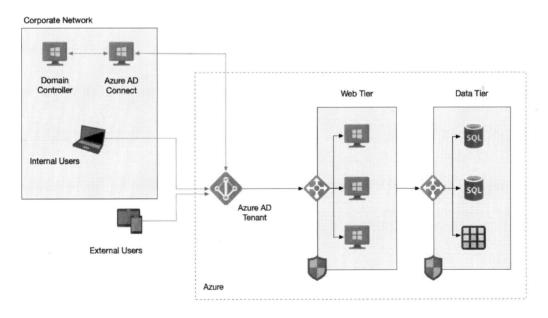

Figure 3.7 – Hybrid authentication

Azure AD Connect provides a way of keeping your user details (such as login name and password) in sync with the accounts in Azure AD.

Also, note there is no VNET integration—that is, the web apps themselves are not connected to a VNET that is accessed via a **VPN** or **express route**. When users try to access the web app, they will authenticate against Azure AD.

When setting up AD Connect, you have several options. You can set up AD Connect to only replicate a *subset* of users using filtering—so, you should carefully consider which accounts are actually needed and only sync those required.

The AD Connect agent is installed on a server in your environment. The only requirement is that it must have access to the AD by being installed on a domain-connected computer.

The download link for the AD Connect agent can be retrieved by going to the **AD Connect** menu option in the **Azure AD** blade in the Azure portal. To access it, perform the following steps:

1. Navigate to the Azure portal at `https://portal.azure.com`.

2. In the top bar, search for and select **Active Directory**.

3. In the left-hand menu, click **AD Connect**.

4. You will see the link to the **AD Connect** agent, as in the following example:

PROVISION FROM ACTIVE DIRECTORY

 Azure AD Connect cloud provisioning

This feature allows you to manage provisioning from the cloud.

Manage provisioning (Preview)

Azure AD Connect sync

Not Installed	Download Azure AD Connect
Last Sync	Sync has never run
Password Hash Sync	Disabled

Figure 3.8 – Getting the AD Connect agent download link

5. Copy the agent onto the server you wish to install it and run it, then follow through the installation wizard.

It is recommended that you install the agent on at least two or, preferably, three servers in your environment to protect the synchronization process should the primary server fail.

> **Important note**
> The AD Connect agent cannot be actively synchronizing on more than one server. When installing the agent on the standby servers, you must configure them to be in stand-by mode. In the event of the primary server failing, you need to manually reconfigure one of the secondary servers and take them out of stand-by mode.

An important aspect of Azure AD Connect is how users' passwords are validated, which in turn defines *where* the password is stored.

Password Hash Synchronization

Password Hash Synchronization (PHS) ensures a *hash* of the user's password is copied from the directory into the Azure AD. When a user's password is stored in AD, it is stored as a *hash*; that is, the password has a mathematical algorithm applied to it that effectively scrambles it. A user's password is prevented from being readable if the underlying database is compromised.

With Azure PHS, the password that is already hashed is hashed once again—a hash of a hash—before it is then stored in the Azure AD, providing an extra level of protection, as per the example shown in the following diagram:

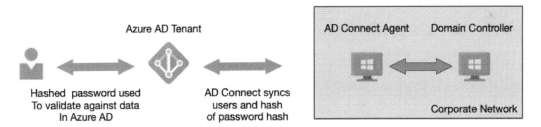

Figure 3.9 – Azure PHS

The result of all this is that when a user authenticates against Azure AD, it does so *directly* against the information stored in the Azure AD database.

An AD Connect synchronization client is required on a computer in your organization if communications to your domain are severed for whatever reason. Users can still authenticate because they are doing so against information in Azure AD.

One potential downside, however, is that this synchronization process is not immediate. Therefore, if a user updates their details, it won't reflect in the Azure AD accounts until the sync process has taken place, which by default takes 30 minutes. However, this can be changed, or synchronizations can be forced, which is useful if a bulk update is performed, especially on disabling accounts.

Note that some premium features such as Identity Protection and Azure AD DS require PHS.

For some organizations, storing the password hash in Azure AD is simply not an option. For these scenarios, one option would be **pass-through authentication** (**PTA**).

Azure AD PTA

With PTA, when a user needs to authenticate, the request is forwarded to an agent that performs the authentication and returns the result and authentication token, as in the example shown in the following diagram:

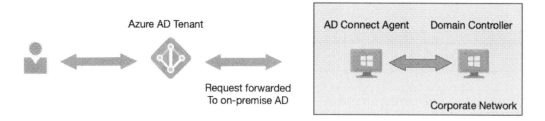

Figure 3.10 – Azure PTA

Another reason you may wish to go for this option is if any changes to user accounts must be enforced across the enterprise immediately.

These agents must have access to your AD, including *unconstrained* access to your domain controllers, and they need access to the internet. You therefore need to consider the security implications of this, and the effort involved; for example, opening firewall ports. All traffic is, of course, encrypted and limited to authentication requests.

Because PTA works by handing off the process to an agent, you need to consider resilience. It is recommended you install the AD Connect agent on at least three servers to both distribute the load and provide a backup should one of the agents go offline.

If you still lose connectivity to your agents, authentication will fail. Another failsafe is to use PHS, although this, of course, requires storing password hashes in Azure AD, so you need to consider why you opted for PTA in the first place.

Password Writeback

As we have already mentioned, one of the benefits Azure AD provides is self-service password resets—that is, the ability for users to reset their passwords by completing an online process. This process results in the user's credentials being reset in the cloud—however, if you have hybrid scenarios with those same accounts, you would typically want to have a password reset performed in the cloud to write that change back to the directory.

To achieve this, we use an *optional* feature in AD Connect called **Password Writeback**.

Password Writeback is supported in all three hybrid scenarios—PHS, PTA, and AD Federation.

Using Password Writeback enables enforcement of password policies and zero-delay feedback—that is, if there is an issue resetting the password in the AD, the user is informed straightaway rather than waiting for a sync process. It doesn't require any additional firewall rules over and above those needed for AD Connect (which works over port 443).

Note, however, that this is an optional feature, and to use it, the account that AD Connect uses to integrate with your AD must be set with specific access rights—these are the following:

- *Reset password*
- *Write permissions* on `lockoutTime`
- *Write permissions* on `pwdLastSet`

AD Connect ensures that the user login experience is consistent between cloud and hybrid systems. However, AD Connect has an additional option—the ability to enable a user already authenticated to the cloud without the need to sign in again. This is known as Seamless SSO.

Seamless SSO

Either PHS or PTA can be combined with an option called **Seamless SSO**. With Seamless SSO, users who are already authenticated to the corporate network will be automatically signed in to Azure AD when challenged.

As we can see in the example in the following diagram, if you have a cloud-based application that uses Azure AD for authentication and you have Seamless SSO enabled, users won't be prompted again for a username and password if they have already signed in to an AD:

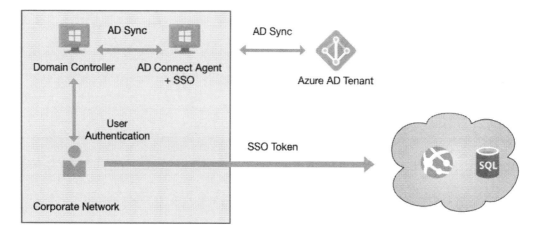

Figure 3.11 – SSO

However, it's important to note that Seamless SSO is for the user's device that *is domain-joined*—that is, domain-joined to a network. Devices that are joined to Azure AD or Hybrid Azure AD-joined use primary refresh tokens also to enable SSO, which is a slightly different method of achieving the same SSO experience but using **JSON web tokens (JWT)**.

In other words, Seamless SSO is a feature of *hybrid* scenarios where you are using AD Connect. SSO is a single sign-on for *pure cloud-managed* devices.

Federated authentication

Federated authentication uses an entirely separate authentication system such as **Active Directory Federation Services (AD FS)**. AD FS has been available for some time to enable enterprises to provide SSO capabilities for users by extending access management to the internet.

Therefore, some organizations may already make use of this, and it would therefore make sense to leverage it.

AD FS provides additional advanced authentication services, such as smartcard-based authentication and/or third-party MFA.

Generally speaking, it is recommended to use PHS or PTA. You should only consider federated authentication if you already have a *specific* requirement to use it, such as the need to use smartcard-based authentication.

Azure AD Connect Health

Before we leave authentication and, specifically, AD Connect, we must look at one last aspect of the service: **AD Connect Health**.

Azure AD Connect Health provides different types of health monitoring, as follows:

- **AD Connect Health for Sync**, which monitors the health of your AD DS to Azure AD.
- **AD Connect Health for AD DS**, which monitors your domain controllers and AD.
- **AD Connect Health for AD FS**, which monitors AD FS servers.

There are three separate agents, one for each scenario; as with the main AD Connect agent, the download link for the AD Connect Health agent can be accessed in the Azure portal, as follows:

1. Navigate to the Azure portal at `https://portal.azure.com`.
2. In the top bar, search for and select **Active Directory**.
3. In the left-hand menu, click **AD Connect**.
4. On the main page, click **Azure AD Connect Health** under **Health and Analytics**.

5. You will see the links to the AD Connect Health agents under **Get tools**, as in the following example:

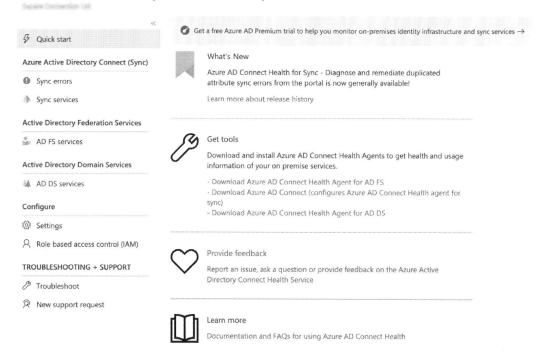

Figure 3.12 – Downloading the AD Connect Health agents

The **AD Connect Health** blade also gives you a view on any alerts, performance statistics, usage analytics, and other information related to the AD.

Some of the benefits include the following:

- Reports on these issues:
    - --Extranet lockouts
    - --Failed sign-ins
    - --Privacy compliance
- Alerts on the following:
    - --Server configuration and availability
    - --Performance
    - --Connectivity

Finally, you need to know that to use AD Connect Health, the following must apply:

- You must install an agent on your infrastructure on any identity servers you wish to monitor.

- You must have an **Azure AD P1** license.

- You must be a **global administrator** to install and configure the agent.

- You must have connectivity from your services to Azure AD Connect Health service endpoints (these endpoints can be found on the Microsoft website).

As we can see, Azure provides a range of options to manage authentication, ensure user details are synchronized between and cloud, and enable easier sign-on. We also looked at how we can monitor and ensure the health of the different services we use for integration.

In the next section, we will look at ways, other than just with passwords, we can control and manage user authentication.

Understanding conditional access, MFA and security defaults

In today's environments that often expand beyond an organization's network into the cloud, controlling access while still enabling users to access their resources becomes more complicated.

An additional complication is the fact that different users may have other requirements. For example, a system's administrators most definitely need the most secure access policies in place. In contrast, an account that will always have more limited access anyway may not need quite as stringent measures because they won't be accessing (or be granted access to) particularly risky systems should they be compromised.

Another example is where a user is signing in from—if a user is on the corporate network, you already have physical boundaries in place; therefore, you don't need to be as concerned as a user accessing from a public network.

You could argue that you should always take the most secure baseline; however, the more security measures you introduce, the more complex a user's sign-on becomes, which in turn can impact a business.

It is, therefore, imperative that you get the right mix of security for who the user is, what their role is, the sensitivity of what they are accessing, and from where they are signing in.

MFA

Traditional usernames and passwords can be (relatively) easily compromised. Many solutions have been used to counteract this risk, such as requiring long and complex passwords, forcing periodic changes, and so on.

Another, more secure way is to provide an additional piece of information—generally, one that is randomly generated and delivered to you via a pre-approved device such as a mobile phone. This is known as MFA.

Usually, this additional *token* is provided to the approved device via a phone call, text message, or mobile app, often called an **authentication app**.

When setting up MFA, a user must *register* the mobile device with the provider. Initially, a text message will be sent to verify that the user registering the device owns it.

From that point on, authentication tokens can only be received by that device. We can see the process in action in the following diagram:

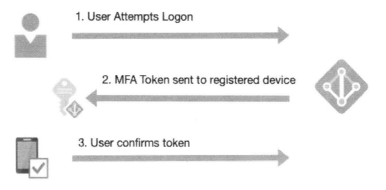

Figure 3.13 – MFA

Microsoft Azure provides MFA for free; however, the paid tiers of Azure AD offer more granular control.

On the Azure AD free tier, you can use a feature called **Security Defaults** to enable MFA for ALL users, or at the very least on all *Azure Global Administrators* when Security Defaults isn't enabled. However, the free tier for non-global administrators only supports a mobile authenticator app for providing the token.

With an **Azure AD Premium P1** license, you can have more granular control over MFA through the use of CA, which allows you only to use MFA based on specific scenarios—for example, when accessing publicly over the internet, but not from a trusted location such as a corporate network.

Azure AD Premium P2 extends MFA support by introducing *risk-based* conditional access. We will explore these concepts shortly, but first we will delve into what is available with Security Defaults.

Security Defaults

Microsoft provides a set of tools called CA—however, these require configuration and ongoing management, plus you must upgrade to the Azure AD Premium P1 tier to use it.

For some organizations, this may either involve too much effort (perhaps you are a small team) or possibly cost too much.

Because security is so important, Microsoft offers Security Defaults—these are a set of built-in policies than protect your organization against common threats. Essentially, enabling this feature preconfigures your AD tenant with the following:

- Requires all users to register and use MFA
- Requires administrators to perform MFA
- Blocks legacy authentication protocols
- Protects privileged activities such as accessing the Azure portal

An important note to consider is that Security Defaults is completely free and does NOT require a premium AD license.

It's also important to understand that because this is a free tier, it's an all-or-nothing package. It's also worth noting that the MFA mechanism only works using security codes through a mobile app authenticator (such as Microsoft Authenticator) or a hardware token. In other words, you cannot use the text message or calling features.

Security Defaults is enabled by default on new subscriptions, and therefore you don't need to do anything. However, for organizations that require more control, you should consider CA.

Understanding and setting up CA

For organizations that want more control over security or that already have an Azure AD Premium P1 or P2 license, CA can provide a much more granular control over security, with better reporting capabilities.

Azure uses several security-based services that can be applied depending on various attributes, known as *signals*, which are then used to make decisions around which security policies need to be applied.

This process and set of tools are called CA, and this can be accessed in the Azure portal via the **AD Security** blade.

> **Tip**
> For the exam, Azure CA requires an *Azure AD Premium P1 license.*

Standard signals you can use when making decisions include the following:

- **User or group membership**: For example, if users are in a group that will give them access to particularly sensitive systems or high levels of access—that is, an admin group.

- **IP location**: For example, when users are signing in from a controlled IP range such as a corporate network, or if users are signing in from a particular geography that has specific local requirements.

- **Device-specific** platforms, such as mobile devices, may need different security measures.

- **Application**: Similar to groups, specific applications, regardless of role, may need additional protective measures—for example, a payroll application.

- **Real-time risk detection**: **Azure Identity Protection** monitors user activity for "risky" behavior. If triggered, this can force particular policies to be activated, such as a forced password reset.

- **Microsoft Cloud App Security**: Enables application sessions to be monitored, which again can trigger policies to be applied.

- **Terms of use**: Before accessing your systems, you might need to get consent from users by requesting a terms-of-use policy to be signed. A specific Azure AD policy can be defined, requiring users to sign this before they can sign in.

Once a signal has been matched, various decisions can then be made regarding a user's access. These include the following:

- **Block Access**

    --Block the user from proceeding entirely.

- **Grant Access**, which is further broken down into the following:

    --Require MFA

    --Require device compliancy (via device policies)

--Require device to be Hybrid Azure AD-joined

--Requirement an approved client app

--Requirement of an app protection policy—that is, a review

To set up CA, you first need to disable Security Defaults. To perform this, follow these steps:

1. Navigate to the Azure portal at `https://portal.azure.com`.

2. In the top bar, search for and select **Active Directory**.

3. On the left-hand menu, click **Properties**.

4. At the bottom of the page, click **Manage Security Defaults**.

5. A side window will appear, with an option to disable Security Defaults.

The next step is to purchase AD licenses, as follows:

1. Navigate to the Azure portal at `https://portal.azure.com`.

2. In the top bar, search for and select **Active Directory**.

3. On the left-hand menu, click **Licenses**.

4. On the main page, click **Manage your purchased licenses**.

5. Click **Try / Buy**.

6. A side window will appear; click **Purchase services**.

7. This will open a new browser window: the **Purchase Services** page of the **Microsoft 365 admin center** (`admin.microsoft.com`).

8. Scroll to the bottom of the page and select **Security and Identity** under **Other categories**.

9. Select **Azure Active Directory Premium P2**.

10. Click **Buy**.

11. Choose whether to **pay monthly** or **pay for a full year** and select how many licenses you need. Click **Check out now**.

12. Complete the checkout process.

Once you have completed the checkout process, you need to assign your licenses to your users, as follows:

1. Navigate back to the Azure portal at `https://portal.azure.com`.

2. In the top bar, search for and select **Active Directory**.

3. On the left-hand menu, click **Licenses**.

4. On the main page, click **Manage your purchased licenses**.

5. Click **All products**.

6. Click **Azure Directory Premium P2** (your licenses count has increased by the number of licenses you have purchased).

7. Click **Assign**.

8. Click **Users**.

9. In the side window that appears, select the user(s) you wish to assign licenses to. Click **Select**.

10. Click **Assignment options**.

11. In the side window that appears, set your license options and click **OK**.

12. Click **Assign**.

With Security Defaults disabled and your premium licenses assigned, you can now configure CA policies, as follows:

1. Navigate to the Azure portal at `https://portal.azure.com`.

2. In the top bar, search for and select **Azure AD Conditional Access**.

3. On the left-hand menu, click **Named locations**.

4. Click **+ New location**.

5. On this page, you can define specific **countries** or **IP ranges** that users can sign in from. Click the *back* button in your browser to return to the **CA** page, or click the **CA** breadcrumb.

6. On the left-hand menu, click **Policies**.

7. Click **New Policy**.

8. Enter `Managers` under **name**.

9. Click **Users and groups**.

10. Click the **Users and groups** checkbox, and then select a user. Click **OK**.

11. Click **Conditions**. You can choose different risk profiles depending on your needs—for example, click **Sign-In risk**, and then click the **Medium** checkbox, as in the following example. Click **Select**:

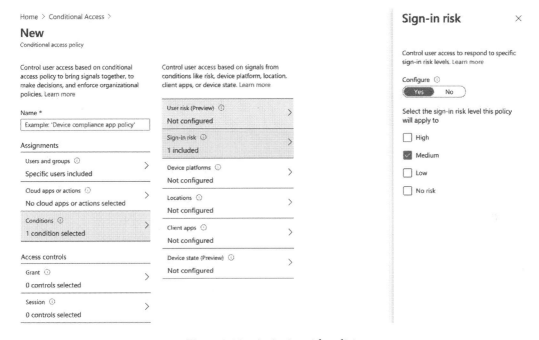

Figure 3.14 – Assigning risk policies

12. Choose the action to perform when the policy is triggered. Click **Grant** under **Access controls**, and then click the **Require multi-factor authentication** checkbox. Click **Select**.

13. Set the **Enable policy** to **Report-only**.

14. Click **Create**.

In this example, we have created a simple access policy that only applies to a single user. The policy will trigger if the user's activity is deemed medium risk, and will then enforce MFA. However, we set the policy to **Report-only**, meaning that the actual MFA enforcement won't take place. This is advised when first creating policies in order to ensure that you do not inadvertently lock users out. In other words, it gives you the ability to test policies before applying them.

In this section, we examined how to provide greater control over the user authentication process for internal users. Sometimes, however, we will want to provide access to external users.

Using external identities

So far, we've looked at integrating our corporate users into an **Azure AD tenant**. However, for may web applications, there will be a need to authenticate customers as well.

Traditionally, this would be provided on a per-application basis using a simple username/password combination stored in a local database. However, given that you may expose multiple applications and you would want to leverage the security benefits we've so far discussed, it would make more sense to leverage the highly secure capabilities of Azure AD.

Of course, what we don't want to do is create user accounts in our domain; they still need to be completely separate from your corporate users. A single authentication mechanism for apps you are responsible for certainly makes sense, both from a management perspective (only having one user database to manage) and from an ease-of-integration perspective—why build a security mechanism for every app?

There are three main ways we can provide this access, listed as follows:

- Multi-tenancy
- B2C
- **Business to Business (B2B)**

We will look at each option in turn.

Multi-tenancy

With multi-tenancy, your applications support *external Azure AD tenants*—that is, as well as allowing our application to authenticate your users, you can also authorize against an external (that is, not yours) Azure AD tenant.

The following diagram shows the differences between the two models:

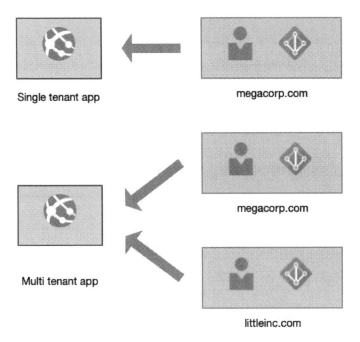

Figure 3.15 – Azure multi-tenancy

This option is excellent for *enterprise-class* applications for organizations—that is, when you've built a SaaS platform that is offered to companies as opposed to individuals. For example, **Office 365** is an enterprise application design for companies and is always tied to an AD tenant, and therefore is available to employees of that company. In comparison, Facebook is for *individual* users who will sign in using personal email accounts.

Because of this, users *must* have an existing Azure AD account, either by having their own Azure tenant or an Office 365 tenant.

Consumer applications – B2C

B2C is essentially designed for *individual customer* applications—for example, a storefront or social site. Users would generally link their existing email to your B2C tenant, and their app would be built to authenticate against your app. Whenever you are signing up for a website and are given the option to **Sign in with Facebook** or **Sign In with your Microsoft Account**, this is B2C.

Azure provides the ability to easily integrate third-party **identity providers** (**IDP**) such as Facebook, Google, LinkedIn, Twitter, and more.

Integrating third-party providers is as simple as registering the client ID and secrets from your external IDP into an Azure B2C tenant.

Users then authenticate directly against the IDP and not your tenant. Your tenant simply confirms with the IDP that your sign-in is valid.

Note that Azure B2C tenants are separate from your regular AD tenant—in other words, to set it up, you must create a new tenant as a B2C tenant.

External user collaboration – B2B

B2B collaboration essentially extends the multi-tenant scenario; however, it will authenticate users who *don't* have an Azure AD account but have some other form of corporate credential instead.

We've already seen these types of users—they are the ones for whom we create guest accounts in our Azure AD. In other words, the email can be from some other external provider.

The following diagram shows the different authentication flows used in B2C and B2B:

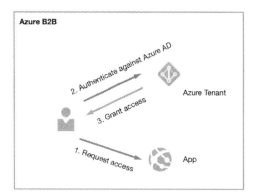
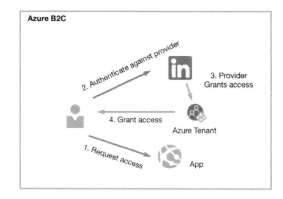

Figure 3.16 – Azure B2B versus B2C

We have seen in this section how we can leverage Azure's authentication mechanisms to authenticate external users as well as internal users.

In the final section of this chapter, we will present an example scenario and discuss which tools and technologies can be used to meet the requirements.

Summary

In this chapter, we have looked at the distinction between authentication and authorization, and the challenges traditional username/password mechanisms present.

We explored Microsoft AD and Azure AD, the differences between them, and how we integrate them through AD Connect, including using AD Connect Health to monitor the connection.

We also saw how Azure provides Security Defaults to provide more advanced options such as MFA, and how through the use of CA we can implement finer-grained controls to tailor and control the user experience.

Finally, we considered the tools available for authenticating external users.

In the next chapter, we will continue this theme and see how we can continue to control the actions our authenticated users can perform through the use of authorization.

Exam scenario

The solutions to the exam scenarios can be found at the end of this book

Mega Corp is looking to begin its migration to Azure.

They currently have an existing AD and are looking to extend this into the cloud to support their workloads.

Because they have a mixture of office-based and remote workers, they need a robust solution that can withstand an interruption to the VPN that will connect them to their Azure tenant.

Remote users must have two-factor authentication, but Office users don't want to be prompted for additional credentials when accessing apps in Azure.

Which options can be implemented to support these requirements?

4
Managing User Authorization

In the previous chapter, we covered how users are authenticated in solutions; this is the act of proving who you are. Once they have access, you must continually ensure that authenticated users can only access what they should – this is known as authorization.

At its simplest, some users may need administrative access to do everything within the Azure portal. In contrast, some users may only want to be able to read or view a specific resource.

In reality, you will have a vast mix of requirements everywhere between those two extremes – and of course, it's not just access to the Azure portal you will want to control, but all the apps and services you created in it.

In this chapter, we will examine how access control is performed using **Active Directory (AD)** roles and Azure roles.

Then, we'll look at how to manage the flow of access, using AD groups, management groups, subscriptions, and resource groups.

We'll then look at how to further tighten security through the use of **Privileged Identity Management (PIM)** before moving on to using **Identity Protection** to help identify and manage risk.

In this chapter, we're going to cover the following main topics:

- Understanding Azure roles
- Managing users with hierarchies
- Controlling access with PIM
- Managing risk with Identity Protection

Technical requirements

This chapter requires internet access to the Azure portal and an Azure subscription:

```
https://portal.azure.com
```

Understanding Azure roles

There are three distinct ways of managing user access in Azure, classic roles, Azure roles, and Azure AD roles. Each controls a different aspect of the platform and is used in different ways. We will examine the three types, how they are different, and how you use them.

Classic roles

When Azure was first introduced, access to resources was controlled using just three roles, which are discussed in the following sections.

Account Administrator

Only one per Azure account. This role grants access to the Azure Account Center for managing all subscriptions within an account. When you sign up for your Azure account, you are granted this role, and it enables you to create, cancel, and manage billing for subscriptions. It also allows you to change the **Service Administrator** role.

Service Administrator

Only one per subscription. This role allows you to manage the services in your Azure subscription, including canceling it. It is also the only role that will enable you to assign the **Co-Administrator** role. By default, when you create your first subscription, this is automatically set to the Account Administrator.

Co-Administrator

Up to 200 per subscription. Grants the same rights as the Service Administrator role, but it can't change the association of subscriptions. You can assign other Co-Administrators, but you can't change the Service Administrator.

To view and manage classic roles, perform the following steps:

1. Navigate to the Azure portal by opening `https://portal.azure.com`.

2. In the left-hand menu, select or search for **Subscriptions**.

3. Select the subscription you wish to manage.

4. On the left-hand menu, select **Access control (IAM)**.

5. On the horizontal menu, choose **Classic Administrators**.

6. To add a new classic administrator, click **+ Add**, followed by **Add co-Administrator**. *Figure 4.1* shows an example:

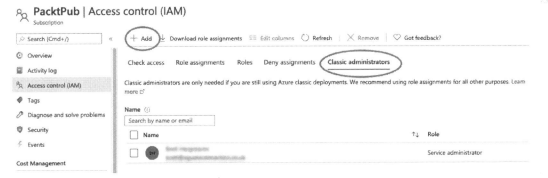

Figure 4.1 – Managing classic administrators

If you need to change the Service Administrator, you must use the Azure account portal:

- Navigate to `https://account.windowsazure.com/subscriptions`.

- Select your subscription.

- Click **Edit Subscription Details** to change the Service Administrator.

As you can see, the original classic roles do not provide much granular access! So, Microsoft introduced **Role-Based Access Control** roles or **RBAC** roles, which we shall look at next.

Azure roles

RBAC roles provide much more control as they give a series of options and can be applied at different scopes – from management groups, subscriptions, right down to individual resources.

They are also based on **Azure Resource Manager (ARM)** templates – and can be defined in code and applied via the portal, script, or DevOps pipelines.

> **Important note**
>
> ARM templates are used throughout Azure to define everything from roles to resources. Built as JSON documents, they are literally the building blocks of Azure.

There are over 70 built-in roles, or you can define your own. The most commonly used built-in roles are the following:

- **Owner**: Full access to all resources with the ability to assign RBAC roles to other users

- **Contributor**: Can create and manage all resources and create new AD tenants, but cannot grant access to other users

- **Reader**: Read access to all resources

- **User Account Administrator**: Can grant access to other users

Other than User Account Administrator, these roles apply to all resource types and can be applied at any scope.

It's also worth mentioning that the Reader role gives access to the resources, but not the data in those resources. For example, a user with a **Reader** role for a storage account can see the storage account and its properties, but it *can't* read the data stored within it.

The rest of the built-in roles provide specific access to specific types of resources. For example, the **Storage Account Contributor** gives access to view and manage storage accounts, but again, not the data *within* them. In contrast, the **Storage Blob Data Contributor** role allows a user to manage containers within a storage account and access the data within them but does not create and manage the storage accounts themselves.

We can examine the individual rights each role provides through the portal, which we will do next.

Managing roles

To view a list of all available roles, who has been assigned to them, and the details around what access they provide, perform the following steps:

1. Navigate to the Azure portal by opening `https://portal.azure.com`.

2. In the left-hand menu, select or search for **Subscriptions**.

3. Select the subscription you wish to manage.

4. On the left-hand menu, select **Access control (IAM)**.

5. On the horizontal menu, choose **Roles**.

6. Select or search for the role **Storage Blob Data Contributor** by typing into the search box (see *Figure 4.2*):

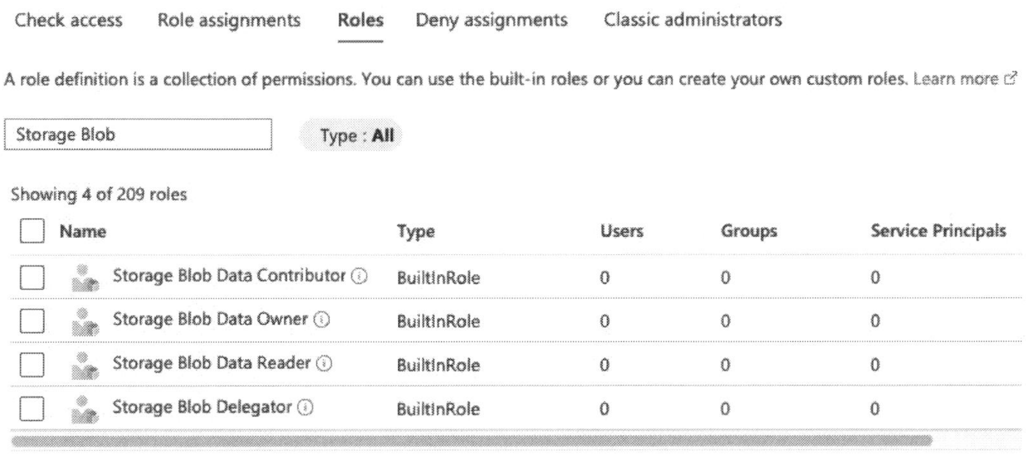

Check access   Role assignments   **Roles**   Deny assignments   Classic administrators

A role definition is a collection of permissions. You can use the built-in roles or you can create your own custom roles. Learn more ⬀

| Storage Blob | | Type : **All** | | | |

Showing 4 of 209 roles

Name	Type	Users	Groups	Service Principals
Storage Blob Data Contributor ⓘ	BuiltInRole	0	0	0
Storage Blob Data Owner ⓘ	BuiltInRole	0	0	0
Storage Blob Data Reader ⓘ	BuiltInRole	0	0	0
Storage Blob Delegator ⓘ	BuiltInRole	0	0	0

Figure 4.2 – Azure Roles List

7. Click on the **Storage Blob Data Contributor** role.

8. This will display a list of all users who have been assigned to the role. **Click Permissions**.

9. Permissions are grouped by resource type; click **Microsoft Storage** to expand all the roles within that type.

10. Scroll down the page to see which roles have been granted. As in the following figure, we can see that the **Storage Blob Data Contributor** role has **Read**, **Write** and **Delete** on **Storage Blob Service Containers** and **Read**, **Write**, **Delete**, and **Other** on **Storage Blob Service Blobs** for data:

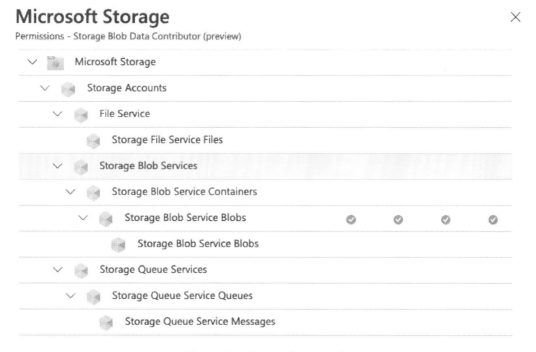

Figure 4.3 – Azure roles example

Creating custom roles

Sometimes the built-in roles don't accommodate your requirements; therefore, we need to create a custom role.

This can be performed in the portal, via PowerShell, or even via a DevOps pipeline. Custom roles are JSON documents that define all the permissions you wish the user to have.

You can build a custom role from scratch; however, the easiest way is to start from an existing role and then modify it as in the following example:

1. Navigate to the Azure portal by opening `https://portal.azure.com`.

2. In the left-hand menu, select or search for **Subscriptions**.

3. Select the·subscription you wish to manage.

4. On the left-hand menu, select **Access control (IAM)**.

5. On the horizontal menu, click **+ Add** followed by **Add custom role**.

6. Enter a name, for example, `StorageManagerDenyDelete`.

7. Next to **Baseline Permissions**, choose **Clone a Role**.

8. In the **Role to clone** drop-down, select **Storage Blob Data Contributor**.

9. Click **Next**.

10. Remove the delete permissions by clicking on the **Trash icon** by the following:

    `Microsoft.Storage/storageAccounts/blobServices/containers/delete`

    `Microsoft.Storage/storageAccounts/blobServices/containers/blobs/delete`

11. Click **Next**.

12. Click **Next** again on assignable scopes as we will allow this to be used at the subscription level.

13. You will be presented with the JSON that defines your new role, which should look like the following:

```json
{
    "properties": {
        "roleName": "StorageManagerDenyDelete",
        "description": "",
        "assignableScopes": [
            "/subscriptions/xxxxxxxx-xxxx-xxxx-xxxx-xxxxxxxxxxxx"
        ],
        "permissions": [
            {
                "actions": [
                    "Microsoft.Storage/storageAccounts/blobServices/containers/read",
                    "Microsoft.Storage/storageAccounts/blobServices/containers/write",
                    "Microsoft.Storage/storageAccounts/blobServices/generateUserDelegationKey/action"
                ],
```

```
                "notActions": [],
                "dataActions": [
                        "Microsoft.Storage/storageAccounts/
    blobServices/containers/blobs/read",
                        "Microsoft.Storage/storageAccounts/
    blobServices/containers/blobs/move/action",
                        "Microsoft.Storage/storageAccounts/
    blobServices/containers/blobs/write"
                ],
                "notDataActions": []
            }
        ]
    }
}
```

14. If you wish to download this JSON, click the **Download** button.

15. To create the role, click **Review + create**.

16. Confirm you wish to create the role by clicking **Create**.

We have seen from these examples that Azure roles allow you to grant access to individual Azure services at a very granular level. Next, we will examine the third type of role – Azure AD roles.

Azure AD roles

Azure AD roles allow us to manage other user accounts, such as creating them, editing them, and deleting them, within Azure AD.

As with Azure roles, Azure AD roles have a range of built-in templates, and you can also create custom roles; however, this requires an **AD Premium P1** or **P2** license:

- **Global Administrator**: Manage access to all features in Azure AD, assign roles to others, and reset the password for all users, including other administrators

- **User Administrator**: Create and manage users, manage support tickets and service health, and change the password for users, Helpdesk administrators, or other User Administrators (but not Global Administrators)

- **Billing Administrator**: Make purchases, manage subscriptions and support tickets, and monitor service health

Again, we can go for more granular roles, and we can get a complete list of those roles through the portal by performing the following steps:

1. Navigate to the Azure portal by opening `https://portal.azure.com`.

2. Select or search for **Azure Active Directory**.

3. In the left-hand menu, click **Roles and administrators**.

4. A list of all existing roles is listed. Click a role, for example, **Application administrator**.

5. On the next window, you are presented with a list of users who have the role assigned to them (if any). To view what actions members of the role can perform, click **Description** in the left-hand menu.

6. Scroll down to see the roles and permissions, as per the following figure:

Figure 4.4 – Application Administrator role permissions

Creating a custom Azure AD role is similar to creating a custom Azure role – but the option is only available if you have purchased an Azure AD Premium P1 or P2 license:

1. Navigate to the Azure portal by opening `https://portal.azure.com`.

2. Select or search for **Azure Active Directory**.

3. In the left-hand menu, click **Roles and Administrators**.

4. On the horizontal menu, click **New custom role**.

5. Give the role a name, such as `MyCustomRole`.

6. For **Baseline permissions**, select **Start from scratch**.

7. Click **Next**.

8. Select the permissions you wish to assign.

9. Click **Next**.

10. Click **Create**.

There is a distinct difference between Azure roles and Azure AD roles; Azure roles are for managing access to resources, whereas Azure AD roles are for managing users.

Using a mixture of role types, you can grant granular access to your users. However, with so much flexibility, it can be challenging to manage, especially in complex or large organizations. For this reason, Azure provides management hierarchies to enable access to be set at different levels.

Managing users with hierarchies

A core principle for any system should be **Least Privileged Access** – that is, only allow access to something if it is required. Or, to put it another way, don't just give every user full owner access to everything! If a user only needs to manage storage accounts, only provide access to storage accounts.

To help manage access, a strategy of how these roles can be applied must be considered and designed.

After all, if you have thousands of users, granting access to each user on a per resource type basis would be unmanageable!

Management groups, subscriptions, and resource groups

We can assign user access to the resources they need at different **scopes** – management groups, subscriptions, resource groups, or individual resources. As we can see in the following figure, the relationships between these scopes are hierarchical, and permissions or roles set at the highest **management group** scope flow down to the child levels:

Figure 4.5 – Azure access scopes

Management groups can also be nested within other management groups to mirror your corporate structure.

The scope of all access is the Azure AD tenant, which contains a top-level **Root Management Group**. By combining management groups and subscriptions, you can build up a structure that maps to your company's departments or geographic locations, or a mixture of both. The following figure shows a possible example of how this might look:

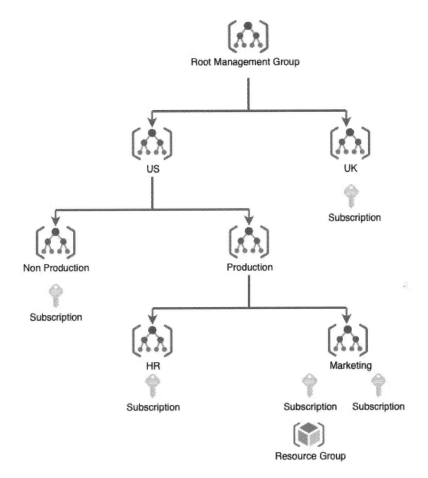

Figure 4.6 – Management group hierarchies

Once we have our structure, we can then assign our RBAC roles at the appropriate level, and those roles will then flow down through all subsequent groups, subscriptions, and resource groups.

The following figure shows another example of how roles can be assigned at different levels, which are then combined at the relevant subscription, resource group, or even resource being accessed:

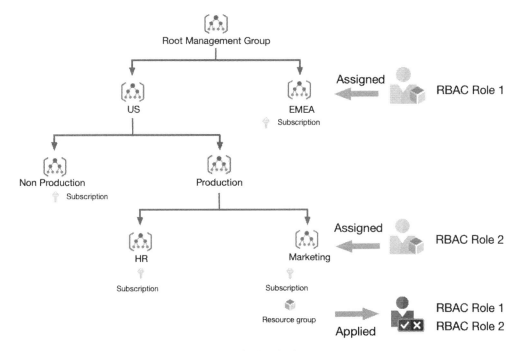

Figure 4.7 – Multi-level role assignment

Because rights flow down through the tree, we need to think about the highest levels and decide at any particular level if there is a group of people who would need the same level of access all the way down.

Naturally, we need to be careful; setting a user as an **Owner** at the root means they have the highest level of access, including the ability to read data, all the way down. Not only do we need to carefully consider whether a user should have this, but we also need to be wary of what it would mean should that account be comprised.

Finally, you can group users themselves by AD groups; that is, if you wanted to assign the HR users read access to the HR department, you could add all those users to an HR AD user group and grant the rights to the group at the appropriate level.

Designing a good management structure will help control your user access levels. However, in large companies with many departments and a mix of authorities, it is still possible to lose track of who has access to what. This can result in users having improper access – especially as they may change roles and take on or lose responsibilities during their time with your company.

Azure provides a collection of tools grouped under **Privileged Identity Management (PIM)** that help secure your organization by granting fine-grained control over how users can get access to your systems.

Controlling access with PIM

The traditional security model defines policies such as *least privileged access*, meaning you should always assign the least amount of rights to any one user. However, you still need to assign administrator rights to some users.

With PIM, you can control *when* and for *how long* those rights are granted. In other words, users have to request elevated access as they need it explicitly, and this access can then be time-boxed to be automatically removed after a defined period.

This way, even if an individual account were compromised, an attacker would still not have high levels of access.

Specifically, PIM can help you by doing the following:

- Providing **just-in-time** elevated access to Azure AD and resources
- Assigning accounts with **time-boxed** start and end dates/times
- Requiring an **additional approval step** for elevated access
- Enforcing **MFA**
- Requesting **justification** for why access is required
- You getting **notified** when privileged roles are granted
- Conducting **Access Reviews**
- Providing an **audit** history

A typical scenario might be as follows.

A manager needs to create a new guest account. By default, the manager does not have access to do this. Rather than grant the manager the role to do this, they are marked as *eligible* to have that role; they can then request access to complete the task, including why they need access.

The request can either be set to auto-approve or be directed to an authorizer for approval. The access is then granted but with only a 1-hour window. Once the window has expired, the elevated rights are automatically removed.

Activating PIM

To use PIM, you need a **P2 license** for every account that wishes to use the service – this includes users who need to manage/authorize others or accounts that need to be managed.

> **Important note**
>
> Example: If you have five accounts that will authorize access or perform access reviews, and you have five different accounts that will be managed or have access reviews run against them, you will need 10 P2 licenses.
>
> Note that PIM can manage Azure roles and Azure AD roles, but *not* classic administrator roles – Account Administrator, Service Administrator, or Co-Administrators.

As PIM is very different from the traditional method of authorizing access to systems, simply "switching it on" is not a simple task. You need to activate and enforce its use gradually, but at the same time, ensure your systems are adequately secured as quickly as possible.

You must first activate PIM within Azure by searching for `Privileged Access Management` in the portal. The first account to use and set up PIM must be assigned as the **Security Administrator** and **Privileged Role Administrator** for your tenant.

Next, review all users who have elevated roles – that is, those who are one of the following:

- **Global Administrator**
- **Privileged Role Administrator**
- **Exchange Administrator**
- **SharePoint Administrator**

Ensure users with those roles do need it and remove any who don't.

To help achieve this, you can use the Discovery and Insights tool:

1. Navigate to the Azure portal by opening `https://portal.azure.com`.
2. Select or search for **Privileged Identity Management (or PIM)**.
3. In the left-hand menu, select **Azure AD roles**.
4. In the left-hand menu, select **Discovery and Insights**.
5. For each of the discovered assignments, click the **Reduce** option, as shown in the following figure (**Reduce global administrators**).

6. Remove the **Administrator** role from users who do not need it:

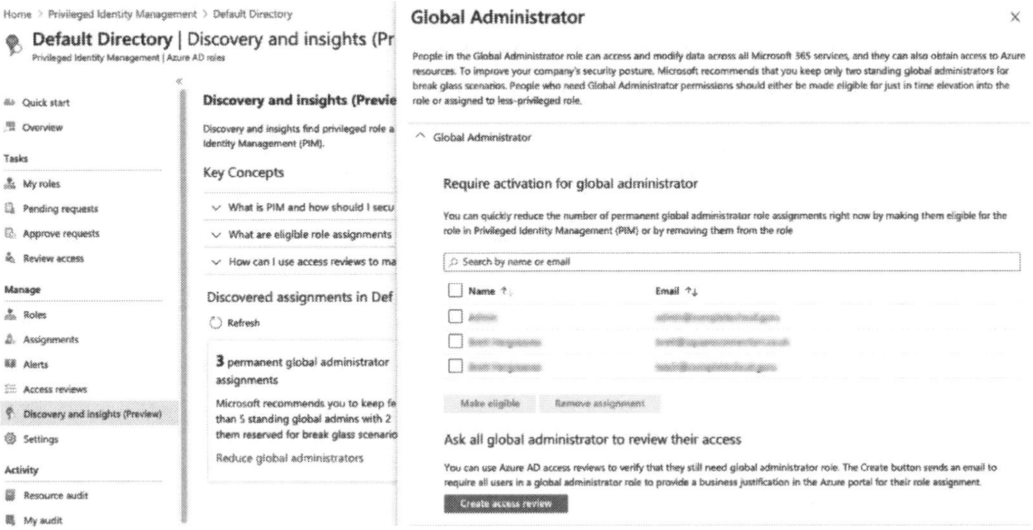

Figure 4.8 – PIM

Removing the roles can be achieved in several different ways. First, the assignment can simply be removed.

The second option is to make the role **eligible**; this means the user can have that role, but they have to request it first, which we will cover shortly.

Finally, to have the users confirm or deny whether they need the role, you can create an **Access Review**. Again, we shall cover this shortly.

Just-In-Time elevated access

As discussed, with PIM, rather than assigning roles to users that are always active, you instead make users eligible to use a role. Users then activate the roles as required.

> **Important note**
> This is *not* the same as just-in-time virtual machine access, which allows access to virtual machines on a per request basis by opening firewalls as required.

For the following walk-through, that demonstrates using just-in-time elevated access, I have created a user called ITManager, which I will use to demonstrate the process. You also need a P1 or P2 license and PIM activated.

Assigning an eligible role

1. Navigate to the Azure portal by opening `https://portal.azure.com`.

2. Select or search for **Azure Active Directory**.

3. In the left-hand menu, click **Roles and administrators**.

4. Select the role you wish to assign, for example, **User administrator**.

5. On the left-hand menu, click **Role Settings**.

6. Click **Edit** at the top.

7. Set the activation settings, such as changing the duration to 1 hour and tick **Require approval to activate**, then add your admin user as an approver. See *Figure 4.9*, for example:

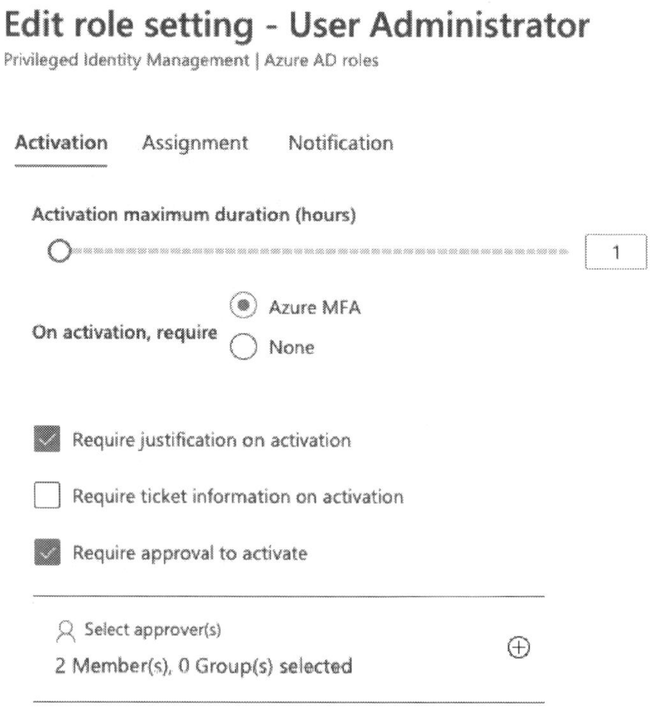

Figure 4.9 – Example activation settings

8. Click **Update**.

9. You will be taken back to the **Role** list; select the **User administrator** role again.

10. From the horizontal menu, click **Add assignment**.

11. Under **Select members**, click the **No member selected** link.

12. In the **Select a member** box that appears, find and select the user you want to assign the role to and click **Select**

13. Click **Next**.

14. Under **Assignment type** ensure **Eligible** is selected.

15. Optionally, untick **Permanently eligible** and set a date range such as 1 year to limit the period the user has the assignment.

16. Click **Assign**.

17. You will be taken back to the **User administrator | Assignments** window, click **Eligible assignments** on the horizontal menu, and confirm the user is now listed. See *Figure 4.10*, for example:

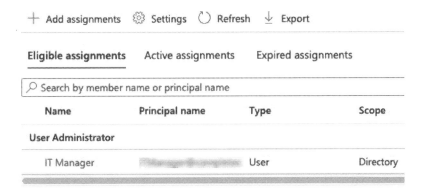

Figure 4.10 – PIM eligible users

Activating eligible roles

When a user wants to use an eligible role, they must first activate it. The options you set in the previous walk-through will determine whether or not the role is automatically activated on request or whether it needs to be approved. In our example, we set the requirement for an approver:

1. In another browser, or in a private window, log in to the Azure portal by opening `https://portal.azure.com` as the assigned user.

2. Search for then select **Privileged Identity Management** or **PIM**.

3. From the left-hand menu, click **Users**.

4. Select a user.

5. Note that the options are grayed out. (**Reset Password** isn't, but if you click it, you will receive an error.)

6. In the resource search bar, search for PIM and select **Privileged Identity Management**.

7. Click **My Roles**.

8. Click **Eligible assignments**.

9. Click **Activate** by the **User Administrator** role:

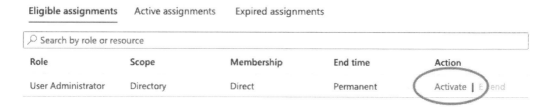

Figure 4.11 – Eligible assignments

10. In the dialog that appears, enter a duration for the role activation and justification as in the following figure:

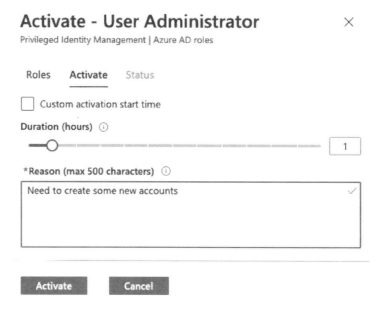

Figure 4.12 – Role activation request

11. The request will now be sent to the approver.

Once a role has been requested, the approver will receive an email containing a link to approve or reject it. Alternatively, this can be performed in the portal, as we shall see next.

Role approval

To approve a role request in the portal, perform the following steps:

1. Navigate to the Azure portal by opening `https://portal.azure.com`.

2. Search for or select **Privileged Identity Management** or **PIM**.

3. On the left-hand menu, choose **Approve Requests**.

4. Select the approval request and click **Approve** as per the example in *Figure 4.13*:

Figure 4.13 – Eligible role approval

5. Enter a justification and click **Confirm**. The role has now been activated.

PIM provides a much safer mechanism for granting elevated access to users. You will always need at least one account, but preferably two that have the global administrator role accessible at all times – but these accounts should be used only when necessary.

Although PIM is beneficial, you must still ensure the eligible roles are kept up to date. To help with this process, you should perform periodic access reviews.

Understanding access reviews

Throughout an employee's time at a company, their role may change. People get promoted or even demoted; they make sideways moves to other departments, take on more responsibilities, or delegate existing ones.

As users' work-related tasks change, so do their access requirements to the systems they need to perform their work. To help keep track of changing requirements, you can use access reviews to periodically confirm accounts' existing rights are adequate for the job, based on the least privileged principle.

Access reviews can be used in two different ways. First, an access review can request that users confirm their access levels; the other option is to request that an administrator or line manager perform the review. The latter needs more granular planning and setup, but does, of course, lead to more accurate responses.

You can also set up access reviews as a one-off task, or you can automatically schedule them at set periods – weekly, monthly, quarterly, semi-annually, or annually.

You need a Premium P2 License for users who are assigned as reviewers – including self-reviewers. You do not need a license to create an access review.

For example, if you create an access review for 100 users, but identify a single user as the reviewer, you only need one license. However, if you set the access review to have everybody perform their review, you would need 100 licenses.

The easiest way to understand the access review process is to step through an example. There are two types of access reviews, and they are performed through different blades. The first is a review of group membership – this is useful if you assign roles to groups rather than directly to users, and this is performed through the **Identity Governance** blade.

Creating an access review

In this example, we'll perform an access review of a role in the **Privileged Identity Management** blade:

1. Log in to the Azure portal by opening `https://portal.azure.com`.

2. Search for or select **Privileged Identity Management** or **PIM**.

3. On the left-hand menu, click **Azure AD Roles**.

4. On the left-hand menu, click **Access Reviews**.

5. At the top of the page, click **New**.

6. Enter a name, for example, `User Administrator Access review`.

7. Leave **Start date** and **End date** as the default and **frequency** at **One time**.

8. Set **Scope** to **Everyone.**

9. Under **Review role membership**, select **User Account Administrator**.

10. Set **Reviewers** to **Selected users**.

11. Select your admin account in **Select reviewers**.

12. Expand **Upon Completion settings**:

    a) **Auto apply results to resource** will automatically remove a role from a user if the review action is to deny the role. The default is **Disable**, meaning that any roles must be manually removed.

    b) You can set a default action if reviewers don't respond – for example, **Remove access** or **Approve access**.

13. Click **Start**.

The specified reviewers will then receive an email similar to the following screenshot:

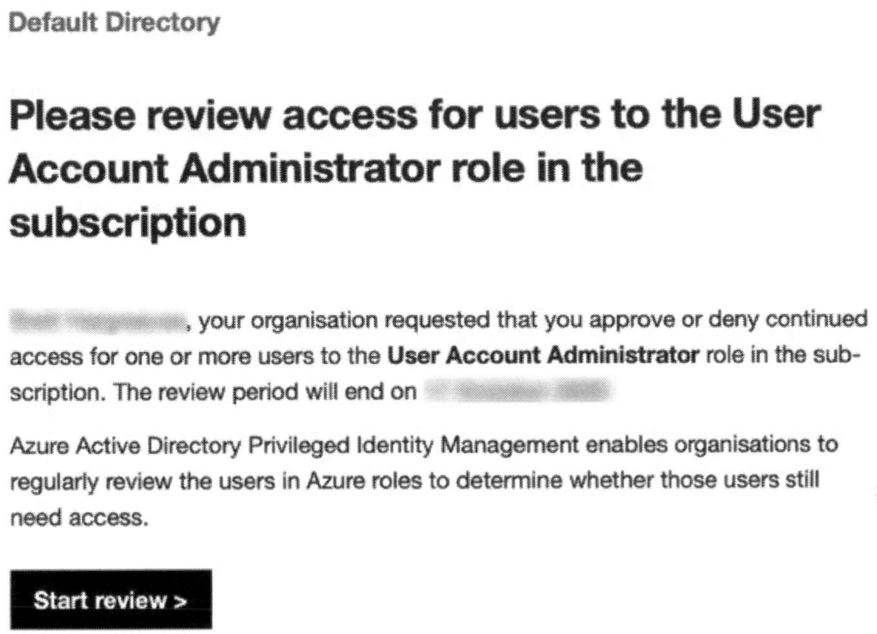

Default Directory

Please review access for users to the User Account Administrator role in the subscription

, your organisation requested that you approve or deny continued access for one or more users to the **User Account Administrator** role in the subscription. The review period will end on

Azure Active Directory Privileged Identity Management enables organisations to regularly review the users in Azure roles to determine whether those users still need access.

Start review >

Figure 4.14 – Access review email

The next step is to perform the access review.

Performing an access review

Although you can go directly to perform the review by clicking the link in the email, in this example, we will go through the Azure portal directly:

1. Go to the Azure portal by opening `https://portal.azure.com`.

2. Search for or select **Privileged Identity Management** or **PIM**.

3. On the left-hand menu, click **Azure AD Roles**.

4. On the left-hand menu, click **Review Access**.

5. Select the access review you just created.

6. Select the users you action and click either the **Approve** or **Deny** button. To approve, enter a reason in the dialog box first, detailing why you are approving the request.

Once an access review has been created, you will want to keep track of the status and see who has been approved or denied.

Access review reporting

In the following example, we will look at an access review report:

1. Go to the Azure portal by opening `https://portal.azure.com`.

2. Search for or select **Privileged Identity Management** or **PIM**.

3. On the left-hand menu, click **Azure AD Roles**.

4. On the left-hand menu, click **Access Reviews**.

5. Select the access review you just created.

6. You will see details of the access review, including a chart of the current progress (see *Figure 4.15*):

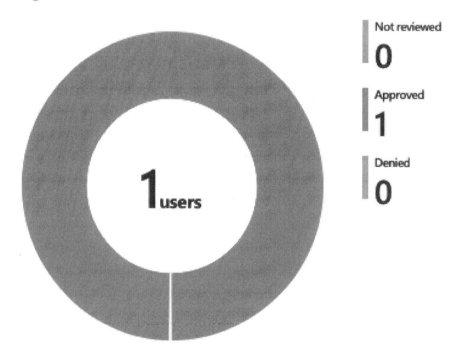

Figure 4.15 – Example access review chart

7. On the left-hand menu, click **Results** to see a detailed list of all users in the review and their status.

Access reviews are a great way to ensure least privileged access for your users over time, and this will help protect you if a user's account details are stolen.

In the next section, we will look at a set of tools to look for, notify you of, and take automatic actions if an account is suspected of being compromised.

Managing risk with Identity Protection

To further support security for users, Microsoft employs an AI-based system for monitoring *risky sign-ins*. Known as **Identity Protection**, it continually monitors your users for known and new vulnerabilities and patterns that might indicate a compromised account.

Identity Protection monitors for two specific types of risk – **User risk** and **Sign-in risk**.

User risk

User risk is the probability that a user's account has been compromised. A **risk score** is calculated based on Microsoft's internal and external threat intelligence systems, such as security researchers, Microsoft's security teams, and other trusted services.

These types of risks are calculated offline – that is, they are based on information obtained from the above sources.

An example of the kind of threat it looks for are leaked credentials – when cybercriminals compromise a user's details, they are often shared on the dark web and traded. Microsoft actively looks for and acquires these details, which it can then use to inform the risk detection system.

Another type of detection is by examining user activity. Again, using offline resources and research, Microsoft can determine whether an activity is consistent with known attack patterns.

By using information from Microsoft's research teams, Identity Protection can detect a whole range of potential threats; however, as with all criminal activity, new methods are continually being developed. Therefore, Azure also uses another set of detection tools – monitoring user login activity.

Sign-in risk

A lot of information can be obtained from a user's actual sign-in details – by this, we mean things such as the IP address they are signing in from, the geographical location, and so on. These risks are calculated in real time and also use the same offline resources as user risk. With both toolsets, Microsoft can detect the following types of risk:

- **Anonymous IP Address**: This detects if users are signing in using an anonymous IP address from a VPN or Tor browser, often used by cybercriminals trying to hide their tracks.

- **Atypical Travel**: Identifies a user signing in from two different geographies. The system learns a user's "normal" geography but also learns common geographies of other users in the organization to prevent false positives.

- **Impossible Travel**: Similar to the previous one, this considers the time it would take a user to travel between two locations to determine how likely it is that this could be a compromised account.

- **Unfamiliar Sign-in**: Similar to **Atypical Travel** – Microsoft considers past IPs and locations to look for anomalous sign-ins. The system also looks for users attempting to sign in with basic authentication of legacy protocols that do not have modern properties such as client ID.

- **Malware Linked IPs**: Determines if a user is signing in from a known IP range associated with malware sites.

- **Admin Confirmed User Compromised**: A manual risk activation whereby administrators can flag an account as compromised.

- **Malicious IP**: Any IP can be considered malicious if associated with multiple invalid credentials, not just from your users, but from other IP reputation sources.

- **Suspicious Inbox Manipulation Rules**: Powered by **Microsoft Cloud App Security** (**MCAS**), this profiles your environment and triggers alerts when unusual activity occurs within a user's mailbox.

All these properties are combined into a risk score, which then feeds into a **risk report**.

Risk score

Through all of the preceding measures, a risk score is calculated – giving a user a **High**, **Medium**, **Low**, or **No Risk** – which can be used with Conditional Access policies as part of a **risk policy** to take action.

Risk policies

A risk score for a user can change minute by minute, especially for sign-in events, and you may want to take immediate action depending on the score. Risk policies define these actions, and you can define different policies for user risk and sign-in risk. Both these policies provide the same options, which is to define the following:

- Who is covered by the policy? You can include or exclude all users, individual users, or groups.

- What risk score will trigger the policy? Set the policy to trigger based on high, medium and above, or low and above scores.

- What action should be taken? Choose to block the user, allow access, or allow access but enforce a password change.

You can define multiple policies to cover a mixture of users and risk scores. As well as setting automated actions, you will also want to report on risky users.

Risk reports

Three reports are available to help you identify and remediate issues, and these are mapped to specific areas – they are as follows:

- **Risky User**: Reports on individual accounts at risk, details of the detections, and history of risky sign-ins. From the report, administrators can reset passwords, confirm whether a user has been compromised, dismiss identified risks, block users, or investigate further using Azure Advanced Threat Protection.

- **Risky Sign-Ins**: This report lists all detected risky sign-ins, displaying the type of risk, what policies have been applied, device information, location information, and the status (dismissed, confirmed safe, or confirmed compromised).

- **Risk Detections**: The risk detections report shows information about each risk detection, including the type, other triggered risks, the sign-in attempt location, and a link to (**MCAS**) for more information about the individual risk.

Azure Identity Protection and Azure PIM together provide tools to help you keep your users secure and to react to common threats automatically.

Summary

In this chapter, we have covered authorization in Azure and how to manage user access, and introduced tools that will help you scale your user base without it becoming unmanageable.

We have covered the different types of roles available – Classic, Azure, and Azure AD, what the differences are, and how to create custom roles. We then looked at how to use management groups, subscriptions, and resource groups to manage the assignment of roles and, in particular, how rights flow down through hierarchies.

Using PIM, we saw how you can manage and grant time-boxed access to roles and run regular reports to ensure that the least privileged principle is adhered to.

Finally, we looked at advanced tooling for detecting and responding to common threats using Identity Protection.

With what you have learned in this chapter, you can now decide on the best authorization and security options for your own solutions.

In the next chapter, we will learn another complementary set of tools for controlling access to resources – tagging, Azure policies, and blueprints.

Exam solution

The solutions to the exam scenarios can be found at the end of this book.

Mega Corp is a global company with a head office in the US and satellite offices in Europe. They have separate IT teams for the US and Europe, responsible for their regions in general, but ultimately the US IT Team has overall accountability.

Each region has a Sales, Marketing, and HR department, and each has its own IT Champions who support them by having the ability to create and manage resources and assign rights to other users.

The company is risk-averse and therefore demands that administrative roles be granted on the least privileged principle. They are also looking at automation options for responding to any external threats to their user accounts.

5
Ensuring Platform Governance

In *Chapter 2*, *Principles of Modern Architecture*, we discussed the need for an IT strategy that would define many aspects of your cloud platform, particularly around security, and would state different requisites, such as encryption, data residency, sign-on locations, use of **Multi-Factor Authentication** (**MFA**), and so on.

Within Azure, you can provide different teams within the business direct access to build solutions. With a relatively open and dynamic system, how can you ensure that the IT strategies and rules you have defined are observed?

Governance and compliance are terms used to describe what users of a system should and should not perform, and Azure provides a range of tools to enforce adherence to these rules.

To support this, we will look at how we can use **tagging** to define and manage metadata against resources, which in turn can be used in reporting and automated processes to help with governance.

Next, we will look at how Azure policies can provide compliance reporting and even control what actions can be performed by users.

Finally, we will see how Azure Blueprints provides a further layer of protection and standards-based governance to your solutions.

This chapter will cover the main tools that will help you achieve these goals:

- Applying tagging
- Understanding Azure policies
- Using Azure Blueprints

Technical requirements

This chapter will use the Azure portal (`https://portal.azure.com`) and Azure PowerShell (`https://docs.microsoft.com/en-us/powershell/azure`) for examples.

The source code for our sample application can be downloaded from `https://github.com/PacktPublishing/Exam-Ref-AZ-304-Microsoft-Azure-Architect-Design-Certification-and-Beyond/tree/master/ch5`.

Applying tagging

Every subscription, resource group, and resource within Azure can have metadata assigned in the form of **tags**. Tags are essentially a set of key/value string pairs that can be applied either via the portal, PowerShell, or **Azure Resource Manager** (**ARM**) templates.

There are a few limitations to be aware of. Most resources can use tags, but there are exceptions. See `https://docs.microsoft.com/en-us/azure/azure-resource-manager/management/tag-support` for details of services that don't.

Tags can only be applied to **resource model** components, not **classic models**:

- Tag names are limited to 512 characters, except for storage accounts, which are limited to 256.

- Tag values are limited to 256 characters, except for storage accounts, which are limited to 128.

- A maximum of 50 tags can be used on a resource.

- Tags on a component do not automatically inherit tags from a resource group (but this can be set using a policy).

- Tags cannot contain the following symbols: <, >, %, &, \, ?, and /.

Because tags are plain text key/value pairs, you can store any information you want in them, which can then be used for reporting or as part of automation tools such as Azure Policy.

Tags are, therefore, a great option to mark different components with a variety of information, such as the following:

- **Description**: Resource names often cannot describe what a component is used for. A description tag can provide a human-readable format for quick reference. For example, you may use a naming convention to give some limited details, such as VM-UKS-API-01 (virtual machine, UK south, Web API). Using a description tag allows you to provide more information, such as *payroll system Web API endpoint*.

- **Workload/function**: Similar to the description, but a more constrained approach using common values such as payroll, webapi, and so on. This is useful for report generation as it provides an easy way to categorize your resources.

- **Contact**: Provide contact information such as a technical owner or business owner.

- **Environment**: Tag resources to state whether they are **production** systems or **test**, **development**, or **QA**.

- **Cost center**: Suppose you need to apportion the costs of a service to individual departments or cost centers. This can be used in reporting to provide totals across resources.

- **Department**: Group resources by the department that owns or manages them.

- **Classification**: Business or data classification is increasingly important for many compliance responsibilities, for example, GDPR in Europe. Tag resources with values such as Public, Private, Confidential, or Personal Information.

- **Operational**: Tag resources to help with operational processes, such as patching schedules or whether a component should be included in backup routines or not.

We will cover using tags with Azure Policy shortly, but first, you must apply the tags. We can add tags in different ways; first, we will manually add them through the Azure portal.

Adding tags manually

When creating resources using the Azure portal, the final screen will allow you to enter tags before the validation screen. Because tags are used for reporting, the names and sometimes the values must be consistent across your platform. For this reason, when you click in the **Name** field of the **Tags** section, a list of previously used tags will appear, as follows:

Figure 5.1 – Tag names are remembered for more accessible reuse

Some resources, such as virtual machines, are made up of multiple different components. In these cases, you have the option to select all or some of the individual resources by clicking on the **Resource** drop-down menu within the **Tags** section, as you can see in the following screenshot:

Create a virtual machine

Basics   Disks   Networking   Management   Advanced   **Tags**   Review + create

Tags are name/value pairs that enable you to categorize resources and view consolidated billing by applying the same tag to multiple resources and resource groups. Learn more about tags

Note that if you create tags and then change resource settings on other tabs, your tags will be automatically updated.

Name	Value	Resource
CostCenter	001	12 selected

☑ Select all
☑ Auto-shutdown schedule
☑ Availability set
☑ Disk
☑ Network interface
☑ Network security group
☑ Public IP address
☑ Recovery Services vault
☑ SSH key
☑ Storage account
☑ Virtual machine
☑ Virtual machine extension
☑ Virtual network

Review + create   < Previous   Next : Review + create >

Figure 5.2 – Selecting multiple resources for tagging

Tags you have added appear on the overview screen of your resources, as follows:

Resource group (change) : PACKVMGROUP

Status   : Running

Location   : East US

Subscription (change)   : PacktPub

Subscription ID   : f9483dab-48b4-4a40-9420-8b916e6b33c9

Tags (change)   : CostCenter : 001

Figure 5.3 – Tags are displayed on the overview page of resources

If you need to modify or add additional tags to an existing resource, this can be performed by either clicking on the **change** option next to **Tags** (see the preceding screenshot) or by clicking on the **Tags** left-hand menu option, as shown in the following screenshot. When adding additional tags, you will again be presented with a list of previously used ones:

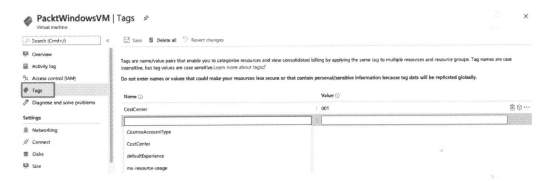

Figure 5.4 – Adding tags to an existing resource

Using the portal, we can also add tags to new and existing resources through Azure PowerShell commands.

Managing tags through Azure PowerShell

Applying tags through PowerShell or the Azure CLI is simple and more manageable when you need to use many tags.

When adding tags to new resources as you create them, you add the `-Tag` option followed by the tags you wish to apply in the following format: `@{"TagName" ="TagValue";" Tag2Name=" Tag2Value"}`.

The following code block shows an example of how to create a storage account with tags added using Azure PowerShell. This code assumes the resource group already exists:

```
New-AzStorageAccount -ResourceGroupName
'packtstorageresourcegroup' -Name 'packtstoragewithtags'
-Location 'eastus' -SkuName 'Standard_LRS' -Kind 'StorageV2'
-Tags @{"Dept"="Finance"; "CostCenter"="001"}
```

If you need to modify the tags on an existing resource, we can update them on an individual resource, a resource group, or even a subscription. This makes it easy to update lots of resources in one command.

To update the tags on a resource(s), you must select it/them using the `Get-AzResource`, `Get-AzResourceGroup`, or `Get-AzSubscription` command, as in the following example:

```
$resource = Get-AzResource -Name 'packtstoragewithtags'
-ResourceGroup 'packtstorageresourcegroup'
```

We can then see what tags are currently applied by querying the `.tags` property, as follows:

```
$resource.tags
```

Apply new tags using `New-AzTag` like this:

```
$newtags = @{"Environment"="Dev"}
New-AzTag -ResourceId $resource.id -Tag $newtags
```

Similarly, you can update tags with `Update-AzTag` to replace all tags with the new ones you supply. Note that this replaces all tags – in other words, it will remove all existing tags, and then add the specified ones. If you wish to merge tags using an update command, you can use `Update-AzTag -Operation Merge`.

Managing tags in ARM templates

Finally, we will add tags when we deploy infrastructure using ARM templates.

To add tags, we simply add the list of tags as a tags section under resources. A simple example template to create a storage account with tags might look like this:

```
{
    "$schema": "https://schema.management.azure.com/
schemas/2019-04-01/deploymentTemplate.json#",
```

```
"contentVersion": "1.0.0.0",
"resources": [
    {
        "type": "Microsoft.Storage/storageAccounts",
        "apiVersion": "2019-04-01",
        "name": "packstoragewithtags",
        "location": "eastus",
"tags": {
                "Dept": "Finance",
                "CostCenter": "001"
            },
        "sku": {
            "name": "Standard_LRS"
        },
        "kind": "StorageV2"
    }
]
}
```

Once you have defined and applied tags to your resources, the next step is to make use of them through different mechanisms.

Using tags

On their own, tags do not provide enforcement. Still, they can be used with reporting mechanisms, automated processes such as Azure Functions or runbooks, or other compliance tools such as Azure Policy.

As an example of how tags can be used in reporting, we can perform a simple search within the Azure portal:

1. Navigate to the Azure portal at https://portal.azure.com.

2. In the top search bar, type Tags.

3. A list of used tags and their values will appear. Select one of the tags.

You will now be presented with a list of all resources using that tag/value combination, as follows:

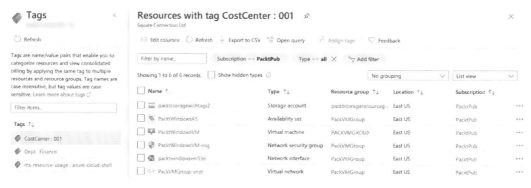

Figure 5.5 – Viewing tagged resources

Tagging can help with your platform's governance and compliance as part of your wider solution design. Although the portal, PowerShell, and ARM templates make it easy to manage them, it can still become tedious, especially if you have lots of resources and the tags have not been applied correctly.

Luckily, with Azure Policy, we can use tagging not only to apply and manage security controls but also to enforce and automate the use of tagging itself.

In this section, we have seen how tagging can be applied and managed. Next, we will look at another way to drive compliance through the use of policies.

Understanding Azure policies

Your IT strategy and governance rules will define ways of working and what should and should not be allowed in your solutions.

An example may be for all resources to be tagged with a cost center so that the associated costs can be billed back to a product owner. Another example could be a requirement to send all diagnostics logs to a centralized management workspace for use by monitoring and security teams.

Whatever the rule, you need some way to either enforce it or report that a component does not implement it – that is, that it is non-compliant. This could be performed manually, and in a traditional on-premise environment, this might be the only option. But when building enterprise-wide systems, manual checks and balances do not scale easily; therefore, an automated method is preferable.

With Azure Policy, we can define and codify the rules of the system in JSON policy definitions. In contrast, authentication and authorization controls such as **MFA** and **Role-Based Access Control** (**RBAC**) are used to manage what actions users can perform, for example, the ability to edit or view a type of resource. Policies set system-wide rules on how resources can be configured regardless of the user's RBAC role. In other words, even if a user has the **Owner** role over a resource, a policy will still prevent or report on that resource being configured in a particular way.

Using policies and initiatives

Using Azure policies involves two steps – first, you *define* the policy. Then, you *assign* the policy to either a **management group**, **subscription**, or **resource group** in the same way you assign RBAC roles.

As with RBAC roles, you also have several built-in policies that cover a wide range of Azure resource types, or you can create custom policies.

Policies are usually written to report or constrain a particular configuration setting of a resource. You then group multiple policies into an **initiative**. For example, you could create a policy that determines what types of storage accounts are used, another to define what kind of redundancy level to use, and a third to ensure secure transfer should always be enabled. All the policies would be grouped into a single storage initiative so that when you assign the initiative, all the policies within it take effect.

Policy definitions can either report non-compliance, prevent the non-compliant resource from being created, or automatically set a configuration. Finally, should a particular resource or group need to be excluded from a policy, individual exemptions can be made. In this way, we can assign policies higher in our hierarchy but still have the flexibility to create exceptions.

The first step of the process is to define a policy document.

Policy structure

An Azure policy definition has a set structure that must be followed and formatted as JSON. At the root of the document is a properties element, with the following child elements:

- **displayName**: A short and straightforward display name.
- **Description**: A verbose description defining what the policy achieves.

- **mode**: Depends on whether the resource you want to apply the policy to is a resource manager property or a resource provider property:

  a) **all**: Applies to resources groups, subscriptions, and resource types – in the majority of cases, you would use this.

  b) **indexed**: Only applies to resource types that support tags and locations.

- **Metadata**: Optional. It can track information about the policy, such as the versions, the category, and whether it is in preview or deprecated.

- **Parameters**: Enables policies to be built generically so that different rules can be set depending on where it is being applied. Parameters will contain the following child elements:

  a) **name**: The name of the parameter.

  b) **type**: **string**, **array**, **boolean**, **object**, **integer**, **float**, or **datetime**.

  c) **metadata**: Optional. Can be used to display user-friendly information.

  d) **defaultValue**: If no value is defined, this will be used.

  e) **allowedValues**: Constrain the allowable values.

- **policyRule**: Definition of the component or element we are checking.

displayName, **description**, **mode**, and **metaData** are relatively straightforward; however, we will cover parameters and policy rules in more detail.

Parameters

Policies can be built to be very specific. For example, a policy could be written to ensure that all resources can only be deployed in a particular region, such as *US East*. However, in larger organizations, you may want to apply different rules to different departments, environments, or teams. Teams based in Europe will most likely want to deploy to a European region, for example.

Policies can be applied to management groups, which, as we covered in *Chapter 4, Managing User Authorization*, can be set up to match your company's geographical structure. Therefore, you could create individual policies for each region. A more straightforward option would be defining a policy that constrains the regions we can use but defines that constraint as a parameter. That parameter would then be set when the policy is assigned.

Thus, the same policy definition can be used multiple times, with a different parameter being set depending on the management group the policy is assigned to. We shall see an example of this shortly in the *Creating a policy and initiative definition* and *Assigning an initiative* sections.

Policy rules

Finally, we must define the actual rule, and this is performed by creating an `if-then` block to determine what actions will be executed when a condition is met. The structure of the policy rule is as follows:

```
{
    "if": {
        <condition> | <logical operator>
    },
    "then": {
        "effect": "deny | audit | append | auditIfNotExists |
deployIfNotExists | disabled"
    }
}
```

The condition is an evaluation of a field within a resource against a particular value, and uses the following format:

```
"if": {
    "allOf": [
        {
            "field": "type",
            "equals": "Microsoft.Storage/storageAccounts"
        }
    ]
}
```

Logical operators are used to provide further control. The supported operators are as follows:

- `not`: Match if the condition results in false.

- `allOf`: Match if all the conditions are met.

- `anyOf`: Match if any of the conditions are met.

Finally, the effect states what will happen when the rule is matched. The available options are as follows:

- `Append`: Adds the defined set of fields.
- `Audit`: Creates a warning event in the activity log
- `AuditIfNotExists`: Creates a warning event in the activity log if a related resource doesn't exist
- `Deny`: Creates an event in the activity log and prevents the resource from being created or modified
- `DeployIfNotExists`: Deploys a resource if it doesn't exist
- `Disabled`: Doesn't evaluate resources for compliance with the policy rule
- `Modify`: Adds, updates, or removes the defined tags from a resource

The easiest way to understand policies is to see them in action, so next, we will create a policy definition, add it to an initiative, and then apply it.

Creating a policy and initiative definition

In this example, we will assume that all resources have to be tagged with a cost center as part of our IT governance rules. To support this, we will create a policy that denies creating a resource group without a `CostCenter` tag, and a second one that automatically applies that tag to resources within the resource group:

1. Navigate to the Azure portal: `https://portal.azure.com`.
2. In the top search bar, type `Policy` and select **Policy** under **Services**.
3. On the left-hand menu, select **Definitions**.
4. A list of built-in definitions and initiatives are presented. We will first create an initiative to hold our policies. Click **+Initiative definition**. Complete the following details:

   a) **Initiative location**: Click the ellipsis next to the input box and then select your subscription.

   b) **Name**: Name the initiative `TaggingEnforcement`.

   c) **Category**: **Use existing**; select **Tags**.

   d) **Version**: **1.0**.

5. Click **Next**.

6. Click **Add policy definition(s)**.

7. With **Automated** selected, type Tag in the search bar, then click **Require a tag on resource groups** and **Inherit a tag from the resource group if missing**. See the following screenshot for an example:

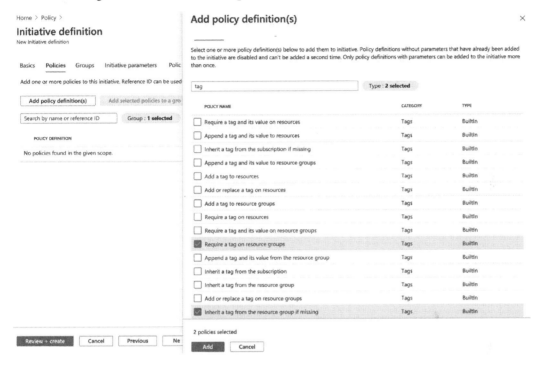

Figure 5.6 – Adding a policy to an initiative

8. Click **Add**.

9. To see what's in a policy, click on the policy; for example, click on **Require a tag on resources**. Then, click **Definition**. You will be shown the policy definition, as follows:

Details   Definition

⎙ Duplicate this policy definition

```
 1   {
 2     "properties": {
 3       "displayName": "Require a tag on resource groups",
 4       "policyType": "BuiltIn",
 5       "mode": "All",
 6       "description": "Enforces existence of a tag on resource groups.",
 7       "metadata": {
 8         "version": "1.0.0",
 9         "category": "Tags"
10       },
11       "parameters": {
12         "tagName": {
13           "type": "String",
14           "metadata": {
15             "displayName": "Tag Name",
16             "description": "Name of the tag, such as 'environment'"
17           }
18         }
19       },
20       "policyRule": {
21         "if": {
22           "allOf": [
23             {
24               "field": "type",
25               "equals": "Microsoft.Resources/subscriptions/resourceGroups"
26             },
27             {
28               "field": "[concat('tags[', parameters('tagName'), ']')]",
29               "exists": "false"
30             }
31           ]
32         },
33         "then": {
34           "effect": "deny"
35         }
36       }
37     },
```

Figure 5.7 – Example policy definition

10. Close the policy window by clicking **X** at the top right, then click **Next**.

11. Ignore the **Groups** option and click **Next**.

12. We now need to add a parameter that will be passed through to the required parameters in the policies. Click **Create initiative parameter**.

13. Enter the following details, then click **Save**:

   a) **Name**: TagName

   b) **Display name**: TagName

   c) **Type**: **String**

14. On the next screen, we see that a parameter on each policy is required. Next to each one, set **VALUE TYPE** to **Use Initiative Parameter** and **VALUE(S)** to **TagName**. See the following screenshot for an example:

Figure 5.8 – Setting initiative parameters to policy parameters

15. Click **Create**.

Once the initiative has been created, you will be taken back to the **Definitions** page, and your new initiative will be displayed at the top. The next step is to assign it.

Assigning an initiative

Follow these steps to assign an initiative:

1. Still on the **Definitions** view, click on the policy you just created.

2. Click **Assign**.

3. Set **Scope** to your subscription.

4. Don't add any exclusions.

5. Set **Policy enforcement** to **Enabled** – we will come back and change this later. Click **Next**.

6. Next, we set a value in the **TagName** parameter. Set this to CostCenter. Click **Next**.

7. Click **Next** to ignore remediation, then click **Create**.

These policies will now take effect, but only when creating new resources and resource groups. Any existing resources will not be affected; however, we can still use the compliance view to see any items that are not compliant with this initiative.

Viewing the compliance dashboard

Earlier, we stated that policies could either report on non-compliant resources, deny their creation, or change the resource. The policies we have applied as part of the initiative will prevent a resource group from being created and automatically apply the cost center tag to new resources.

However, these only affect new resource groups and resources; what about the existing resources that do not fit the policies we have set?

The compliance dashboard in the Azure Policy blade will display all resources that do not match the set's policies. This includes any new and existing resources. This is why not all policies necessarily restrict what we can and cannot do; sometimes, it may be acceptable to report and manually remediate compliant resources.

To view the compliance reports, perform the following steps:

1. Navigate to the Azure portal: `https://portal.azure.com`.

2. In the top search bar, type `Policy` and select **Policy** under **Services**.

3. On the left-hand menu, select **Compliance**.

The compliance dashboard shows all the initiatives applied along with the compliance state across your organization. The following screenshot shows an example compliance view of the `TaggingEnforcement` initiative we created earlier:

Figure 5.9 – Example compliance dashboard

Click on the **TaggingEnforcement** initiative to view more details. This will display more granular details of the compliance of individual policies within that initiative. Clicking on a policy will display a list of all the resources that are not compliant. See the following screenshot for an example:

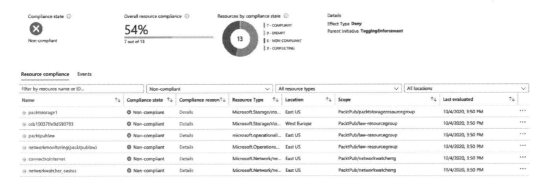

Figure 5.10 – Policy non-compliance details

Clicking the **Details** link against each resource will display further details about why it is non-compliant. You can use this information to fix the problem manually, or we can create an auto-remediation task to fix it for us.

Creating a remediation task

When creating a policy, there are various options for the policy's effect, such as *modify*, which updates the resource when it is being created. An example is the **inherit tag** policy we deployed earlier. Because this is performed whenever a new resource is deployed, the modify effect occurs under the context of the user who is trying to create the resource.

If we need to apply such a modification to an existing resource as part of an automated task, we need to define an identity that the remediation will run as. We use **Managed Identity**, a built-in identity controlled by the Azure platform, to perform this.

Remediation tasks can be created as part of a policy definition, or via the remediation view, as we will see in the following example:

1. Navigate to the Azure portal: `https://portal.azure.com`.

2. In the top search bar, type `Policy` and select **Policy** under **Services**.

3. In the left-hand menu, select **Remediation**.

4. Select the policy you wish to remediate.

5. Set the scope to your subscription.

6. Tick **Re-evaluate resource compliance before remediating**.

7. Click **Remediate**.

It can take 10–30 minutes for the new remediation task to process. You can view the remediation task's status in the **Policy** blade by clicking **Remediation** on the left-hand menu and then clicking **Remediation tasks**.

Azure Policy is incredibly flexible and is used to keep your Azure assets compliant. As well as the preceding example, other example uses cases include the following:

- Limit or automatically apply configuration changes such as enforcing transparent data encryption on SQL Server or SSL on storage transfers.

- Configure diagnostics and logging settings resources. For example, every time a SQL server is created, automatically configure it to output its diagnostics logs to a centralized Log Analytics workspace.

- Automatically deploy supporting resources, such as a backup job, when a virtual machine is created.

So far, these examples apply to Azure resources; there is also a set of policies called virtual machine guest configurations that offer much deeper integration with Windows and Linux virtual machines.

Using virtual machine guest configurations

Virtual machine guest configurations enable the same level of compliance control at the operating system level of a virtual machine. Again, there are several built-in policies and initiatives available, or custom ones can be created.

Some example policies that might be applied are as follows:

- Ensure remote connections from accounts without passwords are not allowed or flagged.

- Report Linux servers that are not using SSH keys for authentication.

- Report Windows servers with specified services not in the **Running** state (for example, ensure software is installed and running).

- Report Windows servers that are not domain-joined.

These are just a few examples. With virtual machine guest configuration policies, you can take precise control over your Windows and Linux virtual machines; however, to use them, there are a few requirements that need to be set:

- The guest configuration extension must be installed on the virtual machine.
- Virtual machines need connectivity to the Azure data centers on HTTPS (port 443).
- System-assigned managed identities are required on the virtual machine.

Using policies and initiatives, you can gain deep insights and control over how your company uses Azure at a very granular level; therefore, they must be used correctly.

Best practices

When working with Azure policies and initiatives, the following best practice guidelines will help ensure a successful deployment:

- Start with an audit effect instead of a deny effect. Then, track the impact of your policy definition on resources.
- Consider organizational hierarchies when creating definitions and assignments.
- Create and assign initiative definitions, even for a single policy definition.
- When an initiative assignment is evaluated, all policies within the initiative are also evaluated. If you need to evaluate a policy individually, it's better not to include it in an initiative.

As we have seen in this section, Azure policies and tagging help control what is deployed and ensure it is deployed in a compliant manner according to your company's governance policies. However, there are some elements that you will always want to be deployed in a subscription. In the next section, we will examine Azure Blueprints and see how it provides an additional control layer.

Using Azure Blueprints

In the previous two sections, we looked at how to apply rules so that deployed resources meet the compliance rules as defined by the business. However, these constraints are on the resources themselves.

When new subscriptions are created within an Azure tenant, there will often be a set of components that always need to be in place. For example, every new subscription may need a VNet with a pre-defined set of network security group rules, a user-defined route table, a storage account to store encryption certificates, and so on.

One option would be to create a set of ARM templates within which all these items are defined and deploy them through a DevOps pipeline for each new subscription. The problem with this method is that once the components have been deployed, they can be modified. For some services, especially networking and security-related artifacts, this is not what we want.

Azure Blueprints allows us to define and deploy resource groups, resources, role assignments, and policy assignments automatically as a subscription is created. A key feature of Blueprints is that the connection between what is defined and what is deployed is kept. In other words, through Blueprints, you can check for and correct any configuration drift.

For more control, a resource lock can be set on the components to prevent users from modifying them, which is essential when setting default routing and firewalls.

In the following example, we will create a blueprint definition to enforce a VNet and then apply it to a subscription.

Creating a blueprint definition

Follow these steps to create a blueprint definition:

1. Navigate to the Azure portal: `https://portal.azure.com`.

2. In the top search bar, type `Blueprints` and select **Blueprints** under **Services**.

3. On the left-hand menu, select **Blueprint definitions**.

4. Click **+Create blueprint**.

5. A list of sample and standard blueprints is listed, or you can create one from scratch. To make things easier, select **Basic Networking (VNET)**.

6. Give your blueprint a name such as `CoreSystems` and set **Definition location** to either a management group or a subscription.

7. Click **Next: Artifacts**.

You will be presented with a list of resources that will be deployed along with this blueprint. If you click on one of the artifacts, you will then be shown an ARM template that will be used, as in the example shown in the following screenshot:

Figure 5.11 – Example blueprint

If you created and assigned the `CostCenter` tag policy, you will need to modify the resource group. See the following screenshot for an example:

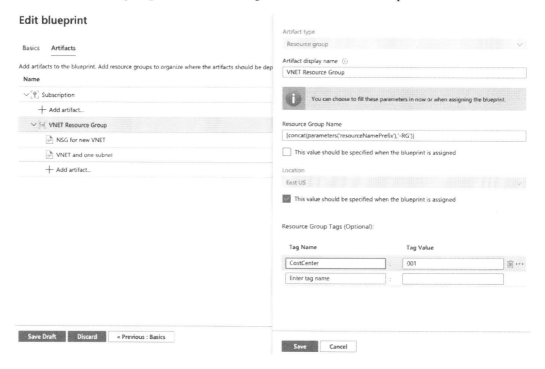

Figure 5.12 – Editing the resource group

8. Click **VNET Resource Group**.

9. Enter a tag name of `CostCenter` and set the value to `001`.

10. Click **Save**.

11. Click **Save Draft**.

Now that we have defined a blueprint, it will be in the draft state. Before we can assign it, we must publish the blueprint. When publishing a blueprint, you must set a version – this enables you to progressively update your blueprints as your platform matures; however, the versioning allows you to keep a history of your changes.

Publishing and assigning a blueprint

Follow these steps to publish and assign a blueprint:

1. Still in the **Blueprints** blade, click **Blueprint definitions** on the left-hand menu.

2. Click your recently created blueprint.

3. Click **Publish blueprint**.

4. Enter a **version number**, for example, 1.0.

5. Click **Publish**.

6. Click **Assign Blueprint**.

7. Select a subscription to assign the blueprint to.

8. Select the location, for example, **East US**.

9. Note the version number is 1.0. Set **Lock Assignment** to **Do Not Delete**. See the following screenshot for an example:

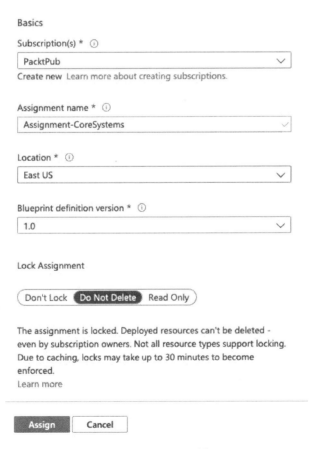

Figure 5.13 – Assigning a blueprint

10. Scroll down the page to see a list of blueprint parameters that must be set:

   a) **Resource name prefix**: **BP**

   b) **Resource Group: Location**: **East US**

   c) **Address space for vnet**: `10.0.0.0/16`

   d) **Address space for subnet**: `10.0.0.0/24`

   See the following screenshot for an example:

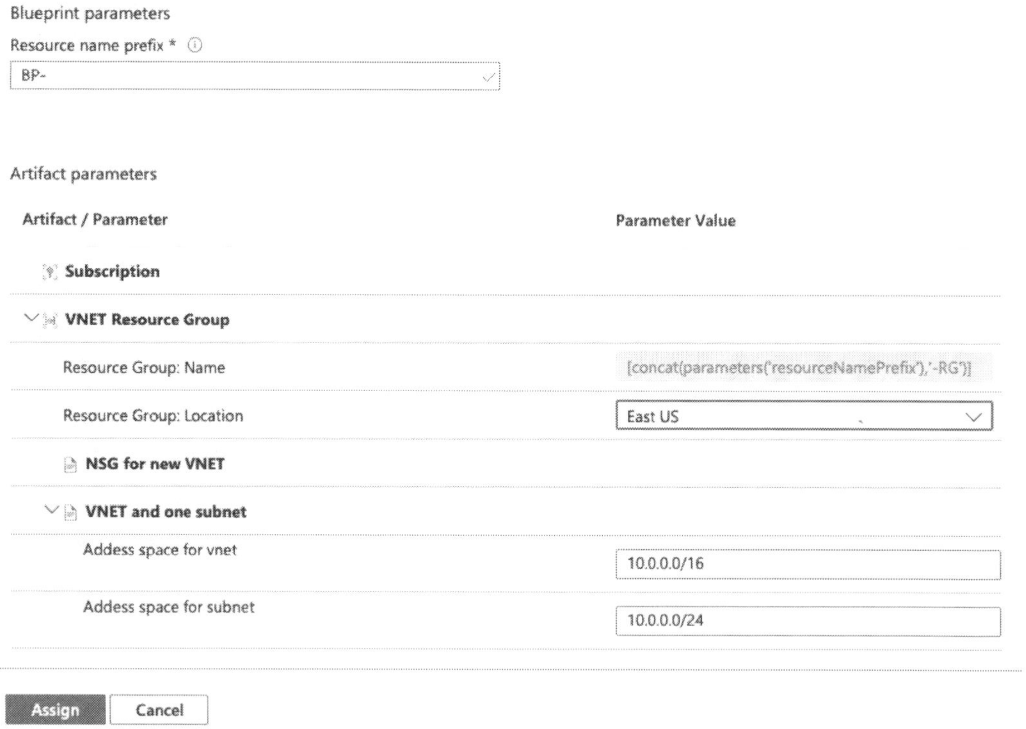

Blueprint parameters

Resource name prefix * ⓘ

| BP- |

Artifact parameters

Artifact / Parameter	Parameter Value
🔑 **Subscription**	
∨ 🔲 **VNET Resource Group**	
Resource Group: Name	[concat(parameters('resourceNamePrefix'),'-RG')]
Resource Group: Location	East US
📄 **NSG for new VNET**	
∨ 📄 **VNET and one subnet**	
Addess space for vnet	10.0.0.0/16
Addess space for subnet	10.0.0.0/24

Assign   Cancel

Figure 5.14 – Assigning blueprint parameters

11. Click **Assign**.

The new resource group and the VNet will now be deployed to the subscription you selected; however, the process can take a few minutes. The **Do Not Delete** lock assignment will ensure that users cannot delete the resource group and VNet or any other resources created as part of this subscription.

Go to the new resource group in the Azure portal. You will see the new VNet and associated network security group. Any attempt to delete either the VNet, network security group, or resource group results in an error. See the following screenshot for an example:

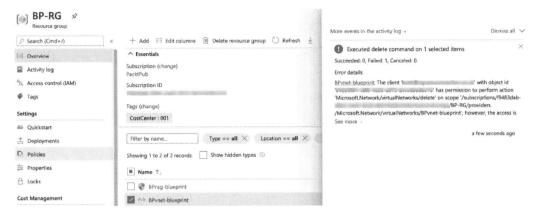

Figure 5.15 – Resource group and resources are locked for deletion

In this section, we have seen how Blueprints can help build standardized subscriptions that can enforce the use of resources and prevent them from being modified.

Summary

This chapter has investigated how we can apply and control solutions according to governance rules laid out by the business.

By using tagging, we can add metadata to resources that can be used for reporting and management purposes. Azure policies allow control over all resources to either prevent, modify, or report on non-compliancy.

Finally, through Azure Blueprints, we can ensure core infrastructure, policies, and roles are always applied, and if need be locked down, to subscriptions.

In the next chapter, we look at how we can secure applications through Azure Key Vault, security principles, and managed identities.

Exam scenario

Your customer, Mega Corp, has asked you to ensure all the solutions built within their Azure platform conform to corporate standards. Specifically, they need to ensure the following:

- All virtual machines are domain-joined.

- All virtual machines have the Windows firewall installed and running.

- All resources are tagged to state what environment they belong to (Prod, Dev, Test).

- All subscriptions have a VNet with a default network security group applied that cannot be modified.

- All subscriptions have a storage account deployed to them that cannot be deleted.

They would like to have very few manual steps involved. What options would you suggest?

Further reading

You can check out the following links for more information about the topics that were covered in this chapter:

- Azure tags: `https://docs.microsoft.com/en-us/azure/azure-resource-manager/management/tag-resources`

- Virtual machine guest configuration: `https://docs.microsoft.com/en-us/azure/governance/policy/samples/built-in-policies#guest-configuration`

- Azure Blueprints: `https://docs.microsoft.com/en-us/azure/governance/blueprints/overview`

6
Building Application Security

In the previous chapter, we explained how to manage and control user access through the use of **management groups**, **policies**, and **Azure Blueprints**.

In *Chapter 2*, *Principles of Modern Architecture*, we also discussed the need for security in depth – that is, the need for multiple layers of security to protect us in the event one layer is compromised.

Two such additional areas of control involve the encryption of data and the security of communications between services. This has become more important in recent years due to the increased use of **microservice** architectures that demand multiple smaller services, working together and transferring data between them.

Encryption of data is often performed using either SSL/TLS certificates or encryption keys and is applied while at rest or in transit.

Another data protection mechanism is how we control and authenticate *between* one system and another. One example is a website communicating with a database; a connection string would typically be used to define a username and password. The connection string itself is considered sensitive, and therefore consideration must be given to how you can provide it to the system without exposing it to developers or system administrators.

This chapter will cover three tools in Azure that can help with these aspects. We will first look at **Azure Key Vault**, a mechanism for generating, securely storing, and managing the life cycle of secrets, keys, and certificates.

Next, we will look at how we can use **Azure security principals** to provide application-level access to secrets and other Azure components, and how they can also to used to enable OAuth-based authentication to your apps quickly.

Finally, we will examine **managed identities**, which provide an alternative to service principals for authenticating between some of Azure's services such as Web Apps, Virtual Machines, Key Vault, and storage accounts.

Specifically, we will be covering the following topics:

- Introducing Azure Key Vault
- Working with Security Principals
- Using managed identities

Technical requirements

This chapter will use the Azure portal (`https://portal.azure.com`) for examples, and Azure PowerShell (`https://docs.Microsoft.com/en-us/powershell/azure/install-az-ps`).

Coding is performed using Visual Studio Code, which can be downloaded here: `https://code.visualstudio.com`.

The source code for our examples can be downloaded from `https://github.com/PacktPublishing/Exam-Ref-AZ-304-Microsoft-Azure-Architect-Design-Certification-and-Beyond/tree/master/ch6`.

Introducing Azure Key Vault

Encrypting data in some form is a core requirement for many solutions; however, there are different ways we can encrypt data.

The most basic is encryption at rest. Storage services in Azure use encryption at rest by default – this includes Virtual Machine disks, storage accounts, and even SQL Server. To encrypt data, Azure uses Microsoft-managed keys; however, there is the option to use keys managed by yourself. When using customer-managed keys, you need to store them in a safe place that your services can access in a tightly controlled manner – because if you can get access to the keys, you can decrypt the data.

> **Important note**
> Data encryption at rest uses a key, a randomly generated set of bits used with a mathematical algorithm to scramble data. The same key is then used to decrypt (unscramble) the data. Much like a password, the length and complexity of the key determine its strength.

As well as encrypting data at rest, virtual machines can also use additional tools such as **BitLocker** to encrypt the data at the operating system level. Known as **full-disk encryption**, this uses a separate key that is always managed by you. Again, a safe place to store and manage keys is therefore required.

Encrypting data is only one way to protect an application. Most systems must communicate with another component at some point – for example, a database or another web service. These connections are sometimes secured with a connection string, which is stored in a configuration file. This is considered insecure as the configuration file is often open and easily compromised. The most secure method is storing items like this as secrets in a safe location that can then be accessed and controlled.

Finally, encryption of data when moving between systems is essential. **Encryption in transit** uses an **SSL/TLS certificate** to encrypt data between points.

For the preceding scenarios and more, Azure offers the **Key Vault** service.

Azure Key Vault enables you to store, generate, and manage access to keys, secrets, and certificates. By storing sensitive data such as this in a key vault, you can control who can access a key, certificate, or secret using Azure's built-in RBAC roles. Access is also separated between the **management plane** (who can administer the vault) and the **data plane** (who can create, read, and delete keys, secrets, and certificates).

Because a key vault is a component of your subscription, you can also limit access to the data stored within it to other components within that subscription. For example, a key vault can be locked to only allow access over an internal VNet, which would mean only devices such as virtual machines would be able to access it.

The following diagram shows an example of how you can secure access to your key vault at the network level:

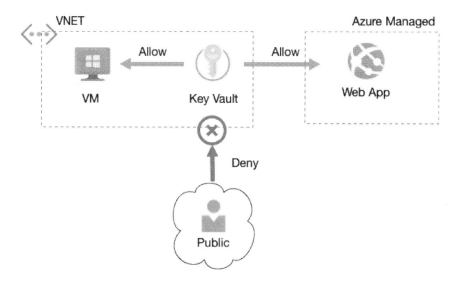

Figure 6.1 – Network-level access restrictions for key vaults

A recommended approach to any form of security is that secrets and keys are rotated regularly, for example, every 90 days.

> **Important note**
>
> **Key rotation** is a standard security strategy to protect against keys or secrets being compromised. Enforcing passwords in connection strings to be changed limits the amount of time a hacker could potentially have to access your data.

When creating a key vault, there are two pricing tiers that you can choose from, **Standard** and **Premium**. Standard encrypts data and information using software-generated keys, whereas Premium uses **Hardware Security Modules** (**HSM**) to protect your keys, which is more secure.

Everything stored in a key vault is automatically replicated to a paired region to protect your secrets, keys, and certificates to protect them from a region outage.

Finally, Azure Key Vault provides monitoring capabilities to log all actions, such as creating, reading, updating, or deleting keys, secrets, and certificates. Log entries can be sent to Azure Monitor, archived in a storage account, or streamed to an event hub. This enables any security events to be thoroughly investigated and tracked, down to the identity of who/what acted.

Next, we will run through the process of creating a key vault.

Creating a key vault

Let's follow these steps for creating a key vault. The following key vault will then be used throughout the chapter to demonstrate some typical use cases:

1. Navigate to the Azure portal at `https://portal.azure.com`.

2. Click the burger menu at the top left and click **Create a resource**.

3. Search for and select **Key Vault**.

4. Click **Create**.

5. Enter the following details:

    a) **Subscription**: Select your subscription.

    b) **Resource group**: Click **Create new** – enter `KeyVaultResourceGroup`.

    c) **Key vault name**: `PacktPubKeyVault`.

    d) **Region**: **East US**.

    e) **Pricing Tier**: **Standard**.

    f) **Days to retain deleted vaults**: `90`.

    g) **Purge protection**: **Disable**.

6. Click **Next: access policy**.

7. Under **Enable Access to**, click all three checkboxes: **Azure Virtual Machines for deployment, Azure Resource Manager for template deployment**, and **Azure Disk Encryption for volume encryption**.

8. Next to **Permission model**, select **Vault access policy**.

9. An access policy is created that grants your account full management and data plane access. Leave this as the default.

10. Click **Next: Networking**.

11. Keep the **Connectivity** option as the default and click **Next: Tags**.

12. Click **Next: Review and create**.

13. Click **Create**.

Once the new key vault has been created, you can select it from the deployment page or by searching for Key Vault in the top Azure search bar. Your key vault should look similar to the following screenshot:

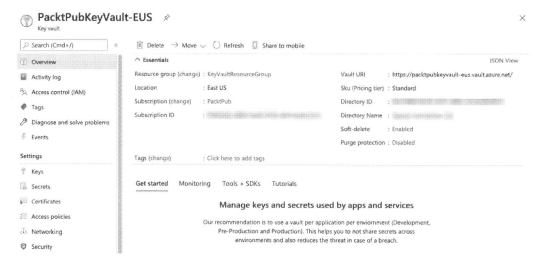

Figure 6.2 – An Azure key vault

With the key vault created, we can create and manage keys, secrets, and certificates within it. So now, let's investigate how to do this.

Managing Key Vault secrets

We will start with a simple example of creating and reading a secret using PowerShell:

1. First, we need to log in to our Azure account:

    ```
    Connect-AzAccount
    ```

2. Select the subscription that you created the key vault in:

    ```
    Select-AzSubscription -SubscriptionId "********-****-
    ****-****-************"
    ```

3. Create a key in a PowerShell variable using the `ConvertTo-SecureString` command:

```
$secret = ConvertTo-SecureString
'MyReallySecureConnectionString' -AsPlainText -Force
```

4. Now store the string in your key vault:

```
Set-AzKeyVaultSecret -VaultName 'PacktPubKeyVault' -Name
'SecureConnectionString' -SecretValue $secret
```

5. We can retrieve the secret through PowerShell as well using `Get-AzKeyVault` as follows:

```
$retreivedSecret = Get-AzKeyVaultSecret -VaultName
'PacktPubKeyVault' -name 'SecureConnectionString'
$retreivedSecret.SecretValueText
```

6. Your decrypted secret should be displayed.

We can also view the key vault's secret through the portal, as we will see next:

1. Navigate to the Azure portal at `https://portal.azure.com`.

2. In the top search bar, search for and select **Key vault**.

3. Click on your key vault.

4. On the left-hand menu, click **Secrets**.

5. The secret you created in steps *1-4* of *Managing Key Vault secrets* will be listed. Click on the secret.

6. You will see a list of versions; in our case, there will only be one. Select it.

7. You will see the details of your secret – in particular, note **Secret Identifier** – this is a **URI** that you will use to access the secret from applications. Copy the identifier and store it somewhere safe for later.

8. At the bottom of the page, click **Show Secret Value**. The value will be decrypted and displayed as in the following example:

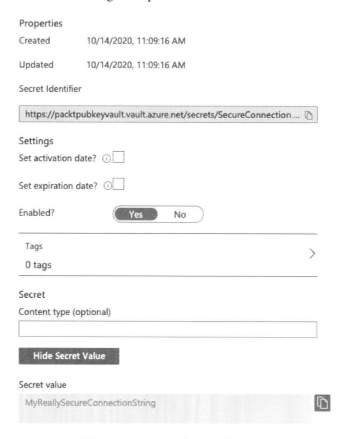

Figure 6.3 – Key Vault example secret

As well as secrets, we can also store keys. Keys can be used for various purposes, but in the next example, we will see how we can generate and store a key that we then use to replace the Microsoft-managed key on a key vault.

Using Key Vault keys

In the following example, we will create a storage account and then replace the default Microsoft-managed key with a customer-managed key, which will be stored in our key vault. We will start by creating the storage account via PowerShell:

1. First, we need to log in to our Azure account:

```
Connect-AzAccount
```

2. If necessary, select the right subscription:

```
Select-AzSubscription -SubscriptionId "********-****-
****-****-************"
```

3. Create a resource group and key vault:

```
$resourceGroup = "cs-managedstorage-resourcegroup"
$location = "eastus"
New-AzResourceGroup -Name $resourceGroup -Location
$location
New-AzStorageAccount -ResourceGroupName $resourceGroup
-Name csmanagedstorage101 -Location $location -SkuName
Standard_LRS -Kind StorageV2
```

This will create a basic storage account in your subscription. Next, we will use the portal to update the encryption key:

1. Navigate to the Azure portal at `https://portal.azure.com`.
2. In the top search bar, search for and select **Storage Accounts**.
3. Click on the storage account you created in *Step 3*.
4. On the left-hand menu, click **Encryption**.
5. Change **Microsoft-managed Keys** to **Customer-managed Keys**.
6. By **Encryption key** choose **Select from the key vault**.
7. Click **Select a key vault and key**.
8. Select your subscription.
9. Select your key vault from the list.
10. Next to **Key**, click **Create new**.
11. Enter the following details:

    a) **Options: Generate**.

    b) **Name**: MyManagedStorageKey.

    c) **Key Type: RSA**.

    d) **RSA Key Size: 2048**.

    e) **Set activation date?**: leave unticked.

f) **Set expiration date?**: leave unticked.

g) **Enabled?**: **Yes**.

12. Click **Create**.

13. Click **Select**.

14. Click **Save**.

The screen will refresh and show the updated configuration – note as well that automated key rotation is enabled, meaning that Azure will automatically generate new keys for you and rotate them.

Using customer-managed keys on services such as storage accounts and SQL databases can sometimes require highly sensitive data.

Using Key Vault certificates

SSL certificates digitally bind cryptographic keys to an organization. They are often used in websites to provide secure HTTPS communications or to encrypt services.

Azure Key Vault provides an easy store to help manage and maintain your certificates. Precisely, it can do the following:

- Create certificates through a certificate creation process. Both self-signed and Certificate Authority-generated certificates can be created.

- Import existing certificates for management.

- Automatically renew certificates with selected issuers.

Therefore, certificates can be stored in a key vault and then accessed either manually through the portal or via programmatic means. For example, they can be referenced as part of an ARM deployment template to automatically install the certificate within a DevOps pipeline.

When we created the key vault, one of the steps involved in creating an **access policy** defined what actions you can access. We chose the default to give your account full access to all certificates, keys, and secrets.

Access policies

Access policies can be assigned to **users**, **security principals**, **managed identities**, and **applications**. Each policy can be a combination of rights broken down into the three data planes. Following the *Least Privileged Access principle*, you should apply only the minimum actions to each user or application.

To add a new policy, perform the following steps:

1. Navigate to the Azure portal at `https://portal.azure.com`.

2. In the top search bar, search for and select **Key vaults**.

3. Click on your key vault.

4. On the left-hand menu, click **Access policies**.

5. Click **Add access policy**.

6. Click the drop-down list next to **Configure from template** and choose **Secret Management**. There are several optional templates you can choose to cover most scenarios, or you can start from scratch.

7. Note that **Key Permissions** has **0** selected. Click the dropdown to view a list of options.

8. Note that **Secret Permissions** has **7** selected. Click the dropdown to view a list of options, including those chosen as part of the template.

9. Note that **Certificate Permissions** has **0** selected. Click the dropdown to view a list of options.

10. Next to **Select Principal**, click **None Selected**. A side window will open, showing you a list of all identities. This list includes not just users but **Security Principals** as well. Select a user, then click **Select**.

11. Click **Add**.

12. From the top menu, click **Save**.

The new policy is now assigned to the user, and you can see that they can be easily edited by clicking the drop-down list for each option and selecting or de-selecting options.

> **Important note**
> You must click the **Save** button when making any changes, *including* when adding new policies.

So far, the access policies have involved user accounts performing actions in either PowerShell or the portal. This has worked okay because they have all taken place under the *context* of your signed-in account.

In many scenarios, an application or other services, such as a virtual machine or Azure function, need to access the key vault. We can't use a user account; instead, we can use either a **Security Principal** or a **Managed Identity**. We will look at Security Principals first.

Working with security principals

Security principals are used primarily for two scenarios: **system access** and **identity integration**.

System access is the ability for one system to access another and is closer to traditional methods for providing application or service access to other systems. A typical example is a database-specific username and password that an application would use to access the backend database.

One of the use cases for secret management in Key Vault is storing a database connection string containing the database username and password as a secret in the vault. However, we must first authenticate to the key vault for our application to access it, which can be performed using a username and password for the vault.

This may seem counter-intuitive, but in reality, this process helps protect our data. Security Principals in Azure can only be used programmatically; that is, you cannot use the credentials directly. It also allows one set of credentials to access multiple secrets, which removes the need to store various secrets within the application configuration itself.

The easiest way to understand the process is to step through it.

We will start by creating a service principal and then a simple **.NET Core web app**.

Creating the service principal

The first step we need to perform is creating a service principal and generating a *client ID* and *secret*, which affects a username and password:

1. Navigate to the Azure portal at `https://portal.azure.com`.
2. In the top search bar, search for and select **Azure Active Directory**.
3. On the left-hand menu, click **App registrations**.
4. Click **+New registration**.
5. On the **Register and application** page, enter a friendly name to refer to your app – for example, `SecureWebApp`.

6. Choose the account type; for now, leave the default of **Accounts in this organizational directory only**.

7. Click **Register**.

8. You will be taken to the **Overview** page for your new service principal; make a note of the **Application (client) ID** – as in the following example:

Figure 6.4 – Creating a service principal

9. On the left-hand menu, click **Certificates & Secrets**.

10. Click + **New client secret**.

11. Give the secret a name such as `WebAppAccess`; leave the expiration at **one year**.

12. Copy the client secret – this is also used in your web app. See the following figure for an example:

Figure 6.5 – Security Principal secret

The next step is to create an **access policy** to allow the security principal we have just created to read secrets, and then finally, we will create our secret.

Setting the access policy

Now we have a service principal, we need to define and assign an access policy to it:

1. Navigate to the Azure portal at `https://portal.azure.com`.

2. In the top search bar, search for and select **Key vaults**.

3. Click on your key vault.

4. On the **Overview** page, copy down the **Vault URI** – this is the final piece of information we will need, along with the *client ID* and *client secret*. See the following example:

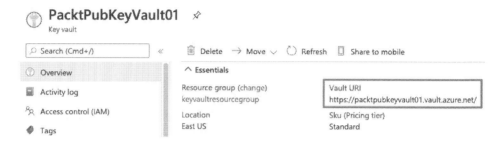

Figure 6.6 – Getting the key vault URI

5. On the left-hand menu, click **Access policies**.

6. Click **Add Access policy**.

7. Click the drop-down list under **Configure from template** and choose **Secret Management**.

8. Under **Select principal**, click **None selected**. Search for the name of the service principal you created in the previous section – *Creating the service principal*. See the example in the following figure. Click **Select**.

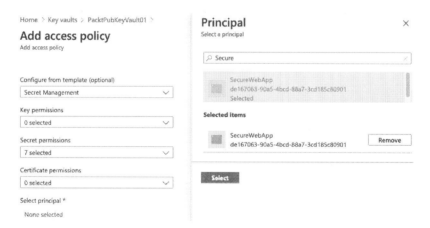

Figure 6.7 – Assigning the access policy

9. Click **Add**.

10. From the top menu, click **Save**.

11. On the left-hand menu, click **Secrets**.

12. Click **Generate/Import**.

13. Complete the following details:

    a) **Upload options**: **Manual**.

    b) **Name**: `SecureConnectionString`.

    c) **Value**: `AreallySecureConnectionString` (details will be masked).

14. Click **Create**.

The final step in the process is to use the service principal we have just created within a web app to access the secret.

Creating the web app

We will use Visual Studio Code to create a basic .NET Core MVC web app:

1. Open Visual Studio Code.

2. Click **Open Folder**.

3. Navigate to a folder to store your project. If necessary, create a new folder (for example, `SecureWebApp`, as in the following figure), then open it.

Figure 6.8 – Creating a new web app project

4. Open a Terminal window by going to the **Terminal** menu and clicking **New Terminal**.

5. In the Terminal window that opens, create a new project by typing the following command:

```
dotnet new mvc
```

The output of the preceding command can be seen in the following screenshot:

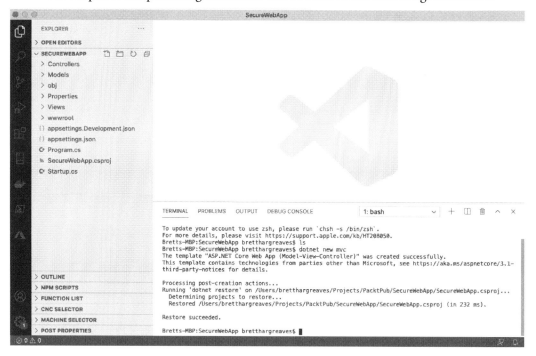

Figure 6.9 – Creating a .NET MVC app

6. Add the **Microsoft Key Vault** NuGet package, and key vault extensions. In the Terminal window, type the following:

```
dotnet add package Microsoft.Azure.KeyVault
dotnet add package Microsoft.Extensions.Configuration.
AzureKeyVault
```

7. Open the `Program.cs` file. Amend the `BuildWebHost` function as follows, replacing `<keyvault-Uri>`, `<client_id>`, and `<client_secret>` with the values you have recorded:

```
public static IHostBuilder CreateHostBuilder(string[]
args) =>
            Host.CreateDefaultBuilder(args)
                .ConfigureAppConfiguration((ctx, builder) =>
                {
                    builder.AddAzureKeyVault("<keyvault-
Uri>", "<client-id>", "<client-secret>");
                })
                .ConfigureWebHostDefaults(webBuilder =>
                {
                    webBuilder.UseStartup<Startup>();
                });
```

8. Open `HomeController.cs` in the **Controllers** folder. Add the following line to the top of the file with the other `using` statements:

```
using Microsoft.Extensions.Configuration;
```

9. Underneath the line `private readonly Ilogger<HomeController> _ logger`, add the following:

```
private readonly IConfiguration _configuration;
```

10. Update the public `HomeController` method as follows:

```
public HomeController(ILogger<HomeController> logger,
IConfiguration configuration)
        {
            _logger = logger;
            _configuration = configuration;
        }
```

11. Update the `Index IActionResult` method as follows:

```
public IActionResult Index()
    {
        ViewBag.ConnectionString = _
configuration["SecureConnectionString"];
        return View();
    }
```

12. Open the `Index.cshtml` page in the `Views/Home` folder as follows:

```
@{
    ViewData["Title"] = "Home Page";
}


<div class="text-center">
    <p>Connection String is @ViewBag.ConnectionString</p>
</div>
```

13. In the **Visual Studio Code Terminal** window, enter the following:

```
dotnet build
dotnet run
```

14. The website will now run, and you can browse to it in the port indicated (usually `localhost:5000`). The index page should show the connection string you added to the key vault as a secret, as in the following example:

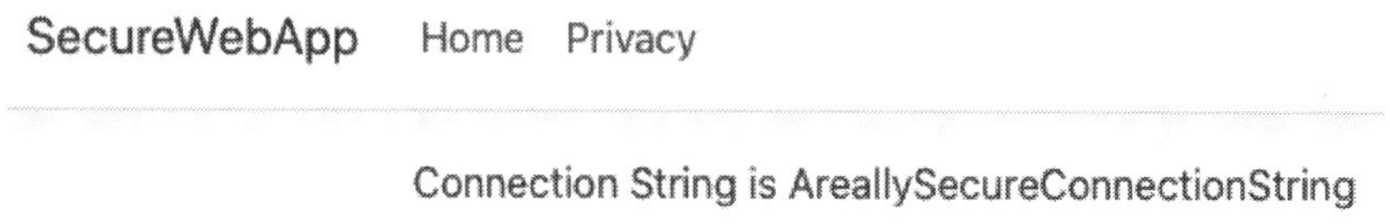

SecureWebApp   Home   Privacy

Connection String is AreallySecureConnectionString

Figure 6.10 – Example of website showing connection string

The preceding processes show how to store and retrieve secrets from the key vault programmatically using a service principal. It is the recommended approach to store sensitive information such as connection strings.

The service principal was created as an App Registration within Azure AD. App Registrations also have another use – to integrate your web applications into Azure AD for authentication and authorization.

Integrating applications into Azure Active Directory

Web applications often need to be secured against unauthorized access, and as we discussed in *Chapter 3, Understanding User Authentication*, Azure Active Directory can be used to provide this security.

Integration is performed through an **OAuth authentication flow**. When a web app is secured with Azure Active Directory, any attempt to access it will trigger the OAuth mechanism. The web app will expect an authentication token to be provided with a request; if that token is missing, the user will be redirected to an authentication endpoint. If Azure AD is integrated with an on-premise directory and **Seamless Single Sign-On** is enabled, this process will be invisible. Otherwise, the user will be redirected to the Microsoft web-based authentication pages.

As part of the authentication process, a token will be provided to the user, then passed with any further requests to the web app. The web app will confirm the supplied token is valid by contacting Azure AD – as in the following diagram:

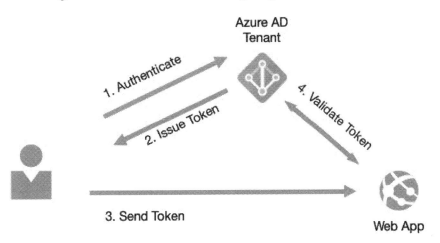

Figure 6.11 – Active Directory integration with web apps

Another advantage of using an OAuth mechanism for authentication is that the validation tokens that identify a user and their access levels can be passed *between* services in a distributed application.

For example, consider an application consisting of a frontend user interface and multiple backend services that perform different processes. Users may have varying levels of access to information; therefore, each service needs to know who the user is and what they should and should not access.

Using OAuth, the user signs in to the Azure tenant, which provides a unique token containing information about the user and their access levels. This token is then passed around within the system as part of each service call; each service then validates the token against Azure AD, as in the following example:

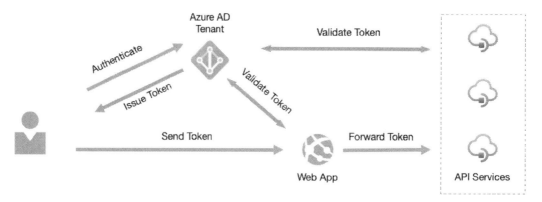

Figure 6.12 – OAuth in a multi-tier system

This process may seem complicated, however, setting it up is relatively easy. In the next example, we will publish the web app we created in the previous example and then enable AD integration.

Deploying a web app

To publish from Visual Studio Code, we first need to install an extension, which we will cover in the walk-through:

1. Open the web app project you created in Visual Studio, then go to the **View** menu and select **Extensions**.

2. Search for `Azure App Service`, then click **Install** – see the following screenshot for an example:

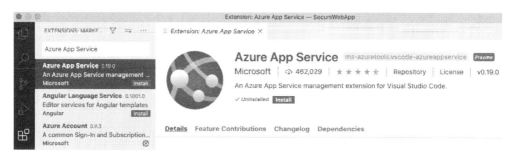

Figure 6.13 – Installing the Azure App Service extension

3. Open a terminal window in Visual Studio Code and publish your website to the local file system by issuing the following command:

```
dotnet publish -c Release -o ./publish
```

4. A folder called `publish` will now appear in the project. Right-click the folder and click **Deploy to Web App...** as in the following screenshot:

publish		
> wwwroot	New File	
{} appsettings.Development.jso	New Folder	
{} appsettings.json	Reveal in Finder	⌥⌘R
≡ Microsoft.Azure.KeyVault.dll	Open in Integrated Terminal	
≡ Microsoft.Azure.KeyVault.Web	Find in Folder...	⌥⇧F
≡ Microsoft.Azure.Services.App		
≡ Microsoft.Extensions.Configu	Cut	⌘X
≡ Microsoft.Extensions.Configu	Copy	⌘C
≡ Microsoft.Extensions.Configu	Paste	⌘V
≡ Microsoft.Extensions.Configu	Copy Path	⌥⌘C
≡ Microsoft.Extensions.FileProv	Copy Relative Path	⌥⇧⌘C
≡ Microsoft.Extensions.FileProv	Rename	↵
≡ Microsoft.Extensions.FileSyst	Delete	⌘⌫
	Deploy to Web App...	

Figure 6.14 – Initiating a web app deployment

5. At the top of the window, a web app deployment wizard will take you through the process of defining the web app details. First, you will be prompted to choose your subscription, as in the following screenshot:

Figure 6.15 – VS Code deploy web app wizard

6. Next, click **Create Web App (Advanced)**.

7. Enter a unique name for your web app – for example, `packtpub-secureapp`, then press *Enter*.

8. Either select an existing resource group or click **+Create new resource group** and enter a new name such as `secureapp-resourcegroup`.

9. Choose Linux or Windows for the underlying OS. Because we are using a .NET application, we can choose **Linux**.

10. Choose the runtime – for example, **.NET Core 3.1**.

11. Click **+ Create new App Service Plan**.

12. Give the new service plan a name, for example, `pactpub-secureapp-serviceplan` – press *Enter*.

13. Choose **F1** for the pricing tier.

14. Click **Skip for now** when prompted to create a new Application Insights resource.

15. Select your region, for example, **East US** – press *Enter*.

16. Once the web app is deployed, you will be prompted to browse to it. Click **Browse Website**.

17. The deployed website will now be opened in a browser window. Copy the URL of the website – we will need this later.

Our web app has been deployed into Azure; you will notice that you can access it without logging in. In the next part of the process, we will enable the app to use **Azure AD integration**.

Enabling AD integration

To enable AD integration, we must first set a login redirect URI for our new website on the service principal we created earlier, and then configure the web app to use that principal:

1. Navigate to the Azure portal at `https://portal.azure.com`.

2. In the top search bar, search for and select **Azure Active Directory**.

3. On the left-hand menu, click **App registrations**.

4. Select the `SecureWebApp` registration.

5. On the left-hand menu, click **Authentication**.

6. Click **+ Add a Platform**.

7. In the **Configure Platforms** window that appears, choose **Web**.

8. Paste in the URL from your web app into **Redirect URIs** and add the following to it: `/.auth/login/aad/callback`. In this example, the URI would be `https://packtpub-secureapp.azurewebsites.net/.auth/login/aad/callback`.

9. Click **Configure**.

10. Scroll down the page to **Implicit grant**, tick the **ID tokens** box, then click **Save**. The page should look like this:

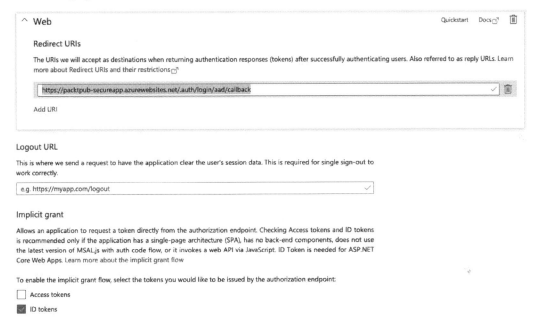

Figure 6.16 – Setting app authentication

11. We now need to configure your app to use the app registration – in the top search bar, search for and select **App Services**.

12. Select your web app – for example, `packtpub-secureapp`.

13. On the left-hand menu, click **Authentication/Authorization**.

14. Set **App Service Authentication** to **On**.

15. Under **Action to take when a request is not authenticated**, choose **Log in with Azure Active Directory**.

16. Under **Authentication Providers**, click **Active Directory**.

17. On the next page, set the first **Management mode** option to **Express**, and the second **Management mode** option to **Select Existing AD App**.

18. Click **Azure AD App**, and select the app registration we created in *Creating the service principal* in the *Working with Security Principals* section.

19. Click **OK**. The page should look like the following. Click **Save**.

Figure 6.17 – Setting authentication

Wait a few minutes for the changes to take effect, then browse to the web app; for example, `https://packtpub-secureapp.azurewebsites.net`. You will now be prompted to log in with your Active Directory account, and once authenticated, you will be directed back to your application. If you are not prompted to sign in, open a private browsing window instead, as your credentials may already be cached in the browser.

As you can see, integrating your application into your Azure Active Directory tenant is very easy and provides a secure and seamless login experience for your users.

The first half of this section involved using a security principal to access the key vault. service principals can be used to access many different services; however, they do rely on a client ID and secret being generated and shared.

Next, we will look at an alternative and more secure method of providing authenticated access to many Azure resources, called **managed identities**.

Using managed identities

In the previous section, we looked at working with security principals that can provide programmatic access to key vaults from our applications. There are a couple of problems with them – you must generate and provide a client ID and secret, and you must manage the rotation of those secrets yourself.

Managed identities provides a similar access option but is fully managed by Azure – there is no need to generate IDs or passwords; you set the appropriate access through role-based access controls. The managed identity mechanism can also be used to provide access to the following:

- Azure Data Lake
- Azure SQL
- Azure Storage (Blobs and Queues)
- Azure Analysis Services
- Azure Event Hubs
- Azure Service Bus

We have the option of using either a **system-assigned** or **user-assigned identity**. System-assigned is the easiest route – and is ideal for simple scenarios – but they are tied to the resource in question – that is, a virtual machine or web app. User-assigned identities are discrete objects and can be assigned to multiple resources – this can be useful if your application uses numerous components to give them all the same managed identity.

As well as Web Apps and Virtual Machines, the following services can also be set to use managed identities:

- Azure Functions
- Azure Logic Apps
- Azure Kubernetes Service
- Azure Data Explorer
- Azure Data Factory

As with security principals, working through using a managed identity is the easiest way to understand it.

Assigning a managed identity

In the next example, we will modify the web app we created in the *Working with security principals* section to use a managed identity instead:

1. Navigate to the Azure portal at `https://portal.azure.com`.

2. In the top search bar, search for and select **App Services**.

3. Select your web app – for example, `packtpub-secureapp`.

4. On the left-hand menu, click **Identity**.

5. **System assigned** is the default identity type; set the status to **On** as in the following example:

Figure 6.18 – Setting the app identity

6. Click **Save**.

7. In the top search bar, search for and select **Key vaults**.

8. Click on your key vault.

9. On the left-hand menu, click **Access policies**.

10. Click **Add Access Policy**.

11. Click the drop-down list next to **Configure from template** and choose **Secret Management**.

12. Under **Select Principal**, click **None selected**. Search for the name of the web app you created earlier in **Deploying a web app** – in our example, `packtpub-secureapp`.

13. Click **Add**.

14. Click **Save**.

With the managed identity set up on our web app, and the necessary policy linked in our key vault, we can update our code to use the identity instead of the security principal.

Using managed identities in web apps

We will replace the key vault that used a client ID and secret in the following walk-through. This time, we will use an `AzureServiceTokenProvider`, which will use the assigned managed identity instead:

1. Open your web app in Visual Studio Code.

2. Open a Terminal window within Visual Studio Code and enter the following to install an additional NuGet package:

    ```
    dotnet add package Microsoft.Azure.Services.
    AppAuthentication
    ```

3. Open the `Program.cs` file and add the following `using` statements to the top of the page:

    ```
    using Microsoft.Azure.KeyVault;
    using Microsoft.Azure.Services.AppAuthentication;
    using Microsoft.Extensions.Configuration.AzureKeyVault;
    ```

4. Modify the `CreateHostBuilder` method as follows:

    ```
    public static IHostBuilder CreateHostBuilder(string[]
    args) =>
                    Host.CreateDefaultBuilder(args)
                    .ConfigureAppConfiguration((ctx, builder) =>
                    {
                        var azureServiceTokenProvider = new
    AzureServiceTokenProvider();
                        var keyVaultClient = new
    KeyVaultClient(
                            new KeyVaultClient.
    AuthenticationCallback(

    azureServiceTokenProvider.KeyVaultTokenCallback));
                        builder.AddAzureKeyVault("https://
    packtpubkeyvault01.vault.azure.net/", new
    DefaultKeyVaultSecretManager());
                    })
    ```

```
      .ConfigureWebHostDefaults(webBuilder =>
      {
            webBuilder.UseStartup<Startup>();
      });
```

5. Open a Terminal window in Visual Studio Code to rebuild and republish the application by entering the following:

```
dotnet build
dotnet publish -c Release -o ./publish
```

6. Next, right-click the `publish` folder and select **Deploy Web App**.

7. Select your subscription and web app to deploy, too, when prompted.

8. Once deployed, browse to your website.

Your website is accessing the secret from the key vault as before; only this time, it is using the managed identity.

In this section, we have replaced a service principal with a managed identity. The use of managed identities offers a more secure way of connecting services as login details are never exposed.

Summary

This chapter covered three tools in Azure that can help secure our applications, particularly around managing data encryption keys and authentication between systems.

We looked at how to use key vaults for creating and managing secrets and keys and how we can then secure access to them using Access policies. We also looked at how we can use security principals and managed identities to secure our applications.

This chapter also concluded the *Identity and Security* requirement of the AZ-304 exam, looking at authentication, authorization, system governance, and application-level security.

Next, we will look at how we architect solutions around specific Azure infrastructure and storage components.

Exam Scenario

The solutions to the exam scenarios can be found at the end of the book.

Mega Corp plans a new internal web solution consisting of a frontend web app, multiple middle-tier API apps, and a SQL database.

The database's data is highly sensitive, and the leadership team is concerned that providing database connection strings to the developers would compromise data protection laws and industry compliance regulations.

Part of the application includes the storage of documents in a Blob Storage account; however, the leadership team is not comfortable with Microsoft managing the encryption keys.

As this is an internal application, authentication needs to be integrated into the existing Active Directory. Also, each of the middle-tier services needs to know who the logged-in user is at all times – in other words, any authentication mechanism needs to pass through all layers of the system.

Design a solution that will alleviate the company's security concerns but still provides a robust application.

Further reading

You can check out the following links for more information about the topics that were covered in this chapter:

- Azure key vault: `Azure Tags: https://docs.microsoft.com/en-us/ azure/azure-resource-manager/management/tag-resources`

- Application Registrations: `https://docs.microsoft.com/en-us/ azure/governance/policy/samples/built-in-policies#guest-configuration`

- Managed identities: `https://docs.microsoft.com/en-us/azure/ governance/blueprints/overview`

Section 3: Infrastructure and Storage Components

In this section, you will learn about the different Infrastructure as a Service (IaaS) components and how they work together to achieve security and resilience.

The following chapters will be covered under this section:

7
Designing Compute Solutions

In the previous chapter, we looked at how to secure our Azure applications using key vaults, security principals, and managed identities.

When building solutions in Azure many components use some form of compute – such as a **virtual machine** (**VM**). However, there are many different types of compute, each with its own strengths. Therefore, in this chapter, we focus on the different types of compute services we have available to us and which options are best suited to which scenarios.

We will then maintain the security and health of VMs by ensuring they are always up to date with the latest OS patches.

Finally, we'll look at containerization and how we can use **Azure Kubernetes Service** (**AKS**).

With this in mind, we will be covering the following topics:

- Understanding different types of compute
- Automating virtual machine management
- Architecting for containerization and Kubernetes

Technical requirements

This chapter will use the Azure portal (`https://portal.azure.com`) for examples.

Understanding different types of compute

When we architect solutions, there will often be at least one component that needs to host, or run, an application. The application could be built specifically for the task or an off-the-shelf package bought from a vendor.

Azure provides several compute services for hosting your application; each type can be grouped into one of three kinds of *hosting model*:

- **Infrastructure as a Service** (**IaaS**): VMs are within this category and support services such as storage (that is, disk drives) and networking. IaaS is the closest to a traditional on-premise environment, except Microsoft manages the underlying infrastructure, including hardware and the host operating system. You are still responsible for maintaining the guest operating system, however, including patching, monitoring, anti-virus software, and so on.

- **Platform as a Service** (**PaaS**): Azure App Service is an example of a PaaS component. With PaaS, you do not need to worry about the operating system (other than to ensure what you deploy to it is compatible). Microsoft manages all maintenance, patching, and anti-virus software; you simply deploy your applications to it. When provisioning PaaS components, you generally specify an amount and CPU and RAM, and your costs will be based on this.

- **Serverless** or **Function as a Service** (**FaaS**): FaaS, or serverless, is at the opposite end to IaaS. With FaaS, any notion of CPU, RAM, or management is completely abstracted away; you simply deploy your code, and the required resources are utilized to perform the task. Because of this, FaaS pricing models are calculated on exact usage, for example, the number of executions, as opposed to IaaS, where pricing is based on the specific RAM and CPU.

Some services may appear to blur the line between the hosting options; for example, VMs can be built as scale sets that automatically scale up and down on demand.

Generally, as you move from IaaS to FaaS, management becomes easier; however, control, flexibility, and portability are lost.

When choosing a compute hosting model for your solution, you will need to consider many factors:

- **Deployment and compatibility**

  Not all applications can run on all services without modification. Older applications may have dependencies on installed services or can only be deployed via traditionally installed packages. For these legacy systems, an IaaS approach might be the only option.

  Conversely, a modern application built using Agile DevOps processes, with regularly updated and redeployed components, might be better suited to Web Apps or Azure Functions.

- **Support**

  Existing enterprise systems typically have support teams and processes embedded within the organization and will be used to patch and update systems in line with existing support processes.

  Smaller companies may have fewer IT resources to provide these support tasks. Therefore, they would benefit significantly from PaaS or FaaS systems that do not require maintenance as the Azure platform handles this.

- **Scalability**

  Different services have different methods for scaling. Legacy applications may need to use traditional load balancing methods by building VMs in web farms with load balancers in front to distribute the load.

  Modern web applications can make use of App Service or Azure Functions, which scale automatically without the need for additional components.

- **Availability**

  Each Azure service has a **Service-Level Agreement (SLA)** that determines a baseline for how much uptime a service offers. The mix of components used can also affect this value. For example, a single VM has an SLA of 95%, whereas two VMs across Availability Zones with a load balancer in front has an SLA of 99.99%.

  Azure Functions and App Service have an SLA of 99.95% without any additional components.

> **Important note**
>
> **Service-Level Agreements (SLAs)** define specific metrics by which a service is measured. In Azure, it is the amount of time any particular service is agreed to be available for. This is usually measured as a percentage of that uptime – for example, 99.95% (referred to as three and a half nines) or 99.99% (referred to as four nines). Your choice of components and how they are architected will impact the SLA Microsoft offers.
>
> An SLA of 99.95% means up to 4.38 hours of downtime a year is allowed, whereas 99.99% means only 52.60 minutes are permitted.

- **Security**

  As services move from IaaS to PaaS and FaaS, the security responsibility shifts. For VMs, Microsoft is responsible for the physical security and underlying infrastructure, whereas you are responsible for patching, anti-virus software, and applications that run on them. For PaaS and FaaS, Microsoft is also responsible for security on the service. However, you need to be careful of different configuration elements within the service that may not be compliant with your requirements.

  For some organizations, all traffic flow needs to be tightly controlled, especially for internal services; most PaaS solutions support this but only as a configurable option, which can sometimes increase costs.

- **Cost**

  FaaS provides a very granular cost model in that you pay for execution time. Whereas IaaS and some PaaS demand you provision set resources based on required CPU and RAM. For example, a VM incurs costs as long as it is running, which is continual for many use cases.

  When migrating existing legacy applications, this may be the only option, but it isn't the most efficient from a cost perspective. Refactoring applications may cost more upfront but could be cheaper in the long run as they only consume resources and incur costs periodically.

  Similarly, a new microservice built to respond to events on an ad hoc basis would suit an Azure function, whereas the same process running on a VM would not be cost-effective.

- **Architecture styles**

  How an application is designed can directly impact the choice of technology. VMs are best suited to older architectures such as N-tier, whereas microservice and event-driven patterns are well suited to Azure Functions or containerization.

- **User skills**

  Azure provides several technologies for *no-code* development. **Power Automate**, and the **workflow development system**, is specifically built to allow end users with no development knowledge to quickly create simple apps.

As you can see, to decide on a compute technology, you must factor in many different requirements. The following chart shows a simple workflow to help in this process:

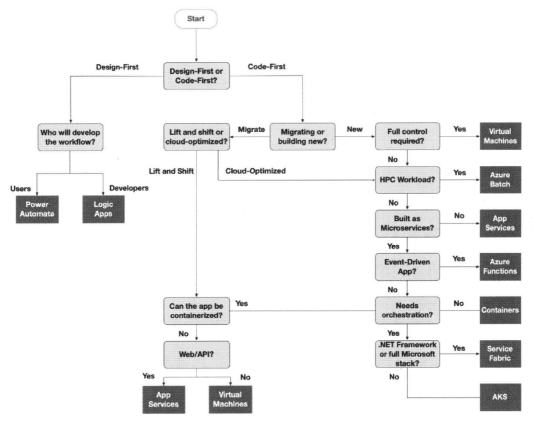

Figure 7.1 – Compute options workflow

Next, we will look in more detail at each service and provide example use cases.

Comparing compute options

Each type of compute has its own set of strengths; however, each also has its primary use cases, and therefore, might not be suitable for some scenarios.

Virtual machines

As the closest technology to existing on-premise systems, VMs are best placed for use cases requiring either fast migration to the cloud or those legacy systems that cannot run on other services without reworking the application.

The ability to quickly provision, test, and destroy a VM makes them ideal for testing and developing products, especially when you need to ascertain how a particular piece of software works on different operating systems.

Sometimes a solution may have stringent requirements around security in that they cannot use shared compute. Running such applications on VMs helps ensure processing is not shared. Through the use of dedicated hosts, you can even provision your physical hardware to run those VMs on.

What to watch out for

To make VMs scalable and resilient, you must architect and deploy supporting technologies or configure the machines accordingly. By default, a single VM is not resilient. Failure of the physical hardware can disrupt services, and the servers do not scale automatically.

Building multiple VMs in availability sets and across Availability Zones can protect you against many such events, and scale sets allow you to configure automatic scaling. However, these are optional configurations and may require additional components such as load balancers. These options require careful planning and can increase costs.

> **Important note**
>
> We will cover availability sets and scale sets in more detail in *Chapter 14, High Availability and Redundancy Concepts*.

Azure Batch

With Azure Batch, you create applications that perform specific tasks, which run in node pools. Node pools can contain thousands of VMs that are created, run a task, and are then decommissioned. No information is stored on the VMs themselves. However, the input and output of datasets can be achieved by reading and writing to Azure storage accounts.

Azure Batch is suited to the parallel processing of tasks and **high-performance computing** (**HPC**) batch jobs. Being able to provision thousands of VMs for short periods, combined with per-second billing, ensures efficient costs for such projects.

The following diagram shows how a typical batch service might work. As we can see, input files can be ingested from Azure Storage by the Batch service, which then distributes it to a node in a node pool for processing. The code that performs the processing is held within Azure Batch as a ZIP file. All output is then sent back out to the storage account:

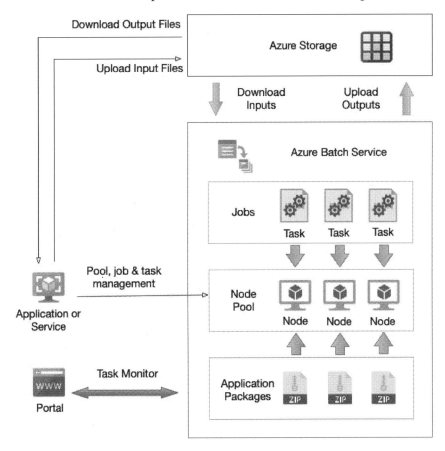

Figure 7.2 – Pool, job, and task management

Some examples of a typical workload may include the following:

- Financial risk modeling

- Image and video rendering

- Media transcoding

- Large data imports and transformation

With Azure Batch, you can also opt for *low-priority* VMs – these are cheaper but do not have guaranteed availability. Instead, they are allocated from surplus capacity within the data center. In other words, you must wait for the surplus compute to become available.

What to watch out for

Azure Batch is, of course, not suited to interactive applications such as websites or services that must store files locally for periods – although, as already discussed, it can output results to Azure Storage.

Service Fabric

Modern applications are often built or run as microservices, smaller components that can be scaled independently of other services. To achieve greater efficiency, it is common to run multiple services on the same VM. However, as an application will be built of numerous services, each of which needs to scale, managing, distributing, and scaling, known as *orchestration*, can become difficult.

Azure Service Fabric is a *container orchestrator* that makes the management and deployment of software packages onto scalable infrastructure easier.

The following diagram shows a typical Service Fabric architecture; applications are deployed to VMs or VM scale sets:

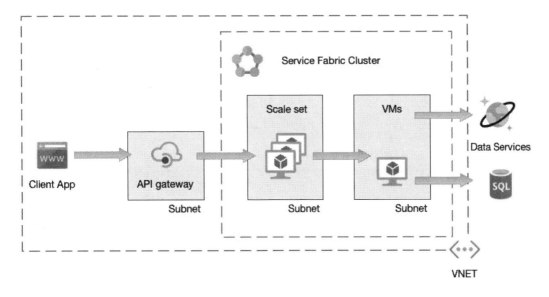

Figure 7.3 – Azure Service Fabric example architecture

It is particularly suited to .NET applications that would traditionally run on a virtual machine, and one of its most significant benefits is that it supports *stateful* services. Service Fabric powers many of Microsoft's services, such as Azure SQL, Cosmos DB, Power BI, and others.

> **Tip**
>
> When building modern applications, there is often discussion around **stateful** and **stateless** applications. When a client is communicating with a backend system, such as a website, you need to keep track of those requests – for example, when you log in, how can you confirm the next request is from that same client? This is known as *state*. *Stateless* applications expect the client to track this information and provide it back to the server with every request – usually in the form of a token validated by the server. With *stateful* applications, the server keeps track of the client, but this requires the client to always to use the same backend server – which is more difficult when your systems are spread across multiple servers.

Using Service Fabric enables developers to build distributed systems without worrying about how those systems scale and communicate. It is an excellent choice for moving existing applications into a scalable environment without the need to completely re-architect.

What to watch out for

You will soon see that there are many similarities between Service Fabric and AKS clusters – one of the most significant differences between the two is portability. Because Service Fabric is tightly integrated into Azure and other Microsoft technologies, it may not work well if you need to move the solution to another platform.

Container Instances

Virtual machines offer a way to run multiple, isolated applications on a single piece of hardware. However, virtual machines are relatively inefficient in that every single instance contains a full copy of the operating system.

Containers wrap and isolate individual applications and their dependencies but still use the same underlying operating systems as other containers running on the host – as we can see in the following diagram:

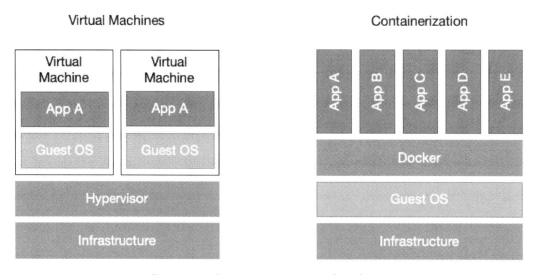

Figure 7.4 – Containers versus virtual machines

This provides several advantages, including speed and the way they are defined. Azure uses Docker as the container engine, and Docker images are built-in code. This enables easier and repeatable deployments.

Because containers are also lightweight, they are much faster to provision and start up, enabling applications based on them to react quickly to demands for resources.

Containers are ideal for a range of scenarios. Many legacy applications can be containerized relatively quickly, making them a great option when migrating to the cloud.

Containers' lightweight and resource-efficient nature also lends itself to microservice architectures whereby applications are broken into smaller services that can scale out with more instances in response to demand.

We cover containers in more detail later in this chapter, in the *Architecting for containerization and Kubernetes* section.

What to watch out for

Not all applications can be containerized, and containerization removes some controls that would otherwise be available on a standard virtual machine.

As the number of images and containers increases in an application, it can become challenging to maintain and manage them; in these cases, an orchestration layer may be required, which we will cover next.

Azure Kubernetes Service (AKS)

Microservice-based applications often require specific capabilities to be effective, such as automated provisioning and deployment, resource allocation, monitoring and responding to container health events, load balancing, traffic routing, and more.

Kubernetes is a service that provides these capabilities, which are often referred to as orchestration.

AKS stands for Azure Kubernetes Service and is the ideal choice for microservice-based applications that need to dynamically respond to events such as individual node outages or automatically scaling resources in response to demand. Because AKS is a managed service, much of the complexity of creating and managing the cluster is taken care of for you.

The following shows a high-level overview of a typical AKS cluster and it is described in more detail in the *Azure Kubernetes Service* section later in this chapter:

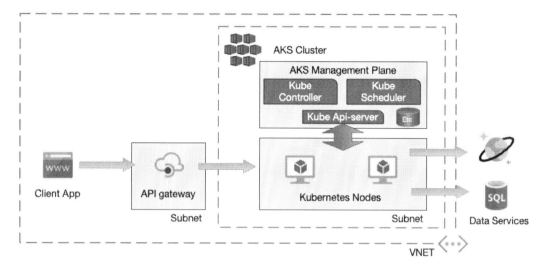

Figure 7.5 – AKS cluster

AKS is also platform-independent – any application built to run on the Kubernetes service can easily be migrated from one cluster to another regardless of whether it is in Azure, on-premise, or even another cloud vendor.

As already stated, we cover containers and AKS in more detail later in this chapter, in the *Architecting for containerization and Kubernetes* section.

What to watch out for

In general, AKS and Kubernetes are more complicated than other technologies, especially Azure native alternatives such as App Service or Azure Functions. Additional tools are often required to better monitor and deploy solutions, which can sometimes lead to security concerns for some organizations. Although these can, of course, be satisfied, there is more work involved in setting up and using AKS for the first time.

Kubernetes is also designed to host multiple services and therefore may not be cost-effective for smaller, more straightforward applications such as a single, basic website. As an example, the recommended minimum number of nodes in a production AKS cluster is three nodes. In comparison, a resilient web app can be run on just a single node when using Azure App Service.

App Service

App Service is a fully managed hosting platform for web applications, RESTful APIs, mobile backend services, and background jobs.

App Service supports applications built in ASP.NET, ASP.NET Core, Java, Ruby, Node.js, PHP, and Python. Applications deployed to App Service are scalable, secure, and adhere to many industry-standard compliance standards.

App Service is linked to an App Service plan, which defines the amount of CPU and RAM available to your applications. You can also assign multiple app services to the same App Service plan to share resources.

For highly secure environments, **Application Service Environments (ASEs)** provide isolated environments built on top of VNets.

App Service is, therefore, best suited to web apps, RESTful APIs, and mobile backend apps. It can be easily scaled by defining CPU and RAM-based thresholds and are fully managed, so you do not need to worry about security patching or resilience within a region.

What to watch out for

Because App Service is always running, is always costs – that is, it is never idle. However, using automated scaling can at least ensure a minimal cost during low usage, and scale-out with additional instances in response to demand.

Azure Functions

Azure Functions falls into the **Functions as a Service (FaaS)** or serverless category. This means that you can run Azure Functions using a consumption plan whereby you only pay for the service as it is being executed. In comparison, Azure App Service runs on a service plan in which you define the CPU and RAM.

With Azure Functions, you don't need to define CPU and RAM as the Azure platform automatically allocates whatever resources are required to complete the operation. Because of this, functions have a default timeout of 5 minutes with a maximum of 10 minutes – in other words, if you have a function that would run for longer than 10 minutes, you may need to consider an alternative approach.

> **Tip**
>
> Azure Functions can be run as an App Service plan the same as App Service. This can be useful if you have functions that will run for longer than 10 minutes, if you have spare capacity in an existing service plan, or if you require support for VNet integration. Using an App Service plan means you pay for the service in the same way as App Service, that is, you pay for the provisioned CPU and RAM whether you are using it or not.

Functions are event-driven; this means they will execute your code in response to a trigger being activated. The following triggers are available:

- **HTTPTrigger**: The function is executed in response to a service calling an API endpoint over HTTP/HTTPS.

- **TimerTrigger**: Executes on a schedule.

- **GitHub webhook**: Responds to events that occur in your GitHub repositories.

- **CosmosDBTrigger**: Processes Azure Cosmos DB documents when added or updated in collections in a NoSQL database.

- **BlobTrigger**: Processes Azure Storage blobs when they are added to containers.

- **QueueTrigger**: Responds to messages as they arrive in an Azure Storage queue.

- **EventHubTrigger**: Responds to events delivered to an Azure Event Hub.

- **ServiceBusQueueTrigger**: Connects your code to other Azure services or on-premises services by listening to message queues.

- **ServiceBusTopicTrigger**: Connects your code to other Azure services or on-premises services by subscribing to topics.

Once triggered, an Azure function can then run code and interact with other Azure services for reading and writing data, including the following:

- Azure Cosmos DB

- Azure Event Hubs

- Azure Event Grid

- Azure Notification Hubs

- Azure Service Bus (queues and topics)

- Azure Storage (blob, queues, and tables)

- On-premises (using Service Bus)

By combining different triggers and outputs, you can easily create a range of possible functions, as we see in the following diagram:

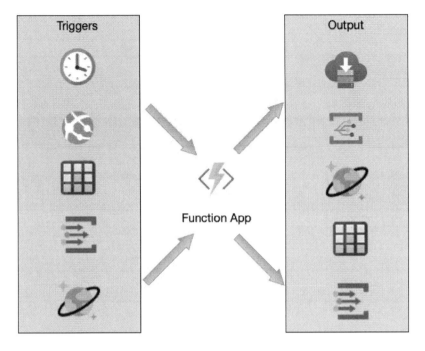

Figure 7.6 – Combining triggers and outputs with a Functions app

Azure Functions is therefore well suited to event-based microservice applications that are short-run and are not continuously activated. As with App Service, Functions supports a range of languages, including C#, F#, JavaScript, Python, and PowerShell Core.

What to watch out for

When running as a consumption plan, Azure Functions is best suited to short-lived tasks – for tasks that run longer than 10 minutes, you should consider alternatives or running them on an App Service plan.

You should also consider how often they will be executed because you pay per execution on a consumption plan. If it is continuously triggered, your costs could increase beyond that of a standard web app. Again, consider alternative approaches or the use of an App Service plan.

Finally, consumption-based apps cannot integrate with VNets. Again, if this is required, running them on an App Service plan can provide this functionality.

Logic Apps

Azure Logic Apps is another serverless option – when creating logic apps, you do not need to be concerned with how much RAM or CPU to provision; instead, you pay per execution or triggering them.

> **Important note**
>
> **Consumption versus fixed price**: Many serverless components, including Logic Apps and Functions, can be run on isolated environments, or in the case of Logic Apps, an **Isolated Service Environment** (**ISE**), whereby you pay for provisioned resources in the same way as a virtual machine.

Logic Apps shares many concepts with Azure Functions; you can define triggers, actions, flow logic, and connectors for communicating with other services. Whereas you define this in code with Functions, Logic Apps provides a drag-and-drop interface that allows you to build workflows quickly.

Logic Apps has hundreds of pre-built connectors that allow you to interface with hundreds of systems – not just in Azure but also externally. By combining these connectors with `if-then-else` style logic flows and either scheduled or action-based triggers, you can develop complex workflows without writing a single line of code.

The following screenshot shows a typical workflow built purely in the Azure portal:

Figure 7.7 – Logic Apps example

With their extensibility features, you can also create your custom logic and connectors for integrating with your services.

Finally, although the solution can be built entirely in the Azure portal, you can also create workflows using traditional development tools such as Visual Studio or Visual Studio Code. This is because solutions are defined as ARM templates – which enables developers to define workflows and store them in code repositories. You can then automate deployments through DevOps pipelines.

What to watch out for

Logic Apps provides a quick and relatively simple mechanism for creating business workflows. When you need to build more complex business logic or create custom connectors, you need to balance the difficulty of doing this versus using an alternative approach such as Azure Functions. Logic Apps still requires a level of developer experience and is not suitable if business users may need to develop and amend the workflows.

Power Automate

Power Automate, previously called Flow, is also a GUI-driven workflow creation tool that allows you to build automated business processes. Like Logic Apps, using Power Automate, you can define triggers and logic flow connected to other services, such as email, storage, or apps, through built-in connectors.

The most significant difference between Power Automate and Logic Apps is that Power Automate workflows can only be built via the drag-and-drop interface – you cannot edit or store the underlying code.

Therefore, the primary use case for Power Automate is for office workers and business analysts to create simple workflows that can use only the built-in connectors.

What to watch out for

Power Automate is only for simpler workflows and is not suitable when deeper or more advanced integration is required.

In this section, we have briefly looked at the many different compute technologies available in Azure. PaaS options are fully managed by the platform, allowing architects and developers to focus on the solution rather than management. However, when traditional IaaS compute options are required, such as virtual machines, security and OS patches must be managed yourself. Next, we will look at the native tooling that Azure provides to make this management easier.

Automating virtual machine management

Virtual machines are part of the IaaS family of components. One of the defining features of VMs in Azure is that you are responsible for keeping the OS up to date with the latest security patches.

In an on-premise environment, this could be achieved by manually configuring individual servers to apply updates as they become available; however, in many organizations, more control is required; such as, for example, the ability to have patches verified and approved before mass roll out to production systems, control when they happen, and control reboots when required.

Typically, this could be achieved using **Windows Server Update Services** (**WSUS**) and Configuration Manager, part of the Microsoft Endpoint Manager suite of products. However, these services require additional management and setup, which can be time-consuming.

As with most services, Azure helps simplify managing VM updates with a native Update Management service. Update Management uses several other Azure components, including the following:

- **Log Analytics**: Along with the Log Analytics agent, reports on the current status of patching for a VM

- **PowerShell Desired State Configuration (DSC)**: Required for Linux patching

- **Automation Hybrid Runbooks / Automation Account**: Used to perform updates

Automation Account and Log Analytics workspaces are not supported together in all regions, and therefore you must plan when setting up **Update Management**. For example, if your Log Analytics workspace is in *East US*, your automation account must be created in *East US 2*.

See the following link for more details on region pairings: `https://docs.microsoft.com/en-gb/azure/automation/how-to/region-mappings`.

When setting up Update Management, you can either create the Log Analytics workspaces and automation accounts yourself or let the Azure portal make them for you. In the following example, we will select an Azure VM and have the portal set up Update Management.

For this example, you will need a Windows VM set up in your subscription:

1. Navigate to the Azure portal at `https://portal.azure.com`.

2. In the search bar, type and select `Virtual Machines` and select the virtual machine you wish to apply Update Management to.

3. On the left-hand menu, click **Guest + host updates** under **Operations**.

4. Click the **Go to Update Management** button.

5. Complete the following details:

   a) **Log Analytics workspace Location**: The location of your VM, for example, **East US**

   b) **Log Analytics workspace**: **Create default workspace**

   c) **Automation account subscription**: Your subscription

   d) **Automation account**: **Create a default account**

6. Click **Enable**.

The process can take around 15 minutes once completed. Go back to the VM view and again select **Guest + host updates** under **Operations**, followed by **Go to Update Management**.

You will see a view similar to the following screenshot:

Figure 7.8 – Update Management blade

You can get to the same view but for all the VMs you wish to manage in the portal by searching for `Automation Accounts` and selecting the automation account that has been created. Then click **Update management**.

If you want to add more VMs, click the **+ Add Azure VMs** button to see a list of VMs in your subscription and enable the agent on multiple machines simultaneously – as we see in the following screenshot:

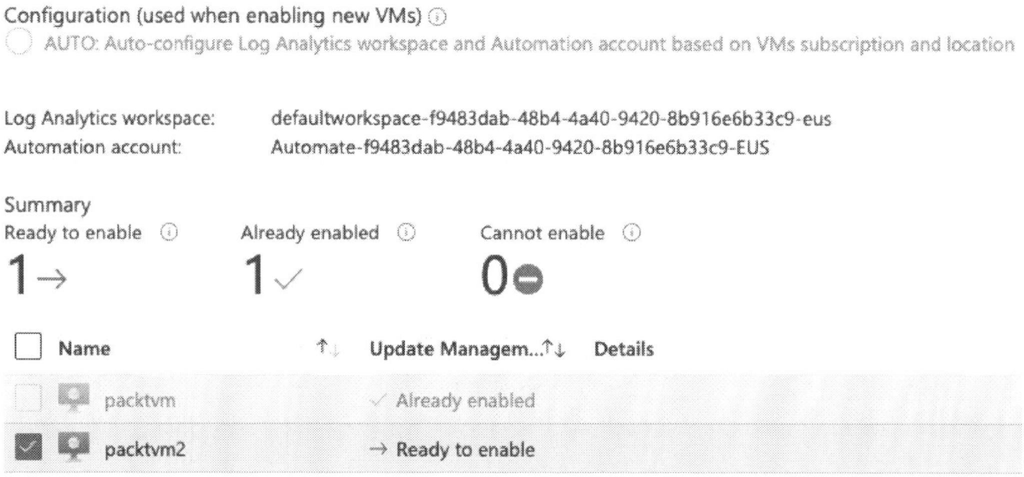

Configuration (used when enabling new VMs) ⓘ
○ AUTO: Auto-configure Log Analytics workspace and Automation account based on VMs subscription and location

Log Analytics workspace: defaultworkspace-f9483dab-48b4-4a40-9420-8b916e6b33c9-eus
Automation account: Automate-f9483dab-48b4-4a40-9420-8b916e6b33c9-EUS

Summary
Ready to enable ⓘ   Already enabled ⓘ   Cannot enable ⓘ
1 →   1 ✓   0 ⊖

☐	Name	↑↓	Update Managem...↑↓	Details
☐	🖥 packtvm		✓ Already enabled	
☑	🖥 packtvm2		→ Ready to enable	

Figure 7.9 – Adding more virtual machines for Update Management

The final step is to schedule the installation of patches:

1. Navigate to the Azure portal by opening `https://portal.azure.com`.

2. Type `Automation` into the search bar and select **Automation Accounts**.

3. Select the automation account.

4. Click **Update Management**.

5. Click **Schedule deployment** and complete the details as follows:

   a) **Name**: `Patch Tuesday`

   b) **Operating System**: **Windows**

   c) **Maintenance Window (minutes)**: `120`

   d) **RebootReboot options: Reboot if required**

6. Under **Groups to update**, click **Click to Configure**.

7. Select your subscription and **Select All** under **Resource Groups**.

8. Click **Add**, then **OK**.

9. Click **Schedule Settings**.

10. Set the following details:

    a) **Start date**: First **Tuesday** of the month

    b) **Recurrence**: **Recurring**

    c) **Recur Every**: 14 days

11. Click **OK**.

12. Click **Create**.

Through the Update Management feature, you can control how your virtual machines are patched and when and what updates to include or exclude. You can also set multiple schedules and group servers by resource group, location, or tag.

In the preceding example, we selected all VMs in our subscription, but as you saw, we had the option to choose a machine based on location, subscription, resource group, or tags.

In this way, you can create separate groups for a variety of purposes. For example, we mentioned earlier that a common practice would be to test patches before applying them to production servers. We can accommodate this by grouping non-production servers into a separate subscription, resource group, or simply tagging them. You can then create one patch group for your test machines, followed by another for production machines a week later – after you've had time to confirm the patches have not adversely affected workloads.

As part of any solution design that utilizes VMs, accommodation must be included to ensure they are always running healthily and securely, and Update Management is a critical part of this. As we have seen, Azure makes the task of managing OS updates easy and straightforward to set up.

Next, we will investigate another form of compute that is becoming increasingly popular – containerization and Kubernetes.

Architecting for containerization and Kubernetes

This section will look in more detail at **AKS**, Microsoft's implementation of **Kubernetes**. To understand what AKS is, we need to take a small step back and understand **containerization** and Kubernetes itself.

Containerization

As we briefly mentioned earlier, containerization is a form of virtualization in that you can run multiple containers upon the same hardware, much like virtual machines. Unlike virtual machines, containers share the underlying OS of the host. This provides much greater efficiency and density. You can run many more containers upon the same hardware than you can run virtual machines because of the lower memory overhead of needing to run multiple copies of the OS – as we can see in the following diagram:

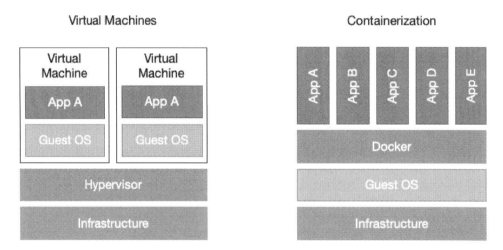

Figure 7.10 – Containers versus virtual machines

In addition to this efficiency, containers are portable. They can easily be moved from one host to another, and this is because containers are self-contained and isolated. A container includes everything it needs to run, including the application code, runtime, system tools, libraries, and settings.

To run containers, you need a container host – the most common is **Docker**, and in fact, container capabilities in Azure use the Docker runtime.

A container is a running instance, and what that instance contains is defined in an **image**. Images can be defined in code; in Docker images, this is called a **Dockerfile**.

The Dockerfile uses a specific syntax that defines what base image you wish you use – that is, either a vanilla OS or an existing image with other tools and components on it, followed by your unique configuration options, which may include additional software to install, networking, file shares, and so on. An example Dockerfile might look like this:

```
FROM node:current-slim

WORKDIR /usr/src/app
COPY package.json .
RUN npm install

EXPOSE 8080
CMD [ "npm", "start" ]

COPY . .
```

In this example, we start with an image called node:current-slim, set a working directory, copy a file into it, and install a package called npm. Finally, we expose the application over port 8080 and issue the npm start command.

This Dockerfile can create a new image but notice how it is based on an existing image. By extending existing images, you can more easily build your containers with consistent patterns.

The images we build, or use as a source, are held in a **container registry**. Docker has its public container registry, but you can create your private registry with the Azure Container Registry service in Azure.

Once we have created our new image and stored it in a container registry, we can deploy that image as a running container. Containers in Azure can be run either using the **Azure Container Instances** (**ACI**), a containerized web app, or an AKS cluster.

Web apps for containers

Web apps for containers are a great choice if your development team is already used to using Azure Web Apps to run monolithic or N-tier apps and you want to start moving toward a containerized platform. Web Apps works best when you only need one or a few *long-running* instances or when you would benefit from a shared or free App Service plan.

An example use case might be when you have an existing .NET app that you wish to containerize that *hasn't* been built as a microservice.

Azure Container Instances

ACI is a fully managed environment for containers, and you are only billed for the time you use them. As such, they suit *short-lived* microservices, although, like web apps for containers, you should only consider this option if you are running a few services.

Web apps for containers and ACI are great for simple services or when you are starting the containerization journey. Once your applications begin to fully embrace microservices and containerized patterns, you will need better control and management; for these scenarios, you should consider using AKS.

Azure Kubernetes Service

We looked at containerization, and specifically with Docker (Azure's default container engine), in the previous section. Now we have container images registered in Azure Container Registry, and from there, we can then use those images to spin up instances or running containers.

Two questions may spring to mind – the first is what now? Or perhaps more broadly, why bother? In theory, we could achieve some of what's in the container with a simple virtual machine image.

Of course, one reason for containerization is that of portability – that is, we can run those images on any platform that runs Docker. However, the other main reason is it now allows us to run many more of those instances on the same underlying hardware because we can have greater density through the shared OS.

This fact, in turn, allows us to create software using a pattern known as **microservices**.

Traditionally, a software service may have been built as monolithic – that is, the software is just one big code base that runs on a server. The problem with this pattern is that it can be quite hard to scale – that is, if you need more power, you can only go so far as adding more RAM and CPU.

The first answer to this issue was to build applications that could be duplicated across multiple servers and then have requests load balanced between them – and in fact, this is still a pervasive pattern.

As software started to be developed in a more modular fashion, those individual modules would be broken up and run as separate services, each being responsible for a particular aspect of the system. For example, we might split off a product ordering component as an individual service that gets called by other parts of the system, and this service could run on its own server.

While we can quickly achieve this by running it on its virtual server, the additional memory overhead means as we break our system into more and more individual services, this memory overhead increases, and we soon run very efficiently from a resource usage point of view.

And here is where containers come in. Because they offer isolation without running a full OS each time, we can run our processes far more efficiently – that is, we can run far more on the same hardware than we could on standard virtual machines.

By this point, you might now be asking how do we manage all this? What controls the spinning up of new containers or shutting them down? And the answer is **orchestration**. Container orchestrators monitor containers and add additional instances in response to usage thresholds or even for resiliency if a running container becomes unhealthy for any reason. Kubernetes is an orchestration service for managing containers.

A Kubernetes cluster consists of worker machines, called **nodes**, that run containerized applications, and every cluster has at least one worker node. The worker node(s) host pods that are the application's components, and a control plane or **cluster master** manages the worker nodes and the pods in the cluster. We can see a logical overview of a typical Kubernetes cluster, with all its components, in the following diagram:

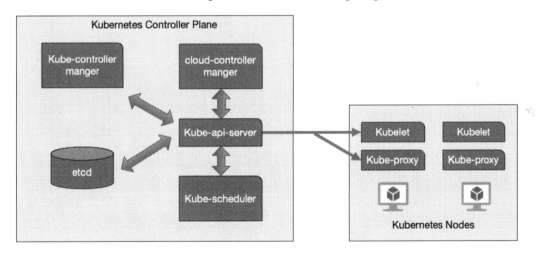

Figure 7.11 – Kubernetes control plane and components

AKS is Microsoft's implementation of a managed Kubernetes cluster. When you create an AKS cluster, a cluster master is automatically created and configured; there is no cost for the cluster master, only the nodes that are part of the AKS cluster.

The cluster master includes the following Kubernetes components:

- **kube-apiserver**: The API server exposes the Kubernetes management services and provides access for management tools such as the `kubectl` command, which is used to manage the service.

- **etcd**: A highly available key-value store that records the state of your cluster.

- **kube-scheduler**: Manages the nodes and what workloads to run on them.

- **kube-controller-manager**: Manages a set of smaller controllers that perform pod and node operations.

You define the nodes' number and size, and the Azure platform configures secure communication between the cluster master and nodes.

Nodes and node pools

An AKS cluster has one or more nodes, which are virtual machines running the Kubernetes node components and container runtime:

- **kubelet** is the Kubernetes agent that responds to requests from the cluster master and runs the requested containers.

- **kube-proxy** manages virtual networking.

- The **container runtime** is the Docker engine that runs your containers.

The following diagram shows these components and their relation to Azure:

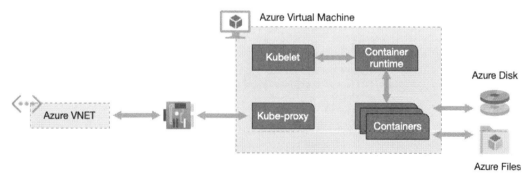

Figure 7.12 – AKS nodes

When you define your AKS nodes, you choose the SKU of the VM you want, which in turn determines the number of CPUs, RAM, and type of disk. You can also run GPU-powered VMs, which are great for mathematical and AI-related workloads.

You can also set up the maximum and the minimum number of nodes to run in your cluster, and AKS will automatically add and remove nodes within those limits.

AKS nodes are built with either Ubuntu Linux or Windows 2019, and because the cluster is managed, you cannot change this. If you need to specify your OS or use a different container runtime, you must build your Kubernetes cluster using the appropriate engine.

When you define your node sizes, you need to be aware that Azure automatically reserves an amount of CPU and RAM to ensure each node performs as expected – these reservations are 60 ms for CPU and 20% of RAM, up to 4 GB So, if your VMs have 7 GB RAM, the reservation will be 1.4 GB but for any VM with 20 GB RAM and above, the reservation will be 4 GB.

This means that the actual RAM and CPU amounts available to your nodes will always be slightly less than the size would otherwise indicate.

When you have more than one node of the same configuration, you group them into a **node pool**, and the first node is created within the *default node pool*. When you upgrade or scale an AKS cluster, the action will be performed against either the default node pool or a specific node pool of your choosing.

Pods

A node runs your applications within pods. Typically, a pod has a one-to-one mapping to a container, that is, a running instance. However, in advanced scenarios, you can run multiple containers within a single pod.

At the pod level, you define the number of resources to assign to your particular services, such as the amount of RAM and CPU. When pods are required to run Kubernetes, the scheduler attempts to run the pod on a node with available resources to match what you have defined.

Deployments and YAML

A pod's resources are defined as a deployment, which is described within a YAML manifest. The manifest defines everything you need to state how many copies or replicas of a pod to run, what resources each pod requires, the container image to use, and other information necessary for your service.

A typical YAML file may look like the following:

```yaml
apiVersion: apps/v1
kind: Deployment
metadata:
  name: nginx
spec:
  replicas: 3
  selector:
    matchLabels:
      app: nginx
  template:
    metadata:
      labels:
        app: nginx
    spec:
      containers:
      - name: nginx
        image: mcr.microsoft.com/oss/nginx/nginx:1.15.2-alpine
        ports:
        - containerPort: 80
        resources:
          requests:
            CPU: 250m
            memory: 64Mi
          limits:
            CPU: 500m
            memory: 256Mi
```

In this example, taken from the docs.microsoft.com site, we see a deployment using the nginx container image, requesting a minimum of 250 m (**millicore**) and 64 Mi (**mebibytes**) of RAM, and a maximum of 500 m and 256 Mi.

> **Tip**
>
> A mebibyte is equal to 1024 KB, whereas a millicore is one-thousandth of a CPU core.

Once we have our pods and applications defined within a YAML file, we can then use that file to tell our AKS cluster to use the information in that file and deploy then run our application. This can be performed by running the deployment commands against the AKS APIs or via DevOps pipelines.

Kubernetes is a powerful tool for building resilient and dynamic applications that use microservices, and using images is incredibly efficient and portable due to their use of containerization; however, they are complex.

AKS abstracts much of the complexity of using and managing a Kubernetes cluster. Still, your development and support teams need to be fully conversant with the unique capabilities and configuration options available.

Summary

This chapter looked at the different compute options available to us in Azure and looked at the strengths and weaknesses of each. With any solution, the choice of technology is dependent on your requirements and the skills of the teams who are building them.

We then looked at how to design update management processes to ensure any VMs we use as part of our solution are kept up to date with the latest security patches.

Finally, we looked at how we can use containerization in our solutions, and specifically how Azure Kubernetes Service provides a flexible and dynamic approach to running microservices.

In the next chapter, we will look at the different networking options in Azure, including load balancing for resilience and performance.

Exam scenario

The solutions to the exam scenarios can be found at the end of this book.

Mega Corp is planning a new multi-service solution to help the business manage expenses. The application development team has decided to break the solution into different services that communicate with each other.

End users will upload expense claims as a Word document to the system, and these documents must flow through to different approvers.

The HR department also wants to amend some of the workflows themselves as they can change often.

The application will have a web frontend, and the application developers are used to building .NET websites. However, they would like to start moving to a more containerized approach.

Suggest some compute components that would be suited to this solution.

Further reading

You can check out the following links for more information about the topics that were covered in this chapter:

- Azure Batch: `https://docs.microsoft.com/en-us/azure/batch/`

- Azure Functions: `https://docs.microsoft.com/en-us/azure/azure-functions/`

- Azure Service Fabric: `https://docs.microsoft.com/en-us/azure/service-fabric/service-fabric-overview`

- Azure Web Apps: `https://azure.microsoft.com/en-gb/services/app-service/web/`

- Azure Logic Apps: `https://azure.microsoft.com/en-gb/services/logic-apps/`

- Azure Kubernetes Service: `https://azure.microsoft.com/en-gb/services/kubernetes-service/`

8
Network Connectivity and Security

In the previous chapter, we examined the different options when building computer services, from the different types of **Virtual Machines** (**VMs**) to web apps and containerization.

All solution components need to be able to communicate effectively and safely; therefore, in this chapter, we will discuss what options we have to control traffic flow using route tables and load balancing components, securing traffic with different firewalling options, and managing IP addressing and resolution.

With this in mind, we will cover the following topics:

- Understanding Azure networking options
- Understanding IP addressing and DNS in Azure
- Implementing network security
- Connectivity
- Load balancing and advanced traffic routing

Technical requirements

This chapter will use the Azure portal (`https://portal.azure.com`) and you need an Azure subscription for the examples.

Understanding Azure networking options

Services in Azure need to communicate, and this communication is performed over a virtual network, or VNET.

There are essentially two types of networking in Azure – private VNETs and the Azure backbone. The Azure backbone is a fully managed service. The underlying details are never exposed to you – although the ranges used by many services are available, grouped by region, for download in a JSON file. The Azure backbone is generally used when non-VNET-connected services communicate with each other; for example, when storage accounts replicate data or when Azure functions communicate with SQL and Cosmos DB, Azure handles all aspects of these communications. This can cause issues when you need more control, especially if you want to limit access to your services at the network level, that is, by implementing firewall rules.

> **Important Note**
>
> The address ranges of services in Azure change continually as the services grow within any particular region, and can be downloaded from this link: `https://www.microsoft.com/en-us/download/details.aspx?id=56519`.

Some services can either be integrated with, or built on top of, a VNET. VMs are the most common example of this, and to build a VM, you must use a VNET. Other services can also be optionally integrated with VNETs in different ways. For example, VMs can communicate with an Azure SQL database using a service endpoint, enabling you to limit access and ensure traffic is kept private and off the public network. We look at service endpoints and other ways to secure internal communications later in this chapter, in the *Implementing network security* section.

The first subject we will need to look at when dealing with VNETs and connectivity is that of addressing and **Doman Name Services** (**DNSes**).

Understanding IP addressing and DNS in Azure

When building services in Azure, you sometimes choose to use internal IP addresses and external IP addresses. Internal IP addresses can only communicate internally and use VNETs. Many services can also use public IP addresses, which allow you to communicate with the service from the internet.

Before we delve into public and internal IP addresses, we need to understand the basics of IP addressing in general, and especially the use of subnets and subnet masks.

Understanding subnets and subnet masks

When devices are connected to a TCP/IP-based network, they are provided with an IP address in the notation xxx.xxx.xxx.xxx. Generally, all devices that are on the same local network can communicate with each other without any additional settings.

When devices on different networks need to communicate, they must do so via a router or gateway. Devices use a subnet mask to differentiate between addresses on the local network and those on a remote network.

The network mask breaks down an IP address into a device or host address component and a network component. It does this by laying a binary mask over the IP address with the host address to the right.

255 in binary is 11111111 and 0 in binary is 00000000. The mask says how many of those bits are the network, with 1 denoting a network address and 0 denoting a host address.

Thus, 255.0.0.0 becomes 11111111.00000000.00000000.0000000, therefore in the address 10.0.0.1, 10 is the network and 0.0.0.1 is the host address. Similarly, with a mask of 255.255.0.0 and an address of 10.0.0.1, 10.0 becomes the network and 0.1 the host. The following diagram shows this concept more clearly:

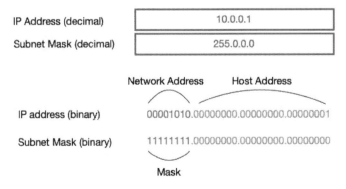

Figure 8.1 – Example subnet mask

Splitting an address space into multiple networks is known as subnetting, and subnets can be broken down into even smaller subnets until the mask becomes too big.

When configuring IP settings for devices, you often supply an IP address, a subnet mask, and the address of the router on the local network that will connect you to other networks.

Sometimes, when denoting an IP address range, the subnet mask and range are written in a shorthand form known as **CIDR notation**. We will cover CIDR notation examples in the *Private IP addresses* sub-section.

This is a relatively simplified overview of network addressing and subnetting, and although the AZ-304 exam will not explicitly ask you questions on this, it does help to better understand the next set of topics.

Public IP addresses

A public IP address is a discrete component that can be created and attached to many services, such as VMs. The public IP component is dedicated to a resource until you un-assign it – in other words, you cannot use the same public IP across multiple resources.

Public IP addresses can be either **static** or **dynamic**. With a static IP, once the resource has been created, the assigned IP address it is given stays the same until that resource is deleted. A dynamic address can change in specific scenarios. For example, if you create a public IP address for a VM as a dynamic address, when you stop the VM, the address is released and is different when assigned once you start the VM up again. With static addresses, the IP is assigned once you attached it to the VM, and it stays until you manually remove it.

Static addresses are useful if you have a firewall device that controls access to the service that can only be configured to use IP addresses or DNS resolution as changing the IP would mean the DNS record would also need updating. You also need to use a static address if you use TLS/SSL certificates linked to IP addresses.

Private IP addresses

Private IP addresses can be assigned to various Azure components, such as VMs, network load balancers, or application gateways. The devices are connected to a VNET, and the IP range you wish to use for your resources is defined at the VNET level.

When creating VNETs, you assign an IP range; the default is `10.0.0.0/16` – which provides 65,536 possible IP addresses. VNETs can contain multiple ranges if you wish; however, you need to be careful that those ranges do not interfere with public addresses.

When assigning IP ranges, you denote the range using **CIDR** notation – a forward slash (/) followed by a number that defines the number of addresses within that range. The following are just some example ranges:

Notation	Subnet Mask	Number of Hosts
/29	255.255.255.248	8
/28	255.255.255.240	16
/27	255.255.255.224	32
/20	255.255.240.0	4096
/16	255.255.0.0	65536
/8	255.0.0.0	16 777 216

> **Tip**
>
> CIDR notation is a more compact way to state an IP address and it's ranged based on a subnet mask. The number after the slash (/) is the count of leading 1 bits in the network mask. The complete range of addresses can be found here: `https://bretthargreaves.com/ip-cheatsheet/`.
>
> For more in-depth details of CIDR, see `https://en.wikipedia.org/wiki/Classless_Inter-Domain_Routing`.

Subnets are then created within the VNET, and each subnet must also be assigned an IP range that is within the range defined at the VNET level, as we can see in the following example diagram:

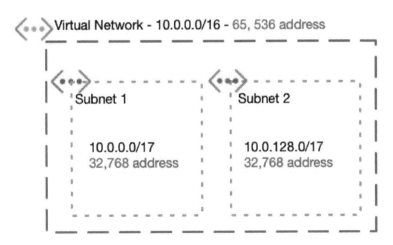

Figure 8.2 – Subnets within VNETs

For every subnet you create, Azure reserves five IPs for internal use – for smaller subnets, this has a significant impact on the number of available addresses. The reservations within a given range are as follows:

Reservation	Used for
x.x.x.0	Network address
x.x.x.1	Default gateway for the subnet
x.x.x.2, x.x.x.3	Mapping Azure DNS IPs to the VNET space
x.x.x.255	Network broadcast

With these reservations in mind, the minimum size of a subnet in Azure is a /29 network with eight IPs, of which only three are useable. The largest allowable range is /8, giving 16,777,216 IPs with 16,777,211 usable.

Private ranges in Azure can be used purely for services within your Azure subscriptions. If you don't connect the VNETs or require communications between them, you can have more than one VNET with the same ranges.

If you plan to allow services within one VNET to communicate with another VNET, you must consider more carefully the ranges you assign to ensure they do not overlap. This is especially crucial if you use VNETs to extend your private corporate network into Azure, as creating ranges that overlap can cause routing and addressing problems.

As with public IPs, private IPs can also be static or dynamic. With dynamic addressing, Azure assigns the next available IP within the given range. For example, if you are using a 10.0.0.0 network, and 10.0.0.3–10.0.0.20 are already used, your new resource will be assigned 10.0.0.21.

Azure DNS

Once we have our resources built in Azure, we need to resolve names with IP addresses to communicate with them. By default, services in Azure use Azure-managed DNS servers. Azure-managed DNS provides name resolution for your Azure resources and doesn't require any specific configuration from you.

Azure-managed DNS servers

Azure-managed DNS is highly available and fully resilient. VMs built in Azure can use Azure-managed DNS to communicate with other Azure services or other VMs in your VNETs without the need for a **Fully Qualified Domain Name** (**FQDN**).

However, this name resolution only works for Azure services; if you wish to communicate with on-premises servers or need more control over DNS, you must build and integrate with your DNS servers.

When configuring a VNET in Azure, you can override the default DNS servers. In this way, you can define your DNS servers to ensure queries to your on-premises resources are resolved correctly. You can also enter the Azure-managed DNS servers as well; if your DNS solution cannot resolve a query, the service would then fall back to the alternate Azure DNS service. The address for the Azure DNS service is 168.63.129.16.

To change the default DNS servers in Azure, perform the following steps:

1. Navigate to the Azure portal at https://portal.azure.com.

2. In the search bar, search for and select **Virtual Networks**.

3. Select your VNET.

4. On the left-hand menu, select **DNS servers**.

5. Change the default option from **Default (Azure-provided)** to **Custom**.

6. Enter your DNS servers, optionally followed by the Azure internal DNS server address.

   The following screenshot shows an example of how this might look:

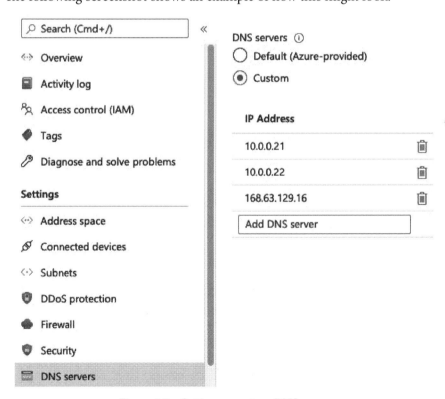

Figure 8.3 – Setting up custom DNS servers

These settings must be set up on each VNET that you wish to set up the custom DNS settings.

> **Tip**
>
> Be careful how many DNS servers you set. Each DNS server will be queried in turn, and if you put too many, the request will time out before it reaches the final server. This can cause issues if you need to fall back to the Azure DNS service for Azure-hosted services.

You can also leverage Azure private DNS, using private zones, for your internal DNS needs, using your custom domain names.

Azure private DNS zones

Using custom DNS allows you to use your domains with your Azure resources without the need to set up and maintain your DNS servers for resolution.

This option can provide much tighter integration with your Azure-hosted resources as it allows automatic record updates and DNS resolution between VNETs. As a managed solution, it is also resilient without maintaining separate VMs to run the DNS server.

Azure also provides you with the ability to manage your external domain records. Using Azure DNS zones, you can delegate the name resolution for your custom domain to Azure's DNS servers.

Private zones are also used with PrivateLink IP services, which we will examine in the next section, *Implementing network security*.

Azure public DNS zones

If you own your domain, `bigcorp.com`, you can create a zone in Azure and then configure your domain to use the Azure name servers. Once set up, you can then use Azure to create, edit, and maintain the records for that domain.

You cannot purchase domain names through Azure DNS, and Azure does not become the registrar. However, using Azure DNS to manage your domain, you can use RBAC roles to control which users can manage DNS, Azure logs to track change, and resource locking to prevent the accidental deletion of records.

We have looked at the different options for setting up VNETs with IP addressing and name resolution; we will now investigate to ensure secure communications to and between our services.

Implementing network security

Ensuring secure traffic flow to and between services is a core requirement for many solutions. An example is an external communication to a VM running a website – you may only want to allow traffic to the server in a particular port such as HTTPS over port 443. All other traffic, such as SMTP, FTP, or file share protocols, need to be blocked.

It isn't just inbound traffic that needs to be controlled; blocking outbound traffic can be just as important. For many organizations today, ensuring you are protected from insider threats is just as crucial, if not more so, than external threats. For this reason, we may want to block all but specific outbound access so that if a service is infected by malware, it cannot send traffic out – known as **data exfiltration**.

> **Important Note**
>
> Data exfiltration is a growing technique for stealing data. Either by manually logging on to a server or through malware infection, data is copied from an internal system to an external system.

As solutions become more distributed, the ability to control data between components has also become a key design element and can often work to our advantage. A typical and well-used architectural pattern is an *n*-tier architecture. The services in a solution are hosted on different layers – a **User Interface (UI)** at the front, a data processing tier in the middle, and a database at the back. Each tier could be hosted on its subnet with security controls between them. In this way, we can tightly control who and what has access to each tier individually, which helps prevent any attacker from gaining direct access to the data, as we can see in the following example:

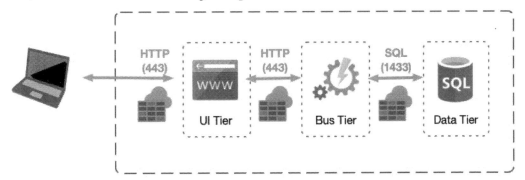

Figure 8.4 – N-tier architecture helps protect resources

In the example, in the preceding figure, the UI tier only allows traffic from the user over HTTP (port 443), and as the UI only contains frontend logic and no data, should an attacker compromise the service, they can only access that code.

The next tier only allows traffic from the UI tier; in other words, an external attacker has no direct access. If the frontend tier was compromised, an attacker could access the business logic tier, but this doesn't contain any actual data.

The final tier only accepts SQL traffic (port 1433) from the business tier; therefore, a hacker would need to get past the first two tiers to gain access to it.

Of course, other security mechanisms such as authentication and authorization would be employed over these systems, but access by the network is often considered the first line of defense.

Firewalls are often employed to provide security at the network level. Although Azure provides discrete firewall services, another option is often used to provide simpler management and security – **Network Security Groups** (**NSGs**).

Network Security Groups

NSGs allow you to define inbound and outbound rules that will allow or deny the flow of traffic from a source to a destination on a specific port. Although you define separate inbound and outbound rules, each rule is stateful. This means that the flow in any one direction is recorded so that the returning traffic can also be allowed using the same rule.

In other words, if you allow HTTPS traffic *into* a service, then that same traffic will be allowed back *out* for the same source and destination.

We create NSGs as components in Azure and then attach them to a subnet or network interface on a VM. Each subnet can only be connected to a single NSG, but any NSG can be attached to multiple subnets. This allows us to define rulesets independently for everyday use cases (such as allowing web traffic) and then reusing them across various subnets.

When NSGs are created, Azure applies several default rules that effectively block all access except essential Azure services.

If you create a VM in Azure, a default NSG is created for you and attached to the network interface of the VM; we can see such an example in the following screenshot:

Resource group (change)	:	PacktLBResourceGroup			Custom security rules	: 2 inbound, 0 outbound
Location	:	East US			Associated with	: 0 subnets, 1 network interfaces
Subscription (change)	:	PacktPub				
Subscription ID	:					
Tags (change)	:	Click here to add tags				

Inbound security rules

Priority	Name	Port	Protocol	Source	Destination	Action	
300	⚠ RDP	3389	TCP	Any	Any	⊘ Allow	•••
310	HTTP	80	TCP	Any	Any	⊘ Allow	•••
65000	AllowVnetInBound	Any	Any	VirtualNetwork	VirtualNetwork	⊘ Allow	•••
65001	AllowAzureLoadBalancerInBound	Any	Any	AzureLoadBalancer	Any	⊘ Allow	•••
65500	DenyAllInBound	Any	Any	Any	Any	⊗ Deny	•••

Outbound security rules

Priority	Name	Port	Protocol	Source	Destination	Action	
65000	AllowVnetOutBound	Any	Any	VirtualNetwork	VirtualNetwork	⊘ Allow	•••
65001	AllowInternetOutBound	Any	Any	Any	Internet	⊘ Allow	•••
65500	DenyAllOutBound	Any	Any	Any	Any	⊗ Deny	•••

Figure 8.5 – Example NSG ruleset

In the preceding figure, we can see five inbound rules and three outbound. The top two inbound rules highlighted in red were created with the VM – in the example, we specified to allow RDP (3389) and HTTP (80).

The three rules in the inbound and outbound highlighted in green are created by Azure and cannot be removed or altered. These define a baseline set of rules that must be applied for the platform to function correctly while blocking everything else. As the name suggests on these rules, AllowVnetInBound allows traffic to flow freely between all devices in that VNET, and the AllowAzureLoadBalancerInBound rule allows any traffic originating from an Azure load balancer. DenyAllInBound blocks everything else.

Each rule requires a set of options to be provided:

- **Name** and **Description**: For reference; these have no bearing on the actual service. They make it easier to determine what it is or what it is for.

- **Source** and **Destination** port: The port is, of course, the network port that a particular service communicates on – for **RDP**, this is 3389; for **HTTP**, it is 80, and for **HTTPS**, it is 443. Some services require port mapping; that is, the source may expect to communicate on one port, but the actual service communicates on a different port.

- **Source** and **Destination** location: The source and destination locations define where traffic is coming *from* (the source) and where it is trying to go *to* (the destination). The most common option is an IP address or list of IP addresses, and these will typically be used to define external services.

  For Azure services, we can either choose the VNET – that is, the destination is any service on the VNET the NSG is attached to – or a service tag, which is a range of IPs managed by Azure. Examples may include the following:

  - **Internet**: Any address that doesn't originate from the Azure platform

  - **AzureLoadBalancer**: An Azure load balancer

  - **AzureActiveDirectory**: Communications from the Azure Active Directory service

  - **AzureCloud.EastUS**: Any Azure service in the East US region

  As we can see from these examples, with the exception of the internet option, they are IP sets that belong to Azure services. Using service tags to allow traffic from Azure services is safer than manually entering the IP ranges (which Microsoft publishes) as you don't need to worry about them changing.

- **Protocol**: **Any**, **TCP**, **UDP**, or **ICMP**. Services use different protocols, and some services require TCP and UDP. You should always define the least access; so, if only TCP is needed, only choose TCP. ICMP protocol is used primarily for Ping.

- **Priority**: Firewall rules are applied one at a time in order, with the lowest number, which is 100, being used last. Azure applies a **Deny All** rule to *all* NSGs with the lowest priority. Therefore, any rule with a *higher* priority will *overrule* this one. **Deny all** is a failsafe rule – this means everything will be blocked by default unless you specifically create a rule to allow access.

Through the use of NSGs, we can create simple rules around our VNET-integrated services and form part of an effective defense strategy. There may be occasions, however, when you want to apply different firewall rules to other components within the same subnet; we can use **Application Security Groups** (**ASGs**) for these scenarios.

Application Security Groups

An ASG is another way of grouping together resources instead of just allowing all traffic to all resources on your VNET. For example, you may want one to define a single NSG that applies to all subnets; however, you may have a mixture of services, such as database servers and web servers, across those subnets.

You can define an ASG and attach your web servers to that ASG, and another ASG that groups your database servers. In your NSG, you then set the HTTPS inbound rule to use the ASG as the destination rather than the whole subnet, VNET, or individual IPs. In this configuration, even though you have a common NSG, you can still uniquely allow access to specific server groups.

The following diagram shows an example of this type of configuration:

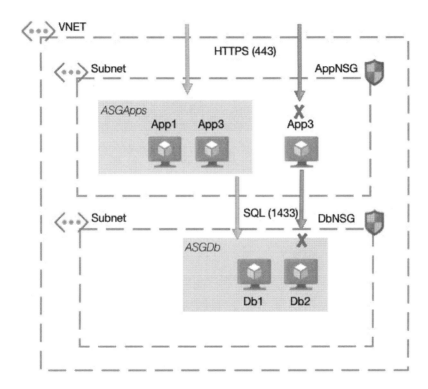

Figure 8.6 – Example architecture using NSGs and ASGs

In the preceding example, **App1** and **App2** are part of the **ASGApps** ASG, and **Db1** and **Db2** are part of the **ASGDb** ASG.

The NSG rulesets would then be as follows:

NSG	Source	Source Port	Destination	Dest. Port
AppNSG	Internet	Any	ASGApps	443
DbNSG	ASGApps	Any	ASGDb	1433

With the preceding in place, HTTPS inbound would only be allowed to **App1** and **App2**, and port 1433 would only be allowed from **App1** and **App2**.

ASGs and NSGs are great for discrete services; however, there are some rules that you may always want to apply, for example, blocking all outbound access to certain services such as FTP. A better option might be to create a central firewall that all your services route through in this scenario.

Azure Firewall

Whereas individual NSGs and ASGs form part of your security strategy, building multiple network security layers, especially in enterprise systems, is even better.

Azure Firewall is a cloud-based, fully managed network security appliance that would typically be placed at the edge of your network. This means that you would not usually have one firewall per solution or even subscription. Instead, you would have one per region and have all other devices, even those in different subscriptions, route through to it, as in the following example:

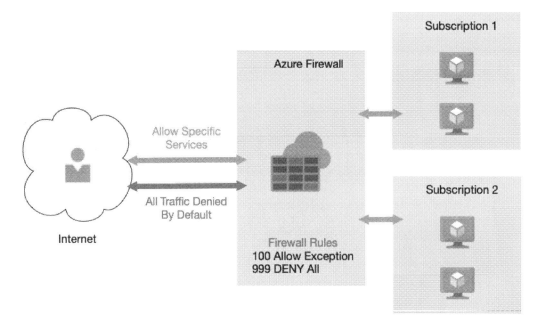

Figure 8.7 – Azure Firewall in a hub/spoke model

Azure Firewall offers some of the functionality you can achieve from NSGs, such as network traffic filtering based on port and IP or service tags. Over and above these basic services, Azure Firewall also offers the following:

- **High availability and scalability**: As a managed offering, you don't need to worry about building multiple VMs with load balancers or how much your peak traffic might be. Azure Firewall will automatically scale as required, is fully resilient, and supports availability zones.

- **FQDN tags and FQDN filters**: As well as IP, addressing, and service tags, Azure Firewall also allows you to define FQDNs. FQDN tags are similar to service tags but support a more comprehensive range of services, such as Windows Update.

- **Outgoing SNAT and inbound DNAT support**: If you use public IP address ranges for private networks, Azure Firewall can perform **Secure Network Address Translation (SNAT)** on your outgoing requests. Incoming traffic can be translated using **Destination Network Address Translation (DNAT)**.

- **Threat intelligence**: Azure Firewall can automatically block incoming traffic originating from IP addresses known to be malicious. These addresses and domains come from Microsoft's threat intelligence feed.

- **Multiple IPs**: Up to 250 IP addresses can be associated with your firewall, which helps with SNAT and DNAT.

- **Monitoring**: Azure Firewall is fully integrated with Azure Monitor for data analysis and alerting.

- **Forced tunneling**: You can route all internet-bound traffic to another device, such as an on-premises edge firewall.

Azure Firewall provides an additional and centralized security boundary to your systems, ensuring an extra layer of safety.

So far, we have looked at securing access into and between services that use VNETs, such as VMs. Some services don't use VNETs directly but instead have their firewall options. These firewall options often include the ability to either block access to the service based on IPs or VNETs, and when this option is selected, it uses a feature called **service endpoints**.

Service endpoints

Many services are exposed via a public address or URL. For example, Blob Storage is accessed via `<accountname>.blob.core.windows.net`. Even if your application is running on a VM connected to a VNET, communication to the default endpoint will be the public address, and full access to all IPs, internal and external, is allowed.

For public-facing systems, this may be desirable; however, if you need the backend service to be protected from the outside and only accessible internally, you can use a **service endpoint**.

Service endpoints provide direct and secure access from one Azure service to another over the Azure backbone. Internally, the service is given a private IP address, which is used instead of the default public IP address. Traffic from the source is then allowed, and external traffic becomes blocked, as we see in the following example:

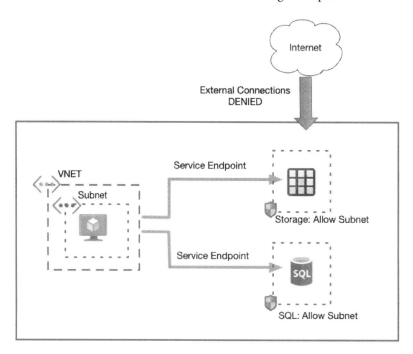

Figure 8.8 – Protecting access with service endpoints

Although using service endpoints enables private IP addresses on the service, this address is not exposed or manageable by you. One effect of this is that although Azure-hosted services can connect to the service, on-premises systems cannot access it over a VPN or ExpressRoute. For these scenarios, an alternative solution called a private endpoint can be used, which we will cover in the next sub-section, or using an ExpressRoute with Microsoft peering using a NAT IP address.

> **Important Note**
>
> When you set up an ExpressRoute into Azure, you have the option of using Microsoft peering or private peering. Microsoft peering ensures all connectivity in the Office 365 platform. Azure goes over the ExpressRoute instead of private peering, sending only traffic destined for internal IP ranges to use the ExpressRoute. In contrast, public services are accessed via public endpoints. The most common form of connectivity is private peering; Microsoft peering is only recommended for specific scenarios. See `https://docs.microsoft.com/en-us/microsoft-365/enterprise/azure-expressroute?view=o365-worldwide` for more details.

To use service endpoints, the service itself must be enabled on the subnet, and the service you wish to lock down must have the public network option turned off and the source subnet added as an allowable source.

> **Important Note**
>
> Service endpoints ignore NSGs – therefore, any rules you have in place and attached to the secure subnet are effectively ignored. This only affects the point-to-point connection between the subnet and the service endpoint. All other NSG rules still hold.

At the time of writing, the following Azure services support service endpoints:

- Azure Storage
- Azure Key Vault
- Azure SQL Database
- Azure Synapse Analytics
- Azure PostgreSQL Server
- Azure MySQL Server
- Azure MariaDB
- Azure Cosmos DB
- Azure Service Bus
- Azure Event Hubs
- Azure App Service
- Azure Cognitive Services
- Azure Container Registry

To enable service endpoints on a subnet, in the Azure portal, go to the properties of the VNET you wish to use, select the **Subnets** blade on the left-hand menu, then select your subnet. The subnet configuration window appears with the option to choose one or more services, as we can see in the following screenshot. Once you have made changes, click **Save**:

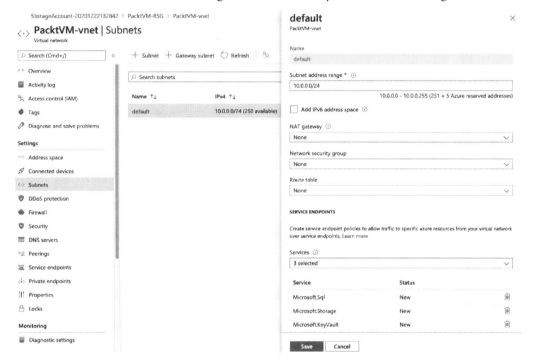

Figure 8.9 – Enabling service endpoints on a subnet

Once enabled, you can then restrict access to your backend service. In the following example, we will limit access to a storage account from a subnet:

1. Go to the Azure portal at `https://portal.azure.com`.

2. In the search bar, search for and select **Storage accounts**.

3. Select the storage account you wish to restrict access to.

4. On the left-hand menu, click the **Networking** option.

5. Change the **Allow access from** option from **All networks** to **Selected networks**.

6. Click **+ Add existing virtual network**.

7. Select the VNET and subnet you want to restrict access to.

8. Click **Save**.

The following screenshot shows an example of a secure storage account:

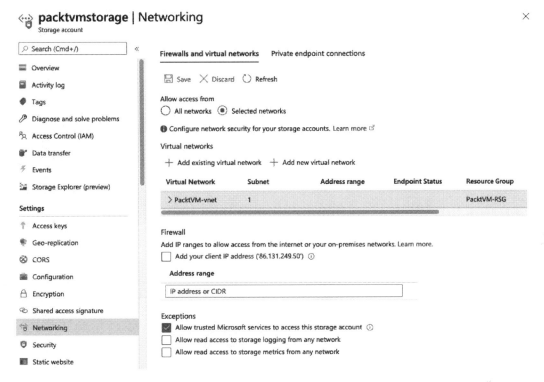

Figure 8.10 – Restricting VNET access

Once set up, any access except the defined VNET will be denied, and any traffic from services on the VNET to the storage account will now be directly over the Azure backbone.

You may have noticed another option in the **Networking** tab – **Private endpoint connections**.

Private endpoint connections

We have said that service endpoints assign an internal IP to services that are then used to direct the flow of traffic to it. However, the actual IP is hidden and can therefore not be referenced by yourself.

There are times when you need to access a service such as SQL or a storage account via a private IP – either for direct connectivity from an on-premises network or when you have strict firewall policies between your users and your solution.

For these scenarios, **Private endpoint connections** can be used to assign private IP addresses to certain Azure services. Private endpoints are very similar to service endpoints, except you have visibility of the underlying IP address and so they can therefore be used across VPNs and ExpressRoute.

However, private endpoints rely on DNS to function correctly. As most services use host headers (that is, an FQDN) to determine your individual backend service, connecting via the IP itself does not work. Instead, you must set up a DNS record that sets your service to the internal IP.

For example, if you create a private endpoint for your storage account called `mystorage` that uses an IP address of `10.0.0.10`, to access the service securely, you must create a DNS record so that `mystorage.blob.core.windows.net` resolves to `10.0.0.10`.

This can be performed by either creating DNS records in your DNS service or forwarding the request to an Azure private zone and having the internal Azure DNS service resolve it for you.

Azure private endpoints support more services than service endpoints and are, therefore, the only option in some circumstances. In addition to the services supported by service endpoints, private endpoints also support the following:

- Azure Automation
- Azure IoT Hub
- Azure Kubernetes Service – Kubernetes API
- Azure Search
- Azure App Configuration
- Azure Backup
- Azure Relay
- Azure Event Grid
- Azure Machine Learning
- SignalR
- Azure Monitor
- Azure File Sync

Using a combination of NSGs, ASGs, Azure Firewall, service endpoints, and private endpoints, you have the tools to secure your workloads internally and externally. Next, we will examine how we can extend the actual VNETs by exploring the different options for connecting into them or connecting different VNETs.

Connectivity

A simple, standalone solution may only require a single VNET, and especially if your service is an externally facing application for clients, you may not need to create anything more complicated.

However, for enterprise applications that contain many different services, or for hybrid scenarios where you need to connect securely to Azure from an on-premises network, you must consider the other options for providing connectivity.

We will start by looking at connecting two VNETs.

Previously, we separated services within different subnets. However, each of those subnets was in the same subnet. Because of this, connectivity between the devices was automatic – other than defining NSG rules, connectivity just happened.

More complex solutions may be built across multiple VNETs, and these VNETs may or may not be in the same region. By default, communication between VNETs is not enabled. Therefore you must set this up if required. The simplest way to achieve this connectivity is with VNET peering.

VNET peering

Any two VNETs can be connected using peering, and there are two types of peering available:

- **VNET peering**, which connects two VNETs in the *same* region
- **Global VNET peering**, which connects two VNETs in *different* regions

You can connect two VNETs that are in different subscriptions. However, you must ensure that the address spaces in each VNET do not overlap. So, if **VNET 1** and **VNET 2** both use the address range of 10.0.0.0/16, the peering will fail.

Peerings between VNETs are also non-transitive – this means that if you have three VNETs – **VNET 1**, **VNET 2**, and **VNET 3** – and you create a peering between **VNET 1** and **VNET 2** and **VNET 2** and **VNET 3**, devices in **VNET 1** will not be able to access a resource in **VNET 3** – in other words, you cannot traverse the two peers. Instead, you would have to explicitly connect **VNET 1** to **VNET 3** as well, as we can see in the following diagram:

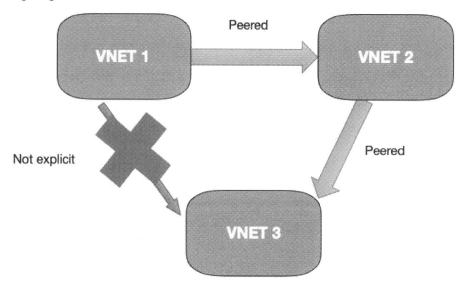

Figure 8.11 – Peerings are not transitive

Peerings between VNETs are not the only type of network you may need to connect; the other common scenario is connecting on-premises networks into Azure. For this, we can use a VPN gateway.

VPN gateways

When you need to connect an on-premises network to Azure, you can use a VPN gateway. A VPN gateway uses a gateway device on your corporate network and a gateway device in Azure. The two are then connected with a VPN that uses the public network to create an encrypted route between your two gateways. In other words, you use the internet but your traffic is encrypted and, therefore, secure.

You can use two types of VPN – a **Point to Site (P2S)** VPN, used by individual clients to connect directly to a remote gateway, and a **Site to Site (S2S)** VPN, used to connect networks.

When creating a VPN connection, you can choose between a policy-based VPN or a route-based VPN.

Policy-based VPNs

Policy-based VPNs are generally used for connections using legacy VPN gateways, as they are not as flexible as route-based. Policy-based VPNs use IKEv1 protocols and static routing to define the source and destination network ranges in the policy, rather than in a routing table.

Route-based VPNs

Route-based VPNs are the preferred choice and should be used unless legacy requirements prevent it. Route-based VPNs use IKEv2 and support dynamic routing protocols whereby routing tables direct traffic based on discovery.

> **Important Note**
>
> **Internet Key Exchange (IKE)** v1 and v2 are VPN encryption protocols that ensure traffic is encrypted between two points by authenticating both the client and the server and then agreeing on an actual encryption method. IKEv2 is the successor to IKEv1. It is faster and provides greater functionality.

When creating a VPN, you have different sizes available, and the choice of size, or SKU, is dependent on your requirements. The following table shows the current differences:

SKU	Max S2S/P2S Tunnels	Throughput	BGP Support
Basic	10	100 Mbps	No
VpnGw1/Az	30	650 Mbps	Yes
VpnGw2/Az	30	1 Gbps	Yes
VpnGw3/Az	30	1.25 bps	Yes

The basic VPN is only recommended for use for dev/test and not for production. Also, basic does not support IKEv2 or RADIUS authentication. This may impact you depending on the clients using the VPN. For example, Mac computers do not support IKEv1 and cannot use a basic VPN for a P2S connection.

When creating a VPN connection, you need several services and components set up.

On-premises resources

To connect to an Azure VPN gateway, you will need a VPN device on your corporate network that supports policy-based or route-based VPN gateways. It also needs to have a public IPv4 network address.

Azure resources

Within Azure, you need to set up the following components:

- **VNET**: The address space used by the VNET must not overlap with your corporate ranges.

- **Gateway subnet**: The VPN gateway must be installed in a specific subnet, and it must be called `GatewaySubnet`. It must have a range of at least /27 (32 addresses).

- **Public IP address**: An IP address that can be connected to from the public network (internet).

- **Local network gateway**: This defines the on-premises gateway and configuration.

- **VNET gateway**: An Azure VPN or ExpressRoute gateway.

The following diagram shows how this might look:

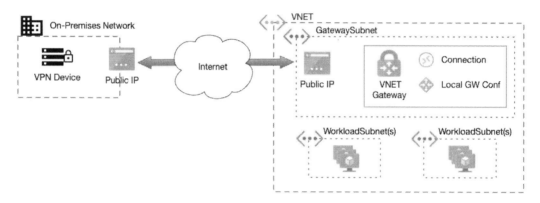

Figure 8.12 – VPN gateway

As we can see from the preceding diagram, a VPN connection is made to a specific subnet and VNET within Azure. In most cases, you would need to connect multiple VNETs to the same connection, which we can perform by peering the connected VNET to your workload VNETs.

This is often called a **hub-spoke model**; we can see an example hub-spoke model in the following diagram:

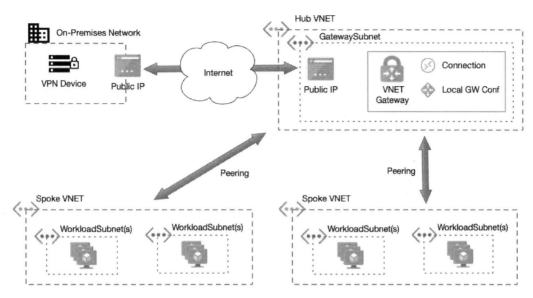

Figure 8.13 – Hub-spoke architecture

Earlier, we stated that connections between VNETs are not transitive, therefore to set up the hub-spoke architecture, we must use a gateway transit – we do this when we create our peering connection between the spoke VNET (which contains our workloads) and the hub VNET (which includes the VNET gateway). On the options when creating a peering request from the spoke to the hub, select the **Use the remote virtual network's gateway** option, as we can see in the following example:

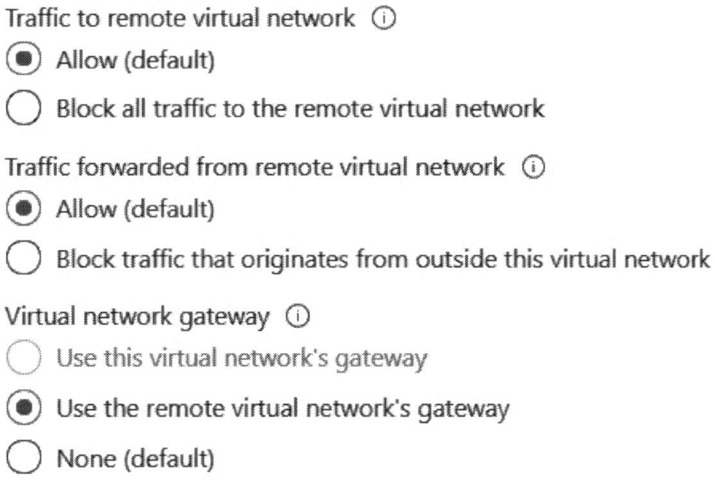

Traffic to remote virtual network ⓘ

◉ Allow (default)

◯ Block all traffic to the remote virtual network

Traffic forwarded from remote virtual network ⓘ

◉ Allow (default)

◯ Block traffic that originates from outside this virtual network

Virtual network gateway ⓘ

◯ Use this virtual network's gateway

◉ Use the remote virtual network's gateway

◯ None (default)

Figure 8.14 – Setting the peering option to use gateway transit

Using a VPN is a simple way to connect securely to Azure. However, you are still using the public network; thus, connectivity and performance cannot be guaranteed. For a more robust and direct connection into Azure, companies can leverage **ExpressRoute**.

ExpressRoute

ExpressRoute provides a dedicated and utterly private connection into Azure, Office 365, and Dynamics 365. Throughput is significantly increased since connections are more reliable with minimal latency.

Connectivity is via authorized network providers who ensure connections are highly available; this means you get redundancy built-in.

There are three different models to choose from when ordering an ExpressRoute – *CloudExchange co-location, point-to-point Ethernet connection,* and *any-to-any connection*:

- CloudExchange co-location is for companies that house their existing data center with an internet service provider.

- Point-to-point connections are dedicated connections between your premises and Azure.

- Any-to-any is for companies that have existing WAN infrastructure. Microsoft can connect to that existing network to provide connectivity from any of your offices.

A key aspect of ExpressRoute is that your connectivity is via private routes; it does not traverse the public internet – except for **Content Delivery Network (CDN)** components, which by design must leverage the internet to function.

As you leverage more advanced network options, you must have tighter control over traffic flow between VNETs and your on-premises network.

Routing

By default, all traffic in Azure follows pre-defined routes that are set up within the VNETs. These routes ensure traffic flows correctly between VNETs and out to the internet as required.

When more advanced routing is required, you can set up your routes to force the traffic through set paths, sometimes known as **service chaining**.

An example is where you need to route your Azure VM traffic back on-premises for your internal ranges. In this instance, you could create a route that sends all traffic destined for your internal ranges to the VPN gateway in your hub VNET.

Another example would be when you wish to have all internet traffic traverse a central firewall; in this instance, you would define a route to send all internet traffic to a firewall device you have in a peered VNET.

When creating routes, you can create either user-defined routes or **Border Gateway Protocol (BGP)**.

BGP automatically exchanges routing information between two or more networks. In Azure, it can be used to advertise routes from your on-premises network to Azure when using ExpressRoute or a site-to-site VPN.

Alternatively, you can create your custom route; although this is more manual and has a higher administrative overhead, it does provide complete control.

When defining a user-defined route, we set a descriptive name, an address prefix that specifies the address range that we will redirect traffic for, and the next hop. The next hop is where traffic will be routed through and can be any of the following:

- **Virtual appliance**: Such as a firewall or other routing device
- **VNET gateway**: Used when directing traffic through a VPN gateway
- **VNET**: Sends all traffic to a specific VNET
- **Internet**: Sends traffic to Azure internet routers
- **None**: Drops all data (that is, blocks all traffic for that range)

For example, if we want to route all traffic through a firewall device with the address of 10.0.0.10, we would create the following custom route:

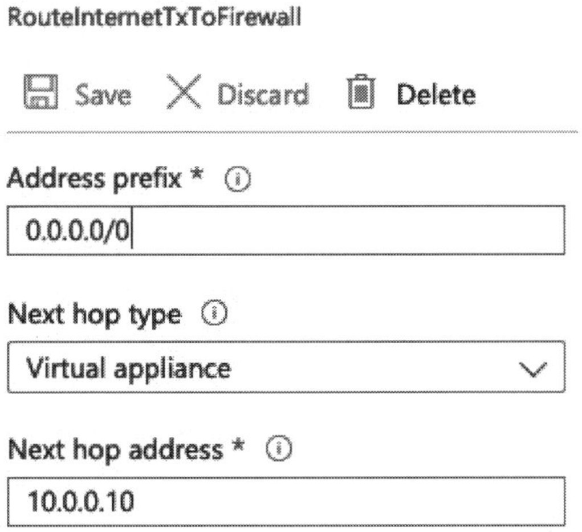

RouteInternetTxToFirewall

🖫 Save   ✕ Discard   🗑 **Delete**

Address prefix ＊ ⓘ

| 0.0.0.0/0 |

Next hop type ⓘ

| Virtual appliance   ⌄ |

Next hop address ＊ ⓘ

| 10.0.0.10 |

Figure 8.15 – Example user-defined route

We can also add additional routes for other rules; for example, routing traffic through the firewall, we could add another rule to route internal bound traffic to a VPN gateway.

Because we can have a mixture of custom routes, system routes, and BGP routes, Azure uses the following order to decide where to send traffic in the event there is a conflict. That order is as follows:

1. User-defined routes

2. BGP routes

3. System routes

By using a combination, we can precisely control traffic depending on our precise requirements.

Another aspect of routing traffic is when we need to use load balancing components to share traffic between one or more services, and we will discuss this in the next section.

Load balancing and advanced traffic routing

Many PaaS options in Azure, such as Web Apps and Functions, automatically scale as demand increases (and within limits you set). For this to function, Azure places services such as these behind a load balancer to distribute the load between them and redirect traffic from unhealthy nodes to healthy ones.

There are times when either a load balancer is not included, such as with VMs, or when you want to provide additional functionality not provided by the standard load balancers – such as the ability to balance between *regions*. In these cases, we have the option to build and configure our load balancers. You can choose several options, each providing its capabilities depending on your requirements.

Azure Load Balancer

Azure Load Balancer allows you to distribute traffic across VMs, allowing you to scale apps by distributing load and offering high availability. If a node becomes unhealthy, traffic is not sent to us, as shown in the following diagram:

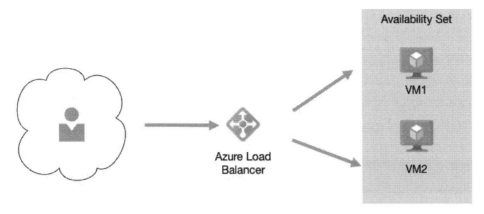

Figure 8.16 – Azure Load Balancer

Load balancers distribute traffic and manage the session persistence between nodes in one of two ways:

- The default is a **five-tuple hash**. The tuple is composed of the source IP, source port, destination IP, destination port, and protocol type. Because the source port is included in the hash and the source port changes for each session, clients might be using different VMs between sessions. This means applications that need to maintain a state for a client between requests will not work.

- The alternative is **source IP affinity**. This is also known as *session affinity* or *client IP affinity*. This mode uses a two-tuple hash (from the source IP address and destination IP address) or a three-tuple hash (from the source IP address, destination IP address, and protocol type). This ensures that a specific client's requests are always sent to the same VM behind the load balancer. Thus, applications that need to maintain state will still function.

Load balancers can be configured to be either internally (private) facing or external (public), and there are two SKUs for load balancers – *Basic* and *Standard*. The Basic tier is free but only supports 300 instances, VMs in availability sets or scale sets, and HTTP and TCP protocols when configuring health probes. The standard tier supports more advanced management features, such as zone-redundant frontends for inbound and outbound traffic and HTTPS probes, and you can have up to 1,000 instances. Finally, the Standard tier has an SLA of 99.99%, whereas the basic tier offers no SLA.

Azure Traffic Manager

When you wish to protect VMs or web apps across regions, for example, East US and West US, you cannot use Azure Load Balancer. Instead, we can use Azure Traffic Manager. Azure Traffic Manager is essentially a DNS router.

This means that unlike Load Balancer, which directs the flow of IP traffic from one address to another, Traffic Manager works by resolving a DNS entry, such as a web address, so a different backend IP address is used, as in the following diagram:

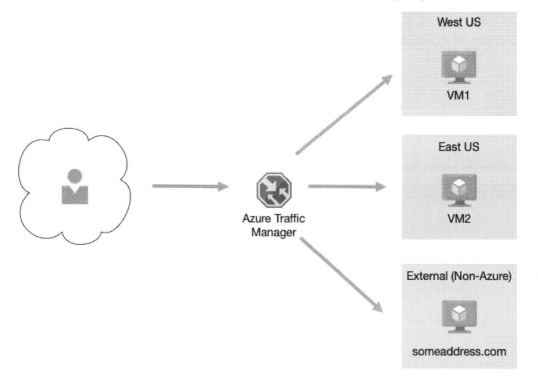

Figure 8.17 – Azure Traffic Manager

This enables us to direct users to the closest server available. Thus, traffic is distributed based on the user location. If a particular region becomes unavailable, then all traffic will be directed to a healthy region.

With Azure Traffic Manager, we have several different options available for defining how to direct traffic and the two just mentioned. They are as follows:

- **Weighted**: Each endpoint is given a weight between 1 and 1,000. Endpoints are randomly assigned but send more traffic to the higher-weighted endpoints.

- **Priority**: Defines a list of endpoints in priority order. All traffic goes to one point until that point degrades; traffic then gets routed to the next highest priority.

- **Performance**: Uses an internet latency table to send traffic to the fastest endpoint for the user.

- **Geographic**: Directed to endpoints based on the user's geographic location.

- **Multivalue**: Traffic Manager sends multiple healthy endpoints to the client. The client can then try each endpoint in turn and is responsible for determining which is the best to use.

- **Subnet**: Route based on a user's subnet. Useful for directing corporate users (that is, those whereby you can pre-determine which network they are on, such as an office location).

Application Gateway

Azure Application Gateway is a web traffic load balancer that can manage traffic to web applications. This web traffic load balancer operates at the application layer (Layer 7 in the OSI network reference stack).

It offers web load balancing, which is for HTTP(S) only. Traditional load balancers operate at the transport layer (Layer 4 in the OSI network reference stack) and route traffic – based on the source IP address and a port number – to a destination IP address and a port number. With Azure Application Gateway, traffic can be routed based on the incoming URL as well. For instance, if /pictures is part of the incoming URL, traffic can be routed to a particular set of servers that have been configured explicitly for pictures. If /audio is part of the incoming URL, the traffic is routed to another set of servers, configured specifically for audio files. The following diagram shows the workflow of Azure Application Gateway:

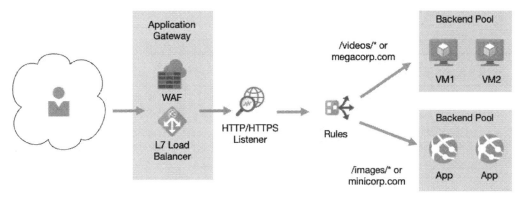

Figure 8.18 – Azure Application Gateway

Azure Application Gateway offers the following features and capabilities:

- **Web application firewall**: One of the features of Application Gateway is its **Web Application Firewall (WAF)**. It offers centralized protection of up to 40 web apps from common vulnerabilities and exploits. It is based on rules from the **Open Web Application Security Project (OWASP)** 3.1, 3.0, or 2.2.9. Common exploits include **Cross-Site Scripting Attacks (XSS)** and SQL injection attacks. With WAF, you can centralize the prevention of such types of attacks, which makes security management a lot easier and gives a better assurance to the administrators than if this is handled in the application code. Also, by patching a known vulnerability at a central location instead of in every application separately, administrators can react a lot faster to security threats.

- **URL path-based routing**: This allows you to route traffic, based on URL paths, to different backend server pools.

- **Autoscaling**: Azure Application Gateway Standard v2 offers autoscaling, whereby the number of application gateway or WAF deployments can scale based on incoming traffic. It also provides **zone redundancy**, whereby the deployment can span multiple availability zones.

- **Static VIP** ensures that the **Virtual IP address (VIP)** associated with the application gateway does not change after a restart. Additionally, it offers faster deployment and update times and five times better **Secure Sockets Layer (SSL)** offload performance than the other pricing tier.

- **SSL termination**: Azure Application Gateway offers SSL termination at the gateway. After the gate, the traffic will be transported unencrypted to the backend servers. This will eliminate the need for costly encryption and decryption overheads. End-to-end SSL encryption is also supported for cases that need encrypted communication, such as when an application can only accept a secure connection or for other security requirements.

- **Connection draining**: This feature will remove backend pool members during planned service updates. You can enable this setting at the backend **HTTP setting** and during rule creation. This setting can be applied to all the members of the backend pool. When this feature is enabled, Azure Application Gateway makes sure that all the deregistering instances in the pool do not receive any new requests.

- **Custom error pages**: You can create custom error pages using your custom layout and branding instead of the displayed default error pages.

- **Multiple-site hosting**: With multiple-site hosting, more than one web app can be configured on the same application gateway. You can add up to 100 web apps to the application gateway, and each web app can be redirected to its pool of backend servers.

- **Redirection**: Azure Application Gateway offers the ability to redirect traffic on the gateway itself. It provides a generic redirection mechanism that can be used for global redirection, whereby traffic is redirected from and to any port you define by using rules. An example of this could be an HTTP to HTTPS redirection. It also offers **path-based redirection**, where the HTTP to HTTPS is only redirected to a specific site area and provides redirection to external sites.

- **Session affinity**: This feature is useful when you want to maintain a user session on the same server. The gateway can direct traffic from the same user session to the same server for processing by using gateway-managed cookies. This is used in cases where session states are stored locally on the server for the user session.

- **WebSocket and HTTP/2 traffic**: Azure Application Gateway natively supports the WebSocket and HTTP/2 protocols. These protocols enable full-duplex communication between the client and the server over a long-running TCP connection, without the need for polling. These protocols can use the same TCP connection for multiple requests and responses, which results in more efficient utilization of resources. These protocols work over the traditional HTTP ports 80 and 443.

- **Rewrite HTTP headers**: Azure Application Gateway can also rewrite the HTTP headers for incoming and outgoing traffic. This way, you can add, update, and remove HTTP headers while the request/response packets are moved between the client and the backend pools.

Azure Application Gateway comes in the following tiers:

- **Standard**: By selecting this tier, you will use Azure Application Gateway as a load balancer for your web apps.

- **Standard v2**: In addition to the previous Standard tier, this tier offers autoscaling, zone redundancy, and support for static VIPs.

- **WAF**: By selecting this tier, you are going to create a web application firewall.

- **WAF v2**: In addition to the previous WAF tier, this tier offers autoscaling, zone redundancy, and support for static VIPs.

Azure Application Gateway comes in three different sizes. The following table shows the average performance throughput for each application gateway:

Page Response Size	Small	Medium	Large
6 KB	7.5 Mbps	13 Mbps	50 Mbps
100 KB	35 Mbps	100 Mbps	200 Mbps

Azure Front Door

Azure Front Door offers a service that also works at the application layer (Layer 7). It is an **Application Delivery Network** (**ADN**) as a service, and it offers various load balancing capabilities for your applications.

Both Azure Front Door and Azure Application Gateway are Layer 7 (HTTP/HTTPS) load balancers. The difference between the two is that Front Door is a global service, whereas Application Gateway is a regional service. This means that Front Door can load balance between different scale units across multiple regions. Application Gateway is designed to load balance between other VMs/containers located inside the same scale unit.

Azure Front Door offers the following features and capabilities:

- **Accelerates application performance**: End users can quickly connect to the nearest Front Door **Point of Presence** (**POP**) using the split TCP-based anycast protocol. It then uses Microsoft's global network to connect the application to the backend.

- **Smart health probes**: Front Door increases application availability with smart health probes. These probes will monitor the backends for both availability and latency and provide instant automatic failover when a backend goes down. This way, you can run planned maintenance operations on your applications without any downtime. Traffic is redirected to alternative backends during maintenance.

- **URL path-based routing**: This allows you to route traffic to backend pools based on the request's URL paths.

- **Multiple-site hosting** allows you to configure more than one web application on the same Front Door configuration. This allows a more efficient topology for deployments. Azure Front Door can be configured to route a single web application to its backend pool or route multiple web applications to the same backend pool.

- **Session affinity**: Azure Front Door offers managed cookies, keeping a user session on the same backend application. This feature is suitable in scenarios where the session state is saved locally on the backend for a user session.

- **Custom domains and certificate management**: If you want your domain name to be visible in the Front Door URL, a custom domain is necessary. This can be useful for branding purposes. Also, HTTPS for custom domain names is supported and can be done by uploading your SSL certificate or implementing Front Door-managed certificates.

- **SSL termination**: Front Door offers SSL termination, which speeds up the decryption process and reduces the processing burden on backend servers. Front Door supports both HTTP and HTTPS connectivity between Front Door environments and your backends. Thus, you can also set up end-to-end SSL encryption if this is required.

- **URL redirection**: To ensure that all the communication between the users and the application occurs over an encrypted path, web applications are expected to redirect any HTTP traffic to HTTPS automatically. Azure Front Door offers the functionality to redirect HTTP traffic to HTTPS. It also allows you to redirect traffic to a different hostname, redirect traffic to a different path, or redirect traffic to a new query string in the URL.

- **Azure DDoS Protection Basic protects application-layer security**: The Front Door platform also allows you to create rate-limiting rules to battle malicious bot traffic and configures custom web application firewall rules for access control. This can protect your HTTP/HTTPS workload from exploitation based on client IP addresses, HTTP parameters, and the country code.

- **URL rewrite**: You can configure an optional custom forwarding path to support URL rewrite in Front Door. This path can be used when the request is made from the frontend to the backend. You can configure host headers when forwarding this request.

- **Protocol support – IPv6 and HTTP/2 traffic**: Front Door natively offers end-to-end IPv6 connectivity and the HTTP/2 protocol. The HTTP/2 protocol enables full-duplex communication between application backends and a client over a long-running TCP connection.

Many load balancing options can perform similar roles, so we will look at how to differentiate between them in the next section.

Choosing the right options

Each of the four load balancing options has its own use cases. Therefore, you can use the following flow chart to determine which to use based on your requirements:

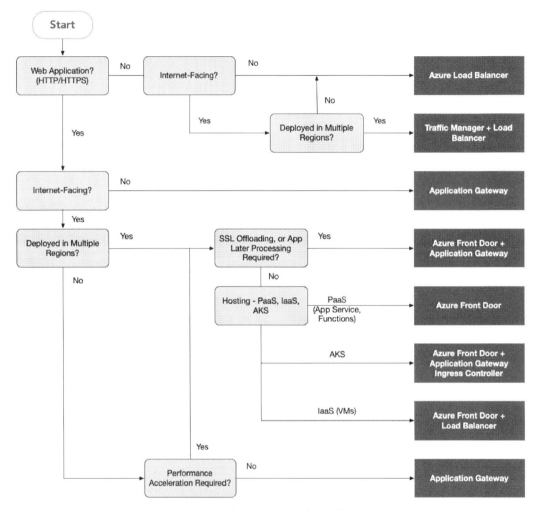

Figure 8.19 – Choosing the right load balancer

As you can see, on some occasions it makes sense to combine one or more options to meet your needs. One example may be when your application needs to be redundant and scalable within a region and across regions – as we can see in the following diagram, we can combine both Azure Traffic Manager and Azure Load Balancer in this scenario:

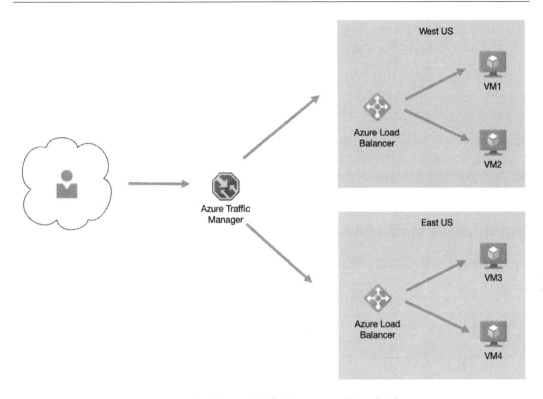

Figure 8.20 – Combining Traffic Manager and Load Balancer

As with most architectural decisions, no one rule or pattern will suit all scenarios, and the mix of technologies and options you need will be entirely dependent on your specific requirements.

Summary

This chapter has looked at many different options and configurations for ensuring connectivity across Azure and hybrid scenarios. We examined how to use public and private DNS in Azure and how we can then control inbound and outbound access using a combination of NSGs, ASGs, and Azure Firewalls.

We have seen how user-defined routes can help us strictly manage traffic flow to support different requirements. Finally, we looked at how to use other Azure services such as Azure Load Balancer, Traffic Manager, Application Gateway, and Azure Front Door to spread traffic over services for better resilience and performance.

In the next chapter, we will look in detail at the different storage options available for use in Azure, including the types of storage, how we can secure our data on it, and what tools we can use to manage it.

Exam scenario

The solutions to the exam scenarios can be found at the end of this book.

MegaCorp Inc. wants to start migrating several on-premises applications into Azure. They want a hybrid configuration whereby VMs in Azure can connect to services on-premises and vice versa.

Any connection into Azure must be resilient, private, and stable with guaranteed throughput.

All VMs in Azure must route any internet-bound traffic through a central firewall to have complete control.

Suggest a solution that achieves these requirements. You need to consider the best connectivity options, how DNS resolution will work, and what sort of firewalls and NSGs you may need.

Further reading

- Azure Virtual Network: `https://docs.microsoft.com/en-us/azure/virtual-network/`

- Network security groups: `https://docs.microsoft.com/en-us/azure/virtual-network/network-security-groups-overview`

- VPN gateways: `https://docs.microsoft.com/en-us/azure/vpn-gateway/vpn-gateway-about-vpngateways`

- Azure Load Balancer: `https://docs.microsoft.com/en-us/azure/load-balancer/load-balancer-overview`

- Azure Application Gateway: `https://docs.microsoft.com/en-us/azure/application-gateway/`

- Azure Traffic Manager: `https://docs.microsoft.com/en-us/azure/traffic-manager/traffic-manager-overview`

- Service endpoints: `https://docs.microsoft.com/en-us/azure/virtual-network/virtual-network-service-endpoints-overview`

- Private endpoints: `https://docs.microsoft.com/en-us/azure/private-link/private-endpoint-overview`

- Azure Firewall: `https://docs.microsoft.com/en-us/azure/firewall/overview`

9

Exploring Storage Solutions

In the previous chapter, we looked at network connectivity and security, including how IP addresses and the **Domain Name System (DNS)** work, and how to control traffic with network security groups, application groups, and routing. We then looked at advanced traffic flow tools, such as Azure Load Balancer, Traffic Manager, and Application Gateway.

Most solutions, at some point, need to store data, and choosing the right type of storage is dependent on many factors such as the kind of data it is, how it needs to be managed, and its lifecycle.

In this chapter, we will continue the *Infrastructure and Storage Components* topic by looking at storage. We will look at different storage types, mainly focusing on Azure Storage accounts and how to choose the right options for your requirements.

We will then investigate how to secure access to your storage accounts before examining the different tooling that is available to manipulate the data stored inside.

In this chapter, we will focus on the following topics:

- Understanding storage types
- Designing storage security
- Using storage management tools

Technical requirements

This chapter will use the Azure portal (`https://portal.azure.com`) for examples.

Understanding storage types

When designing Azure solutions, at some point, you will be required to store data. Azure has several options for storing data, and the choice of which to use depends on several different factors.

This section will examine the various options and which option is best suited to which scenario.

First, we will take a high-level look at one of the most common non-database storage mechanisms – Azure Storage accounts.

Azure Storage accounts

Azure Storage accounts are the main form of managed data storage. They can store different types of data depending on how you configure them on initial creation.

When creating a storage account, you must choose an **Account Kind** – the options are **General Purpose V2 (GPv2)**, **General Purpose V1 (GPv1)**, **Blob Storage**, or **File Storage**.

Storage accounts are grouped into two performance tiers – **Standard** or **Premium**.

Performance tiers

To make sense of the options, we will first consider the performance tier. Generally speaking, the **Premium Tier** is primarily used for storing **Virtual Machine (VM)** disks – specifically, unmanaged VM disks. Later in this section, when we discuss VM disks, you'll understand why this is the case, and why you would not usually choose these!

The **Standard Tier** is the one that you will use the most. So next, we will consider the account kind.

Account kind

Depending on the chosen tier, you will have the option for File Storage and Blob Storage.

File Storage offers Azure file shares, very similar to a regular share you would create on Windows File Server. The File Storage kind, part of the Premium Tier, is a specialized high throughput file share service that supports high **Input-Output Operations (IOPS)**.

We have already mentioned that the GPv1 and GPv2 support file shares, so it is useful to take note of some of the main differences:

Resource	Standard File Share (GPv1, GPv2)	Premium File Share
Maximum account capacity	5 PiB	100 TiB
Minimum size of the share	No minimum	100 GiB
Maximum file size	1 TiB	4 TiB
IOPS per share	Up to 10,000 IOPS	100,000 IOPS
Maximum IOPS per file	1,000	4,000

> **Important note**
>
> You might be expecting the sizes in GB, TB, or PB (that is, gigabyte, terabyte, or petabyte); however, these tables show **TiB**, **GiB**, and **PiB** (that is, **gibibyte**, **tebibyte**, and **pebibyte**). This isn't a type; it's a slightly different notation used when measuring certain storage types. It's down to the fact that GB, TB, and PB are Base 10, whereas GiB, TiB, and PiB are base 2 (that is, binary). As an example, 1 GB is 1,073,741,824 bytes, whereas 1 GiB is 1,000,000,000 bytes. You don't need to worry about this too much and certainly not for the exam; the important point is to note the differences between each tier's relative sizes.

Blob Storage is a similar story. Again, Blob Storage is also included with GPv1 and GPv2 accounts, but the Blob Storage account kind is a premium version that is specifically optimized for smaller, kilobyte-sized data. It's ideal for an application that has a high number of transactions and requires low-latency storage.

> **Important note**
>
> A **Blob** is an acronym for a **Binary Large Object**. In Azure, it refers to files, especially non-text files such as executables, images, videos, disk files, and more. However, since text files and structured data files, such as **comma-separated values** (**CSV**), can also be stored as blobs, this can be a confusing definition! In Azure, blobs can also be **Block**, **Page**, and **Append** blobs – block blobs are optimized for large uploads; page blobs are fixed byte-sized and are optimized for random I/O – often used for disk images; and append blobs are optimized for – well, appending! Typically, if you see the term "Blob," think file.

As you can see, both Blob and File storage account kinds are generally only used for specific scenarios that require the capabilities that we have mentioned.

General Purpose V1 supports blobs, files, disks, queues, and tables. Usually, you would only choose GPv1 if your application is transaction-intensive but does need a large capacity. It also supports older versions of the storage services REST API, which is used to access the account programmatically.

Finally, we come to **General Purpose V2**. As you can probably guess, GPv2 is the newest version and is recommended for most scenarios. GPv2 supports blobs, files, disks, queues, tables, and Azure Data Lake Gen 2, which is a particular type of Blob Storage mainly aimed at big data analytics.

To ensure your data is always available, each option supports different replication options.

Storage replication

To help protect your data against hardware failure, storage accounts replicate your information to two other locations within any one region – this means that you always have at least three copies. Although they are all in the same region, each copy is in a different physical location within the availability zone. This is known as **locally redundant storage (LRS)**. LRS is not the only option – if you need better protection, you can also choose other options.

Zone-redundant storage (**ZRS**) copies data synchronously across availability zones (for example, in separate data centers) within a region.

Geo-redundant storage (**GRS**) protects against regional failures by using LRS in the primary regions and creating three replicas in another region. This can be a read/write replica or a read-only replica with **read-access geo-redundant storage** (**RA-GRS**). In both cases, data is copied asynchronously to the other region.

Geo-zone-redundant storage (**GZRS**) is similar to GRS except that the local region's data uses ZRS rather than LRS. Again, a read-only option is available with **read-access geo-zone-redundant storage** (**RA-GZRS**). At the time of writing, GZRS and RA-GZRS are relatively new and are now available in all regions.

> **Important note**
>
> The difference between synchronous writes and asynchronous writes is essential. Synchronous writes with LRS and ZRS happen *simultaneously* – in other words, the loss of one replica means the data in the other two will always be up to date. Asynchronous copies used in GRS and AZGRS happen *after* the primary replicas have been written – this means there is a time delay. Microsoft does not offer an SLA for the asynchronous copy but typically takes less than 15 minutes. In other words, the replica in the second region could be up to 15 minutes out of date from the primary replica.

Not all storage accounts support all redundancy options as the following table shows:

Account type	Redundancy options
GP v2	LRS, GRS, RA-GRS, ZRS, GZRS, and RA-GZRS
GP v1	LRS, GRS, and RA-GRS
BlockBlobStorage	LRS and ZRS
FileStorage	LRS and ZRS
BlobStorage	LRS, GRS, and RA-GRS

Using replicas help protects your data against hardware failure or regional outages; however, it does not protect against accidental or malicious deletion. Fortunately, Azure provides additional tools to help with this.

Data protection

Storage accounts offer several services to help you protect your data from accidental deletion or updates – these include the following:

- **Soft delete**: This is just like a recycle bin on your computer. When you delete data, it is not physically removed; instead, it is effectively hidden. You can then recover data if it has been accidentally removed. The soft delete can be activated at the blob or container level (that is, to protect against file deletion or complete container deletion).

- **Versioning**: With versioning, every time you change a file, a copy of the previous file is also kept. Each change causes the updated file to have a version increment. In this way, you are protected against data changes.

> **Important note**
> At the time of writing, both soft delete and versioning are not available with Data Lake Gen 2 when using hierarchical namespaces.

Both of these options cost more as you are effectively using more space within the storage; therefore, as with other options, careful consideration must be given to whether the cost of these services warrants the benefit.

Access tiers

When provisioning GPv2 or Blob Storage accounts, you can choose between access tiers with different prices and speed characteristics based on how often you need to access your data:

- **Hot**: This is for regular everyday use – such as data that is accessed frequently. It is the most expensive storage costs but has the cheapest access costs.

- **Cool**: This is for infrequently accessed data and has lower storage costs, but reading and writing operations cost more.

- **Archive**: This storage type is also designed for writing to but rarely reading or updating. As the name suggests, this is designed for storing archival information. For example, data that you must keep for historical or legal reasons long term but may never actually need to read. This has the cheapest storage costs, but reading back is relatively expensive and can take some time - it can take hours to move the data to the hot tier and then be able to read it.

Storage accounts offer a feature called **life cycle management**. With life cycle management, you can define rules that will automatically move data from one access tier to another or even delete it, based on when data was last accessed. For example, if you have data that hasn't been accessed for six months, it will automatically move to an archive storage tier.

Storage accounts can be used for various purposes; however, sometimes, a database might make more sense depending on the type of data you are storing. We will go into detail regarding the different database storage options in *Chapter 12, Creating Scaleable and Secure Databases*. In this chapter, we will just look at why you might choose a database over a storage account, which we shall investigate next, starting with the need for data classification.

Data classification

The first question you need to ask when choosing a storage technology is *what kind of data you are storing?* In other words, we need to classify our data. Typically, data could be classified as one of the following types.

Structured data

Structured data is data that follows a strict definition or schema. Typically, this means information is stored in a table with columns defining the type and size of that data. Sometimes, one or more tables might be linked together with some form of a key. This type of data is typically stored inside a SQL database.

Semi-structured data

Semi-structured data is similar to structured data in that it often (but doesn't have to) conforms to a set structure. This might be in a hierarchical format rather than "flat" tables:

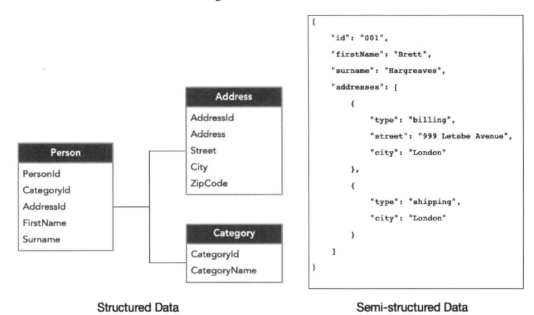

Structured Data   Semi-structured Data

Figure 9.1 – Structured versus semi-structured data

As you can see from the preceding diagram, semi-structured data still has a structure, but it is not as strict as structured data. Finally, we have data that conforms to no structure at all.

Unstructured data

Unstructured data is also known as raw data. Typically, it is not in a set format as you find with structured and semi-structured, or it might use a propriety file type – for example, a media file or a Word document. Typical examples include (but are not limited to) the following:

- Media files such as videos, images, and audio
- Application files, such as Word documents, Excel files, or PowerPoint
- Disk images such as **Virtual Hard Disk (VHD)** files used by VMs.
- Pure text files (without any structure)
- Log files (but not in tabular format)

Data classification, on its own, will not necessarily tell you the storage you should choose. For example, you might be using structured data which would normally be stored in a SQL database. However, you could always receive the data as comma-separated text files that you want to manage as text files. Conversely, you might be receiving Excel files, but you need to query data across them.

Therefore, the next question we need to ask is *what operations will we be performing with the data?*

Operational decisions

As we have discussed already, for each data type, there are also other factors that will determine which storage mechanism we choose.

We need to think about how we will receive the data, how we will interact with the data, and how we will present it back to the user.

User-interactive applications

If data will be used as a backend to a business application, such as an e-commerce site, then our data is typically product information, customer records, and order records. This data is highly structured and needs to be quickly queried, and be managed through a user interface (for example, the web page). You might also want to batch import data or store reports, but these are secondary mechanisms, as they are not what the application does minute by minute or day to day.

A database is an obvious choice; however, it might not be the only mechanism. An e-commerce site will usually store and display product images. Although it is possible to store images directly inside a database, this is often not the best choice as additional computing will be required to convert the data from a database field type into an image type.

In this scenario, we can consider using a hybrid of a database and a traditional file store. A field in a database's product table will hold a reference to the image (that is, its filename), but the image itself could be stored and retrieved from Azure Blob Storage.

Other media files or document file types can also be used in a similar way. For example, a database record holds a reference, but the actual file is stored or retrieved from a file-based storage container, such as Azure Blob Storage or Azure File Storage:

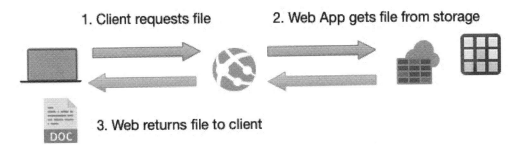

Figure 9.2 – An example of a user-interactive application

As well as web-based interactive pages, another increasingly common use case for Azure is to analyze big data.

Data analytics solutions

Another common scenario is a data analysis application. Here, data might be received in bulk as structured or semi-structured files. These files need to be read, queried, and maybe even reformatted to produce a report or data model.

The initial storage mechanism could be a file store such as Azure Blob Storage or Azure Data Lake. From there, you could ingest the data into a database store such as Azure SQL or Cosmos DB. Again, we use a mixture of technologies, but each has its specific use case – for instance, is it being used purely for storage or for querying? Take a look at the following diagram:

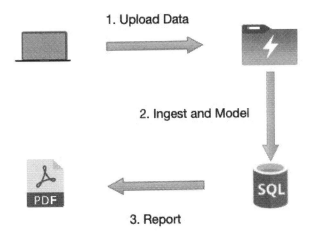

Figure 9.3 – An example of a data analytics solution

Most solutions will also need to store logs. Either for troubleshooting or performance monitoring, logging needs to be carefully planned.

Logging systems

Many applications and systems emit logging information that can be used for performance or diagnostics analysis.

This type of data is typically a combination of structured and semi-structured data – but not always. This log data can be sent out in many different ways and from numerous sources, such as applications, VM operating systems, and even the Azure platform itself. To make sense of the data, you need to collate it and then be able to visualize it.

Again, we could use Azure Blob or even Azure File Storage. Then, an external logging viewer could be used to make sense of the data, or you could opt for Azure's logging analytics solution – Azure Log Analytics, which uses the Kusto query language and enables data to be easily formatted and visualized.

We will cover Log Analytics and Application Insights, which is an application-specific monitoring and logging tool, in more detail in *Chapter 15, Designing for Logging and Monitoring*:

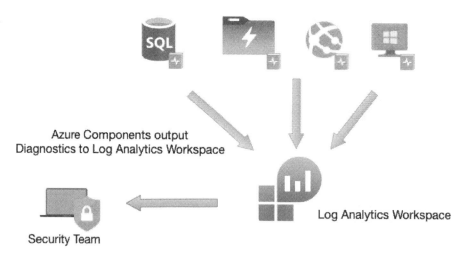

Figure 9.4 – An example logging solution

The next use case we will consider is a programming pattern for decoupling application components from each other.

Queuing mechanisms

Sometimes, data is transient and only used by the application to keep track of state or process information. This type of data still needs to be persisted but only temporarily – and often, a mechanism is required to ensure the data is removed once the process or task has been completed so that it isn't duplicated.

A typical application development pattern is message queuing, which does just that – a task that needs to be performed is recorded, along with the relevant parameters, by one part of a solution, to be read and actioned by another component.

You can build your application to manage this queuing process, or you can use a technology that manages it for you.

Azure Storage accounts contain tables and queues. Tables could store temporary messages, but the application would need to manage the process entirely. Storage queues are a better option, as they are built specifically for this task and provide messaging-specific capabilities.

We will cover queuing and messaging from a technology perspective in more detail in *Chapter 11, Comparing Application Components*; however, the following diagram shows a high-level view of how this might work:

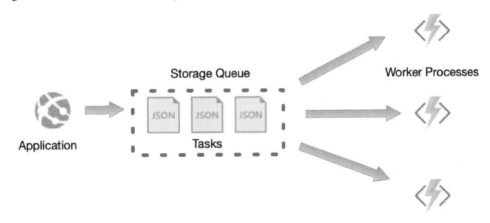

Figure 9.5 – A messaging architecture example

Many Azure services are built on top of these native storage mechanisms, such as Azure SQL, Azure Cosmos DB and Azure Storage accounts. However, another use case is specific to Azure VMs. VMs use virtual hard disks for the operating system, and as data disks, we will examine these next.

Archiving

Sometimes, data needs to be stored for long periods for compliance and legal reasons, or simply just as a long-term record. Savings can be made by separating this data from live data.

Azure Storage accounts support differing access tiers – hot, cold, and archive, which we looked at in detail at the beginning of this chapter.

By considering how often data will be accessed, and with a well-thought-out data life cycle management plan, you can achieve the best cost to performance ratio.

So far, we have looked at these requirements from a pure data perspective. Next, we will examine a different use case for storage – that is, VM disk storage.

VM disks

Windows and Linux servers must have at least one hard disk drive to store the operating system on and, sometimes, you might also need separate data disks.

When virtualization was introduced, those disks also become virtual but were stored on physical drives as disk image files used by the Hypervisor. In the case of Windows Hyper-V (Microsoft's Virtualization software), these files had the .VHD extension (that is, **VHD** for **Virtual Hard Disk**).

VMs, in Azure, are no different; the OS and data disks are just files that must be stored on a physical disk. When VMs were first introduced in Azure, these files, now with the .VHDX extension, were created and stored in an Azure Storage account as blobs in a container. Today, they are known as **Unmanaged Disks**.

However, today, when you create a VM, you have the option to create disks as **Managed Disks**. Managed disks are just regular vhdx files, but they are not stored in a storage account that you have direct access to; instead, they are managed by Azure in a storage account that only the system has access to. Managed disks offer the following features:

- **Scalable**: You can have up to 50,000 disks in each region with a subscription.

- **High Availability**: Managed disks store three replicas within a region, providing an SLA of 99.999% (that is, five nines).

- **Availability Sets and Zones**: When building VMs in Availability Sets or Availability Zones, the disks will be automatically distributed across fault domains or availability zones.

- **Azure Backup Support**: Using Azure Backup, OS and data disks can be included in backup routines.

- **Granular Access**: Managed disks allow you to use RBAC to manage access for individual users and groups for set operations.

- **Encryption**: You can use **Storage Service Encryption** (**SSE**) to protect data on the physical disk, known as **data at rest**. You also have the option to use **Azure Disk Encryption**, which protects disks at the OS level.

Generally, for most use cases, you should use managed disks. Unmanaged disks should only be used for legacy requirements as they don't support the scalability and other management features you get from managed disks.

The third type of disk you can use is an **ephemeral** OS disk. Ephemeral disks are faster for read and write operations; however, if the attached VM fails, it can corrupt the data, leaving the server unable to boot. They are handy for applications built using microservices, where your solution expects individual instances of a service to be either short-lived or scalable, for example, when using scale sets. Ephemeral disks use local storage on the underlying host and don't incur costs.

Disk types

When using disks on VMs, you also choose the disk type, that is, HDD, Standard SSD, Premium SSD, or Ultra SSD.

Each option offers different performance levels, with HDD at the lower end and Ultra SSD being the fastest. This, of course, impacts cost, and therefore choosing the correct type is a dependent on your required **Input/Output Operations per Second** (**IOPS**) throughput (that is, the rate at which data can be moved between the disk and host) and what you are prepared to pay for it. Additionally, note that not all VM sizes support all disk types:

- **Standard HDDs** use magnetic drives and are available on all VMs SKUs. They are the slowest but cheapest option, and so they are ideal for Dev/Test machines.

- **Standard SSDs** are generally considered the entry level for production workloads. They are faster than HDDs offering increased IOPS while still being relatively low cost.

- **Premium SSDs** are the next tier up, providing faster throughput, higher IOPS, and lower latency than Standard SSDs.

- **Ultra SSDs** are the fastest and most expensive option. However, they are not available in all regions yet (at the time of writing) and can only be used on the VM's built-in Availability Zones. They are also only available on ES and DS v3 VMs. They can only be used as data disks and don't support backup options such as snapshots, Azure Backup, Site Recovery, or even encryption.

As you can see, Ultra SSDs have many limitations; however, if your application requires high throughput and low latency, and Premium SSDs cannot provide the levels you need, then Ultra SSDs might be the only option. Use cases for Ultra SSDs are top-tier databases and applications such as SAP HANA.

Once you have chosen your storage mechanism and decided on the various options within that mechanism, we must think about controlling access to the data that resides upon it.

Designing storage security

Protecting your data is a crucial consideration with any storage mechanism. Luckily, security is at the heart of Azure components, and storage solutions implement various protection levels by default.

We will take a look at the different security options for Cosmos DB and Azure SQL in *Chapter 12, Creating Saleable and Secure Databases*. In this section, we will look at how to secure Azure Storage accounts.

Securing your data can be achieved in four different ways:

- **Network protection**: First, we need to protect your data against unauthorized access at the network level – only allow access from the applications that need access and no more.

- **Authorization**: Next, ensure that any system or person who can access the network level also has to access the data based on their account—in other words, use **Role-Based Access Controls (RBAC)**.

- **Encryption**: Ensure data is encrypted so that if a hacker were able to bypass the network and role-based controls, they cannot access the data itself without access to the relevant encryption keys.

- **Auditing and threat detection**: If a breach does occur, auditing enables you to track down who, when, and how the data was accessed.

We will start with how to protect storage at the network level.

Network protection

The first step in access prevention is to stop applications or systems from accessing the data if they don't need to. For example, an application might use a web interface to read and write the data – end users don't need direct access. In this scenario, we should lock down access to the application itself.

By default, storage accounts allow access from all network devices, so anyone with the URL to a file in the storage account can access it. This is not required in the preceding example; instead, we can configure Azure storage to only allow traffic from a selected IP range or Azure subnet.

The following screenshot shows the **Networking** blade of a storage account configured to allow access from a set subnet:

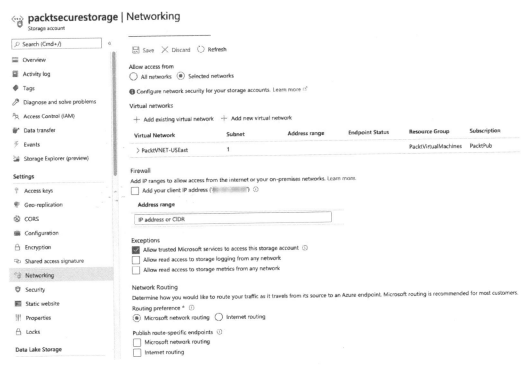

Figure 9.6 – Configuring storage network protection

Here, note the **Exceptions** section – by default, the option to **Allow trusted Microsoft services to access this storage account** is checked. This is useful because when you lock down a storage account, you might need to provide access to Azure Event Grid, Azure Data Factory, or a range of other Azure services. Although Microsoft does publish the IP ranges for these services, they are subject to change; therefore, checking this box opens the storage account to all of those services. Please refer to the following link for an up-to-date list of what is included: `https://docs.microsoft.com/en-gb/azure/storage/common/storage-network-security`.

Choosing whether to turn on network-level security requires some thought in terms of how your solution will work.

For example, a website might contain images and videos; however, these might all be stored in a storage account. To serve the media to end users, the web application can either get the files from the storage account and pass them to the user or supply a URL link to the asset directly in the storage account. In this situation, the account must be set to allow all networks, as the client could come from anywhere.

Authorization

The next layer of protection ensures the person or application trying to access the data is authorized to. There are several different mechanisms in which to achieve this.

RBAC

Using RBAC, we can ensure a user or other type of identity (such as a managed identity or service principal) is authorized to perform a task on that data. We covered RBAC in detail in *Chapter 4, Managing User Authorization*, and we looked at managed identities and service principals in *Chapter 6, Building Application Security*.

Individual users, groups, or identities can be assigned roles like any other Azure resource, and there are several built-in roles that are available specifically for storage accounts – these include the following:

- Storage Account Contributor
- Storage Blob Data Contributor
- Storage Blob Data Owner
- Storage Blob Data Reader
- Storage Queue Data Contributor
- Storage Queue Data Reader

There are others too, and the complete list, along with the details for each role, can be found at `https://docs.microsoft.com/en-us/azure/role-based-access-control/built-in-roles#storage`.

The key thing to understand about these roles is that the data and queues are separate from the account's management. To view the storage account at all, a user must have the general Reader role in place. In order to manage the account, they must have at least the Storage Account Contributor role, but this does not automatically grant access to the data or queues within the accounts. Instead, these have specific blob data and queue data roles.

RBAC only comes into play with storage blob containers if containers and folders within those containers are set to private access levels. When you create a container in a storage account, you must set the access level. The options are as follows:

- **Private (no anonymous access)**: Full RBAC is in play to control who can access an account.

- **Blob (anonymous read access for blobs only)**: With this set, you can provide a direct link to a file in the container, and a user can access a file for reading without needing to authenticate.

- **Container (anonymous read access for containers and blob)**: This is similar to Blob, but users can enumerate files in a container without needing to authenticate.

Access can be set at the container level or the folder level; however, be aware of setting a container to use Blob or Container access only affects whether an authenticated user can read or write the data based on an assigned role; you also need to allow access in the network level settings.

RBAC controls are not the only way to provide access to storage accounts – we can also use a **Shared Access Signature (SAS)**.

SASes

A SAS is a unique URL that you can generate that provides time-limited access to your storage account. An account SAS is created at the storage account level, granting access to all containers within that account. Alternatively, you can create a SAS for a container, a folder, or even an individual object, which is known as a service SAS. A SAS can also be generated through the portal or code.

As you can see in the following screenshot of a storage account's SAS blade in the Azure portal, when generating a SAS, you can define the allowed services and resource type, set a start and expiry date for the SAS, and even specify allowed IP ranges:

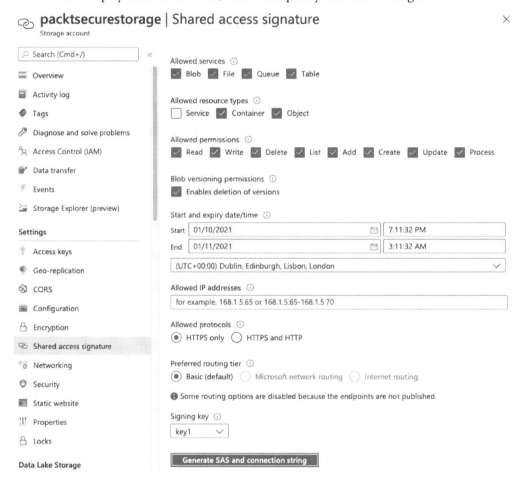

Figure 9.7 – Generating a SAS URL

Once you click on **Generate SAS and connection string**, a series of URLs and connection strings will be generated, which can then be used to access the service without the need to authenticate.

You can also generate a SAS for an individual file – by navigating to the file through the Azure portal; we can select the file and click on the option to generate a SAS for it, as shown in the following screenshot:

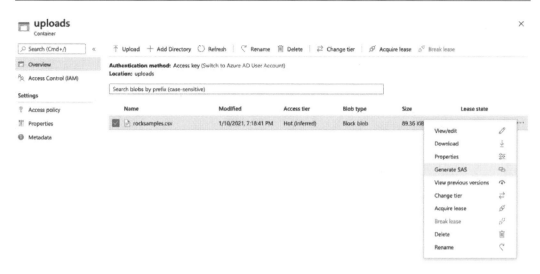

Figure 9.8 – Generating a SAS for an individual file

The URL generated can then directly access the file through a web browser, again without authenticating.

As mentioned earlier, these tasks can also be achieved in code. This is a great way to secure access to assets in your storage accounts without requiring users to sign in but still giving direct access (as opposed to your application retrieving the file and passing it on). A typical workflow could look like this:

1. A user requests access to a secure file from your application.

2. Your application generates a time-limited, IP-restricted SAS and returns the URL to the user.

3. The user uses that URL to download the file directly, but they only have a short timeframe to download it and can only download it from their current IP address.

A SAS is generated using a storage account key – and each storage account has two keys available. When you generate a SAS, you have to option to use either key.

The storage account key can also directly access a storage account without generating a SAS – this is synonymous with using a connection string for a SQL database. The keys and connection string can be viewed in the Azure portal by navigating to the **Access keys** left-hand menu option in the **Storage Account** blade.

Occasionally, you might need to regenerate these access keys – for example, if you are worried a connection string or SAS has been compromised. You can regenerate these keys through the Access key's view, which can disable a previously generated SAS or connection string.

As well as creating individual SAS tokens, an access policy, defined at the container level, provides an additional level of security.

Encryption

All storage accounts in Azure are encrypted by **Storage Service Encryption** (**SSE**) using a 256-bit **Advanced Encryption Standard** (**AES**) cipher. This makes Azure storage **FIPS 140-2** compliant.

> **Important note**
>
> **FIPS 140-2** is a US government security standard for the approval of cryptographic processes.

By default, the keys used to encrypt the storage are managed by Microsoft; however, there is also the option to use customer-managed keys instead. These keys can be provided by you or generated by Azure and stored in an Azure key vault. Some organizations demand that all data should be encrypted using individually managed keys.

Access to storage accounts also uses transport-level security in HTTPS to secure communications to the account. HTTPS connections are enforced by default; however, this can be disabled to allow HTTP if required.

Auditing

Auditing is another requirement for some organizations, especially for highly sensitive data. Breaches can happen. And even with well-defined security in place, a breach could occur from insider threats (for example, authorized users).

The Azure event logger logs control-plane events (for example when a storage account is created or deleted). Transactional logs can be activated and sent to an Azure Log Analytics account.

Azure Defender for Storage is another optional advanced threat protection service that can detect and alert unusual activity. Integrated into Azure Security Center, alerts can be sent via email to administrators with details of the event and advice on investigating and remediating.

Through a combination of network, authorization, and encryption, you can ensure your data is safe and secure. In the final section of this chapter, we will investigate the different tools available for managing the data in storage accounts.

Using storage management tools

You will need to copy data into and out of a storage account; therefore, we will examine the different tools available in this final section.

All data operations can be actioned by calling the **Azure Storage REST APIs** – in fact, all of the other tools that we will explore through this section use the REST APIs themselves.

Azure Storage REST APIs

Each storage service – Blob Storage, Data Lake, Files, Queues, and Tables – all have their endpoint URLs, as follows:

Service	Endpoint
Blobs	HTTPS://<storage-account>.blob.core.windows.net
Data Lake Gen 2	HTTPS://<storage-account>.dfs.core.windows.net
Azure Files	HTTPS://<storage-account>.file.core.windows.net
Queues	HTTPS://<storage-account>.queue.core.windows.net
Table	HTTPS://<storage-account>.table.core.windows.net

Each service, then, has its own unique set of calls that can be made depending on the action you are trying to take. For example, to get a list of all blobs within a folder, you can follow the GET call:

```
https://mystor.blob.core.windows.net/?comp=list&maxresults=3
```

Here, `mystor` is the name of the storage account. Note that if the storage account or container is set to private, you first need to make a call to the Azure authentication service to obtain an authorization token and then pass that token through to the REST endpoint header.

Although you could perform these actions manually, the REST APIs are meant for use programmatically.

Microsoft also provides several client libraries that you can use in your applications to make using them more manageable.

However, if you want to access it without writing your software, you can use the `azcopy` command.

AzCopy

AzCopy is a command-line tool available for Windows, Linus, and macOS that wraps some of the REST APIs calls to make it easier to perform actions against storage accounts.

AzCopy has a login command to authenticate you to your Azure subscription and obtain an authorization token. You could use SAS to grant access without the need to authenticate.

You can then use the following command to copy a file from your local computer to the blob container:

```
azcopy copy ''mylocalfile'' https://mystorageaccount.blob.core.windows.net/destinationfolder
```

Although AzCopy makes it much easier to manage storage account data from a command line, this is particularly friendly for many users.

Therefore, Microsoft also offers an even easier option – Azure Storage Explorer.

Azure Storage Explorer

Azure Storage Explorer is a user-friendly **Graphical User Interface (GUI)** that manages the data in Azure Storage simply and easily and is available for Windows, macOS, and Linux.

Azure Storage Explorer allows you to connect and authenticate against multiple subscriptions; therefore, authorization is seamless. However, as well as AD authentication, you can also connect using connection strings and SAS URLs.

As you can see from the following screenshot, Azure Storage Explorer allows you to interact with storage accounts such as Windows File Manager. You can upload and download, copy, delete, and even modify files if they are in plain text:

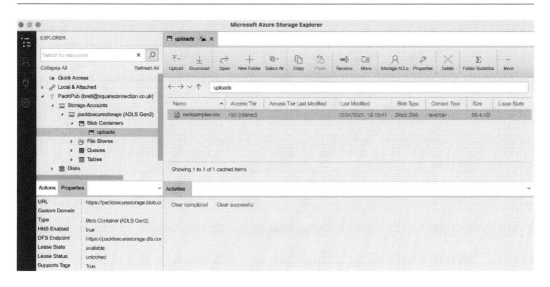

Figure 9.9 – Blob access in Storage Explorer

Storage Explorer also enables you to access tables, queues, files, and data lakes. You can even use it to connect to Azure's NoSQL implementation Cosmos DB.

In this section, we looked at many different ways to interact with Azure Storage, from direct REST API access to a user-friendly GUI that uses Azure Storage as easily as using a local filesystem.

Summary

This chapter has explored the different configuration options of Azure Storage, including when to choose which. Designing applications for storage involves thinking about many other aspects of your data – from the speed at which you need to read and write to cost and availability – all of which we have looked at.

We've also delved into how to secure access to our storage at the network level, with identities and encryption. Finally, we learned the different options for manipulating and managing data in our storage accounts, from the user-friendly GUI of Azure Storage Explorer to the more manual methods of AzCopy. We also saw how they all use Storage REST APIs under the hood.

In the next chapter, we will consider the various options that are available for migrating workloads into Azure, including VMs.

Exam scenario

The solution to the exam scenario can be found in the *Assessments* section at the end of the book.

MegaCorp Inc. is building a new insurance application that allows users to enter details and then generates a PDF quote that users can download.

Security is essential because the data and reports contain **Personally Identifiable Information** (**PII**).

Quotes older than 6 months must be kept for 7 years if users ever want to look back at their past quotations; however, this rarely happens.

Live data (that is, 6 months or newer) should also be protected against a single availability zone failure; however, historical quotes are not critical and, therefore, don't require any additional resilience.

Recommend a storage solution that meets the customer's requirements.

Further reading

- Azure Storage Accounts: https://docs.microsoft.com/en-us/azure/storage/common/storage-account-overview

- Azure Managed Disks: https://docs.microsoft.com/en-gb/azure/virtual-machines/managed-disks-overview

- Azure Storage REST API reference: https://docs.microsoft.com/en-us/rest/api/storageservices/

- AzCopy: https://docs.microsoft.com/en-us/azure/storage/common/storage-ref-azcopy-copy

- Azure Storage Explorer: https://azure.microsoft.com/en-gb/features/storage-explorer/

10
Migrating Workloads to Azure

In the previous chapter, we examined Azure storage use, looking at the different types available, including their benefits, and how to secure them.

In this chapter, we will focus on migrating workloads from on-premises systems into Azure. The process starts with an analysis of your current environment. We will discuss the areas you must consider, including the communication, dependencies, business drivers, and tools we can use to assist in this process.

Next, we will look at the different options when considering the would-be architecture and how we can perform migrations of VMs and databases.

Finally, we will consider how to monitor the migrated systems to optimize your new platform.

With this in mind, in this chapter, we will cover the following:

- Assessing on-premises systems
- Migration options
- Migrating virtual machines and databases
- Monitoring and optimization

Technical requirements

This chapter will use the Azure portal (`https://portal.azure.com`) for examples.

Assessing on-premises systems

When an organization decides to migrate its existing systems from on-premises to the cloud, the migration must be well planned and well designed. An architect's role is not just limited to the end state's design; they must also be involved from the very beginning of the process and throughout.

At a high level, any successful migration consists of the following steps:

1. Assessing
2. Migrating
3. Optimizing
4. Monitoring

The fact that the actual migration is not the final step may come as a surprise to some. However, all organizations are unique – they have different requirements, infrastructure, and various reasons for migrating.

This means that there is no *one-size-fits-all* solution for migrating, and once the migration is complete, you cannot wholly predict how your systems will perform. Therefore, to ensure a move is successful, you must monitor and tweak your components once your applications have migrated.

The first step of the migration process is the assessment of your existing environment. This involves both the discovery and evaluation of your on-premises servers, databases, and the applications that run on them.

The discovery phase

Very few applications run in isolation on a single server. The majority will be split across multiple servers; for example, web applications may consist of a web server frontend and a backend database. To further complicate matters, some systems may share resources – multiple applications may share the same backend databases, and web servers may host multiple websites. There might also be a crossover in this sharing, as depicted in the following diagram:

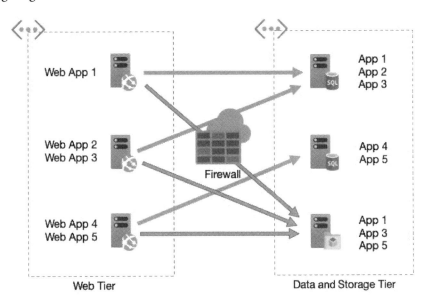

Figure 10.1 – Applications are often spread across shared servers

Therefore, the discovery phase of the migration involves not only producing an inventory of servers, databases, and services in scope but a dependency matrix as well.

Once you have identified the components of the systems, you must investigate how they communicate. Firewalls and routers may exist between different layers of any one solution, and therefore the rules also need to be captured to ensure they can still communicate post-migration. Consideration must also be made for IP addressing and DNS – will your on-premises network extend into Azure as a *flat network* (a single subnet), or will it be segregated using a different subnet?

Your network schema will determine whether services will receive a new IP address once migrated or use the current address, which has an impact on the DNS and potentially the configuration of n-tier systems – have tiers been configured to contact upstream and downstream tiers directly via an IP address, a DNS name, or some other means?

Finally, you will also need to consider the impact the actual migration will have on end users. There will be service interruption at some point, and depending on the complexity, more than one system may be impacted when you switch over.

There are several tools to assist with the technical discovery of your systems – including several third-party applications such as Movere (recently acquired by Microsoft), Cloudamize, Current Tech, and ATADATA, as well as Azure's own **Azure Migrate**.

However, in many organizations, systems will have business owners – stakeholders who manage and understand your applications at a detailed level, including the history and potential problems you might encounter.

You should also collate any documentation and service designs to aid in the process to help map out the end-to-end architecture of each solution.

As mentioned, there are several tools to assist with the discovery exercise, including Azure Migrate. The Azure Migrate tool consists of an appliance (a virtual machine with a collector and discovery tool pre-installed) that must be installed and run on your on-premises environment.

There are two versions of the appliance, one for Hyper-V and one for VMware – in either case, the process for downloading and configuring the tool is as follows:

1. Create an `Azure Migrate: Server Assessment` project in the **Azure Migrate** blade of the Azure portal.

2. Download the appliance.

3. Install and run the appliance by importing it as a VM into either Hyper-V or VMware.

4. Start the discovery process.

5. Once the discovery has finished, create an assessment.

The final assessment step creates a report similar to the one in the following screenshot:

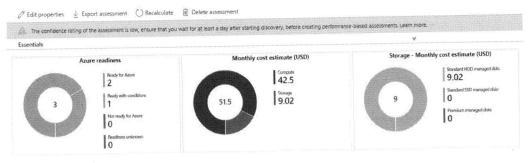

Figure 10.2 – Example Azure Migrate assessment report

The assessment report shows how many VMs have been discovered and are ready for migration, an estimate of the monthly cost of each VM when migrated to Azure, and an estimate of the monthly storage costs.

> **Tip**
> The complete end-to-end process for creating and running a full assessment is documented in the book *Implement Microsoft Azure Architect technologies: AZ303 Exam Prep and Beyond*, by myself, Brett Hargreaves, and Sjouke Zaal – also by Packt Publishing.

The Azure Migrate tool is not the only way to help assess your on-premises servers and solutions. We mentioned earlier that understanding dependencies between servers is also an essential requisite.

Azure **Service Map** is an optional add-on solution available for **Log Analytics workspaces**. When enabled, the Service Map tool works with a dependency agent and the Log Analytics agent that must be installed on all your on-premises VMs. The tool will then create a visual map of all identified services and how they relate to each other.

> **Tip**
> Log Analytics workspaces are covered in *Chapter 15, Designing for Logging and Monitoring*.

Another useful tool is the Azure **Total Cost of Ownership (TCO)** calculator. Whereas the Azure Migrate assessment report will provide an estimate of run costs for each virtual machine, the TCO calculator takes detailed information on your on-premises workloads and provides a breakdown estimate of what a comparable service in Azure might cost.

The TCO calculator is a free tool available at `https://azure.microsoft.com/en-gb/pricing/tco/calculator/` and produces reports similar to that in the following screenshot:

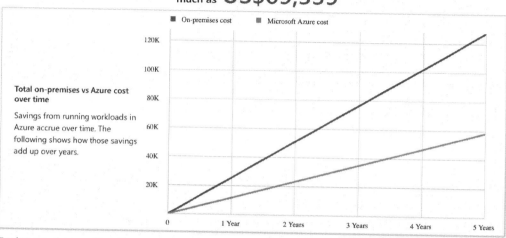

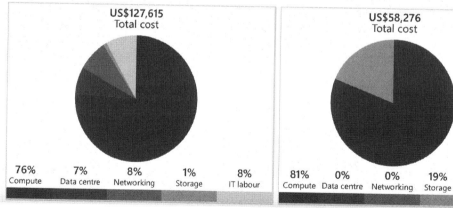

Figure 10.3 – TCO calculator report

Once you understand your on-premises environment, you can start to plan how your new environment will look.

Understanding migration options

The next phase of the migration planning is to determine how your migrated services will be built. This may be a simple lift-and-shift of one VM to a new VM in Azure, or you may take the opportunity to modify the technologies you use.

This part of the process is more than just technical decisions – you need to understand the reasons for moving to Azure; therefore, you must involve the senior decision-makers to help define the scope.

Depending on the motivation for the move, you may want to move some or all of your infrastructure. This also plays a vital role in determining *how* your systems migrate – not from the physical move's point of view, but the actual process you choose.

The options available when choosing your end-state architecture can be grouped as follows:

- **Rehost**: Also known as lift-and-shift. This is the simplest – you simply move your on-premises VM to a VM in Azure. It will also be the easiest as no other work is required for the applications that run on the VM. However, the rehost approach doesn't provide many automated scaling and cost-saving opportunities in Azure.

- **Refactor**: Depending on your application, it may be possible to leverage one of Azure's many PaaS components. The obvious examples would be moving databases to Azure SQL or an IIS hosted web application to an Azure web app. Not all applications are quite so simple, and some systems leverage more advanced Microsoft SQL options such as SSIS, which are not as straightforward to move; in these cases, the lift-and-shift approach may still be the best option. Moving to PaaS, however, does provide greater cost efficiencies, resilience options, and scalability.

- **Re-architect**: If you have the time and aspiration, completely re-architecting an application can bring the most significant benefits. By employing different architectures such as messaged-based, containerization, or using other serverless technologies, you can make your solution fully cloud-native, save costs, and get greater performance, resilience, and flexibility.

- **Rebuild or decommission**: You may need to entirely rebuild an application from the ground up. Or you may decide the application is no longer required. Business needs change over time, and a migration to the cloud and the necessary planning can be an excellent opportunity to re-evaluate applications.

- **Replace**: As part of the evaluation process, you may decide that your business needs could be better served by replacing applications with other systems or third-party products.

The option you choose should take into account business motivation, budget, and timescales. It may be better to spend more time and money upfront on re-architecting services to save money and provide greater flexibility in the long term.

Alternatively, speed may be the most critical factor, in which case a simple lift-and-shift could be the best option. Finally, a hybrid or phased approach may suit – many organizations perform a rehost as an initial step in a migration project, followed by a re-architecture of systems once everything is in Azure.

Whichever path is chosen, once you know what and how you wish to move, the next step is to select a methodology and tool to perform the actual migration.

Migrating virtual machines and databases

Depending on how you plan to migrate into Azure, determine your next steps and what tools are required.

Refactorization, re-architecting, rebuilding, and replacing are manual processes and will need to be managed as individual projects.

There are several tools available for VM migrations, and again, the Azure Migrate tool can perform this task for you.

Migrating virtual machines

The migration step consists of three stages:

1. Replicate
2. Test
3. Migrate

From the Azure portal, in the Azure Migrate blade, in the **Migration Goals | Windows, Linux and SQL Server** section, you can start a replication process. The following screenshot shows the portal view after you have added the Azure assessment tool:

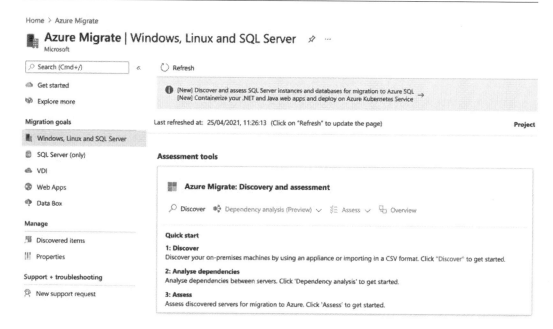

Figure 10.4 – Azure Migrate server assessment

You can choose to replicate up to 100 VMs at a time. Therefore, if you have more than 100 VMs to migrate, you will have to perform the process in batches.

Once replication has been completed (which can take some time depending on the size of your connection to Azure), you can perform a test migration. This runs a check on the VM, then starts it – but does not migrate it.

Once you are satisfied with any VMs you test, you can perform the actual migration. This is achieved by choosing the **Migration** option from the replicating machines view in the Azure portal. The process will prompt you to shut down the source (on-premises) VM and perform the final replication of any changed data. Once completed, an Azure VM is created and started.

Of course, most organizations will also need to migrate databases – and there are arguably many more options than just using, for example, SQL installed on a VM. For this reason, Azure provides additional tools specifically for this task.

Migrating databases

Like the VM migration service, you must create a database migration project in the **Azure Migrate** blade in the Azure portal to get started with the database migration service.

The first step is to download the **Data Migration Assessment (DMA)** tool. Unlike the VM migration tool that comes pre-installed on a VM image, the DMA tool is installed on an existing server that can connect to your SQL databases.

The process takes place on the VM. Once you launch the tool, perform the following steps:

1. Download and install the DMA tool on a server that can connect to your on-premises databases.

2. Run the DMA tool and create a new `Assessment` project.

3. Choose your **Source server type** from SQL Server or AWS RDS for SQL Server.

4. Choose your **Target server type** – the options are as follows:

    - **Azure SQL Database**

    - **Azure SQL Database Managed Instance**

    - **SQL Server on Azure Virtual Machines**

    - **SQL Server**

5. Depending on the **Target Server type**, you will see a list of report options; for example, if you choose **Azure SQL Database**, you will see the following options:

    - **Check database compatibility**: This option will report on any features you are currently using that are not supported in the target type that will prevent a migration.

    - **Check feature parity**: Report on unsupported features that won't block a migration but could prevent your database from functioning as expected.

6. Click **Next**, then click **Add sources**.

7. Enter your source database details and click **Connect**.

8. Click **Start Assessment**.

Depending on the options you chose, the report will show you a list of issues along with potential fixes – as you can see in the following screenshot:

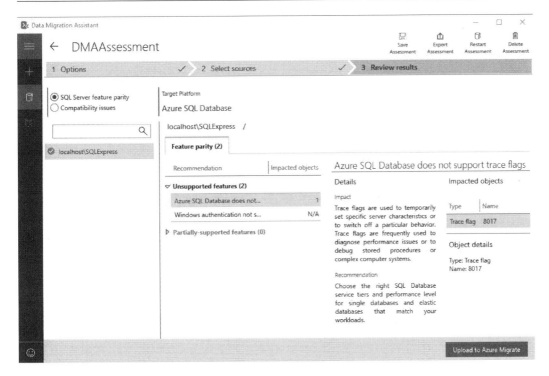

Figure 10.5 – Database Migration Assessment

As indicated in the target options, on-premises databases can be migrated to different destinations, including the following:

- A single Azure SQL Database

- Azure SQL Database Managed Instance

- SQL Server on an Azure VM

- Azure Database for MySQL

- Azure Database for PostgresSQL

- Azure Cosmos DB

You can save the assessment report or upload it to Azure for visibility in the portal. To perform the latter, simply click the **Upload to Azure Migrate** button, then **Connect**. You will be prompted to sign in and select a target subscription.

Once you have decided how you want to migrate your database, you can use the DMA tool to copy it.

You can perform either an offline migration – whereby the source server must be shut down for the migration – or an online migration that can be performed while the server is running. Regardless of which option you choose, several pre-requisite actions must take place:

- Create an Azure VNET in your subscription for connectivity back to your on-premises network.

- Configure the VNET Network Security Groups to allow ports `443`, `53`, `9354`, `445`, and `1200`.

- Open the VM Windows firewall to allow `1433` (single database instances) and `1434` named cases used on dynamic ports.

- Grant `CONTROL SERVER` permissions to the account used to connect to the source SQL server.

- Grant `CONTROL DATABASE` permissions to the account used to connect to the destination SQL database in Azure.

- Create a SQL database in Azure – this is the target that your database will be migrated to.

Once the preceding actions have been completed, create a new project in the DMA tool, but this time you do a **Migration** project.

You again select the source database, but this time you also choose the new SQL database you created in Azure. You can also choose to migrate either just the database schema or the schema and the data.

As you have seen, Microsoft provides a range of tools to assess and migrate VMs and databases into Azure. Once completed, you should monitor and optimize your workloads – again, there are several tools available to help with this.

Monitoring and optimizing your migration

Azure has several opportunities for enhancing performance and security that you may not have used with your on-premises systems. It is also possible that your existing servers were underutilized or even overutilized, which can impact costs.

Therefore, once migrated, you should monitor your workloads for performance trends, security enhancements, or cost optimizations.

To support these tasks, Azure provides the following tools:

- Azure Monitor

- Azure Cost Management

- Azure Advisor

Let's look at each one to see how they can help optimize your environment.

Azure Monitor

We cover Azure Monitor in more detail in *Chapter 15, Designing for Logging and Monitoring*; however, you can use Azure Monitor to record and report on performance metrics as a brief introduction. By analyzing trends over time, you can gain deep insights into a VM's usage, as you can see in the following example screenshot:

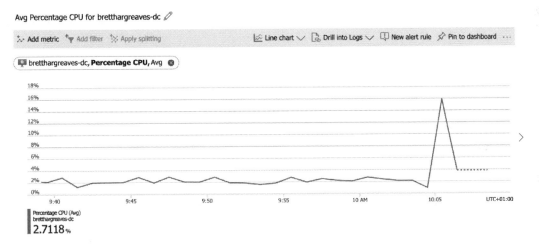

Figure 10.6 – Monitoring VM CPU performance

Suppose you see over some time that CPU, RAM, and disk I/O are all consistently under a low threshold (for example, never going above 10%). In that case, this can be a good indication that your VM is a higher specification than required. By reducing the size to a small version, you can substantially reduce costs.

Similarly, the inverse may be true – in other words, if you consistently see CPU and RAM over 80%, you may need to increase the size to gain performance.

Azure Cost Management

Azure Cost Management will show you Azure costs over time and also allows you to define views to help understand where your highest costs are. The following screenshot shows the default view displaying spend by service, location, and resource group:

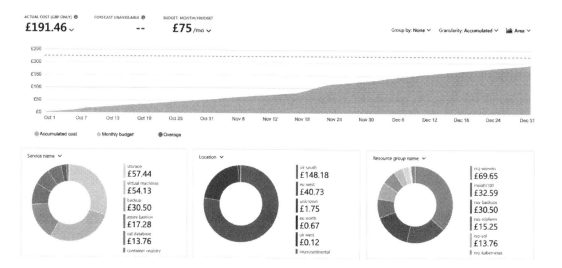

Figure 10.7 – Azure Cost Management

You can tailor this view as you see fit – filter or group by **Service Name**, **Metric**, **Meter**, **Service Tier**, and more. You can also visualize your costs through different chart types or even output the entire list in a table.

By closely monitoring costs and spending by resource over time, you gain a unique insight into your highest utilized, most expensive, and fastest-growing components.

For example, by drilling down through the different filter options, you might discover that a particular storage account is increasing in costs month on month, which in turn can help you investigate why and potentially reduce costs.

Azure Advisor

Perhaps the most useful tool, Azure Advisor makes suggestions for you based on your services' many different aspects.

Categorized by cost, security, reliability, operational excellence, and performance, you can quickly see a series of opportunities to optimize your service. Some of these recommendations include cost and performance options. As we discussed earlier, however, Azure Advisor performs this analysis automatically and continually.

The following screenshot shows an example Advisor overview page:

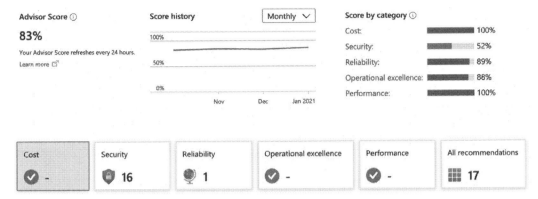

Figure 10.8 – Azure Advisor overview page

By clicking on a heading, you can drill down into each recommendation. Next, click on the recommendation itself, and you are given detailed information, and in some cases can click through wizards, to implement the suggestions.

As we can see in the following screenshot, recommendations are easy to view and show you how many resources they affect:

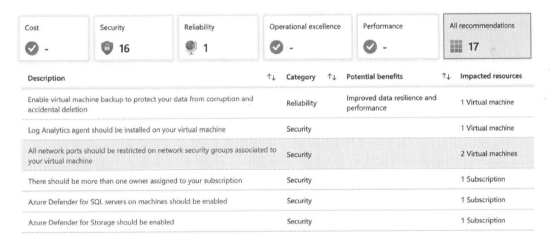

Figure 10.9 – Azure Advisor recommendation details

Through automated tools and your investigations, you can optimize your environment and ensure your services are running efficiently and reliably over time.

Summary

In this chapter, we have examined how to build a strategy for migrating workloads into Azure. We looked at the types of issues you must consider and the available tools for collating and documenting an as-is environment.

We then looked at what tools are available to perform VM and database migrations, including the different options available. Finally, we investigated the need to monitor and optimize post-migration, again looking at the other tools available to achieve this.

In the next chapter, we begin *Section 4, Applications and Databases*, and we start by comparing the different types of application components to choose from when building modern, cloud-native solutions.

Exam scenario

The solutions to the exam scenarios can be found on the Assessments page at the end of the book.

MegaCorp Inc. currently leases space in a third-party data center, but their current contract is coming to an end in 6 months. They have decided to migrate some of their workloads to Azure to reduce costs. However, any move must be completed before the contract end date.

Much of their server estate consists of web applications running on Windows Server 2018 with Internet Information Services server installed, file servers, and Windows SQL servers.

Some websites run on web server farms – multiple web servers built as load-balanced clusters running various websites.

Most of the SQL servers are running standard databases, but they are concerned some older databases may be using outdated features and procedures.

Develop a migration strategy, suggestion tooling, and highlight any potential issues they might encounter.

Further reading

For more information on topics covered in this chapter, refer to the following:

- Azure Migrate: `https://docs.microsoft.com/en-us/azure/migrate/migrate-overview`

- Azure Database Migration Service: `https://docs.microsoft.com/en-us/azure/dms/dms-overview`

- Azure TCO Calculator: `https://azure.microsoft.com/pricing/tco/calculator`

- Azure Advisor: `https://azure.microsoft.com/services/advisor/`

- Azure Service Map: `https://docs.microsoft.com/en-us/azure/azure-monitor/insights/service-map`

Section 4: Applications and Databases

This section covers how to build solutions using Platform as a Service (PaaS) components and when each is best suited for which scenario. It will also look at the two main database options in Azure, SQL and Cosmos DB.

The following chapters will be covered under this section:

- *Chapter 11, Comparing Application Components*
- *Chapter 12, Creating Scalable and Secure Databases*
- *Chapter 13, Options for Data Integration*
- *Chapter 14, High Availability and Redundancy Concepts*

11
Comparing Application Components

In the previous chapter, we concluded *Section 3, Infrastructure and Storage Components,* by looking at how to migrate existing on-premises workloads into Azure and what different options were available from an architectural and strategic perspective. With this chapter, we begin *Section 4, Applications and Databases,* by looking at the different options and architectural patterns for building apps in Azure – from essential web apps to microservices and messaging.

In *Chapter 7, Designing Compute Solutions,* we looked at the different compute technologies in Azure that can be used to run our applications. This chapter will examine some of these again; however, we will see how they affect our overall solution's architectural choices.

By understanding how to combine web apps, API apps, microservices, and messaging patterns, we will learn how to structure our environment to enable secure, flexible, and cost-efficient solutions.

In particular, we will examine the following topics:

- Working with web applications
- Managing APIs with Azure API Gateway
- Understanding microservices
- Using messaging and events

Technical requirements

This chapter will use the Azure portal (`https://portal.azure.com`) for its examples.

Working with web applications

Azure web apps, or more generally **Azure app services**, are the first step in migrating from VM-based solutions toward a more flexible, fully managed offering.

They are essentially a managed **Internet Information Services (IIS)** offering for hosting web applications built with standard web technologies and programming languages.

App services are split into two types of apps – **web apps** and **API apps**. Web apps are UI-driven applications whereby the result of any backend programming language is to produce HTML and JavaScript that can be consumed by an end user through a browser.

API apps use the same technologies and programming language as web apps; however, they send pure data in either JSON or XML, rather than sending HTML to a web browser.

> **Note**
>
> XML and JSON are text-based formats for storing and sending information. Technically, XML is a self-describing markup language – this means you can define the data format of a field in a structured way. When used to transfer data between systems, it is commonly used in conjunction with **Simple Object Access Protocol (SOAP)**.
>
> JSON is a much simpler key-value notation, resulting in much smaller and arguably more comfortable files for reading. **Representational State Transfer (REST)** uses JSON to define a standard for also allowing systems to communicate. However, REST is easier to use and more flexible and has gradually become the more popular option.

Both web apps and API apps can be built using the following languages and frameworks: ASP.NET, ASP.NET Core, Java, Ruby, Node.js, PHP, and Python.

App services are linked to an **App Service plan**, which defines the amount of CPU and RAM that is available to your applications. You can also assign multiple app services to the same App Service plan to share resources. In some ways, an app service is analogous to a VM running various websites. Therefore, hosting multiple app services on a single App Service plan can be cost-efficient; however, you will have more applications competing for the same CPU and RAM resources.

App services can be easily scaled by defining CPU- and RAM-based thresholds so that as additional resources are required, additional instances of an app can be added. This is known as scaling out, unlike scaling up, which consists of adding more RAM and CPU to an existing instance.

Scaling out is far quicker and more flexible (scaling up is a manual process). However, your applications need to be written in such a way as to be aware that the end compute device serving your user may change from one request to the next. In essence, this means that applications should be built to be stateless, that is, to not store information on the backend needed to track the user interaction.

App services offer features over and above simple hosting and scaling, such as deployment slots.

Using deployment slots

A powerful feature of app services in Azure is deployment slots. When publishing updates to app services, you need to be confident that your latest changes do not break the existing running application.

Although you should always test changes in lower environments such as a development or test environment first, a final production deployment can still cause unexpected outages. For example, a connection string and configuration may be incorrectly configured.

Whereas development or test deployments of your systems are used to check for functional or user acceptance, final pre-check or staging environments can be used to confirm configuration elements before the final go-live.

The best way to confirm such elements would be to connect your deployment to live systems. Deployment slots allow us to perform this live check without overwriting our running production code.

When you create an additional deployment slot for an app service, one will be the production slot on your main URL and the others (you can create multiple) are given unique URLs. When publishing your code, you can then deploy to one of the non-production slots and then test your newly deployed code on the test URL.

The configuration is considered to release code, and therefore configurations such as database connection strings are the production versions. All your tests are consequently made against the production databases and other services. Once you have validated the deployment, you then swap the slots – the non-production slot becomes production, and the production slot becomes non-production. Therefore, the code you deployed now becomes the live code.

Another critical aspect to consider when building app service solutions is connecting to backend services such as databases or Azure storage accounts. To help with this, you can use a feature called VNet Integration and service endpoints.

App services VNet Integration

App services rarely work independently; they often need to store and retrieve data from storage services as files or database records. Azure storage accounts and Azure SQL databases are great options for these scenarios; however, the connection is made via public endpoints by default.

For some organizations, this is not acceptable, and those services need to be locked down to only allow access from specific services, such as your frontend app service. Many Azure components supporting service endpoints services are direct communication lines between services using the Azure internal backbone instead of public endpoints.

This is achieved in the backend storage component by authorizing specific VNets and subnets in the firewalls view of the service you wish to protect, as we can see in the following example for securing a storage account:

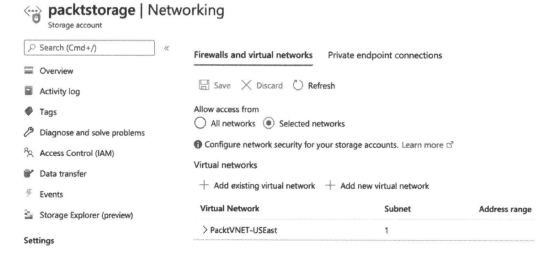

Figure 11.1 – Securing a storage account

This works for VMs that connect natively to VNets, but for app services, you must enable VNet Integration. VNet Integration allows you to connect your app service to a VNet in your subscription, and doing so will let you take advantage of VNet services.

VNet services offer the following benefits:

- **Service endpoints**: Allow secure, direct communication between Azure services.

- **Network security groups**: Block and allow specific *outbound* communications from your deployed apps.

- **User-defined routes**: Force *outbound* traffic via specified routes, for example, an Azure Firewall appliance.

By integrating your app services with VNets, you gain greater security and control, which in turn can help you adhere to stricter organization requirements.

We mentioned earlier that app services cover both web apps and API apps. In the next section, we will look into more details about API apps.

Managing APIs with Azure API Gateway

When building cloud solutions and web applications, it is common to use APIs – specific types of apps that only return data in JSON or XML. This data is then used by a consuming application, a desktop application, a mobile application, or even a website.

APIs can be used internally or to expose your data to external customers or partners.

An example would be a distribution organization that supplies products to resellers, and therefore needs to provide details of those products and up-to-date pricing and stock levels.

The reseller would use that feed on their website or mobile app to display products to their customers.

In such a scenario, the distribution company can expose its products via an API. However, they need to ensure they only provide details to registered resellers, and each reseller may have their own pricing bands.

The data provider will also use other APIs for internal use only. Each system that provides all these APIs may be hosted across platforms and may even be built using different technologies and formats.

Azure API Gateway is a service that helps address all these issues and more. Azure API Gateway provides a façade that can front multiple APIs and expose them as a single service or set of APIs, as you can see in the following diagram:

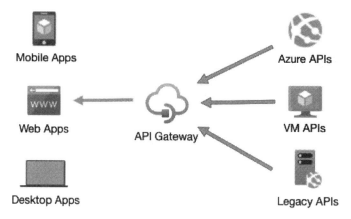

Figure 11.2 – Combining APIs behind Azure API Gateway

Azure API Gateway also provides the following features:

- **API documentation**: Automatically generates OpenAPI standards documentation that enables consuming developers to understand how to use your APIs.

- **Rate limiting**: Controls how much data can be retrieved in any one call. This is useful if a consumer could inadvertently request large amounts of data.

- **Health monitoring**: Logs and searches for issues generated by your APIs.

- **Format exchange**: APIs can expose data in a range of formats, for example, XML or CSV. Azure API Gateway can convert these to JSON to provide a consistent data format.

- **Combine APIs**: APIs can be combined from multiple locations into a single set.

- **Analytics**: Gains insights into your APIs as they are consumed to see how often they are being used and their source systems.

- **Security**: Wraps security around your APIs using OAuth 2.0 and Azure **Active Directory** (**AD**) integration.

When creating an API gateway and choosing pricing plans, however, each plan supports a different set of features:

- **Developer**: Primarily used for development and evaluation purposes. The Developer plan supports most features except for multi-region deployment. It has no **Service Level Agreement** (**SLA**) and is restricted to 500 requests a second.

- **Basic**: Entry-level but production use cases. 99.9% SLA and low scalability. It supports 1,000 requests per second but doesn't offer VNet Integration, Azure AD integration, or multi-region deployments.

- **Standard**: Standard use with a 99.9% SLA and supports 2,500 requests per second. Standard is easier to scale but doesn't support VNets or multi-region deployments, although it does offer Azure AD integration for identity support.

- **Premium**: High-volume production use with a 99.95% SLA. It supports 4,000 requests per second, is scalable, and supports all features such as multi-region deployments.

- **Consumption**: A serverless offering whereby there are no limits imposed and you pay for what you use (for example, per million calls). Consumption plans are ideal for lightweight or intermittent use and offer 99.95% SLA. However, it does not support Azure AD integration, VNet Integration, or multi-region deployments.

As you can see, choosing the correct pricing tier depends on the features you need to access. For example, if you have APIs running on internal VNets or enforce internal communication over VNets, only the Premium and Developer plans support this.

Once you have decided which plan will meet your needs, you must consider how to secure your APIs. The first step in this process is to implement policies.

Using API policies

Azure API Management policies allow you to change how your APIs function and behave. Typical examples include rate-limiting responses, converting one format to another, such as XML to JSON, or even modifying the contents of the data returned.

Azure API Management offers a range of built-in policies, or you can create custom ones.

The following are some examples of use cases and policies:

- Restrict who can access your APIs by specifying allowed IP ranges (whitelisting) or denied IP ranges (blacklisting).

- Set rate limits on calls to prevent too much data from being sent in one call, or limit how many times an API can be called. This can help protect you from hackers or consumers who have called the API incorrectly.

- Check HTTP headers to ensure they contain specific values. For example, ensure all requests include the authorization header.

- Create mock responses. Ideal for testing, an API policy can prevent the call from returning real data and supply mock data instead.

- Transform data from XML to JSON, which is especially useful if you expose older XML APIs and need a consistent data format returned to your consumers.

- Override data in the HTTP headers to add or remove information. A standard security requirement is to not expose data in the HTTP header that might provide hackers with the information they can use, such as the **X-Powered-By** or **Server** headers.

- Override content data. Suppose an API returns content you don't want it to, rather than modifying the API (which may need to supply the data for internal systems). In that case, you can overwrite that information using a find-and-replace statement.

- Allow **Cross-Origin Resource Sharing** (**CORS**). You can use a policy to override an API's native CORS ability by adding the allow origins and allowing HTTP header methods.

Using API policies is a powerful tool for many transformations and security-related tasks without updating the source APIs, modifying behavior for internal or external calls only.

When exposing your APIs to consumers, you may want to control who has access. This control is sometimes required when developing the API itself. However, if you have multiple APIs, or if those APIs were initially built for internal use, access control mechanisms may not have been built into them.

Using Azure API Gateway, you can restrict access to all your APIs without writing any additional code. When securing APIs, you have three options – subscription keys, client certificates, or authentication.

Securing your APIs with subscription keys

By default, when you import APIs into an Azure API gateway, subscription keys are required. A subscription key is an alpha-numeric key generated for you and must be supplied with every request.

Subscription keys can be scoped to all APIs, a single API, or a product, which is a collection of one or more APIs.

When your consumers request one of your APIs, the key must then be included in a header as an `Ocp-Apim-Subscription-Key` key or as part of a query string using the `subscription-key` parameter. Both the key and parameter names can be changed if required.

Each subscription has two keys – a primary and a secondary key. Having two keys helps prevent downtime if you need to regenerate a key. For example, you could regenerate the secondary key and transition consumers over to the new key before regenerating the primary.

Client certificates

You can configure the Azure API gateway so that it requires a certificate when making calls. Whereas subscription keys are generated by you and can be quickly supplied, certificates provide greater security. However, the certificate must be generated by a certificate authority and securely provided to your consumers. But when security and control are of the utmost importance, this administrative overhead is worth the effort.

OAuth 2.0 and OpenID Connect

Azure API Gateway also supports user authentication flows. You can choose to define either an OAuth 2.0 or OpenID Connect identity provider. These providers could be external providers such as Google, Facebook, or LinkedIn, or you can use Azure AD integration (depending on the pricing tier you chose).

By setting up authentication flows, you can quickly and easily wrap and protect your APIs, making it possible not just to restrict who can access the APIs but also what actions they can perform once they gain access.

Another form of protection for your APIs can be achieved at the network level using VNet Integration.

VNet Integration

The Developer and Premium service plans support VNet Integration, wherein you can choose to connect it to internal VNets. With VNet Integration, you can also decide whether the gateway will be internal only or externally accessible as well.

Making the gateway externally accessible with VNet Integration means you can expose any APIs running on a VNet, for example, VMs that only have internal IP addresses.

Alternatively, using VNet Integration with internal-only connectivity allows you to expose natively external services, such as web apps and functions, to your internal network. This is an excellent way of securing internal access when you want to completely block off external access to your APIs but make use of **PaaS** and serverless components such as Azure app services and Azure Functions. The following diagram shows an example of how this might look:

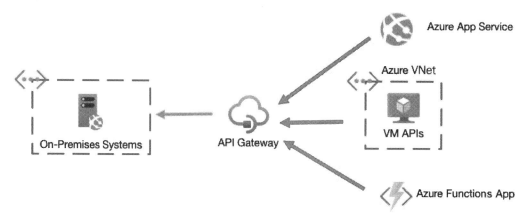

Figure 11.3 – Using Azure API Gateway to provide internal connectivity to app services

When connecting to services in the same region, you use regional VNet Integration with a dedicated subnet for the services you are attaching. If you need to connect to a service in another region, or if you need to integrate with a classic VNet, then you must use an Azure VNet gateway – this is known as gateway-required VNet Integration.

Finally, it is possible to combine the security of forcing internal connectivity and exposing services to the public network using an application gateway. Because the application gateway includes a web application firewall, you get greater security and more control. You can also use the application gateway with the API gateway to expose some APIs internally and externally, as shown in the following diagram:

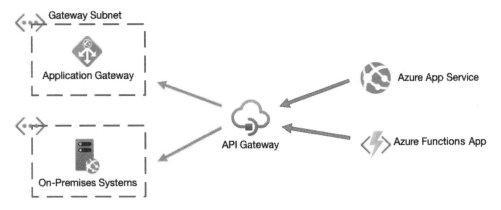

Figure 11.4 – Using an application gateway with an API gateway

Using APIs in your solutions is a common method for exposing data to various application types, from desktop apps to mobile or web apps. A typical pattern is to build those APIs as smaller services that perform discrete tasks – these are known as microservices.

Understanding microservices

One of the goals of cloud computing is to provide cost-effective solutions that are dynamic and reliable. In *Chapter 7, Designing Compute Solutions*, we looked at several different components: containers, Kubernetes, Azure Functions, and Logic Apps.

One of the key differences between these services and more traditional compute options, such as VMs, is the ability to scale the resources they use up and down, dynamically – that is, in response to demand.

This scaling ability is most effectively used when combined with the microservice pattern of development. Understanding microservices helps to review the problems associated with applications that *don't* use them.

A typical solution comprises a user interface, a backend database or storage mechanism, and some business logic in between. Each of these components has to run on some form of computer, which could be a VM. Using N-tier architectures, we break these components up so that each tier can run on its own VM, which allows us to configure those VMs according to the demand placed on them. For example, the user interface may not need much power at all, the business tier may need lots of CPU to perform complex calculations, and the storage may want more RAM to better cache data.

However, even with N-tier, the relevant process is still running on one or more VMs with a static amount of RAM and CPU configured. The application may have varying requirements depending on how much it is being used at any given moment. For example, an internal business application will have high usage during working hours but not outside working hours.

Hosting applications must accommodate the peak usage times, meaning that the compute and RAM resources are wasted during off-peak times.

Microservices seek to address this problem by using technologies that can dynamically expand and contract the resources they need in response to the demand being placed on them.

To help achieve this, hosting technology should expand *out* rather than *up*. This means that more copies of the instance running the service should be created, rather than adding more RAM and CPU to an individual service.

To get the most significant benefit from this pattern and ensure that the most efficient number of resources are used at any one time, each instance needs to use as few resources as possible. In other words, rather than a service that requires a *minimum* of two CPUs and 4 GB of RAM, services should seek to use a fraction of CPU and memory in the KB range. In this way, resources can be managed in a more granular, more efficient, and cost-effective manner.

If processes are to use as few resources as possible, they must be smaller, which means the functions they perform should be discrete and specific.

Thus, microservice architectures ensure individual services are built to be small and fast. The minimum resources can be allocated where required when needed, as depicted in the following diagram:

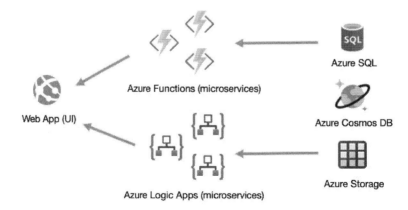

Figure 11.5 – Microservice-based architecture example

In Azure, there are many options for helping with this, and in *Chapter 7, Designing Compute Solutions*, we saw how containerization and orchestration technologies could help with this. However, they still require a minimal amount of compute to be running at all times.

Serverless technologies, such as Azure Functions and Azure Logic Apps, provide the most flexible and cost-effective options as they can be billed on a per-execution basis, meaning you only ever pay for the service when it is running.

From an architectural perspective, and for the AZ-304 exam, the key point is that serverless components such as Azure Functions and Logic Apps are ideally suited to microservice solutions as they automatically scale in response to demand; however, to get the most benefit out of it, code must be built with the microservice pattern in mind.

Another feature of Azure Logic Apps and Azure Functions is that they are event-driven, meaning that the logic is called in demand to events happening elsewhere – either in response to a user clicking a button or another service triggering them. The Azure platform uses events throughout many of its components, allowing you to set triggers for various actions on many services.

For example, when a file is uploaded to a Blob storage container, it triggers an event that can be hooked into using Azure Functions or Logic Apps to perform another action. This event-driven nature, combined with the fact that actions should be fast and responsive, leads to other best-employed patterns, such as messaging and events.

Using messaging and events

Microservice components need to send information between each other; however, traditionally, the sender would wait for a reply from the recipient before continuing. An example would be an application that accepts user input and returns a result.

This behavior can cause blocking as one component depends on another, and the more pieces you have that are responsible for discreet operations, the more they must communicate.

To prevent blocking, two alternate patterns are available – events and messaging. Both mechanisms work at a basic level in the same way – they inform other components, either directly or indirectly, but they don't wait for a reply.

Events are notifications to other system components that have happened, but they do not contain any data, although they may include a reference. When events are triggered, they don't expect another component to necessarily do something. It is the job of a consuming component to decide what actions must be taken in response.

A typical example of this scenario is that of an image being uploaded to Blob storage. The upload event is triggered, and an Azure function may be configured to wait for that event. When the event happens, the Azure function reads the newly uploaded image, performs an image resize, and stores the new image back in the storage account. The key is that the event's sender – the storage account – is not dependent on the Azure function doing anything.

Messaging works slightly differently. With messaging, a component will write data to a queue in a particular format. A consumer will be monitoring that queue, and when an item arrives, it will perform an action with that data and then remove it from the queue. An example is an email service. A user enters text into a box and clicks send, and the user interface component then sends that data to an email queue. A separate email service component then reads the data and acts by sending the email. In this scenario, the user interface does not expect a response to say the message has been sent; it relies on a consumer to process it.

Messaging and events often work together. When a message is written to a queue, the queue may trigger an event to notify a consumer to go and read the queue.

Because the sender doesn't wait for a response, you often need the consumer to trigger another event or write another message once it has been completed that responds. In the example of a user sending an email, the email service triggering an email sends an event that the user interface is monitoring to update the user of success or failure.

Azure provides a series of components to help with both messaging and events, and for the AZ-304 exam, you must know when to use which component. First, we shall look at two options for triggering events – Azure Event Grid and Azure Event Hubs.

Azure Event Grid

When one component needs to inform another component that an event has happened, you need a mechanism to route that information from the sender to the consumer. Azure Event Grid provides this routing mechanism by routing events from an event source (the sender) to an event handler (the consumer), as we can see in the following diagram:

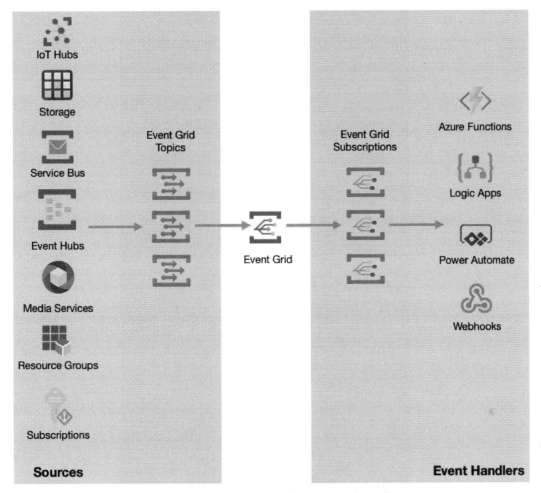

Figure 11.6 – Azure Event Grid sources and handlers

The following Azure components can all be event sources for Event Grid:

- **Subscriptions and resource groups**: Events are created within subscriptions and resource groups whenever an operation occurs within Azure, such as creating a VM, starting and stopping a VM, or deleting a VM.

- **Azure Container Registry**: When images are uploaded, changed, or removed, an event is triggered.

- **Storage**: When data is uploaded, changed, or removed in blobs, files, tables, and queues, an event is triggered.

- **Media Services**: Specific events for processing video and image media, such as job started or job completed.

- **Service Bus**: A messaging component can trigger events to inform subscribers that a message has been written to its queue.

- **IoT Hub**: Used to inform other Azure components about communication events occurring on IoT devices.

- **Event Hubs**: Used for ingesting large amounts of data.

- **Customer events**: Build custom events using the Azure SDK or REST API in the language of your choice.

An event is a lightweight JSON message, no larger than 64 KB in size, containing information about the occasion. The message always adheres to the following format:

```
[
  {
    "topic": string,
    "subject": string,
    "id": string,
    "eventType": string,
    "eventTime": string,
    "data":{
      object-unique-to-each-publisher
    },
    "dataVersion": string,
    "metadataVersion": string
  }
]
```

The details for each field are as follows:

Field	Details
topic	The source of the event (for example, `Microsoft.storage`).
subject	Details of the event. For example, for storage, this might be a filename and path.
id	Unique identifier for the event.
eventType	Registered event type for the source. For example, for storage, this might be `BlobCreated` or `BlobDeleted`.
eventTime	The time at which the event triggered.
data	Specific information about the event, which is unique to each source.
dataVersion	Schema version of the preceding `data` field.
metadataVersion	Schema version of the event's top-level properties.

Event Grid uses a publish and subscription mechanism. When a source triggers an event, it is defined in a topic. Consider a topic as a grouping for events, and your application may have one or more topics depending on the complexity and size.

There are two types of topics in Azure: system topics and custom topics. System topics are built into Azure sources, whereas custom topics are those you can build yourself.

Once a source has published an event to a topic, a consumer must subscribe to that event; in other words, it informs Event Grid that it wishes to be notified when events occur. The consumer then uses one or more event handlers that will perform some action.

Event handlers can be one or more of the following components in Azure:

- Azure Functions

- Webhooks

- Azure Logic Apps

- Microsoft Power Automate

We covered how to choose the best service from the preceding list in *Chapter 7, Designing Compute Solutions.*

Azure Event Grid is a simple mechanism for connecting sources to subscribers, and you can configure as many subscribers to an event as you need. Event Grid is a serverless product and, as such, is reliable, scalable, and cost-effective as you only pay for events as you transmit them.

For more advanced scenarios, for example, when you expect to deal with large volumes of events, Azure Event Hubs provides an intermediary for Event Grid.

Event Hubs

Event Hubs is optimized for high volumes and throughput of events and data, for example, when using hundreds of IoT devices that may continually send high volumes of data.

Event Hubs groups incoming data into partitions that buffer the information, ensuring that subscribers can keep up with the traffic. Each partition can also have its own distinct set of subscribers, which is useful for scaling out work among multiple consumers.

Event Hubs also supports authentication and saves the data stream to Azure Data Lake or Blob storage.

We mentioned earlier that events and messaging are best used together, so next, we will examine message queues in Azure Queue Storage and Service Bus.

Storage queues

Azure Storage contains a simple message queue mechanism called storage queues. Queues act as an intermediary for different system components to communicate with each other. Rather than one component talking directly to another, which would mean both ends need to be free and available, sending data to a queue allows the different components to work on tasks as they become free without impacting the broader system. In other words, using queues helps solution components become *independent* of each other.

Azure Storage Queues are the most straightforward option and offer a **First In First Out (FIFO)** queuing system. However, the actual order of messages is not guaranteed.

Azure components needing to send a message write the messages to a queue, and consumers pick up the messages from the queue one at a time to process them, as in the following example:

Figure 11.7 – Azure storage queues

Azure Storage Queues also provide an audit trail, and the queue messages can be up to 64 KB in size, but you can store millions of messages.

Azure Service Bus

Azure Service Bus is an enterprise-scale message queuing mechanism that enables you to use it either as a straightforward queuing mechanism or as a topic and subscriber mechanism. The publish/subscribe pattern allows multiple consumers rather than a single consumer, which is the case with a single queue. Filters can also be set on the subscriptions, enabling different consumers to process various topics.

For example, an order management system may need orders to be processed by different systems based on the product type or location. Orders for the US would be processed by a US-based Azure function, whereas orders bound for Europe would be processed by a European-based function, as in the following diagram:

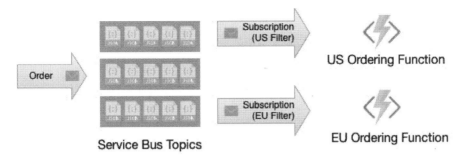

Figure 11.8 – Service Bus topics and subscriptions

The first question to consider when choosing between these options is whether to use Storage Queues or Service Bus queues. The following table can help with this:

Comparison Criteria	Storage Queues	Service Bus Queues
Ordering guarantee	No	Yes – FIFO
Delivery guarantee	At least once	At least once At most once
Message size	Up to 64 KB	64 KB–256 KB, 1 MB for Premium tier
Queue size	Only limited by the size of the storage account	Up to 80 GB
Scheduled delivery	Yes	Yes
Automatic dead lettering	No	Yes
Message auto-forwarding	No	Yes
Message groups	No	Yes
Duplicate detection	No	Yes

Two of the critical decisions are around ordering guarantee and delivery guarantee. A typical exam question is where you're asked to ensure the FIFO pattern is used for message delivery. For this, you need to use Service Bus, and also, to enforce this, you need to enable sessions – which is one of the options when creating queues or subscriptions to a topic.

It's also useful to remember that sessions require the Standard pricing tier or above; Basic does *not* support them.

You also need to consider that Service Bus only supports message queues of up to 80 GB compared to storage queues, which are only limited by the storage account's capacity.

Other reasons to use Service Bus queues over Storage Queues are when you want to ensure FIFO delivery and when you need automatic de-duplication of messages.

The next decision to make is whether to use simple queues or topics and subscriptions. You should choose queues when you want to ensure *one* consumer only consumes each message. Conversely, select a topic when you want multiple consumers to read the messages or when you need to apply filtering.

Through the correct use of Event Grid, Event Hubs, Storage Queues, and Service Bus, you can architect robust applications whose components are independent of each other and therefore more reliable and robust.

Summary

In this chapter, we revisited some of the Azure native compute options and introduced queues, Service Bus, and API gateways, and how these components can be used in modern solutions that follow development patterns such as microservices, messaging, and events.

We looked at how you can use deployment slots to validate application updates before going live and how to use VNet Integration to securely connect backend data services such as storage accounts.

We also examined how you can collate and secure both new and existing API services behind an API gateway and modify and control the access to and the response from your APIs without needing to make any code changes.

Finally, we looked at microservices and messaging patterns to create flexible, cost-efficient, and independent solutions that scale automatically in response to user demand.

In the next chapter, we will look at the options when using databases – both SQL and NoSQL options – and when to choose one over the other.

Exam scenario

MegaCorp is re-developing an order management tool for their global operations. The solution will be built on Azure with teams in Europe, the US, and India.

Customers will place orders through a global website but they will be processed in the closest geographical region.

The website will need a web frontend that will make calls to APIs to retrieve the product data and place orders.

As this is a new system, hosting costs need to be kept at a minimum, but with the ability to scale automatically as demand increases. The business wishes to ensure that modern development techniques are used and that all the components are resilient and secure.

The site will also be developed iteratively, with updates rolled out once a month, and the business needs to ensure that those updates do not disrupt live services.

Design an architecture that meets the business needs.

Further reading

You can check out the following links for more information about the topics that were covered in this chapter:

- **Azure web app deployment slots**: `https://docs.microsoft.com/en-us/azure/app-service/deploy-staging-slots`

- **Azure Service Bus**: `https://docs.microsoft.com/en-us/azure/service-bus-messaging/service-bus-messaging-overview`

- **Azure Storage Queues**: `https://docs.microsoft.com/en-us/azure/storage/queues/storage-queues-introduction`

- **Azure Event Grid**: `https://docs.microsoft.com/en-us/azure/event-grid/overview`

- **Azure Event Hubs**: `https://docs.microsoft.com/en-us/azure/event-hubs/event-hubs-about`

12
Creating Scalable and Secure Databases

In the previous chapter, we began *Section 4, Applications and Databases*, by looking at web-based application components in Azure and the different architectural patterns that can be leveraged to create resilient and performant applications.

Nearly all applications use a database to hold information, and therefore this chapter looks at the data tier. We start by examining the two main database options in Azure— **Azure Structured Query Language (Azure SQL)** and Azure Cosmos DB. We then progress into the different pricing and service tiers available for each service and look at how these impact scalability and resilience.

Finally, we look at how to secure database services through encryption and the different areas where this can be applied.

With this in mind, this chapter covers the following four topics:

- Selecting a database platform
- Understanding database service tiers
- Designing scalable databases
- Securing databases with encryption

Technical requirements

This chapter will use the Azure portal (`https://portal.azure.com`) for examples throughout.

Selecting a database platform

Within Azure, there are two main types of database—Azure Cosmos DB and Azure SQL. There are also several different kinds of SQL databases—Azure SQL Database, Azure SQL Managed Instance, or even traditional Microsoft SQL running on a **virtual machine** (**VM**). In this section, however, we will consider why you might choose Cosmos DB over SQL Server.

With the choice between Cosmos DB and SQL and a choice between relational SQL databases and hierarchical NoSQL databases, we need to understand the differences between them. We will start with SQL.

Understanding SQL databases

SQL databases are built around the concept of tables, and within each table, you would have rows of data split into cells. Each cell would contain an individual piece of data within a record, and each row would be an entire record.

SQL databases have a **schema** that lays out your data structure in tables, columns, and rows. The schema must be defined *before* you can enter data into it. If you want to store a customer record containing a name and address, you first need to create a table with each of the columns defined for each data type, such as the first name, address line, city, country, and so on.

Traditionally, SQL tables are built as **relational**—this means that rather than having extensive records containing all the information, you split the records into multiple tables and then join them as part of a query. For example, you could store core personal information, such as first and last name, in one table but the address details in another table, with a link in each record to join the related tables together.

There are many reasons why databases used a relational structure, one being because of the computing resources available. Years ago, computer components were costly, and the technology available meant computers only had a limited amount of **random-access memory (RAM)**, **central processing units (CPUs)**, and storage. This meant that creating tables with lots of columns caused them to become slow and difficult to manage. Large records therefore needed to be broken down into smaller schemas and linked together.

Another useful facet of relational data is the ability to create constraints on the data you enter. Elements that need to be consistent across records—for example, a *category*—would be defined in a separate table, with a category ID link in the person record rather than the category itself. When users needed to create a record that uses a category, they would select the category from the category table's values. The category would then be stored in the *parent* record as a link to the record's ID in the category table.

The following screenshot shows an example of how this might look:

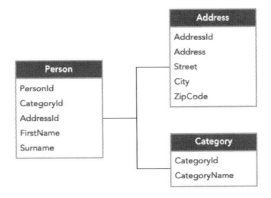

Example Combined Query

Person.PersonId	Person.FirstName	Person.Surname	Category.Name	Address.Street	Address.City
100	Brett	Hargreaves	Active	999 Letsbe Avenue	London

Figure 12.1 – Example relational table

Another benefit of a relational table is that any change to a category name would automatically be reflected across all parent records. You only need to update the data in the category table.

Relational tables can also have **one-to-many relationships**—this means that rather than linking a single address record to a person, you can link multiple address records. This could be used to store separate addresses for billing and shipping, for example.

Some downsides to SQL are that it requires a lot of planning upfront because you must define the schema before entering data. Any changes to that structure can then be challenging to manage, especially when tables are related and you need to change those relationships. Querying across tables can result in very complex queries, which, as well as being tricky to write, results in them running slower.

As computing power became more powerful and cheaper, some of the reasoning for using relational tables became not just redundant but also constraining. This became especially true for reporting. Because complex relational structures are slow to query but great for management, many systems started to move data between the core database and a second reporting database. The reporting database's structure is simplified and therefore optimized for querying, but there is additional overhead in the movement of data between them. This process is often performed once or twice a day, meaning there would be a lag between the live data and the ability to report on it.

Despite these issues, SQL is still extremely popular and sometimes the best choice, depending on your requirements. However, in recent years, new technology has emerged—NoSQL.

NoSQL databases

NoSQL databases, as the name suggests, do not follow relational patterns. NoSQL databases store data as **JavaScript Object Notation (JSON)** documents, which are *hierarchical* in structure. This means that related information such as an address can be stored with the primary record but *embedded* as a child object. Embedding data can also be used for multiple related records; for example, multiple addresses can be stored within the primary record.

With this in mind, a typical NoSQL JSON document might look like this:

```
{
    "id": "001",
    "firstName": "Brett",
    "surname": "Hargreaves",
    "category": "Active",
    "addresses": [
        {
            "type": "billing",
            "street": "999 Letsbe Avenue",
            "city": "London"
        },
```

```
        {
            "type": "shipping",
            "street": "20 Docklands Road",
            "city": "London"
        }
    ]
}
```

NoSQL databases can perform much faster than their SQL counterparts for specific scenarios, manage far greater volumes of data, and are considerably more scalable.

Another benefit is that you can easily mix records of completely different schemas.

For example, a container, which is synonymous to a table in SQL parlance, might contain the following records—and this would be perfectly valid:

```
[
    {
        "id": "001",
        "firstName": "Brett",
        "Surname": "Hargreaves",
        "category": "Active",
    },
    {
        "id": "002",
        "title": "Microsoft Azure Architect Design - AZ-304
    Certification & Beyond",
        "publisher": "Packt Publishing",
    }
]
```

The mixing of completely different record types, as in the prior example, would not be recommended. But it highlights the ability to have a flexible schema, which is immensely powerful, especially for applications built in an Agile manner.

Because a data schema in NoSQL does not need to be defined upfront, systems can be built interactively over time, adding to the data structure more easily.

Another benefit of a flexible schema is that your applications can be more dynamic. For example, in a **Human Resources** (**HR**) system that stores employee data, any requirement to add new fields to the employee record would typically need to be performed by a developer. The developer would need to change the database schema and update their code to take this change into account.

With a NoSQL schema, the system could be designed so that the data structure itself could be defined as a record. As new fields are required, the schema is updated within the definition record, and that additional piece of information starts getting stored in the primary collection. No redevelopment or database schema changes are required, and no downtime is necessary to update the system.

Flexibility can, of course, have its downside too. More programming effort is required to enforce data integrity, ensuring only certain types of data can be added.

With this in mind, SQL can be a better choice over NoSQL if a well-defined structure is essential or if a mistake that led to inconsistent data might be dangerous.

SQL can also be faster for multi-record updates—for example, if you must regularly update rows in large batches.

Now that we understand SQL and NoSQL, we will look in more detail at the differences between Azure SQL and Cosmos DB.

Understanding database service tiers

Usage patterns and requirements for any type of database vary greatly depending on the application that uses them. In an on-premises scenario, you would need to calculate the optimum amount of RAM, CPU cores, and disk configurations to best optimize a database or set of databases for any given solution.

In Azure, unless you opt for running SQL on a VM, many of these configuration details are abstracted away, and instead you must choose a pricing model and a service tier.

Because Cosmos DB and Azure SQL Database are different platforms, the configuration options are also different. Therefore, the options for each must be considered separately. We will start by understanding Azure SQL pricing tiers.

SQL Database tiers

Azure SQL has the most options available; you must decide between a pricing model, a service tier, and even different SQL products.

You essentially have two options when it comes to choosing a **Platform-as-a-Service (PaaS)** SQL product. When creating a SQL database in Azure, you must decide whether to use Azure SQL Database or Azure SQL Managed Instance.

Azure SQL Database options

Both options are fully managed versions of SQL, and by this we mean that the Azure platform takes care of availability, security patches, updates, and so on.

Azure SQL Database was introduced first and abstracted away more of the underlying infrastructure; it is much more granular in the options you can choose, especially when it comes to scaling. Because of this, some applications may not be compatible with Azure SQL Database.

Azure SQL Managed Instance offers less flexibility but offers near 100% compatibility with older, legacy databases. Some of the main differences between Azure SQL Managed Instance and Azure SQL Database are outlined here:

Feature	Azure SQL Database	Azure SQL Managed Instance
Backup command	No. Backup is controlled through the Azure management plane.	Yes.
Collation	Only `SQL_Latin1_General_CP1_CI_AS` is supported.	Supports other SQL collations and is set on initial creation.
Common Language Runtime (CLR) support	No	Yes
Cross-database queries	No (but can use elastic queries, which provide an alternative option).	Yes
Cross-database transactions	No	Yes
Database mail	No	Yes
Linked servers	No	Yes

Another core difference between Azure SQL Database and Azure SQL Managed Instance is how they integrate at the network level.

An Azure SQL Database is built and exposed via Azure's internal network backbone. Although through the firewalls and virtual networks blade you can restrict access via **virtual networks (VNets)**, the SQL Server component's **Internet Protocol (IP)** address is not exposed.

This can cause problems in some organizations if traffic needs to be carefully controlled or if you wish to connect on-premises systems to the Azure SQL Database via private endpoints. A PrivateLink IP can address this issue by connecting a separate internal network connection to the service. However, this service requires modifications to your corporate **Domain Name System (DNS)** zones, as you must override the public **Uniform Resource Locator (URL)** address to resolve to the internal IP address.

Azure SQL Managed Instances are built natively on a VNet within your subscription, and therefore internal connectivity is the default.

The next aspect to consider when choosing a SQL option is the pricing model. Azure SQL Database has three options: **virtual core (vCore)**, **Database Transaction Units (DTUs)**, and **serverless**.

SQL pricing models

The vCore pricing model is now the recommended option and allows you to choose the number of virtual CPU cores your database will use. You don't have any choice over the amount of RAM, but storage is separate from a pricing perspective—that is, you pay for the storage you use on top of the vCore costs.

The vCore pricing also enables an option for hybrid benefit, whereby you can save costs if you have an Enterprise license agreement with Microsoft for SQL Server.

Serverless pricing is similar to the vCore pricing. You choose the number of vCores to assign to your database; however, with serverless, the number of vCores are the minimum and maximum number of cores that will be used. With the serverless pricing model, your databases will automatically scale up and down in response to demand. An **Auto-pause** option will cause the database to stop using any compute resources if it has been idle for a set period.

This makes servers an excellent choice for development environments or scenarios where ad hoc access is required—for example, for data analytics solutions.

> **Important note**
> Because storage is billed separately to compute when your database pauses, with the serverless option you will still incur storage costs.

DTUs combine compute, storage, and **input/output (I/O)** resources into a single unit. DTU pricing offers much smaller and granular performance tiers; for example, the smallest **5 DTU** option costs around 5 **US Dollars (USD)** a month. The DTU pricing model is ideal for when you want a more straightforward, preconfigured option.

Serverless and DTU-based pricing are not available for Azure SQL Managed Instance.

The final choice when deciding on an Azure SQL offering is the service tier.

SQL service tiers

Azure SQL service tiers represent different levels of performance, scalability, and redundancy for SQL workloads. The different tiers are General Purpose/Standard, Hyperscale, and Business Critical, although this last option is called Premium when you opt for the DTU pricing model. The Hyperscale tier is only supported on Azure SQL Database, while Azure SQL Managed Instance only supports General and Business Critical tiers.

General tier

The General tier is the default model when creating an Azure SQL Database or Azure SQL Managed Instance and is designed for generic workloads or when cost economies are essential.

The General tier offers a 99.99% **service-level agreement** (**SLA**) and is resilient against failure within its region. It achieves this by separating the compute nodes and the underlying storage. At any one time, a single compute node runs a `sqlservr.exe` process with cached and transient data being stored on **solid-state drives** (**SSDs**) attached to that node. The database files themselves are held in Azure Blob storage, replicated within a region three times. Secondary compute nodes run on standby. In the event of either a system failure or a maintenance task being performed on the primary node, the process will move over to a standby node.

The following diagram shows this concept:

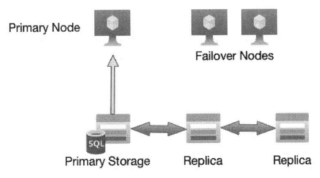

Figure 12.2 – Azure SQL General service tier redundancy

The General service tier supports up to 80 vCores and 4 **terabytes** (**TB**) of storage for Azure SQL Database, and 8 TB storage for Azure SQL Managed Instance. Latency is between 2 and 10 **milliseconds** (**ms**), and this is an essential value as for some applications, this variance may not be acceptable.

Hyperscale tier

The Hyperscale tier is the recommended tier for most production workloads. It offers up to 99.95% availability (when built with multiple database replicas) and is specifically designed to enable massive scale-out when required, supporting up to 100 TB in a single database.

Hyperscale also provides near-instantaneous backups and fast restores, which can be a crucial factor for solutions that demand a low **Recovery Time Objective** (**RTO**).

Latency is similar to General, at 2-10 ms. However, the **I/O operations per second** (**IOPS**) figure, which is the ability to read and write data, is between 500 and 204,800ms, whereas this figure for the General tier is between 500 and 20,000ms. These factors make the Hyperscale tier the best choice for most production workloads.

> **Information note**
>
> IOPS is a common measure for how fast a disk performs. Basically, the higher the IOPS, the faster the disk.

Due to the underlying architecture, both the Hyperscale and General tiers can suffer momentary outages or temporary performance issues if a primary node fails over to a standby node.

If your applications cannot stand any interruption to services or require lower latencies, then the next tier up should be considered.

Business Critical/Premium tier

The Business Critical tier (or Premium tier when using DTU-based pricing) provides the lowest latency and fastest IOPS of the available options.

Whereas the Hyperscale and General tiers use Azure Blob storage for the underlying data files, the Business Critical tier uses locally attached, high-speed SSDs. Built around SQL Always On technologies, the Business Critical tier uses a cluster of servers all connected to the same storage, enabling latencies of 1 to 2 ms and IOPS between 5,000 and 204,800ms. The clustered nature of the platform also offers even better availability, with an SLA of 99.995%.

The following diagram shows an example of the underlying architecture:

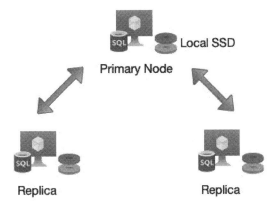

Figure 12.3 – Azure SQL Database Business Critical architecture

Azure SQL Database Business Critical is ideally suited for high-speed solutions such as analytics or applications that perform a lot of read and write operations. However, it is only available for Azure SQL Database; Azure SQL Managed Instance is not supported on this tier.

Azure SQL has the most significant number of options for pricing models, types, and tiers. Azure Cosmos DB, by comparison, has fewer choices.

Cosmos DB service tiers

Technically speaking, Cosmos DB does not have service tiers; all options are classed as a Premium offering, as this is a multi-model and globally distributed database service that is designed to horizontally scale and replicate your data to any number of Azure regions.

High availability and low latency make Cosmos DB most suitable for mobile applications, games, and applications that need to be globally distributed.

Cosmos DB does provide two pricing models, however—Provisioned and Serverless, and the key to understanding these models is to first understand how operations are charged in general.

Unlike Azure SQL, which can be billed on a vCore basis, Cosmos DB billing is based on a **Request Unit**, or **RU** for short. 1 RU is equivalent to performing an action such as a read operation on a 1 **kilobyte (KB)** item. Other operations, such as reading, writing, and querying, are also assigned a relative number of RUs based on the complexity and size of the operations.

Based on the preceding information, the size of the record you are working with has a direct impact on the number of RUs an operation consumes, as well as other factors such as the following:

- **Indexing**: Indexes on items would cost RUs, therefore if you chose not to index items, you would consume fewer RUs.

- **Property count**: The more properties your items have, the greater the cost.

- **Data consistency**: Cosmos DB offers different levels of data consistency, which is the time it takes for replicated data to be copied between one region and another. The highest levels of consistency, strong and bounded staleness, which ensures data is replicated as soon as possible, costs the most in terms of RUs.

- **Query complexity**: Complex queries cost more; simple queries cost less.

Now that we have an understanding of what an RU is, we can better understand the options between the two provisioning models.

Provisioned throughput

When creating a Cosmos DB account, if you choose the Provisioned pricing model, you can set the number of RUs that your storage account will use in increments of 100 RUs per second, with the minimum being 400 RUs.

By setting a defined number of RUs, you can precisely control and predict your costs; however, if your solution is continually using up your RUs, performance will be impacted. Note that setting 400 RUs means you are billed for that number of RUs, whether you use them or not.

When choosing the provisioned throughput model, you therefore have a few additional options to help manage performance and costs. The first is that RUs can be set at the database level or at the container level.

> **Tip**
> A Cosmos DB container is synonymous with a table. Although you can store different record types in a single container, separating out different record types is useful to help manage costs and performance.

Using the database level ensures all operations are equal in performance across all records and also ensures you don't incur additional costs as additional containers are added. However, if you set RU limits at the container level, you can vary the performance of different containers. For example, you could put the minimum RUs on some containers that you know are not used much, but have a higher RU rate for containers that do require more throughput, as in the following example:

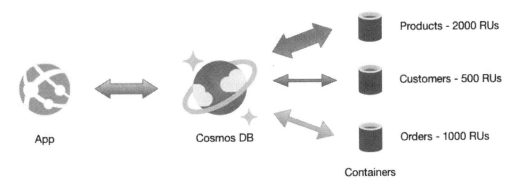

Figure 12.4 – Using different RU rates on other containers

As your application grows, you may need to increase the number of RUs your databases or containers consume. If this growth can be predicted, the standard provisioning described earlier is a good fit. However, if your applications experience variable usage through the month—for example, if certain days are busier than others—you have the option of provisioning your Cosmos DB account with autoscale.

With autoscale, you define an upper limit to the number of RUs your application can use, and your Cosmos DB account will automatically scale up to meet those needs. This option is ideal for critical or variable workloads; however, the minimum starting point is 4,000 RUs. Therefore, if your application is small, manual scaling may be preferable.

The other pricing option when provisioning Cosmos DB is Serverless.

Serverless throughput

In some ways, serverless throughput takes the autoscale option to the next level. With serverless, you do not define any minimum or maximum limits. Your Cosmos DB account will simply use the number of RUs required to perform at peak capacity.

This is an excellent option for applications that may spend long periods of time idle or at low usage but need to be able to burst performance on demand.

The downside of serverless is that you have no control over upper limits, which means that if your database is continually at high usage, your costs would be equally high and uncontrolled.

At the time of writing, serverless is in preview in some regions, and as such, there are certain limitations. One such constraint is that the maximum storage per container is 50 **gigabytes** (**GB**). When the service goes out on general release, this may be lifted.

Although both Cosmos DB and Azure SQL services can be easily scaled, you still need to factor in future growth and how that might happen. In the next section, we will look at the different options for scaling your database services.

Designing scalable databases

As applications grow, you need to be able to accommodate the need for more storage and more processing power to cope with demand. Sometimes, this growth is organic and happens naturally over time as your service becomes more popular.

For some applications, the need to rapidly scale out is known ahead of time—for example, with reporting solutions where you know you will be ingesting large amounts of data.

Within Azure, there are many options for achieving growth. However, the correct choice will, as always, depend on your precise requirements and solution architecture.

Both Cosmos DB and Azure SQL Database design for scale from the outset. As we saw in the previous section, the available tier is built around Azure storage with separate compute nodes. Upgrade to the Hyperscale tier, and your databases can grow up to 100 TB. However, in order to manage additional storage, you must also increase the compute capabilities.

The default options for scaling out compute entail manually increasing the number of vCores or DTUs to meet your needs. For some scenarios, this hands-on process may be adequate for your needs.

However, the scaling process for single databases or a managed instance is not immediate. Behind the scenes, moving from one vCore or DTU level to another, or when moving between tiers, involves copying your database to a new instance of a new size. Once the copy is complete, the compute node then flips over to the new service.

If you have multiple databases and you need databases to be able to scale automatically based on demand, you can instead opt for elastic pools.

With an elastic pool, you can define a number of **elastic DTUs (eDTUs)** or vCores, and then within that pool, you can set the maximum number of DTUs or vCores per database. Once set up, the resources within the pool will be automatically assigned to the database that requires the resources at any one time, as we can see in the following diagram:

Figure 12.5 – Azure SQL elastic pools

The preceding scenarios are only applicable to Azure SQL options; with Azure Cosmos DB, we have already seen that scalability is built in. Cosmos DB automatically replicates, and scales as required. This means Cosmos DB can guarantee low latency, high availability, and high performance anywhere in the world.

Another alternative to elastic pools is the serverless option, which is available for an Azure SQL single database or Cosmos DB. As we saw in the previous section, the serverless tier for Azure SQL Database allows you to define an upper vCore count and have Azure automatically scale on demand. Similarly, the Azure Cosmos DB serverless options also automatically scale on demand but lack the ability to control an upper limit.

Manual scaling or autoscaling is excellent for building solutions that can leverage the power of near-unlimited resources to enable your applications to grow over time (even if it's a short period of time) without needing to invest upfront in hardware.

Some solutions start big, and although Azure provides massive amounts of resources, there are times when you need to employ different architecture patterns to achieve performance at scale. Two such options are read replicas and database sharding.

Using read replicas

In *Chapter 14, High Availability and Redundancy Concepts*, we will look at how we achieve high availability—that is, the ability to automatically recover from a local, zone, or even regional outage, by creating replicas of your database.

When you use the Premium or Business Critical tiers with Azure SQL Server, a read-only replica is automatically created for you within the region, and you can optionally generate more replicas in other regions. Similarly, with the Hyperscale tier, you can also optionally create replicas of your databases.

As well as providing a failover facility, these replicas can also be used by your applications, which can then help spread the load across multiple servers when you only need to read data. This is known as **read scale-out** and, as already indicated, this is automatically enabled on the Premium and Business Critical tiers, while it is optional on the Hyperscale tier.

Within your application, you can configure a database connection string with `ApplicationIntent=ReadOnly`, which redirects the connection to the read-only replica rather than the read-write replica.

An example scenario that makes use of this pattern is where you have separate components of your application being responsible for day-to-day read/write interactions with your data and reporting. By configuring the reporting components to use the read-only replica, you remove the load from the read-write replica, as we can see in the following example:

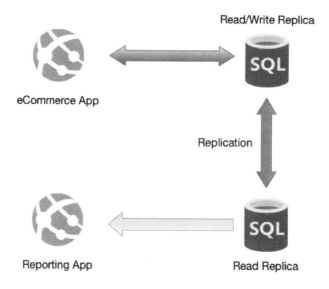

Figure 12.6 – Using read-only replicas to spread the load

Using **read scale-out** replicas is a great way to increase the performance of your applications but only works when your workloads can be easily separated into read and read/write operations; as such, the amount of scale-out you can achieve may be limited.

Another way to achieve scale that can, in theory, be near limitless is to use a pattern called database sharding.

Using database sharding

Database sharding is a process of splitting your data across one or more databases. For sharding to work, the schema of the databases is the same. However, you must find a way to partition the data that enables you to know which database houses which chunk of data; this is sometimes known as a sharding key.

There are two mechanisms that can be used to enable database sharding—application-controlled and database-controlled mechanisms.

With application-controlled sharding, your application is responsible for knowing which database contains which data. A typical example may be an application that provides services for multiple clients. Each client could have its own database on its own server, and the application would be responsible for mapping a particular client to each database, as we can see in the following example:

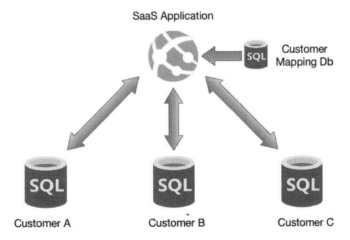

Figure 12.7 – Application-level sharding

With database-controlled sharding, the database platform itself manages the sharding of data between databases. In such situations, there needs to be a key that can be used for sharding the data. One such example could be to use a date key or a name key whereby different databases store data for different time periods; this would be especially useful in an archiving system or genealogy database where records have practical date fields, as in the following example:

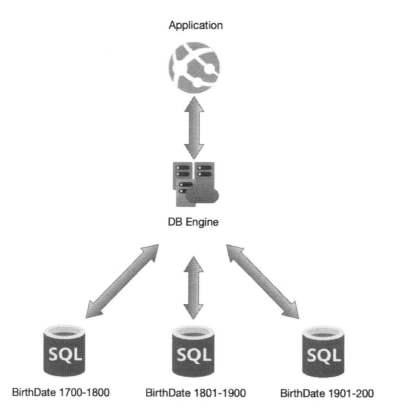

Figure 12.8 – Database-level sharding

Through a combination of database architecture patterns and choosing the correct service tiers, this will help you build a robust and performant database solution.

The next area to consider is security—specifically, encryption.

Securing databases with encryption

When storing data in a database, a key question many organizations will need to know, especially when that data is being held with a public cloud provider such as Azure, is: *How safe is my data?*

Using encryption is a great way to protect data. Encryption protects your data in the event of other protection measures—such as networks, firewalls, or authentication controls— being circumvented. If a hacker were able to bypass other controls, they would not be able to read any encrypted data without the key used to encrypt it.

There are multiple areas where encryption can be used, including the following:

- Encryption in transit
- Encryption at rest
- Encryption in use

First, we will consider in-transit protection.

Encryption in transit

Encrypting data in transit means ensuring that when moving data from point A to point B, any interception of that traffic would not yield anything useful.

Azure SQL Database and Azure SQL Managed Instance both enforce the use of encrypted traffic when connecting to them from a client application. With an on-premises database, you would have to specifically configure this on the server and then configure your applications to use `Encrypt=True` in the connection string.

With Azure SQL, all this is done for you, and the `Encrypt` setting in the connection string is ignored—it is encrypted regardless of what this is set to.

Similarly, connections to Cosmos DB are also encrypted. However, communications to Cosmos DB are performed using the **HyperText Transfer Protocol Secure (HTTPS)** protocol, and—again—your Cosmos DB always has a certificate installed and configured.

Once your communications are secured, we must consider how to protect the data while stored on disk.

Encryption at rest

All storage in Azure is encrypted at rest. This means that any data you write to a storage account is automatically encrypted using an Azure managed key.

Azure SQL Database and Azure SQL Managed Instance use **Transparent Data Encryption** (**TDE**). This means that the data on the disk is encrypted without you having to configure anything, and it is invisible to your applications—in other words, your developers do not need to do anything to ensure data is encrypted or decrypted.

TDE protects your data in the unlikely event that a physical disk is stolen from an Azure data center. The keys used to manage the encryption are automatically rotated periodically for additional protection. For organizations that require more direct control over the encryption keys, there is also the option to use **customer-managed keys** (**CMK**). With CMK, you can store the keys used to perform the encryption in an Azure Key Vault; this ensures that nobody else, including Microsoft, has sight of, or can access, those keys.

Finally, we can employ application-level encryption.

Encryption in use

TDE protects data against physical disk theft. However, there are times when you need the data to be protected within the database itself. You may want to protect sensitive data from some users but make it available to others.

One such example would be a finance application whereby approved users of the finance system can read the data; however, database administrators should not be able to read the data.

In such scenarios, you can employ a feature of SQL called **Always on encrypted**. The SQL **Always on encrypted** feature uses a key or certificate to encrypt data before it is sent to the database. Usually, this would be performed by the application.

The application would therefore use a key or certificate stored in a key vault or certificate store to encrypt the data before writing it to the database. Similarly, the data would be read from the database in its encrypted format and then decrypted by the application.

In this way, any access to the database by a database administrator by issuing direct **Transact-SQL** (**T-SQL**) commands such as a SELECT statement would return encrypted data, as we can see in the following example:

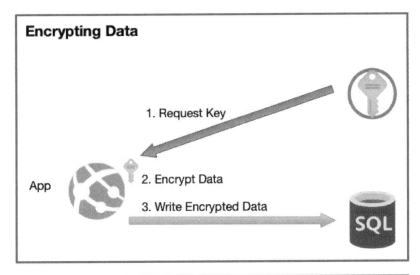

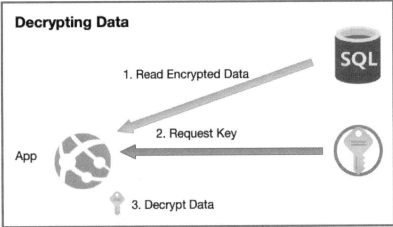

Figure 12.9 – Always Encrypted in use

Only users who had authenticated against the application would then be able to access the data; this split of administrator and authorized user access is known as **segregation of duties (SoD)**.

Another feature of SQL that can help protect data at the field level is **Dynamic data masking**. Dynamic data masking is similar to Always Encrypted, in that individual fields are masked (but not encrypted). This is managed by the SQL server by configuring columns to use the masking feature and then using SQL roles to define who can read the data unmasked or who must read it masked.

Dynamic data masking can therefore be used without the need to modify existing code within an application.

Different organizations have different requirements for the security of their data. However, personal and sensitive data should always employ the highest levels of protection—often, this will involve using multiple layers.

As we have seen, Azure and SQL technologies can be used to provide both resilience and security at all levels.

Summary

In this chapter, we have looked at the two main types of databases available—SQL and NoSQL databases, specifically looking at Azure SQL Database, Azure SQL Managed Instance, and Azure Cosmos DB. We have looked at how the different pricing and service tiers have an impact on multiple areas such as costs, scalability, resilience, and performance.

We also looked at different architectural patterns for ensuring our databases remain performant, based on expected usage scenarios and growth. Finally, we examined the different types of encryption we can employ to secure our data, including encryption in transit, at rest, and in use.

In the next chapter, we continue the data management theme by looking at the different tools available for the integration, movement, and transformation of data.

Exam scenario

MegaCorp Inc. is building a new e-commerce application. Due to the nature of the data, there will be lots of interrelated records, and it is imperative that data across records is kept consistent.

The site will start with a small number of records initially, but is expected to expand quite rapidly. The company wants to keep costs aligned with growth—that is, sales need to fund the scaling-out of the system. Any scaling operation will be managed by the team as they will first analyze usage patterns and sales.

As part of the application, the sales and marketing teams will run regular reports against the database. The management team is concerned the reporting mechanism could affect the performance of the system and have asked if there is some way to separate the customer experience and the sales and marketing teams' access.

You have been tasked with designing a database solution to accommodate their needs.

Further reading

For more information on topics covered in this chapter, you can refer to the following links:

- Azure Cosmos DB: `https://docs.microsoft.com/en-us/azure/cosmos-db/introduction`
- Azure SQL Database: `https://azure.microsoft.com/en-gb/services/sql-database/`
- Azure SQL security: `https://docs.microsoft.com/en-us/azure/azure-sql/database/security-overview`
- Azure SQL service tiers: `https://docs.microsoft.com/en-us/azure/azure-sql/database/service-tiers-general-purpose-business-critical`

13
Options for Data Integration

In the previous chapter, we looked at how to architect database solutions that are scalable and secure. This chapter will look at several options available for architects when designing solutions that must work with large datasets for analysis and reporting.

Big data is an industry term for working with **terabytes (TB)**, or even **petabytes (PB)** of data, to create analytical dashboards and gain insights. Specialist tools are often required to perform this kind of processing, and it would be expensive to build them in your own data center.

Azure provides some of the world's most popular data tools for loading, transforming, and analyzing data. We will examine what a data pipeline looks like and then delve deeper into some of those tools.

Specifically, this chapter will cover the following topics:

- Understanding data flows
- Comparing integration tools
- Exploring data analytics

Technical requirements

This chapter will use the Azure portal (`https://portal.azure.com`) for examples.

Understanding data flows

Many organizations gather massive amounts of data and continue to amass data in many different forms from various systems. This data can be used to bring great value to a company.

One example may be an e-commerce company that collects sales and marketing data from its day-to-day operations. By analyzing the data, customer patterns could be ascertained, as well as the relative success of different advertising campaigns. This information could then be used to develop the company website to create a better customer journey or to identify the strongest performing marketing activities so that these can be honed while less effective ones are dropped.

Scientific organizations also make use of data to create better treatments, drugs, and methodologies.

Manufacturers can use data from **internet of things** (**IoT**) devices and sensors to optimize supply chains, increase operational efficiencies, or identify risks in products or processes.

Data sources include sales and marketing databases, product inventories, **human resources** (**HR**), machinery, heating systems, security devices, and even personal devices that monitor health and well-being. The internet has granted many organizations the ability to make vast amounts of data available to the public, which in turn can be consumed by other companies and combined with their sources to provide even greater insights.

Big data has become big business for many organizations. The act of analyzing data can be broken down into several different areas, including the following:

- **Descriptive**: What is happening now within the business or organization, trial, marketing campaign, and so on.

- **Diagnostic**: Why is this happening? What has led to the current state?

- **Predictive**: What is going to happen next, and how can we influence the outcome? What is the probability?

- **Prescriptive**: Automate and recommend responses to given events to achieve the desired outcome.

The sheer volume of data has led to a few problems, as outlined here:

- The amount of computing power required to process so much data can be costly.
- As information comes from many different sources, it can often be in various formats.
- Data can be incomplete or not follow a prescribed format.

Therefore, organizations wishing to use data for analysis have several issues to overcome. This is achieved by creating data flows, which are end-to-end processes that define the following activities:

- **Ingest**: Pull data in from either a central location in the form of files or continually receive data from a streaming service such as an IoT device.
- **Clean**: Ensure your data is normalized and transformed and that gaps are filled or removed from the dataset.
- **Store**: Once your data has been cleaned and transformed, you may want to store it for further analysis.
- **Train**: Investigate and explore data to derive deeper insights.
- **Model**: Analyze and learn from your data by applying algorithms and data maps.
- **Serve**: Query and visualize data.

Conceptually, a data flow pipeline may look like this:

Figure 13.1 – Data flow pipeline

Now we know at a high level what we are trying to achieve, we can investigate the various tools available to us in Azure.

Comparing integration tools

One of the greatest benefits of using cloud services such as Azure is that it gives you the ability to create the necessary resources required without needing to invest large amounts of capital. The tools you can choose from cover end-to-end processes and are scaled in and out as needed.

One of the first decisions you may need to consider is where to initially store raw data. Except in the case of streaming analytics, whereby you continually ingest data from a source such as an IoT device (for example, a temperature sensor), you need a place to store and retrieve your data files from.

Azure storage accounts provide storage capabilities in the form of file storage or Blob storage; however, a specific type of account called an **Azure Data Lake Storage Gen2 (ADLS Gen2)** account might be better suited to data analytics.

ADLS Gen2

ADLS is an optional configuration feature of a standard storage account. One of the key differences is that it supports filesystem-style hierarchical namespaces. This allows files and objects to be stored in folder structures, thus providing greater performance.

You can still provision ADLS Gen1; however, this is not recommended. Gen2 includes additional features over Gen1. The following table shows the key differences between the two:

Feature	Gen1	Gen2
Namespaces	Files and folders	Containers, files, and folders
Redundancy	**Locally redundant storage (LRS)**	LRS; **zone-redundant storage (ZRS); geo-redundant storage (GRS); read-access GRS (RA-GRS)**
Authentication	Managed identities; service principals	Managed identities; service principals; shared access keys
Authorization	**Access control lists (ACLs)** for data; **role-based access control (RBAC)** for management	ACLs and RBAC for management and data
Networking	**Virtual Network (VNet)** integration	Service and private endpoints

It is also worth noting that you cannot directly upgrade a Gen1 configuration to a Gen2 configuration. If you wish to migrate, you must create a new Gen2 account and manually copy or move the data.

Quite often, large data operations involve enumerating and modifying a large number of files at the same time or modifying a directory name that contains those files. Standard blob storage supports directories; however, these are virtual, so this means that when performing an operation on a directory (such as renaming it), you need to update every file.

With ADLS Gen2, the hierarchical namespace means directory-level operations apply at a directory level. ADLS Gen2 also supports the **Hadoop Distributed File System (HDFS)**, and therefore supports a driver called the **Azure Blob File System (ABFS)** driver. All this essentially means that ADLS Gen2 can be used by Hadoop tools, and Hadoop is one of the most popular big data analytics tools.

ADLS Gen2 also supports **Portable Operating System Interface (POSIX)** permissions and is very cost-effective, yet incredibly fast. Finally, ADLS Gen2 replaces the original ADLS offering, which although still available is no longer recommended.

> **Note**
> POSIX is a standard for defining a portable operating system. This means systems that are POSIX-compliant will also be interoperable.

Because ADLS Gen2 is a configurable item of a standard storage account, you create it by creating a general-purpose Azure storage account and enabling **Hierarchical namespace** in the **Advanced** settings, as per the following screenshot:

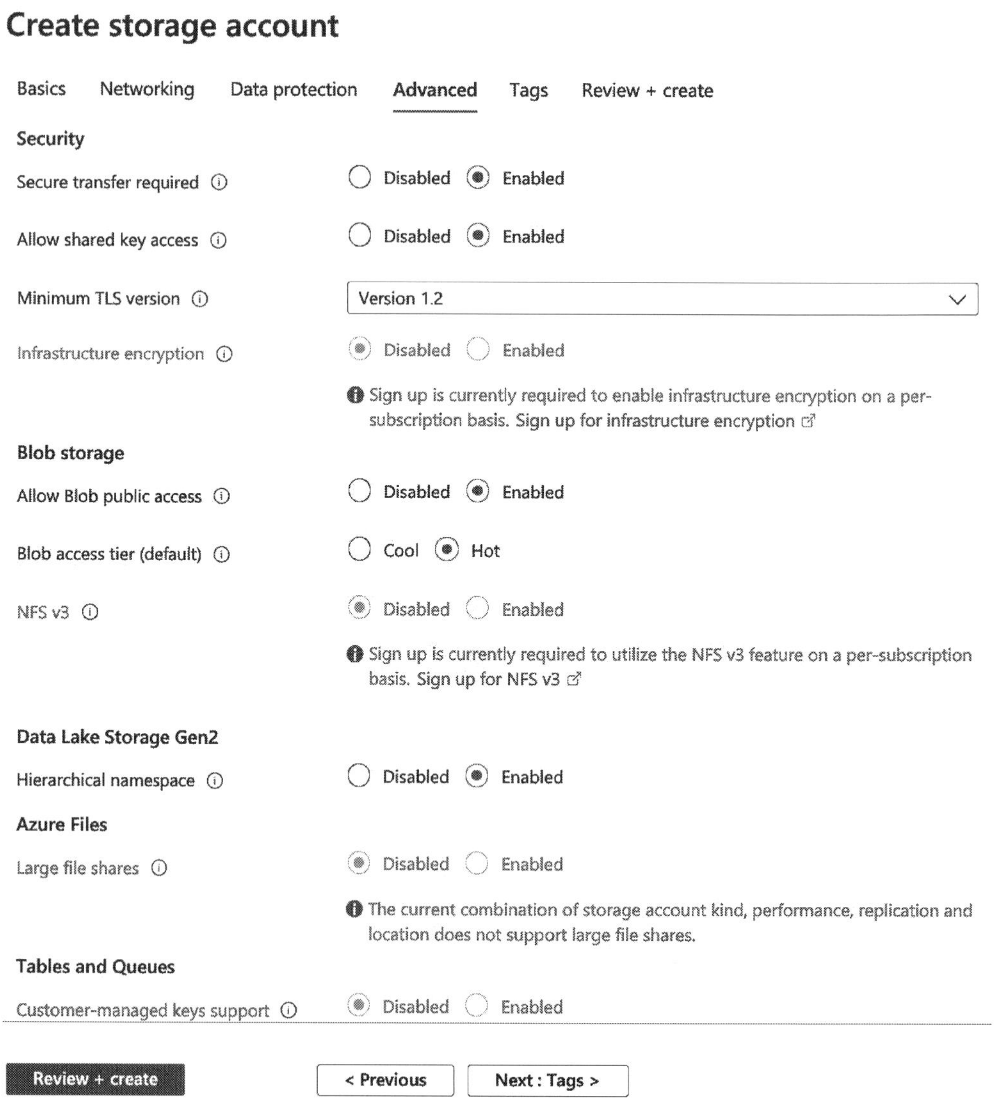

Create storage account

Basics   Networking   Data protection   **Advanced**   Tags   Review + create

Security

Secure transfer required ⓘ   ○ Disabled ◉ Enabled

Allow shared key access ⓘ   ○ Disabled ◉ Enabled

Minimum TLS version ⓘ | Version 1.2   ∨ |

Infrastructure encryption ⓘ   ◉ Disabled ○ Enabled

　　　　　ⓘ Sign up is currently required to enable infrastructure encryption on a per-subscription basis. Sign up for infrastructure encryption ⧉

Blob storage

Allow Blob public access ⓘ   ○ Disabled ◉ Enabled

Blob access tier (default) ⓘ   ○ Cool ◉ Hot

NFS v3 ⓘ   ◉ Disabled ○ Enabled

　　　　　ⓘ Sign up is currently required to utilize the NFS v3 feature on a per-subscription basis. Sign up for NFS v3 ⧉

Data Lake Storage Gen2

Hierarchical namespace ⓘ   ○ Disabled ◉ Enabled

Azure Files

Large file shares ⓘ   ◉ Disabled ○ Enabled

　　　　　ⓘ The current combination of storage account kind, performance, replication and location does not support large file shares.

Tables and Queues

Customer-managed keys support ⓘ   ◉ Disabled ○ Enabled

[Review + create]   [< Previous]   [Next : Tags >]

Figure 13.2 – Configuring an Azure storage account as ADLS Gen2

When a storage account is created as an ADLS Gen2 storage account, the `https://dfs.core.windows.net` **application programming interface (API)** endpoints become available to interact with it. You can also use the ABFS driver that supports Hadoop, using the following **Uniform Resource Identifier (URI)** pattern:

```
abfs[s]://file_system@account_name.dfs.core.windows.
net/<path>/<path>/<file_name>
```

When using the ABFS driver, Azure translates behind the scenes the preceding URI to the **REpresentational State Transfer (REST)** API endpoints.

> **Important note**
> A storage account can only have ADLS Gen2 enabled at the time of creation—you cannot change this setting after it has been deployed.

Although a standard storage account can be used, an ADLS Gen2 account provides the best capabilities for big data and analytics workloads.

ADLS Gen2 therefore provides you with a storage location to ingest data from, and it can also be used to store processed data. Services such as **Power BI** can be connected directly to storage accounts to create visualization dashboards.

Most other Azure tools can either write or read from ADLS Gen2 storage accounts, such as Azure Synapse Analytics or Azure Databricks.

Before we look at some of these services, we will examine another tool that makes orchestrating the end-to-end ingestion and transformation of data easier.

Azure Data Factory

Azure Data Factory is a serverless offering, meaning you only pay for it as you use it, enabling you to automate and simplify many steps in a data flow.

Much of Azure Data Factory's power and flexibility is due to the many connectors that allow you to integrate with a wide range of linked services and tools.

Linked services can include storage accounts and databases, and these form datasets. Datasets are used to define source data—for example, **comma-separated values (CSV)** files or a database table. They are additionally used to describe output data, which can also be CSV files or database tables.

Azure Data Factory supports a wide range of services to create datasets from, including—but not limited to—the following:

- Amazon Redshift
- Amazon **Simple Storage Service (S3)**
- Azure Blob Storage
- Azure Cosmos DB
- ADLS (Gen1 and Gen2)
- Azure Database for MariaDB
- Azure SQL Database
- Microsoft Dynamics 365
- **File Transfer Protocol (FTP)**
- Google BigQuery
- **Google Cloud Storage (GCS)**
- **Systems Applications and Products in Data Processing (SAP)**
- Salesforce
- ServiceNow

Azure Data Factory allows you to use those datasets to create pipelines that define activities and perform a task, such as a simple copy or a transformation. Other services can be linked to achieving end-to-end data ingestion and transformation, such as the ones listed here:

- Azure Functions
- Azure Databricks
- Azure Batch
- Azure HDInsight
- Azure Machine Learning
- Power Query

The following diagram shows a high-level example of this concept:

Figure 13.3 – Azure Data Factory pipelines

A simplest example would be a simple data copy from a raw data file in CSV format to an Azure SQL Database. Using the **Copy data** activity, you can set the source as a CSV file in a linked ADLS-enabled storage account, set the destination or **sink** as an Azure SQL Database, and then define specific mappings between the source and sink data types, as depicted in the following screenshot:

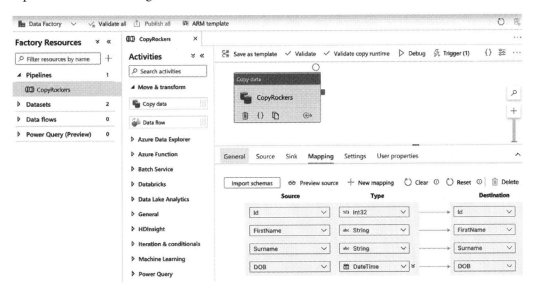

Figure 13.4 – An example Copy data pipeline

A pipeline can then either be run manually or you can create triggers that define when to run it. The triggers can either be configured to a set **Schedule**, or as a **Tumbling window** whereby a pipeline is run every x minutes, hours, or days, or in response to an event. A typical event might be a file being uploaded to a storage account. Such an event can be set to monitor a file pattern or a designated container in the storage account.

More advanced pipelines can be run; for example, a **Data flow** operation can be created rather than a simple **Copy data** operation. **Data flow** activities allow more complex activities to be performed. For instance, in the following screenshot, we read from two different CSV data files and combine the data from them using a related key. The output is then sent to an Azure SQL Database:

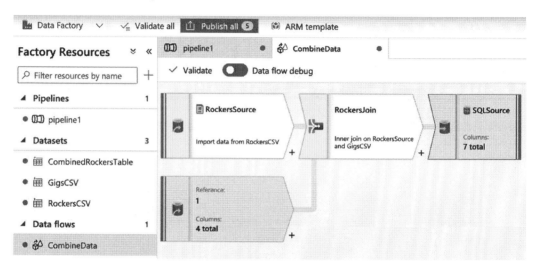

Figure 13.5 – Dataflow pipeline combining multiple sources into a single output

Some form of compute must perform activities. Azure Data Factory uses **integration runtimes (IRs)**, and there are three different runtimes you can use.

Azure-hosted IR

An Azure-hosted IR is fully managed by Azure; these IRs can run **Data flow**, **Data movement**, and **Dispatch** activities both on public and private networks. Azure Dispatch launches and monitors activities such as Azure Databricks. Azure Dispatch activities are those that connect to other services such as Azure Databricks.

An Azure-hosted IR creates **virtual machines (VMs)** in the background to run your pipelines on, and you can configure the type of compute it uses, from general-purpose, compute-optimized, and memory-optimized. You can also configure the number of cores created for use by that VM, from 4 up to 256. Compute resources are automatically shut down when idle.

When creating an Azure-hosted IR, you have the option of using VNets or not. When VNet configuration is disabled, you can only connect to services on public endpoints; however, on enabling it, you can then connect to your Azure-hosted services over private endpoints. This negates the need to configure network firewall rules on services such as Azure SQL Database or Azure Storage accounts. Without a VNet configuration enabled, if your storage and **Structured Query Language** (**SQL**) accounts blocked public access, you would need to manually add the Data Factory **Internet Protocol** (**IP**) ranges for the region they are running in.

Self-hosted IRs

Self-hosted IRs allow you the option of creating a VM yourself and installing the IR on it. This can provide more control, and even allows the IRs to be hosted on-premises. However, the VM must be maintained by you (including the stopping and starting of it). You lose the dynamic ability to easily create massive core-based servers for individual jobs.

Self-hosted IRs *do not* support **Data flow** activities, only **Data movement** and **Dispatch** activities.

Azure SQL Server Integration Services (SSIS)

Azure SSIS hosting is specifically designed for running **SQL Server Integration Services** (**SSIS**) packages. It makes an ideal choice for scenarios where a lot of investment has already been made in developing SSIS packages, and allows you to take these to the cloud more efficiently.

> **Note**
> SSIS is an optional add-on to Microsoft SQL Server and provides the ability to create **extract, transform, and load** (**ETL**) packages for automating data movement and transformation. In many ways, Azure Data Factory can replace such packages; however, businesses often invest a great deal of time and money in developing them, hence why Azure provides the ability to reuse them in Data Factory.

When connecting Azure Data Factory to your services, you must consider how those services will authenticate. For example, when connecting to a storage account that is locked down using RBAC controls, you need to find a way to provide a valid user.

For scenarios such as this, you can either use native connectivity options—for example, **shared access signature (SAS)** tokens with storage accounts or SQL authentication for Azure SQL Database. Alternatively, you can use service principals or managed service identities, which we discussed in more detail in *Chapter 6, Building Application Security*.

An example of building a simple data copy pipeline using managed identities can be found on my blog at `https://bretthargreaves.com/2020/11/10/move-data-securely-with-azure-data-factory`.

Out of the box, Azure Data Factory provides a wide range of tools and activities. However, there are times when advanced tooling is required—specifically, data analytics services. Two analytical tools that can be integrated into Azure Data Factory are Azure Databricks and Azure Synapse Analytics, which we will explore next.

Exploring data analytics

Once data has been ingested, transformed, and aggregated, the next step will be to analyze and explore it. There are many tools available on the market to achieve this, and one of the most popular is **Databricks**.

Databricks uses the Apache Spark engine that is well suited to dealing with massive amounts of data due to its internal architecture. Whereas a traditional database server would typically run workloads, Databricks uses Spark clusters built from multiple nodes. Data analytics processes are then distributed between those nodes to process them in parallel, as shown in the following diagram:

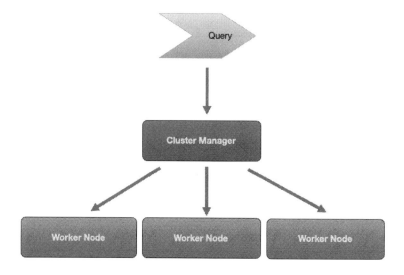

Figure 13.6 – Example Spark cluster architecture

Azure Databricks is a managed Databricks service that provides excellent flexibility for creating and using Spark clusters as and when needed.

Azure Databricks

Azure Databricks provides workspaces that multiple users can use to build and run analytics jobs collaboratively. A Databricks workspace contains notebooks, which are web-based interfaces for running commands executed on a Spark cluster.

Notebooks are written using either Python, SQL, R, or Scala programming languages. Depending on the type of analytical work being performed, you can choose between different Databricks runtimes. These are listed here:

- **Databricks**: A general-purpose runtime using Apache Spark, with additional components for performance, security, and usability on the Azure platform.

- **Databricks Runtime for Machine Learning** (**Databricks Runtime ML**): Using Databricks at its core but optimized for **machine learning** (**ML**) and data science. It includes popular ML libraries such as **TensorFlow**, **Keras**, **PyTorch**, and **XGBoost**.

- **Databricks for Genomics**: A highly specialized runtime built for working with biomedical data.

- **Databricks Light**: A cutdown version of the full Databricks runtime. Particularly suited to smaller jobs that don't require as much performance or reliability.

When you create a Databricks notebook, you can choose the type and size of the cluster that it will run on. Notebooks run as workloads on a cluster and can be one of two types, as outlined here:

- **Data engineering** is for scheduled workloads—for example, jobs that perform specific tasks and that will be repeatedly used. Clusters are created and destroyed as required.

- **Data analytics**, which is for interactive workloads and runs on a general processing cluster. These workloads are run when you are working in a notebook to develop models and analytics.

Azure Databricks provides compute as needed as a serverless offering, and clusters are destroyed when not used.

Notebooks can be executed from Azure Data Factory as part of a pipeline. In this way, you can perform any ingestion, transformation, and aggregation using **Data copy** or **Data workflow** activities, which will then output the result to storage or a database. The Azure Databricks notebook job can then be called, and this will read the processed data to perform other analytics or calculations, as in the following example:

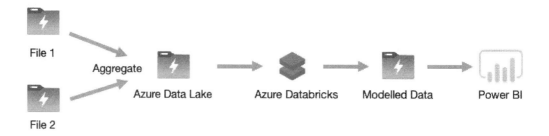

Figure 13.7 – Using Databricks as part of an Azure Data Factory pipeline

Azure Databricks is not the only choice for analytics; Microsoft also offers Azure Synapse Analytics, which can be used independently or as part of a more extensive toolset.

Azure Synapse Analytics

Azure Synapse Analytics was originally called **Azure Data Warehouse**. As the name suggests, it was built as a particular type of SQL database engine for storing large amounts of data that could then be queried by an analytics service such as Databricks.

The solution has been built out to include many new features and therefore was rebranded to highlight that it now does far more.

Azure Synapse Analytics is now a fully integrated service that enables you to ingest, transform, and analyze data. It can be used as a complete replacement for Azure Data Factory and Azure Databricks or used with them.

Azure Synapse Analytics provides access to two engines, **SQL** and **Spark**, and the SQL engine can be serverless or provisioned. As with Azure SQL Database using SQL serverless offers significant cost efficiencies for periodic workloads; however, the provisioned option may be better for continual availability and guaranteed performance levels.

As an integrated service, the Azure Synapse interface is very similar to that of Azure Data Factory. You can use it to create pipelines and the same activities, as you can see in the following screenshot:

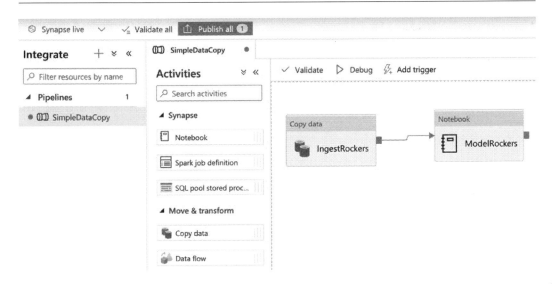

Figure 13.8 – Combining Azure Data Factory pipelines and Azure Synapse Analytics notebooks

As with Azure Data Factory, you use IRs for running some activities, and again these can be Azure-hosted or self-hosted.

As mentioned, Azure Synapse Analytics includes a SQL engine that can create queries and analyze data. Using the familiar **Transact-SQL (T-SQL)** language, data can be ingested, aggregated, and queried using a SQL pool. SQL pools run in a similar way to Apache Spark clusters, in that jobs are distributed among multiple worker nodes to enable much faster processing times.

Alternatively, data can be loaded, transformed, and analyzed using **Apache Spark clusters** by building notebooks, similar to Azure Databricks.

Choosing Azure Synapse Analytics over Azure SQL Database provides many benefits due to SQL pools' serverless nature and the underlying architecture of using distributed nodes. However, choosing this service over Azure Databricks may not seem as obvious.

Although both Azure Databricks and Azure Synapse Analytics use Spark clusters, Azure Synapse Analytics only supports version 2.4. The underlying runtime is based on the open source version of Spark. Conversely, Azure Databricks supports Spark version 3.1, and it includes additional components that provide greater performance and reliability. Because of this, Azure Databricks can perform up to 50x faster.

Azure Synapse Analytics, however, has support for .NET applications running on Spark, includes data pipeline orchestration, and consists of the SQL Pool engine. Therefore, the choice between the two can come down to the type of work you are performing, the level of performance required, and the toolsets you are used to using.

Putting it all together

For many, a combination of tools may be the best option, and, depending on your exact requirements, you may use a combination of toolsets for different projects. As an all-encompassing example, however, the following diagram shows how all these products—and more—can be combined into a single solution:

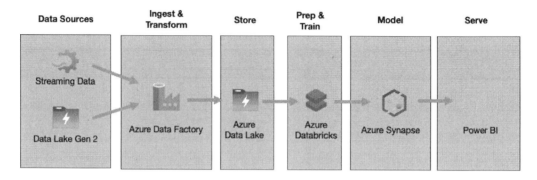

Figure 13.9 – Example solution combining multiple technologies

As you can see, each service can work together as part of an overall data analytics solution, and although there are sometimes overlaps, combining multiple components gives the greatest flexibility.

Summary

This chapter looked at a growing capability in the cloud, especially in Azure—data integration and analytics.

Azure provides a range of tools for creating end-to-end data pipelines for storing, ingesting, transforming, aggregating, and analyzing data. So, we started the chapter with a high-level view of what a typical pipeline might look like.

We looked at how to configure Azure Storage to use ADLS Gen2, what extra capabilities this gives you, and how Azure Data Factory can create automated and secure pipelines for data loading and transformation.

Finally, we looked at the two primary tools for exploring and analyzing data with Azure: Azure Databricks and Azure Synapse Analytics.

After reading this chapter, you should have a better understanding of the different components that comprise a data analytics solution, including the strengths of each service and where one might be a better choice over another.

In the next chapter, we conclude *Part 4, Applications and Databases,* by looking at the different ways to architect solutions that enable automated resilience and redundancy.

Exam scenario

MegaCorp Inc. is building a new data analytics capability to help understand its marketing campaigns' effectiveness and how they relate to product sales.

Marketing campaign data is exported daily and stored as flat CSV files. Sales data is exported overnight from the sales database into a normalized data warehouse database.

The management team would like data to be automatically imported and aggregated, and then modeled. It is expected that large amounts of data will be processed, and this needs to be performed relatively quickly. The data analytics teams are seasoned developers who are currently using the latest version of Spark.

Design an end-to-end solution that can accommodate the management team's requirements.

Further reading

- ADLS: `https://azure.microsoft.com/en-gb/services/storage/data-lake-storage/`

- Azure Data Factory: `https://azure.microsoft.com/en-gb/services/data-factory/`

- Azure Databricks: `https://azure.microsoft.com/en-gb/services/databricks/`

- Azure Synapse Analytics: `https://azure.microsoft.com/en-gb/services/synapse-analytics/`

14

High Availability and Redundancy Concepts

In the previous two chapters, we examined how to create scalable databases and the different options for integrating them using data flows.

This chapter looks at how we can ensure our solutions are highly available and automatically respond to failures.

Many Azure components, especially **Platform as a Service (PaaS)** and serverless options such as Azure Functions, automatically implement high availability. We examined how to best leverage and architect applications to take advantage of those features in *Chapter 11, Comparing Application Components*.

However, **Infrastructure as a Service (IaaS)** components such as virtual machines need more thought to respond to outages. Azure storage and Azure databases offer more options on top of the default configuration to expand the concept of high availability across regions. Again, we touched on this in *Chapter 12, Creating Scalable and Secure Databases*, when investigating the use of data replicas for scalability.

In this chapter, we will re-visit the use of replicas for storage and databases, specifically with high availability in mind. However, as you will see, scalability and redundancy go hand in hand.

We will also look at implementing high-availability options with **virtual machines** (**VM**) by looking at VM scale sets.

This chapter will specifically cover the following concepts:

- Understanding virtual machine availability
- Understanding storage availability
- Understanding SQL database availability
- Understanding Cosmos DB availability

Technical requirements

This chapter will use the Azure portal (`https://portal.azure.com`) for examples.

Understanding virtual machine availability

A common misconception in Azure is that VMs are automatically highly available. Although this may be true to a certain extent as the failure of hardware results in a VM being moved to healthy hardware, this process temporarily interrupts the accessibility of that VM.

Additionally, during maintenance events, the Azure platform may need to forcefully reboot your VM. This is performed gracefully, but again it causes a brief outage for your workload.

Finally, in the unlikely event of an entire region outage, for example, due to networking failure, your VMs will be inaccessible until that outage is rectified.

Another aspect of your VM availability is the type of disks you choose to build it with. Standard magnetic HDDs have the lowest availability, whereas premium SSDs have the greatest due to how they are used and distributed.

These factors can have a significant impact on the **Service-Level Agreement** (**SLA**) of your service. For example, a single-instance VM with a standard HDD has an SLA of 95%, whereas a single VM with a premium **Solid State Drive** (**SSD**) has an SLA of 99.9%. To put this into context, an SLA of 95% means you could have downtime of up to 36.53 hours a month without any compensation, whereas 99.9% reduces this to 44.83 minutes.

This does not mean you will suffer these outages; it means that if your service does fail for longer than these periods, you are eligible for service credits. It is a good measure of the overall potential availability for when (not if) things go wrong.

There are several options for workloads that cannot suffer any outage or as little outage as possible.

First, all options require that you build at least two VMs that run the same service. Typically, these VMs would be placed behind a load balancer so that if one fails, the other will take over, as we can see in the following diagram:

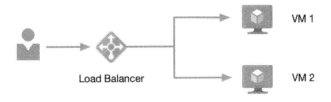

Figure 14.1 – Using Azure Load Balancer to protect VMs

Using a load balancer can help protect a VM, however, on its own, this is not enough.

Fault domains and update domains

Within Azure's data centers, the hardware has built-in fault domains. A fault domain is a group of VMs that share the same power and network switches, which means any failure to those components would affect all VMs in that fault domain. Similarly, update domains are VM groupings that define standard maintenance windows such as patching and reboots.

With this in mind, when building VMs, you can choose to place them in an availability set, which instructs the Azure platform to spread any VMs in that set across update and fault domains. There are up to 3 fault and 20 update domains within any 1 availability set; therefore, if you have more than 3 VMs in a cluster or farm, then at least 2 will reside in the same fault domain.

> **Important note**
> Availability sets only protect your VMs from hardware and power failures, and they do not provide any protection against OS failures or application failures. Generally, these types of issues would need to be mitigated with application-level architecture.

When building a VM, the default and recommended disk type is a managed disk. Managed disks follow a similar pattern for protecting against hardware failure. When a VM is built in an availability set, the disks are also created in different storage fault zones aligned to the VM. The following diagram shows an example of this:

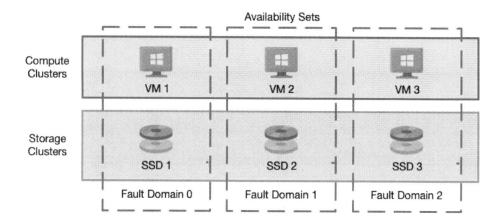

Figure 14.2 – Availability Zones example

Using availability sets with multiple VMs increases the SLA from 99.9% to 99.95% or an allowed outage of 21.92 minutes a month.

Availability sets help protect you against isolated hardware failures. However, Availability Zones can protect you against an entire data center failure.

Availability Zones

Each Azure region contains multiple separate data centers that are at least 10 miles (16 km) apart. Each data center has its power, networking, and security. They are purposefully placed to ensure some protection against possible natural events such as flooding.

Not all regions support Availability Zones. However, the majority of them do. Each region that does support Availability Zones will have at least three zones within the region. For details of each region and whether they support Availability Zones, see the following link: `https://azure.microsoft.com/en-us/global-infrastructure/geographies/#geographies`.

When building VMs, you have the option to build them in set Availability Zones. By spreading your VMs among zones and placing them behind a load balancer, the SLA on them increases to 99.99%, or a potential downtime of only 4.38 minutes per month.

> **Important note**
>
> When building resilient architecture with VMs, you will typically use a load balancer. However, having a load balancer zone redundant is optional and only supported on the standard SKU. Therefore, to ensure resilience against zone failures, you must build your VMs across availability sets and use a zone redundant, standard SKU load balancer.

For many organizations, zone redundancy is adequate as each data center is distanced within that region. For organizations that required regional resilience, either for protection or for performance benefits, services can be built across regions.

To achieve region resilience, additional components are required to distribute traffic accordingly, such as a Azure Traffic Manager or Azure Front Door. These are covered in *Chapter 8, Network Connectivity and Security*.

VMs built across regions are not managed in the same way as VMs in an availability set. The Azure platform will not automatically place VMs or distribute them between the regions. The following diagram shows an example of how this might look:

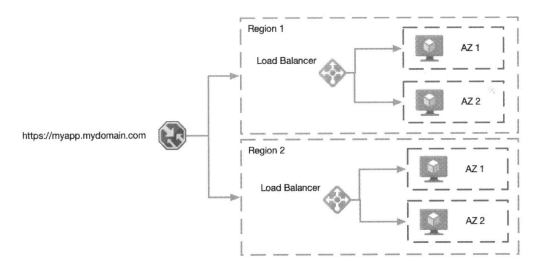

Figure 14.3 – Cross region, zone redundant architecture example

Typically, you would build VMs in both regions across Availability Zones and using load balancers, and then configure the regional network distribution component, such as Traffic Manager, accordingly. In other words, cross-region resilience usually requires more forethought and architecture.

Creating VMs across Availability Zones is a great way to protect your application. However, it is a manual process in which you must configure each VM. Load balancing workloads across VMs also provides performance benefits. However, it can again be cumbersome to create new VMs when you need to scale manually.

Azure provides an automated way of load balancing your apps across VMs using a feature called scale sets.

Azure virtual machine scale sets

Azure VM scale sets automate the process of horizontally scaling your application across multiple VMs automatically. VMs in a scale set are automatically distributed across Availability Zones as new instances are created.

Scale sets can be configured to scale out (that is, add more instances) in response to either set schedules or as pre-configured CPU and RAM thresholds are met. For example, you can create an autoscale rule that will automatically create a new instance of your VM if the average CPU across your exiting instances reaches 80%, and then scale back down when it drops below 20%.

You can also define the minimum and maximum number of VMs to have in a scale set at any one time, enabling you to control costs and ensure that in the event of a VM's failure, a new one will automatically be created.

Because each VM needs to run your application, you must either create a custom image that contains your services or create a custom script that runs on each new VM to automatically install and configure your app.

Creating a custom image involves the following steps:

1. Create a shared image gallery that will contain all your customized images. This can be done through the Azure portal, using PowerShell, or by using the Azure CLI.

2. Create a VM through the normal process, then install and configure your application on it.

3. Prepare your VM for imaging by either running Sysprep on Windows VMs or waagent -deprovision on Linux VMs.

4. Create an image definition from the VM you just created. Again, this can be performed in the Azure portal by going to the shared image gallery you created in *step 1* and clicking **Add new image definition** or using PowerShell or the Azure CLI. When creating an image definition, you define the **publisher name**, **offer name**, and **SKU** information.

5. As part of this process, you must decide whether to create a generalized image or a specialized image. Generalized images have had machine-specific information removed, such as any user accounts and the hostname. Specialized images retain all this information. Specialized images are created much faster as they do not need to go through an initial setup process to create and store this base information. However, because they retain the same hostname, conflicts can occur; therefore, you might need to update this through a post-build script.

6. Now create a version for your image and set the source disk used to create it. Version numbers must be in the format `MajorVersion.MinorVersion.Patch` - for example, 1.0.0.

7. Create your scale set using the image version created in *step 5*.

Either in addition to using an image or instead of using an image, you can use a custom script extension. A custom script extension will download a script such as a Bash script or PowerShell script from an accessible location such as GitHub or a storage account and then run it.

That script will install the necessary additional software such as Windows Internet Information Services or Apache on Linux and then deploy your custom code.

Creating custom scripts can be more complex and is much slower for scale-out operations as each new VM must be initialized and configured. However, the benefits are that you can always use the latest patched base image from the Azure gallery.

Conversely, when building your custom images, you must either manually keep them up to date or ensure the latest patches are installed on a newly created instance.

> **Important note**
>
> When building solutions with a scale set, your applications are best built to be stateless. We covered this concept in *Chapter 11, Comparing Application Components*. As a user may use a different backend server between one request and the next, we should not store information about that user on the server processing the request.

The next component you will want to ensure is resilient is storage. Also, managed disks, which we saw in this section, are automatically resilient when VMs are built across Availability Zones; you may also need to consider your redundancy options for using Azure storage accounts.

Understanding Azure storage resiliency options

Azure storage accounts have several options when creating them to define how the data within them is protected and made available in the event of hardware or even regional failure.

We looked in detail at storage accounts in *Chapter 9, Exploring Storage Solutions*, where we looked at different replication options such as **locally redundant storage (LRS)** and **geo-redundant storage (GRS)**.

To recap, data in Azure is always replicated to ensure durability and high availability. Storage replication can be set during the creation of a storage account; however, you can change the type of replication later by using the Azure portal, PowerShell, or the CLI.

In the event of an outage of the region that contains your storage account, failover is not automatic. You must manually switch your secondary replica to be the primary. Note that because data is copied from one region to another asynchronously, that is, the data is copied to the secondary region after it has been written to the primary, there is still a chance, therefore, that some data could be lost if the outage happens before the data has had an opportunity to replicate.

It is also worth noting that, unlike some other data redundancy options, you do not have a choice as to which region your geo-redundant replica is stored in. Each region has its pair, and when enabling GRS or ZA-GRS, the Azure platform will use that paired region and cannot be changed.

When using regional replication, you can access the secondary endpoints for direct read-only access, but failover is automatic and cannot be manually triggered.

In the next section, we will see what availability options we have for SQL databases.

Understanding SQL database availability

Even when your databases are hosted in Azure, there is still a chance that failures and outages will occur. In the case of an outage (such as a total regional failure, which a natural disaster could cause, an act of terrorism, war, a government action, or a network or device failure external to the data centers of Microsoft), your data still needs to be accessible.

In *Chapter 12, Creating Scalable and Secure Databases*, we looked at database service tiers chosen when creating a SQL Server database – the General tier, Hyperscale tier, and Business Critical tier.

With the General and Hyperscale tiers, by default, data is replicated within a single region. However, it Is not regionally redundant. This is partly due to how data is protected within them. Essentially, data is stored in Azure storage accounts and therefore uses that underlying technology to spread and replicate data among physical disks. However, there is still only ever one database – as we can see in the following diagram:

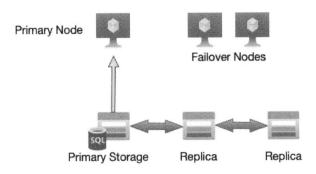

Figure 14.4 – General and Hyperscale data replication

To create highly available SQL Server databases in Azure, you can use failover groups and active geo-replication. By default, the Business Critical tier creates a secondary replica, and with the Hyperscale tier, you can optionally create additional replicas.

Replicas in this sense are additional copies of the database and server. In other words, you essentially have two Azure SQL servers, each serving their copy of the database – as we can see in the following example:

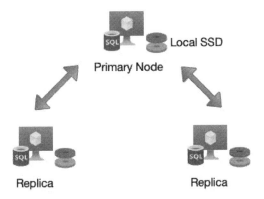

Figure 14.5 – Business Critical tier replication

Replicas can be created within the same region or across regions. Of course, creating a replica within the same region only protects against Availability Zone loss, whereas building your database in another region provides full protection. Unlike an Azure storage account, when creating database replicas, you can choose whichever target region you prefer – this helps when designing solutions that want read-only copies of your database closer to a target audience.

Creating a replica ensures you always have another copy of your database with the required server to present it. On its own, this protects your data; however, if a failure of a region occurs, failover to the replica is not automatic. For automatic failover between your databases, you need a failover group.

The following describes the critical differences between replication and failover groups:

- **Active geo-replication**: Geo-replication is a business continuity feature that allows you to replicate the primary database and up to four read-only secondary databases in the same or different Azure regions. You can use the secondary databases to query data or for failover scenarios when there is a data center outage. Active geo-replication has to be set up by the user or the application manually.

- **Failover groups**: Failover groups are a feature that automatically manages the failover for the database. They automatically manage the geo-replication relationship between the databases, the failover at scale, and the connectivity. The primary and secondary databases need to be created within the same Azure subscription to use failover groups. However, they must be in different regions.

When you create a failover group or a replica in the Azure portal, you have visibility of two separate SQL servers and SQL databases; a failover group simply connects them. You can still connect to either of the original connection strings for either database, but if you do, any failover will result in your application losing connectivity.

Therefore, when using failover groups, you are provided with an additional two connection strings in the failover blade – read/write and read-only, as in the following screenshot:

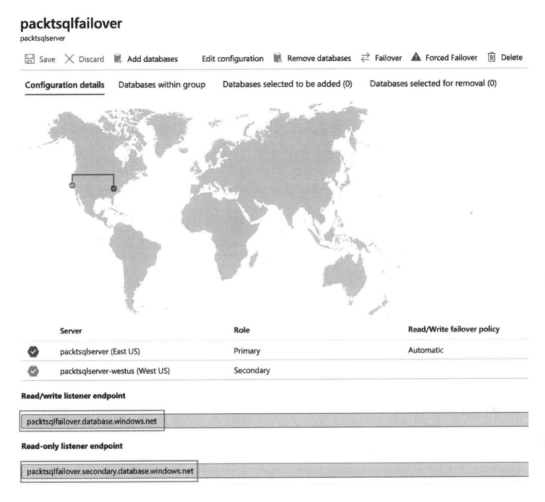

packtsqlfailover
packtsqlserver

🖫 Save   ✕ Discard   🖳 Add databases   Edit configuration   🖳 Remove databases   ⇄ Failover   ⚠ Forced Failover   🗑 Delete

Configuration details   Databases within group   Databases selected to be added (0)   Databases selected for removal (0)

	Server	Role	Read/Write failover policy
✓	packtsqlserver (East US)	Primary	Automatic
✓	packtsqlserver-westus (West US)	Secondary	

Read/write listener endpoint

packtsqlfailover.database.windows.net

Read-only listener endpoint

packtsqlfailover.secondary.database.windows.net

Figure 14.6 – SQL failover groups

By changing your connection string to the read/write listener endpoint, such as
`packtsqlfailover.database.windows.net` in this example, in the event
of a failover, your application will automatically be directed to the active server.

The read-only listener is useful for spreading a load across servers when you only need to
read from your database. In this way, when combined with frontend user interfaces spread
across regions, you can achieve faster response times by directing users to their closest
replica.

Failover will occur automatically in the failure of the primary server, but you can also
trigger a failover yourself.

Understanding the nuances between just having a replica or having a failover group depends on your requirements. The following table shows the main differences between the two options and why you might choose one over the other:

Feature	Geo-Replication	Failover Groups
Read scale-out	Yes	Yes
Use of multiple replicas	Yes	No
Support managed instance	No	Yes
Primary and secondary in the same region	Yes	No
Auto failover	No	Yes

As we can see from the preceding table, geo-replication is therefore useful when you want multiple replicas either within a region or across regions, which in itself makes them ideal when you need reliable infrastructure. You want to leverage options such as read scale-out.

> **Important note**
>
> When dealing with data replication for DR purposes, we need to understand the term **Recovery Point Object (RPO)**. RPO states the point in time when you can be confident your data is kept in sync. For example, an RPO of 5 seconds means there could be a 5-second lag between your data in the primary replica and the secondary. In Azure SQL, the Business Critical tier has a guaranteed 5-second RPO. The other tiers have no such guarantee, meaning there could be a more significant time difference between the replicas. This may be an essential factor for applications that must be kept consistent at all times.

Whereas failover groups are best when you need automatic switching from a primary replica to another, geo-replication is best when you need multiple replicas – for example, when using them for read scale-out for performance reasons.

You can see a complete walk-through of setting up an Azure SQL failover database by following the tutorial in *Implementing Microsoft Azure Architect Technologies: AZ-303 Exam Prep and Beyond* also by Packt Publishing.

Next, we will examine the options for another commonly used database in Azure, Cosmos DB.

Understanding Cosmos DB availability

Azure Cosmos DB is built with availability in mind. The underlying database of a Cosmos DB account is written to four replicas with any given region – this is the default and minimal configuration in regard to availability.

You can optionally create one or more replicas of your databases in any Azure region that supports Cosmos DB. Replicas in other regions are also replicated within that region to four other replicas. For example, suppose you set up your Cosmos DB account to be multi-region across two regions. In that case, you will have eight replicas of your data – four in the primary and four in the secondary regions.

Although data within a region is replicated four times, it is not stored across Availability Zones by default. This is an optional configuration applied to a Cosmos DB account in regions that support high-Availability Zones.

Another factor to consider when using Cosmos DB with global replication is whether to use single-region or multi-region writes. As the name would suggest, with single-region writes, data is written to the primary region only. This is, of course, useful for disaster recovery scenarios – in the event of a region outage, your secondary replica will become available for writing too.

Multi-region writes allow data to be written to multiple replicas at the same time. This is especially useful when you want to use your application's global distribution options to achieve lower latency by enabling applications to write to their closest replica. For example, if your solution serves users in Europe and the USA, you could have replicas in both regions. Users in the USA would read and write from the USA replica, and users in Europe would read and write from the European replica. As writes are made to the closest replica, latency is considerably lower.

Replicas can be added and removed as needed. However, when enabling Availability Zone support, this has to be done when creating the replica. The following screenshot shows an example and the replica management page showing the options and a visual display of where replicas are placed:

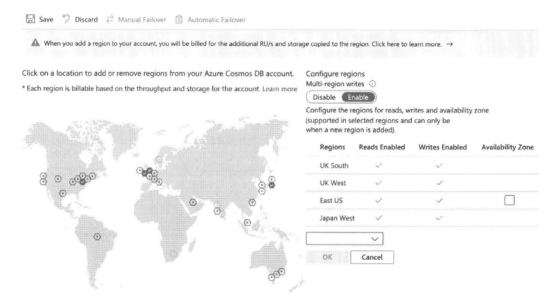

Figure 14.7 – Azure Cosmos DB management

Having a globally distributed database can cause issues with consistency, however. Suppose you have data being replicated between regions. In that case, there will be a delay either in the time it takes to become consistent between replicas or to ensure all replicas are in sync before a write is acknowledged, which can decrease performance.

Whereas some technologies, such as Azure SQL, manage this as part of the service and do not provide any options, Azure Cosmos DB offers a range of consistency options and allows you to choose the best one according to your requirements.

Consistency levels

Azure Cosmos DB offers a range of choices for defining consistency between replicas, known as consistency models. Strong consistency and eventual consistency are at two different ends of the spectrum, and this can help developers make a clear choice concerning high availability and performance.

The five consistency models are as follows:

- **Strong**: Strong consistency is the easiest model to understand. The most recent committed version of an item is returned when the data is read. A partial or uncommitted write is never returned to the client. This will give a lot of overhead because every instance needs to be updated with the latest version of the data, which has a huge price in terms of the data's latency and throughput.

- **Bounded staleness**: This is a compromise that trades delays for strong consistency. This model doesn't guarantee that all the observers have the same data at the same time. Instead, it allows a lag of 5 seconds (100 operations).

- **Session**: This is the default level for newly created databases and collections. It is half as expensive as strong consistency, and it offers good performance and availability. It ensures that everything that is written in the current session is also available for reading. Anything else will be accurate but delayed.

- **Consistent prefix**: With this level, updates that are returned contain accurate data for a specific point in time but won't necessarily be current.

- **Eventual**: There's no ordering guarantee for how long it will take to synchronize (like the consistent prefix), and updates aren't guaranteed to come in order. However, this is the most performant model for response times. When there are no further writes, the replicas will eventually be updated.

You can configure a change of the desired consistency model at any time, either through the portal or programmatically through PowerShell, the CLI, or REST APIs. The portal shows a graphical example of how the consistency models work in practice, as shown in the following screenshot:

Figure 14.8 – Setting the Cosmos DB consistency model

Such fine-grained controls over consistency, the placement of replicas, and the ability to have read/write replicas anywhere in the world make Azure Cosmos DB the ideal solution for globally spanning applications as it enables you to have your data close to your customer while still ensuring uniformity.

Summary

In this chapter, we concluded *Part 4, Applications and Databases* by looking at the options for introducing high availability into our solutions.

Although many Azure components provide a redundancy level by default, some services require availability to be designed in, and others offer different levels of resilience depending on your needs.

We also looked at how we can apply these concepts to Azure VMs using scale sets, which enable us to automate the scaling of VMs based on demand and thresholds we can set.

We also looked at the different Azure storage accounts and databases, namely Azure SQL and Azure Cosmos DB. These services provide a default level of local redundancy, meaning you are protected against hardware failure. However, we examined how this can be extended across regions should it be required.

In the next chapter, we begin *Part 5, Operations and Monitoring*, starting with the different ways to set up logging and monitoring components.

Exam scenario

MegaCorp Inc. has an e-commerce application that they wish to expand to serve global customers, but they are concerned about performance. Local distribution centers in each region (the Americas, Europe, and Asia) perform their order shipping and management. The performance and a local view of stock levels within each region are important. However, a consolidated global view is still required for reporting purposes, but as reports are run in the evening, an up-to-date view of levels across regions is not required.

Currently, the application is built using traditional VMs because it requires specific OS components and custom modules to be installed. The backend database has been built with NoSQL in mind, currently being used on a Mongo DB. The application team has tested and confirmed the solution can be migrated to Cosmos DB using the MongoDB APIs with little effort.

Currently, there are only 2 VMs and a load balancer running the application. Although these VMs are at maximum capacity during busy periods, there are also occasions when they experience very low usage.

All components currently run in Azure but only in the East US region. Tests with customers outside the US have confirmed low response times.

Suggest a potential strategy to the management team that could help improve the application's efficiency and performance.

Further reading

For more information on topics covered in this chapter, you can refer to the following links:

- *Azure Scale Sets*: `https://docs.microsoft.com/en-us/azure/virtual-machine-scale-sets/overview`

- *Azure SQL Availability Groups*: `https://docs.microsoft.com/en-us/azure/azure-sql/database/auto-failover-group-overview`

- *Azure Cosmos DB Consistency Levels*: `https://docs.microsoft.com/en-us/azure/cosmos-db/consistency-levels`

Section 5: Operations and Monitoring

This section will look at how to effectively monitor and manage solutions in order to be notified of problems and events. It includes the different options for backup, cost optimization, and managing how we deploy systems.

The following chapters will be covered under this section:

- *Chapter 15, Designing for Logging and Monitoring*
- *Chapter 16, Developing Business Continuity*
- *Chapter 17, Scripted Deployments and DevOps Automation*

15
Designing for Logging and Monitoring

In the previous chapter, we explored the options for enabling solutions to be highly available and implementing automatic redundancy to ensure that our systems are always running and healthy.

In this chapter, we begin *Section 5, Operations and Monitoring*, by looking at how we ensure we are always aware of what is happening to our platform from a perspective of health, security, and costs.

Azure provides a range of options for collecting logs and metrics that we can continually monitor and alert on so that we can be proactive and also keep the systems running optimally. Some tools are enabled by default; others must be specifically activated. For larger organizations with more complex structures and requirements, how we design those systems can greatly impact the efficiency and scalability of them.

This chapter, therefore, explores the different tools available to us and what the architectural options are when using them. Specifically, we will be covering the following subjects:

- Understanding logs and storage options
- Exploring monitoring tools
- Understanding security and compliance
- Using cost management and reporting

Technical requirements

This chapter will use the Azure portal (`https://portal.azure.com`) for examples.

Understanding logs and storage options

Monitoring and logging in Azure is a key feature of the platform and helps to drive everything from resilience and automated scaling to performance and security.

Monitoring is so important that it is enabled by default. However, this does not mean we don't need to consider monitoring in our designs – each service has its own nuances, and the platform as a whole has a number of options for how you can configure your solutions depending on your organization's needs.

As an example, we will consider two extremes. The first is a start-up company that is developing a modern containerized web service built using a microservice-based architecture. The scalability and health of the service are key, and the solution itself may be built from numerous different components, including storage, databases, service queues, and apps.

As all these components must work harmoniously together, with many interdependencies between them, we need to monitor the whole stack and the communications between them. When problems do arise, we need a monitoring solution that can help us trace from one component to the next where the issue might be. From an organizational perspective, there might be a product owner who is entirely responsible for this application.

At the other end of the scale is a large, multi-national company that is running hundreds of different systems in Azure. Some of these applications may be complex and some simple. Some may use **IaaS** components such as VMs, whereas others may be built around **PaaS** and serverless architectures.

Support and security may be centralized into different teams. For example, a global security team may be responsible for monitoring and responding to all potential threats, whereas local development teams may take responsibility for the performance and overall health of individual apps.

The Azure logging and monitoring ecosystem, therefore, needs to be flexible enough to cope with a multitude of scenarios.

Azure Monitor has matured over the years, and what used to be individual products are merging into one monitoring solution made up of different modules. We will first look at the different types of logs, their sources, and where they can be stored.

Understanding data types and sources

Monitoring data is largely split into two different types – metrics and logs.

Metrics describe an aspect of a system at a particular point in time and are displayed in numerical values. They are capable of supporting near real-time scenarios. Logs are different from metrics. They contain data that is organized into records, with different sets of properties for each type. Data such as events, traces, and performance data is stored as logs.

Metrics and logs can also come from numerous sources; again, these are generally broken down into the following:

- **Application**: Data gathered from a custom-built application such as .NET applications. Applications must be discretely configured to emit their logs and information to an Application Insights instance.

- **Operating system**: Windows and Linux operating systems have their own logging mechanisms, and these can be hooked into. You must install the diagnostics extension, Log Analytics agent, or dependency agent on each VM to receive this data.

- **Azure resources**: All Azure native resources produce their own metrics and logs; however, some must be explicitly captured. This includes VMs when considered from the Azure management plane point of view and are additional to operating system logs. As each resource is different, the types of logs you can receive from them are also different.

- **Azure subscription**: Also known as the **activity log**, events on the Azure management plane for an individual subscription are logged. Examples include the health, deployment, interaction, and modification of Azure services.

- **Azure tenant**: User operations such as the creation, modification, and deletion of users.

- **Custom source**: Some external services or software installed on a VM may produce their own logs. For example, an application may output data to a CSV file on a VM or via a REST API. This data can be mapped, collected, and reported on in Azure Monitor.

Logs and metrics from each source can be used in a variety of ways, and how you wish to view or interact with them will determine what additional configuration may be required.

Understanding log use cases

Logs can help in a number of different ways; the following are some use cases that will be covered in more detail through this chapter:

- **Analysis**: Metrics and logs can be analyzed using Azure Monitor or Log Analytics.

- **Respond**: Alerts can be set up to trigger when specific conditions are met, for example, when a VM's CPU reaches a critical threshold. VM scale sets and App Service scale events use this mechanism to add or remove instances based on these thresholds.

- **Insights**: Specific solutions are available for different sources, for example, Application Insights, Container Insights, and VM insights. Separate monitoring solutions can be installed that configure source-specific workbooks such as Azure SQL or Backup.

- **Visualize**: Logs and metrics can be viewed graphically using workbooks or dashboards, or even by integrating with Power BI.

- **Integrate**: Custom actions can be created in response to logs and metrics using Logic Apps.

The following diagram shows how all these features and sources come together as part of the Azure Monitor ecosystem:

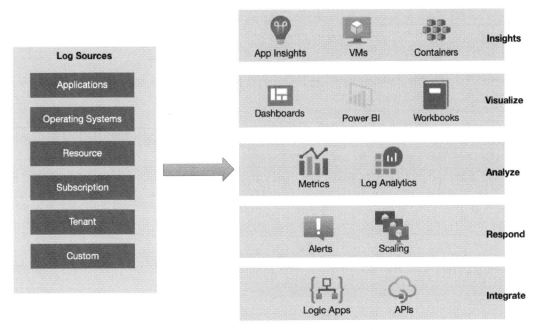

Figure 15.1 – Azure monitoring sources and actions

By default, basic logs and metrics are stored automatically on the platform and you can view up to 30 days of history. These default views also provide basic filtering and monitoring options to get a high-level view of what is happening to your solutions. If you need longer retention of logs or wish to perform deeper analysis or integrate with other services, logs must be directed elsewhere.

At the subscription level, activity and resource logs can additionally be sent to a **Log Analytics workspace**, an Azure storage account, or an Azure Event Hubs instance. To set up the additional destinations, or *sinks*, from the **Activity Log** blade, click **Diagnostics Settings** followed by **+Add diagnostic setting**. The following screenshot shows an example of this page:

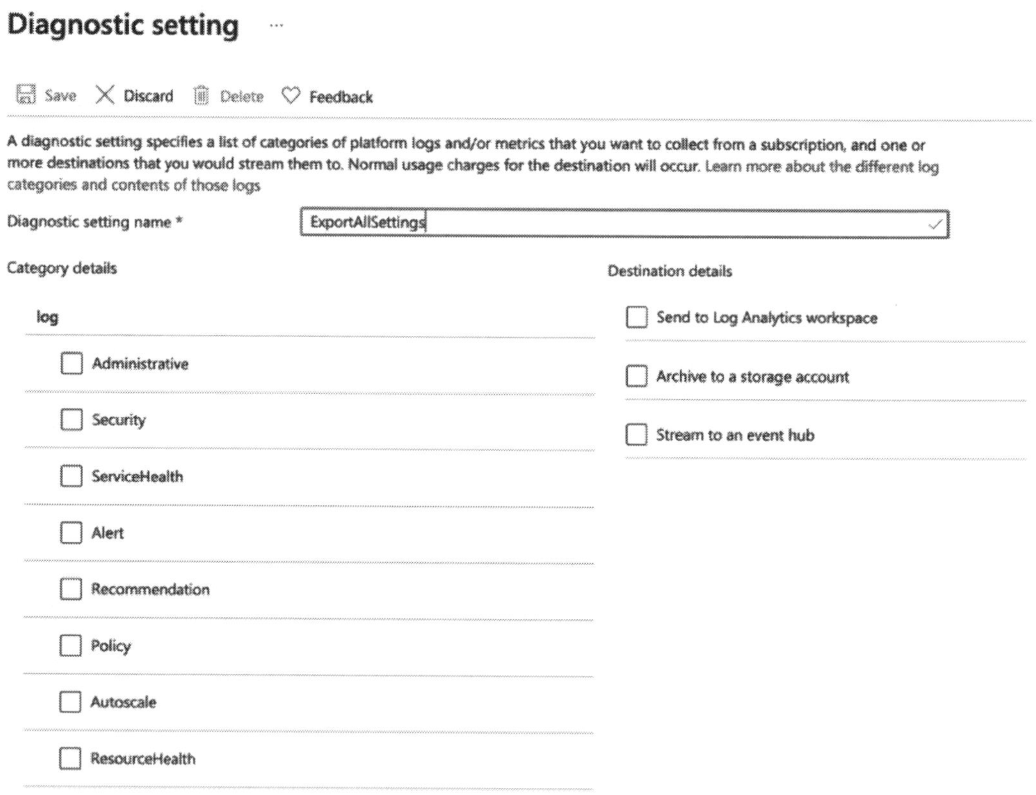

Diagnostic setting   ...

🖫 Save   ✕ Discard   🗑 Delete   ♡ Feedback

A diagnostic setting specifies a list of categories of platform logs and/or metrics that you want to collect from a subscription, and one or more destinations that you would stream them to. Normal usage charges for the destination will occur. Learn more about the different log categories and contents of those logs

Diagnostic setting name *   [ExportAllSettings   ✓]

Category details   Destination details

log   ☐ Send to Log Analytics workspace

☐ Administrative   ☐ Archive to a storage account

☐ Security   ☐ Stream to an event hub

☐ ServiceHealth

☐ Alert

☐ Recommendation

☐ Policy

☐ Autoscale

☐ ResourceHealth

Figure 15.2 – Sending activity logs to additional sinks

For activity logs, setting additional destinations at the subscription level will direct all logs of all components within that subscription. Additional log options can then be set at either the subscription level or the component level; in this way you can configure what logs are sent where at a very granular level.

For example, you could set logs to be sent to a central Log Analytics account at the subscription level, and then create additional sinks at the component level to also send those logs to an application-specific Log Analytics workspace, storage account, or event hub, as we can see in the following example:

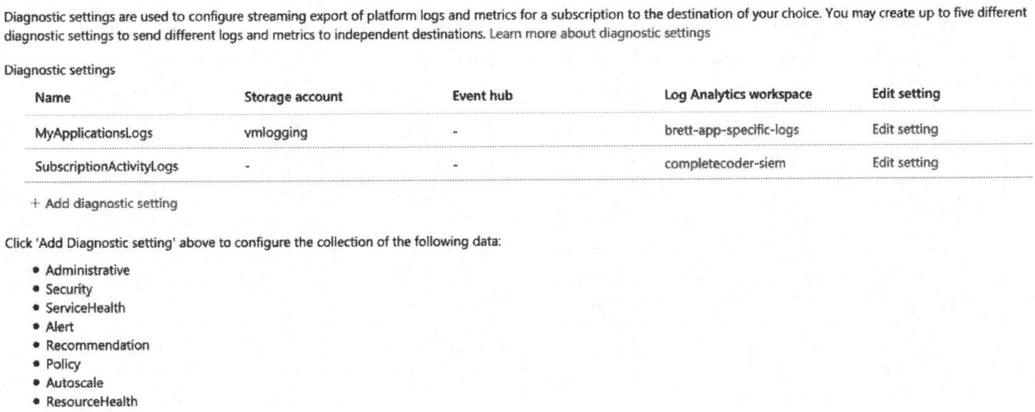

Diagnostic settings are used to configure streaming export of platform logs and metrics for a subscription to the destination of your choice. You may create up to five different diagnostic settings to send different logs and metrics to independent destinations. Learn more about diagnostic settings

Diagnostic settings

Name	Storage account	Event hub	Log Analytics workspace	Edit setting
MyApplicationsLogs	vmlogging	-	brett-app-specific-logs	Edit setting
SubscriptionActivityLogs	-	-	completecoder-siem	Edit setting

+ Add diagnostic setting

Click 'Add Diagnostic setting' above to configure the collection of the following data:

- Administrative
- Security
- ServiceHealth
- Alert
- Recommendation
- Policy
- Autoscale
- ResourceHealth

Figure 15.3 – Configuring multiple log sinks

As we saw in *Figure 15.1*, you can also be selective in the logs you send. Therefore, by configuring specific logs being sent to multiple sinks, you can ensure different teams only receive the logs they are interested in.

Configuring logs from the **Activity Log** blade allows you to collect the following specific log types:

- **Administrative**: Creating, updating, deleting, and actioning events, for example, creating a storage account or starting a VM

- **Security**: Security Center alerts, such as suspicious double extension files executed

- **Service health**: Region-wide health events

- **Alert**: Alerts that you can define, for example, if you create an alert to monitor for high CPU usage

- **Recommendation**: Azure Advisor recommendations

- **Policy**: Events triggered by policies

- **Autoscale**: VM scale sets or apps scaling out or in

- **Resource health**: Resource-specific health issues

Individual services also have their own specific logs. Again, these logs can be directed to a Log Analytics workspace, storage account, or event hub. These additional logs are configured through each component's diagnostics blade.

In the following screenshot, we can see the diagnostics blade for a SQL database. The view is similar to what we saw when configuring activity logs, and again to output the logs to a different destination, we simply click + **Add diagnostic setting** and then select the Log Analytics workspace, storage account, or event hub:

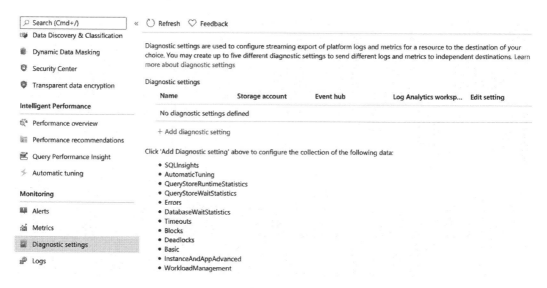

Figure 15.4 – SQL database diagnostics settings

What is different, however, is the logs that are sent; in this example of a SQL database, we see specific options for databases such as **SQLInsights**, **QueryStoreRuntimeStatistics**, and **DatabaseWaitStatistics**.

Again, we can send some or all of these logs to the destination or create multiple settings to have logs sent to multiple sinks for consumption by different teams.

All Azure components emit logs and metrics as described in this section. However, VMs behave differently. Although you can collect Azure management plane events that are still captured through the activity log, a VM can optionally have agents installed to collect additional metrics and logs from the VM.

VM logging and monitoring

Because VMs generate logs as part of the operating system – Windows event logs for Windows servers and syslogs for Linux servers – Microsoft provides agents that must be installed on the VMs.

There are four different agents that can be installed on VMs, and each either collects different logs or can send them to different destinations. The newest, the **Azure Monitor agent**, is in preview at the time of writing; however, it will eventually replace the **Log Analytics** and **Telegraf** agents on Windows and Linux. The following diagram shows at a high level how we can use different agents and settings and where we can send those logs and metrics:

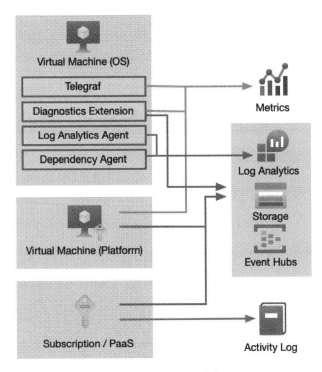

Figure 15.5 – Log sources and destinations

Next, we shall look in more detail at each of the different agents.

Azure Monitor agent

The Azure Monitor agent uses **Data Collection Rules** (**DCRs**), which are configured in the Azure Monitor blade. You can create multiple DCRs for different purposes, and each DCR can have its own set of the following:

- **Data sources**: Define specific performance counters, such as CPU, memory, disk, and network metrics, or event logs, such as application logs, security logs, or system logs.

- **Destinations**: Sets where logs will be sent, for example, Azure Monitor Metrics or an Azure Log Analytics workspace.

- **Resources**: The VMs you wish to collect logs from.

Because you can create multiple DCRs, you can set up complex scenarios for different needs. For example, you could have a DCR for all VMs that collects general metrics and logs and another rule for SQL servers that collects SQL-specific metrics and logs.

Log Analytics agent

The Log Analytics agent also collects monitoring data from the operating system of VMs and sends that data to a Log Analytics workspace. The agent is the same agent that is used by **System Center Operations Manager** (**SCOM**) and can be used in conjunction with an on-premises SCOM implementation. This also means that the agent can be used to collect logs from on-premises VMs and even VMs running on other cloud platforms.

The Log Analytics agent and its data are used by a number of Azure monitoring tools, including the following:

- Log Analytics
- VM insights
- Azure Automation
- Azure Security Center
- Azure Sentinel

Because the Log Analytics agent only sends the data to a Log Analytics workspace and Azure Monitor, if you need to send information to other sources, such as Azure Storage or Event Hubs, you may need additional agents such as the diagnostics or Telegraf agents.

Azure diagnostics agent

The diagnostics agent can collect performance data, operating system logs, and crash dumps. However, the diagnostics agent sends those logs to an Azure storage account and optionally an event hub or Azure Monitor Metrics. This makes the agent ideal when you need a longer-term storage mechanism without built-in querying capabilities or if you want to send logs to external services by integrating with an event hub.

> **Important Note**
> You cannot configure the diagnostics agent to sends logs to an event hub via the portal; this can only be done using PowerShell, the Azure CLI, or via an ARM template.

Another limitation to using the diagnostics agent is that it can only be used on Azure resources.

Telegraf agent

The Telegraf agent is also used to collect performance data; however, it is specifically for Linux computers. The agent can only send data to Azure Monitor Metrics for viewing in the Azure portal via the metrics explorer.

Dependency agent

The dependency agent is an add-on to the Log Analytics agent and is used to collect data about running processes on a VM and track external dependencies on those processes. This agent is used by the VM insights tool or the Service Map solution, which are covered in the next section.

Before we move on to the tools we can use to use our logs, we need to quickly look at the options for deploying the different log options.

Understanding deployment options

By default, only Azure activity logs and platform metrics are enabled. Sending those logs to a Log Analytics workspace or enabling VM agents must be explicitly done.

The VM agents are installed when you activate specific tools, such as VM insights, enabling guest-level monitoring, or enabling **Logs** in the Azure portal. As we see in the following example screenshot, we are installing the Log Analytics agent by enabling logs via the **Logs** blade of an Azure VM:

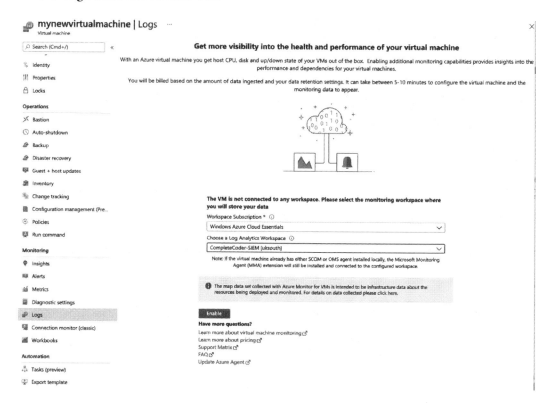

Figure 15.6 – Enabling the Log Analytics agent

Alternatively, agents can be installed via a PowerShell or Azure CLI script or as part of an ARM template when deploying VMs, which is ideal when you want to automate your deployments. The following is an example ARM template snippet we can use:

```
{
    "type": "extensions",
    "name": "OMSExtension",
    "apiVersion": "[variables('apiVersion')]",
    "location": "[resourceGroup().location]",
    "dependsOn": [
        "[concat('Microsoft.Compute/virtualMachines/',
 variables('vmName'))]"
```

```
    ],
    "properties": {
        "publisher": "Microsoft.EnterpriseCloud.Monitoring",
        "type": "MicrosoftMonitoringAgent",
        "typeHandlerVersion": "1.0",
        "autoUpgradeMinorVersion": true,
        "settings": {
            "workspaceId": "xxxxxxxxx"
        },
        "protectedSettings": {
            "workspaceKey": "xxxxxxxxxx"
        }
    }
}
```

Because the configuration can be written as JSON using an ARM template, you can also create an Azure policy with a `deployIfNotExists` setting to automatically configure agents whenever a VM is created. Policies can also be used on other Azure resources to similarly configure the outputs of activity logs and diagnostics settings whenever a resource is defined.

> **Information Tip**
> Azure has a number of built-in policies for setting up the automated configuration of monitoring tools, and you can view them here:
> `https://docs.microsoft.com/en-us/azure/azure-monitor/policy-reference`.

Now that we understand how to collect logs, we need tools that will help us use those logs to understand issues and trigger alerts.

Exploring monitoring tools

There are a number of tools available that help us monitor, alert, analyze, and visualize our logs. Some require additional steps to be configured, as we saw in the previous section when we configured activity logs, to also output them to a Log Analytics workspace; others are available automatically.

By default, basic logs and metrics can be visualized in the Azure portal via the **Metrics** and **Activity Log** blades either at the subscription or component level.

Activity logs

The following screenshot shows the **Activity Log** blade when looking at a VM:

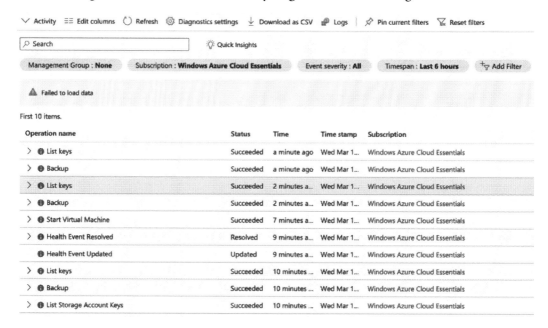

Figure 15.7 – Azure activity log

Here we can see the most recent Azure plane events, which are useful for troubleshooting events; for example, if the VM had been shut down, the event would be listed in the Azure activity log.

Events can be filtered by clicking the menu options to change the scope of **Management Group**, **Subscription**, **Event severity**, and **Timespan**. Additional filters can be added by clicking the **Add Filter** button to also filter on the **Resource type**, **Operation**, **Event initiated by**, and **Event category** options.

Selecting an event will show you granular details of what occurred, when, and perhaps more importantly, who triggered it, by selecting the **JSON** view, as we can see in the following example:

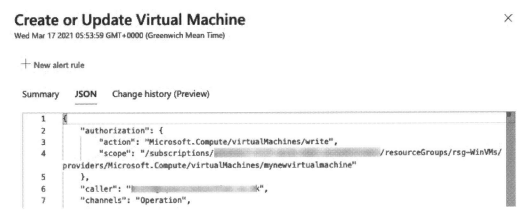

Figure 15.8 – Azure activity log details

From this view, we can also create alerts by clicking **+ New alert rule**, which will take us to the **Create alert** page. Alternatively, we can create alerts directly by going straight to the **Alerts** blade, which we will look at shortly; but first, we will look at the other default tool, the **Metrics** blade.

Azure Metrics

At the start of the chapter, we said that metrics describe an aspect of a system at a particular point in time and are displayed in numerical values. Typical examples include CPU utilization, disk reads and writes, network usage, and storage capacity or usage. As each service in Azure performs different tasks, the metrics we receive are also different. For example, for a storage account, we may be interested in the bytes read, but CPU utilization has no meaning.

As numerical values, metrics are also easiest to visualize graphically and are therefore normally displayed as charts.

The following two screenshots show two examples of the **Metrics** blade for two different Azure components – a VM and a storage account. The first shows a VM, and we have added two metrics – CPU and disk operations:

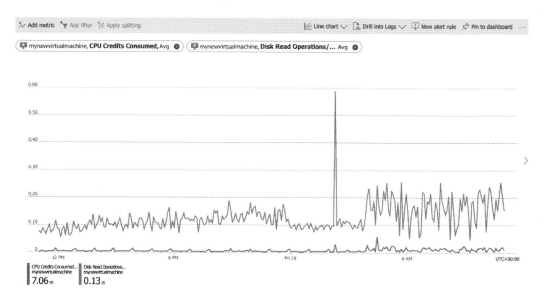

Figure 15.9 – Azure VM metrics example

The next screenshot shows a storage account displaying transactions:

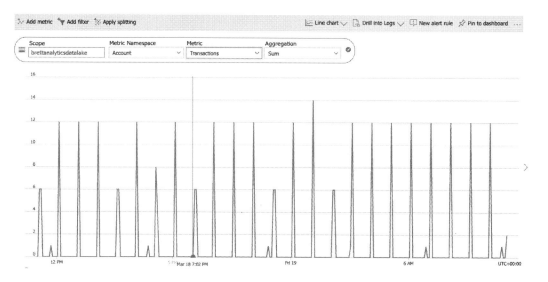

Figure 15.10 – Azure storage account metrics example

In both cases, similarly to the **Activity Log** view earlier, we can add filters, specify which metrics to view, and create alerts, which we will look at next.

Azure alerts

Displaying metrics and logs in the Azure portal is of course extremely useful; however, we sometimes need to be proactively informed when certain events are happening, for example, if a critical VM is shut down, or a storage account grows to a certain size.

Alerts in Azure allow us to specify criteria and automatically inform us when those criteria are triggered. We saw in the earlier sections that we can create alerts from the **Activity Log** view and the **Metrics** view. These links provide a quick way to create alerts based on what you were looking at (for example, a VM shutdown), but we can also just create them from scratch by going to the **Alerts** blade in the Azure portal.

Alerts can be created from a resource by selecting the **Alerts** view on that resource, or by going into Azure Monitor and clicking the **Alerts** view.

For each resource, such as a storage account, a VM, or other resource, alerts start with a signal, which is a piece of information – a metric or a log activity – and they come from either activity logs, Log Analytics, Application Insights, or metrics.

When creating an alert in the Azure portal, we specify the scope, which is the resource in question, and where the signal will come from.

Next, we define the criterion or condition that will trigger the rule, for example, when a specific activity event occurs or CPU utilization reaches a particular threshold.

Now we define what action we will take. Actions are grouped as action groups. An action group allows us to define what will happen, for example, email, SMS, push notification, or voice message, and where to send it, for example, an administrator's phone or email account.

We can also trigger integration actions such as calling an Azure function, logic app, webhook (API endpoint), automation runbooks, and many others.

You can define multiple action groups, each with its own set of recipients and notifications, and then assign multiple action groups to each alert.

Finally, we set a rule name and a description and then either enable or disable the rule. Only enabled rules will trigger.

The following diagram shows a visual representation of the options and flow:

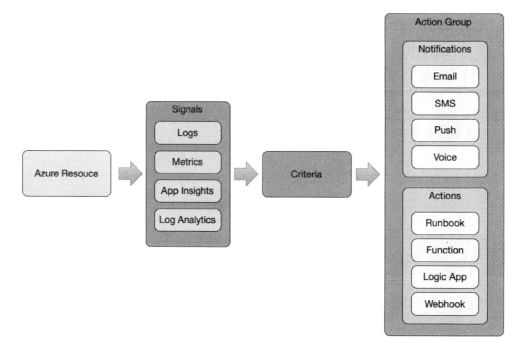

Figure 15.11 – Alert logic

The following screenshot shows what a typical alert rule might look like:

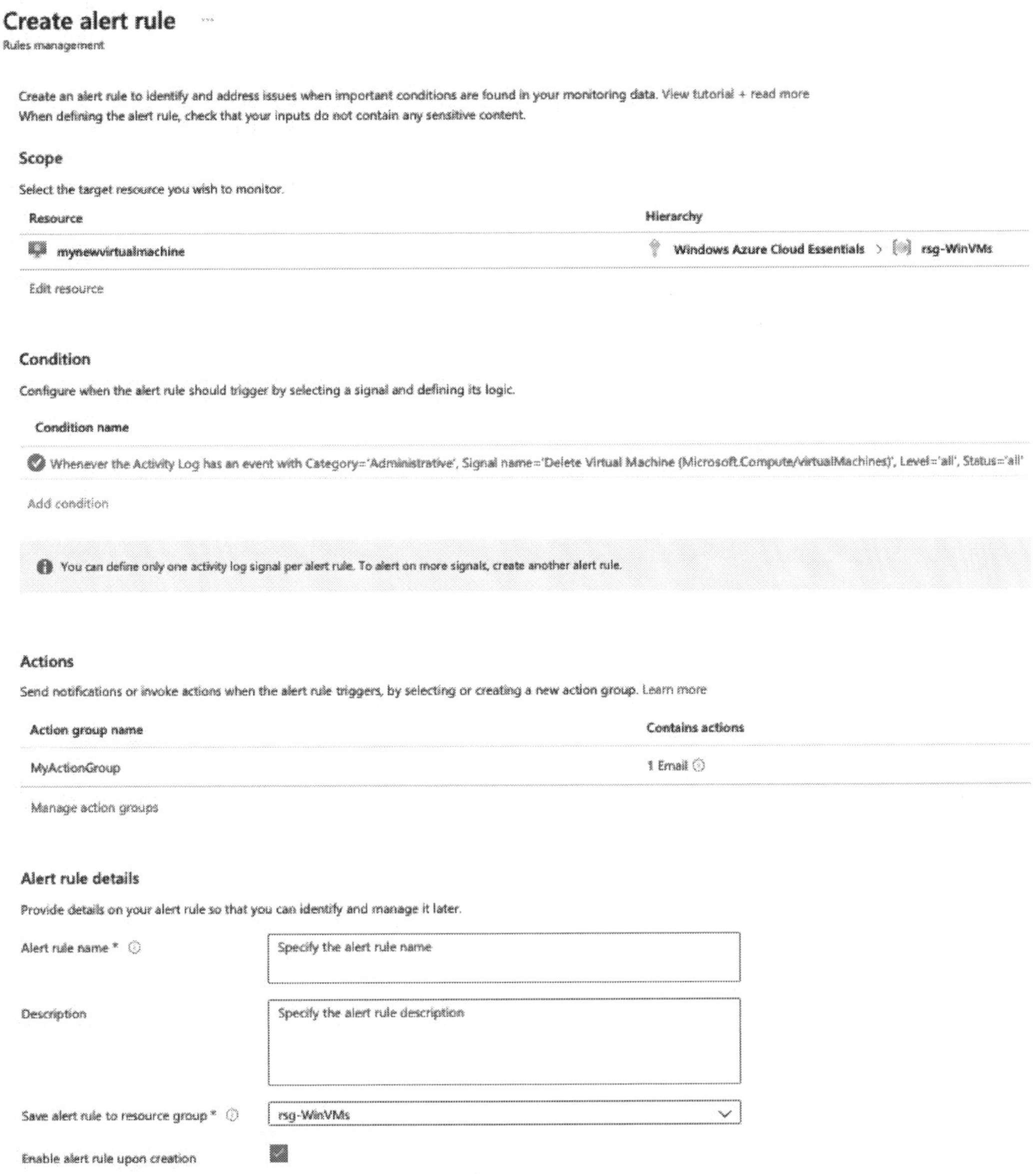

Create alert rule ···
Rules management

Create an alert rule to identify and address issues when important conditions are found in your monitoring data. View tutorial + read more
When defining the alert rule, check that your inputs do not contain any sensitive content.

Scope

Select the target resource you wish to monitor.

Resource	Hierarchy
🖥 mynewvirtualmachine	⚙ Windows Azure Cloud Essentials > 🔘 rsg-WinVMs

Edit resource

Condition

Configure when the alert rule should trigger by selecting a signal and defining its logic.

Condition name

✅ Whenever the Activity Log has an event with Category='Administrative', Signal name='Delete Virtual Machine (Microsoft.Compute/virtualMachines)', Level='all', Status='all'

Add condition

ℹ You can define only one activity log signal per alert rule. To alert on more signals, create another alert rule.

Actions

Send notifications or invoke actions when the alert rule triggers, by selecting or creating a new action group. Learn more

Action group name	Contains actions
MyActionGroup	1 Email ⓘ

Manage action groups

Alert rule details

Provide details on your alert rule so that you can identify and manage it later.

Alert rule name * ⓘ	Specify the alert rule name
Description	Specify the alert rule description
Save alert rule to resource group * ⓘ	rsg-WinVMs ⌄
Enable alert rule upon creation	☑

Figure 15.12 – Creating an alert rule

Through the use of alerts, you can generate complex rules and responses to any event that might happen in Azure. Over and above what we have discussed, some possible scenarios include the following:

- Email administrators if a VM is shut down.
- Send an SMS to on-call personnel if critical CPU thresholds are met.
- Update a status web page via Logic Apps or Functions.
- Raise an incident ticket in a helpdesk solution by calling a webhook (API).

Alerts, metrics, and activity logs are automatically enabled across all your Azure resources, and although the default tools provide many possibilities for being alerted too, or for investigating issues, sometimes you need to explore across resources and aggregate information to get a complete view; for these scenarios, we can use Log Analytics.

Log Analytics workspaces

In this chapter, we have seen how logs and metrics from Azure resources and VMs can be directed to a Log Analytics workspace.

Having logs in a Log Analytics workspace provides a few benefits. First, logs can be retained for longer than 90 days. Second, logs can be more easily filtered using a query language called **Kusto Query Language** (**KQL**), which provides greater flexibility and power when trying to find the data you need. Because data is coming from multiple sources, we can also combine and aggregate that data to provide far greater insights and correlations between services.

Kusto queries are designed to be easily written and therefore quick and easy to learn. For example, a basic query to view the heartbeat of VMs would look like this:

```
Perf
| where CounterName == "% Processor Time"
| where ObjectName == "Processor"
| summarize avg(CounterValue) by bin(TimeGenerated, 15min),
Computer, _ResourceId
```

The first part of the query states the data we want to read, in this case, the `Perf` (performance) logs. Then, we use a pipe (`|`) to separate our commands, followed by `where` statements to provide basic filtering. Finally, we can summarize our data using standard grouping techniques.

Data can be viewed in a variety of ways, including charts, which further help investigations, and for spotting trends, the preceding query, for example, can be easily modified to display the data as a chart by adding the `render timechart` command, as follows:

```
Perf
| where CounterName == "% Processor Time"
| where ObjectName == "Processor"
| summarize avg(CounterValue) by bin(TimeGenerated, 15min),
Computer, _ResourceId // bin is used to set the time grain to
15 minutes
| render timechart
```

When designing solutions that use a Log Analytics workspace, you need to consider who has access, what data you are sending, and how it will be used.

We saw earlier that some logs, such as Azure activity and diagnostics logs, can be sent to multiple Log Analytics workspaces; however, some logs, such as Windows event logs, can only be ingested into a single workspace.

Different organizations and different teams within those organizations may have different requirements.

For example, a small company that uses a single subscription for all its Azure resources would probably only need a single workspace.

A large, multi-national organization may have multiple subscriptions either across regions or departments. We must then consider how systems are managed and monitored. For example, if there is a single team responsible for everything across the enterprise, you would be better off with a single workspace, with all resources, regardless of which subscription they are in, sending the logs to that workspace. This can have implications on network traffic if those services are in different regions as you will incur additional ingress and egress costs.

Alternatively, you would have workspaces per region, or even per subscription, which helps provide more granular control; however, your data is now spread across multiple workspaces.

A hybrid approach could include sending some logs to a central workspace and other logs to individual workspaces. This design pattern is useful where different teams need access to different logs and have different responsibilities. For example, a central workspace may be used by a company-wide monitoring team, but individual service owners need visibility of application-specific information and metrics, as we can see in the following diagram:

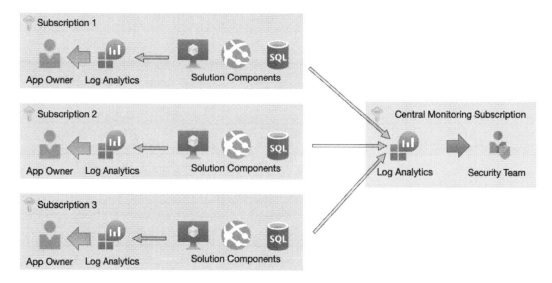

Figure 15.13 – Example hybrid reporting

Azure Log Analytics workspaces are used by other services in Azure for security and compliance monitoring, as we shall explore in the next section.

Understanding security and compliance

Security and compliance are important factors in all organizations. As we move our solutions to the cloud, we need to ensure that the resources we build do not expose data to the public network.

In addition, many organizations define governance policies that must be adhered to; sometimes these are aligned to regulatory compliance, and sometimes they match security policy.

We discussed compliance and governance in *Chapter 5, Ensuring Platform Governance*, and during that chapter, we explored how to create policies and initiatives that encode those needs.

Security Center is an optional addition to your toolset, and when enabled on a subscription, it creates an Azure Security benchmark initiative that gets automatically assigned. The initiative contains audit policies containing industry best practices for ensuring a secure platform.

Azure Security Center

Azure Security Center uses your own policies and the built-in policies to calculate a secure score, along with recommendations on how to improve that score. The following screenshot shows an example of such a report:

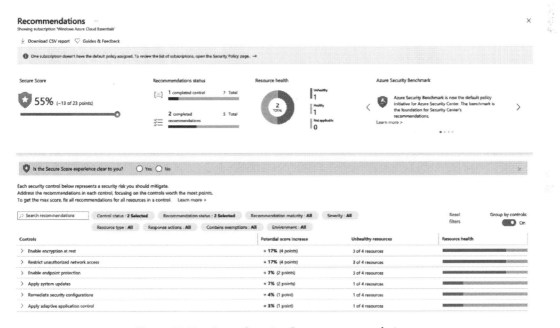

Figure 15.14 – Azure Security Center recommendations

Azure Security Center continually assesses your subscriptions as resources are added or altered. The secure score itself can help security and compliance teams to quickly identify and then investigate resources to secure and make them compliant.

Azure Security Center also reports policy compliance; in other words, you can see each of your policies and see which subscriptions and components adhere to the policy and highlight those that don't. Security Center also helps remediate non-compliant policies from within the reports by providing guidance and tools to bring them in line.

Additionally, Azure Defender can also be activated on subscriptions to provide even greater protection. Azure Defender provides enhanced security and alerting with advanced threat protection on VMs, SQL databases, containers, web applications, storage accounts, and more.

Azure Defender

Azure Defender must be enabled on a per-subscription basis as it incurs additional costs; however, when it is you gain the following benefits:

- **Just-in-time VM access**: Controls the ability to log on to VMs by enforcing a request/accept workflow before ports are opened to the VM.

- **Adaptive application and network controls**: Using AI and automation, suggests enhancements based on all your workloads in the organization. Also includes monitoring of network security group rules and again advises the tightening of them based on usage.

- **Vulnerability assessments**: Scans VMs using Qualys looking for vulnerable software and missing patches.

- **Threat protection**: Scans and alerts on potential threats to your PaaS components, such as storage accounts, Azure SQL, and web apps. For example, SQL databases are monitored for SQL injection and brute-force attacks.

- **Kubernetes and container protection**: Assesses your AKS clusters and container hosts, then alerts on unsafe configuration. Also scans container images in an Azure container registry looking for known vulnerabilities.

Vulnerabilities and alerts, along with coverage (for example, which subscriptions have Azure Defender enabled), are surfaced in the Azure Security Center portal, as in the example in the following screenshot:

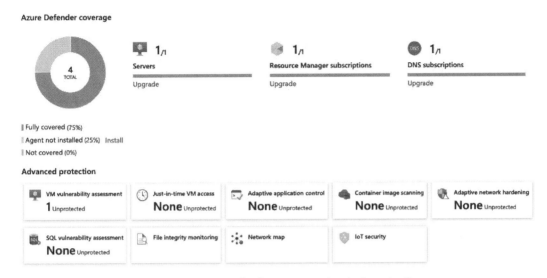

Figure 15.15 – Azure Defender coverage view in Security Center

Although Security Center on its own provides a base layer of security benchmarks, Azure Defender builds on these to further enhance your solutions with industry-standard best practices and continual threat protection.

For even greater protection, and the ability to investigate security incidents, you can use a **Security Information Event Management (SIEM)** tool. There are a number of SIEMs on the market that can be integrated into your Azure resource, often utilizing specific VM agents and event hubs for forwarding traffic. However, Microsoft offers **Azure Sentinel**, an AI-driven SIEM that integrates directly into your Log Analytics workspace to ingest, monitor, and respond to threats.

Azure Sentinel

Azure Sentinel brings together all your logs from all sources, via the Log Analytics workspace, to correlate and search for threats. Sentinel uses connectors to integrate with Microsoft 365, Active Directory, and many third-party vendors such as Cisco, Carbon Black, and F5 networks. By combining information from many different sources, an attack can be tracked and investigated across the entire IT stack.

Azure Sentinel is priced by the amount of log data ingested, and so you can choose which log sources to ingest. Known as a data connector, you configure Sentinel to only ingest the log sources you are interested in, although of course the more you connect, the greater visibility you have.

Once connected, Azure offers a series of analytical templates from which you can easily create rules, or you can use them as a starting point and create your own. Rules are analytical queries that search for specific attack types, which you can then use to generate an alert from.

The following screenshot shows an example of templates you can choose from for a given data connector:

SEVERITY ↑↓	NAME ↑↓	RULE TYPE ↑↓	DATA SOURCES	TACTICS	CREATE RULE
High	Modified domain federation trust settings	Scheduled	Azure Active Directory	Credential Access	Create rule
High	First access credential added to Application or Service Principal where ...	Scheduled	Azure Active Directory	Credential Access	Create rule
High	Suspicious application consent similar to O365 Attack Toolkit	Scheduled	Azure Active Directory		Create rule
High	IN USE Known IRIDIUM IP	Scheduled	Office 365 +7	Command and Control	Create rule
High	Known Barium IP	Scheduled	Office 365 +8	Command and Control	Create rule
Medium	Brute force attack against Azure Portal	Scheduled	Azure Active Directory	Credential Access	Create rule
Medium	MFA disabled for a user	Scheduled	Azure Active Directory +1	Credential Access	Create rule

Figure 15.16 – Creating rules from pre-defined templates

As well as sending alerts when rules are triggered, you can also create automation runbooks to perform automated actions. These can be as simple as integrating with your helpdesk solution to generate tickets, or even responding directly to the threat by performing a specific action. For example, if a source is detected as performing a SQL injection attack, you can create a playbook that would automatically blacklist that IP address on your Azure Firewall.

The Sentinel overview page shows all your ingested events, alerts, and incidents, as you can see in the following example:

Figure 15.17 – Azure Sentinel overview page

When threats are detected, Sentinel provides you with investigative tools that help to trace and hunt down the attack. You can select an incident from the **Incidents** view and locate the root cause by seeing what happened before and after the incident, where it occurred, links, and related information.

The **Hunting** tool allows security professionals to proactively investigate your Azure solutions for potential or in-progress attacks before they happen. Sentinel provides a series of starting queries to help with this, or you can build your own.

Sentinel also provides a series of **Jupyter** notebooks so that you can use machine learning, using an Azure Machine Learning workspace to further enhance your investigations.

Threat detection and remediation are specialist areas and often involve dedicated security teams or a **Security Operations Center** (**SOC**). As an architect, it is your responsibility to ensure the right tools are provided for your organization's needs.

From a monitoring and alerting perspective, you therefore need to understand how Log Analytics, Security Center, Defender, and Sentinel fit together.

The end-to-end process is to log and collect data, identify activities, pro-actively protect, detect anomalies, respond to threats, and then recover. The following diagram shows how each of the available tools works together to achieve this:

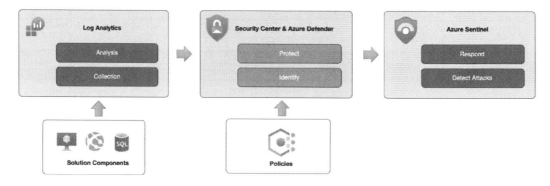

Figure 15.18 – Security ecosystem

The use of security and monitoring tooling is a big subject and detailed knowledge is needed for the AZ-500 Microsoft Azure Security Technologies exam. For the AZ-304 exam, you need to know how the different solutions fit together and what each achieves.

In the final section of this chapter, we will cover another built-in set of tools that help you keep an eye on costs and efficiency.

Using cost management and reporting

Using a cloud platform such as Azure provides great flexibility in costs; that is, you only pay for exactly what you need. However, with such a flexible pricing model, costs could easily spiral out of control, resulting in bill shock.

Luckily, Azure provides you with a number of tools to help keep an eye on costs and even recommends changes to your infrastructure if you're underutilizing any services.

The first of these tools is the **Cost analysis** blade. Select any subscription in the portal and you have a **Cost analysis** option under **Cost Management**. The following screenshot shows an example:

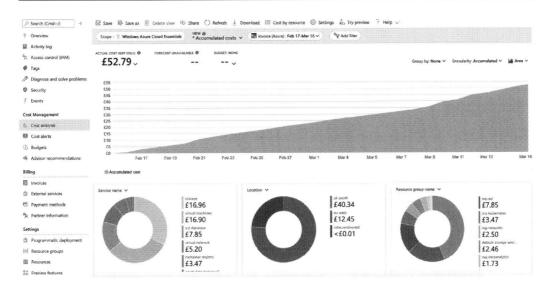

Figure 15.19 – Example cost analysis

The **Cost analysis** panel enables you to tailor your view to show a range of different options. The default view will show the current spend for your billing period and a prediction, based on currently running services, of how much your final bill will be.

The menu options provide the ability to filter on a range of options, including resource group, resource type, and location. You can also group by these options, change the granularity to accumulated, daily, or monthly, and set the range you wish to report over, for example, current billing period, previous billing period, or last 12 months.

You can also change the visualization itself to show the data as bar charts, line charts, donut charts, or even in tabular format. For example, the following screenshot shows daily spend grouped by location and displayed as a bar chart:

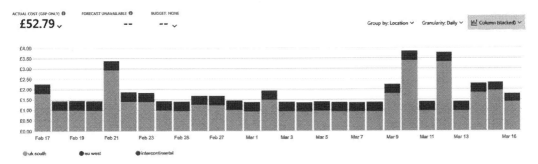

Figure 15.20 – Different cost analysis reports

You can also export your report. This can be performed as a one-off download, either as an image, Excel file, or CSV. Or you can create a regularly scheduled export – daily, weekly, or monthly – and have the report sent to a storage account.

Being able to see your current costs is useful, but sometimes you need to be able to control costs very tightly – for example, if you have a development team that is working on a proof-of-concept solution, you may need to either set a defined monthly budget or at least be alerted if costs go over a particular threshold.

Again, Azure provides the ability to perform both these tasks. From the **Cost alerts** or **Budgets** view, you can set a monthly, quarterly, or yearly budget, and then create an alert that will send an email or other notification should a percentage of that budget be reached. For example, you could set a budget of $100 a month with an alert at 80% so that you can be informed when you are getting close to that budget.

Another tool that can be used to help save costs is the Azure Advisor tool. Azure Advisor continually monitors your subscriptions and makes recommendations for security, reliability, operations, performance, and, of course, costs.

The Advisor tool can be viewed any time and is a great way to quickly see areas for improvement. The following screenshot shows an example of what this might look like:

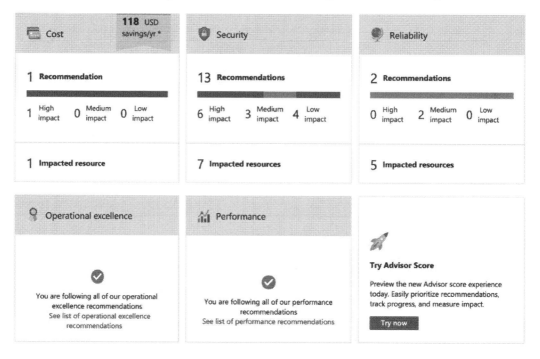

Figure 15.21 – Azure Advisor example

By clicking on one of the areas of improvement, for example, **Cost**, you are then taken to the details, which you can then action. The following screenshot shows a typical cost-saving option for VMs, which is the ability to save money by opting for reserved instances:

Figure 15.22 – Example cost-savings recommendation

Through a combination of reporting, alerts, and acting on recommendations, you can ensure that your Azure subscriptions are always running optimally, efficiently, and, of course, economically.

Summary

In this chapter, we began *Section 5*, *Operations and Monitoring*, by looking at the options available for building robust monitoring and logging solutions.

Azure provides basic capturing of metrics and logs from the platform and its components, including built-in tools for visualizing and exploring them. For more advanced scenarios, we looked at additional options for sending these logs and metrics to other locations, such as storage accounts, Log Analytics workspaces, and event hubs.

We looked at how to also hook into and capture VM operating system logs, and then how we can use tools such as Log Analytics to query across multiple data sources.

We then examined how to use Security Center, Defender, and Sentinel to provide proactive threat detection and remediation, and how each product can work together to enable automation and alerting.

Finally, we looked at the tools available for reporting on and monitoring costs.

In the next chapter, we continue our operations theme by looking at how we can back up our solutions, and what options we have for recovery depending on your business requirements.

Exam scenario

MegaCorp Inc. is a multi-national organization spread across many different divisions, including sales and marketing, HR, and IT. Due to its size and complexity, each division within each country manages its own solutions, which are hosted in Azure, and each division has its own Azure subscription for its applications.

IT and the overall health management is controlled by a central team that has responsibility for all divisions and countries, and as part of this, a separate sub-team is responsible for monitoring and responding to security threats.

The IT team also runs proof-of-concept systems with business areas when developing new solutions, and these are often created as needed and then de-commissioned when no longer in use.

As the lead architect, you must recommend a monitoring and logging solution that addresses the following requirements:

- The security team needs overall visibility of potential threats.

- Over time, the security team wishes to implement automated responses to common threats.

- Individual product teams need to be able to monitor performance and technical issues on their solutions.

- Due to their nature, proof-of-concept solutions need to be tightly controlled from a cost perspective.

Recommend and design a solution that meets the company's requirements.

Further reading

For more information on the topics covered in this chapter, refer to the following links:

- Azure Monitor: `https://docs.microsoft.com/en-us/azure/azure-monitor/overview`

- Kusto Query Language: `https://docs.microsoft.com/en-us/azure/data-explorer/kusto/query/`

- Azure Security Center: `https://docs.microsoft.com/en-us/azure/security-center/`

- Azure Sentinel: `https://docs.microsoft.com/en-gb/azure/sentinel/`

- Azure Advisor: `https://docs.microsoft.com/en-us/azure/advisor/`

16
Developing Business Continuity

In the last chapter, we started the operations and monitoring topic by looking at logging and monitoring. In this chapter, we'll explore another important subject – the ability to recover from a complete outage.

Azure provides a range of recovery solutions that offer different features; these include traditional backup and restore functionality for VMs and the data on them, Azure Site Recovery for continually replicating VMs, and Azure SQL or Azure Cosmos DB backup facilities.

Finally, we will also look at a related feature – the ability to move infrequently accessed data to cheaper storage for long-term retention in a cost-effective way.

By the end of this chapter, you will understand how to choose between the different backup and recovery solutions depending on your organization's needs, taking into account how quickly services must be restored and how much data loss is, or isn't, acceptable.

With this in mind, we will be covering the following subjects:

- Understanding recovery solutions
- Planning for Azure Backup
- Planning for Site Recovery
- Planning for database backups
- Understanding the data archiving options

Technical requirements

This chapter will use the Azure portal (`https://portal.azure.com`) for examples.

Understanding recovery solutions

Throughout this book, we have looked at how to architect solutions that are resilient to failures or outages. Often this has involved duplicating components such as VMs, web apps, and even databases. Sometimes we have duplicated systems within a region to protect against hardware or individual data center failures, or cross-region to protect against entire region outages.

However, this comes at a financial cost – doubling up on a database or VM means doubling the costs as well.

Sometimes the cost of an outage outweighs the cost of duplicate components – if an application is used continually and is revenue-generating, a 1-hour downtime could cost millions, and therefore the increased cost of another database is negligible.

Not all systems are this sensitive. For lower-budget solutions, or systems that are not as critical, potential downtime may be preferable to an increase in hosting costs. Therefore, when architecting solutions, we must understand the business needs. Often, the amount of downtime an application can withstand is expressed in terms of a **Recovery Point Objective (RPO)** and a **Recovery Time Objective (RTO)**.

Understanding the Recovery Time Objective (RTO)

The RTO defines how quickly you must be able to recover from an outage. If your RTO is at or close to 0, then building the highly available solutions we have looked at so far is the best course of action. If, however, your RTO is 24 hours or more, then a traditional backup and restore design may be more suitable and cost-effective.

An RTO of 24 hours means you have a full day to rebuild or restore your solution from backup, which, depending on the backup solution you choose and the size of your application, may be adequate.

Understanding the Recovery Point Objective (RPO)

An RPO is often stated alongside an RTO. If you are architecting a solution that performs regular backups of your platform, then you also need to consider how often those backups are taken. This effectively determines your RPO, which is the maximum amount of time that can pass between backups.

For example, an RPO of 24 hours means a daily backup is sufficient; however, an RPO of 1 hour may rule out some technologies.

It's worth mentioning that even if your solution is built with high availability in mind and will automatically fail over to a different region in the event of failure, many organizations require a backup solution as well.

Understanding Azure Backup options

For extremely critical applications, a full **Disaster Recovery (DR)** may be required to protect you against an unknown design fault in your primary systems that could still result in failure.

Finally, backups of your data may be required for accidental updates or deletions. If your data is replicated to another region, it will not protect you against a user accidentally, or purposefully, deleting or overwriting your data as any such changes will also be replicated. Again, a backup solution is your best protection here.

Azure provides a number of different solutions, and each has its own use cases. You may even need to utilize multiple solutions depending on your organization's needs.

At a high level, your backup options in Azure include the following:

- Disk snapshots
- Azure Backup
- Azure Site Recovery
- Azure Backup for databases

Disk snapshots are often confused with Azure Backup, and although they technically can be used to create a backup solution, it is recommended to use Azure Backup.

Disk snapshots take a point-in-time copy of a VM's disk, and this can be performed while the VM is running and at any time. When creating a snapshot, you can choose between a full snapshot or an incremental one. An incremental snapshot is much smaller as it only stores data that has changed since the last one.

You cannot restore from a snapshot; you can only create a new VM from one. Also, a snapshot is not region-redundant; however, it can be zone-redundant.

Finally, snapshots are manual, if you want to take them at pre-defined periods, you would need to build an Azure function or similar to perform the action for you.

Snapshots are best for quick, one-off backups; for example, if you are making a configuration change and are worried about a failure, in these scenarios a snapshot provides a fast way to recover should something go wrong.

Although you could create a backup solution using a combination of snapshots and automated functions, a far easier and more robust solution would be to use Azure Backup, which we will cover next.

Planning for Azure Backup

Azure Backup is generally the first solution to consider when planning your backup strategy. Azure Backup uses the **Microsoft Azure Recovery Services (MARS)** agent, which is installed on a VM, to back up files, folders, and system state to a **Recovery Services** vault, which, in turn, uses a storage account for persisting those backups.

You can back up both Azure and on-premises VMs using the MARS agent, as well as **Azure Managed Disks**, **Azure file shares**, **SQL Server** on Azure VMs, **PostgreSQL** on Azure VMs, Azure blobs, and SAP HANA on Azure VMs.

Azure Backup can also use System Center **Data Protection Manager (DPM)**, which is an enterprise backup system for on-premises servers. Using either DPM or **Microsoft Azure Backup Server (MABS)** on your existing on-premises infrastructure, you can take local backups and then move them into the cloud.

Exam Tip

When backing up on-premises VMs into Azure, you can use either the MARS agent to directly back up into Azure or the DPM or MABS solutions. However, Linux VMs are not supported using the MARS agent; therefore you must use either DPM or MABS.

The following diagram shows an example of the different sources of possibilities of Azure Backup:

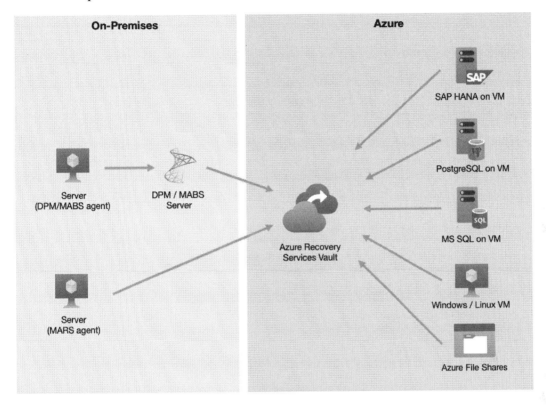

Figure 16.1 – Azure Backup sources

Because Azure Backup is built using cloud resources, especially storage, it scales automatically as you need, and you only pay for what you need. Because the underlying storage mechanism is Azure Storage, it can be used with different levels of protection:

- **Locally Redundant Storage (LRS)**, providing three replicas with a single data center
- **Zone-Redundant Storage (ZRS)**, providing multiple replicas across data centers, or Availability Zones, within a single region
- **Geo-Redundant Storage (GRS)**, providing multiple replicas to a paired region

Although GRS is used as the default, providing ultimate durability of your backups, you must optionally enable **Cross-Region Restores (CRR)** if you need to perform a VM restore from your primary region to the secondary region. CRR is only available for Azure VMs, SQL on Azure VMs, and SAP HANA on Azure VMs.

It is also useful to understand that under the hood, Azure Backup uses snapshots to create backups for Azure VMs. As part of the backup process, a snapshot is taken of the VM and temporarily stored. This snapshot is then sent to the Recovery Services vault.

Once you have created a Recovery Services vault to store your backups, your next step to is define a **backup policy**.

Understanding backup policies

A backup policy is used to define different aspects of how you want to back up your workloads, and multiple policies can be created and used. For example, you may want to use one policy for application VMs that don't change very often, and a separate policy for database VMs, whose data changes continually.

Once a policy has been created, VMs can be onboarded in a number of ways:

- Individually via the **Backup** blade of the VM you wish to backup
- In groups, by associating VMs with backup policies in the Recovery Services vault blade
- During a VM build, either when creating via the portal or when using ARM templates
- Via an Azure policy

When creating a policy, you define the policy type, choosing from either **Azure Virtual Machine**, **Azure File Share**, **SQL Server in Azure VM**, or **SAP HANA in Azure VM**.

Depending on the policy type, you then have different options around the backup schedule and retention:

	VM	File Share	SQL on VM	SAP HANA
Frequency	Weekly or Daily	Daily	Weekly or Daily	Weekly or Daily
Instance Restores	Up to 5 Days	n/a	n/a	n/a
Daily Retention	Between 7 and 9,999 Days	Max 200 Days	Between 7 and 9,999 Days	Between 7 and 9,999 Days
Weekly Retention	Max 5,163 Weeks	Max 200 Weeks	Max 5,163 Weeks	Max 5,163 Weeks
Monthly Retention	Max 1,188 Months	Max 200 Months	Max 1,188 Months	Max 1,188 Months
Yearly Retention	Max 99 Years	Max 10 Years	Max 99 Years	Max 99 Years
Differential Backups	Not Supported	n/a	Supported	Supported
Incremental Backups	Not Supported	n/a	Supported	Supported
Log Backup Frequency	n/a	n/a	15 Mins to 25 Hours	15 Mins to 25 Hours
Log Backup Retention	n/a	n/a	Up to 35 Days	Up to 35 Days

From the preceding table, we can see that we have different options depending on what we are backing up. There are also a few points to consider when defining our overall backup solution.

Backup retention

The first consideration is around retention, which is the length of time any backup is retained for. We can have backups be retained for days, months, or even years; however, the longer you retain backups, the more individual backups you will have at any one time, and therefore your storage costs will increase.

Next, for databases, we can choose to configure full, incremental, or differential backups.

Backup types

A full backup is a complete backup of the database at that point in time. After the first full backup has been taken, we can opt for differential or incremental backups.

Some backup types, such as SQL on VM and SAP HANA, offer a differential backup that only backs up blocks of data that have changed since the last full backup.

An incremental backup only stores blocks changed after the last incremental backup.

Both incremental and differential backups use far less storage and less network bandwidth; however, the downside is that it can take longer to restore.

The final consideration is the frequency of our backups.

Backup frequency

We can only back up VMs on daily or weekly schedules, and a VM can only be associated with a single policy. Database backups can be more granular – by backing up logs every 15 minutes we effectively provide ourselves with an RTO of 15 minutes; however, our VM RTO is 24 hours.

If your VMs do not contain changing data, an RTO of the VM itself would be fine. If, however, your solution stores data on a VM and the RTO of that data is less than 24 hours, the backup mechanism would not cover you.

To overcome this limitation, you could re-architect your application to store such data on a different mechanism, for example, in a database or blob storage with geo-redundancy enabled.

Alternatively, you could use a different backup solution that would provide a continual backup of your VMs – Azure Site Recovery.

Planning for Site Recovery

Business-critical applications may have different backup and recovery requirements to servers that don't change often or store data. For applications that need to be recovered quickly, or that need to be backed up every few minutes or hours, Recovery Services values also provide a tool called Azure Site Recovery. Both Azure Backup and Azure Site Recovery are set up and managed by an Azure Recovery Services vault.

Whereas Azure Backup takes a one-off backup at daily intervals, Azure Site Recovery continually replicates your VM's disks to another region. In the event that you need to failover, a new VM is created and attached to the replicated disk in the paired region, as we can see in the following diagram:

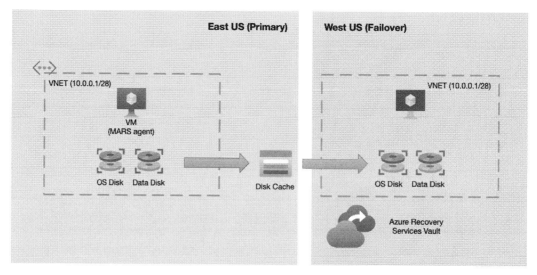

Figure 16.2 – Azure Site Recovery architecture

As we can see from the preceding diagram, Azure Site Recovery requires a VNET and subnet in the paired region that your replicated VMs can attach to. When you set up a VM to use Site Recovery, the setup wizard can either create the VNET and subnet for you or use an existing VNET you have already set up in the paired region.

> **Important Note**
> You must set up an Azure Recovery Services vault in the paired region that you wish to protect. For example, if the workload you wish to protect is in East US, you must create the vault in West US. This is because the replicated VM needs to exist in the paired region.

An important consideration of the network is how you will define your IP ranges. By default, the internal IP ranges that the paired VNET uses are the same as the primary region. If your VMs fail over, they therefore retain their original internal IP address.

If your VMs only use the internal IPs for communicating with each other, this will not cause an issue; however, if you connect to your VMs from an on-premises network over a VPN, you need to consider whether using a separate range and separate VPN to the paired region is required.

Public IP addresses cannot move as part of a failover process. If your VMs are accessed via public IPs, those IPs will change in the event of a failover. To overcome this issue, consider using a service such as Azure Traffic Manager to control connectivity to your services. We looked at using Azure Traffic Manager in *Chapter 8, Network Connectivity and Security*.

The replication process of Site Recovery ensures the lowest possible RTO. Because data is constantly being replicated to another region, when a failover occurs, the data is already where you need it – that is, you don't need to wait for a restore to happen.

Azure Site Recovery works by creating snapshots of your VM and then replicating that data into the Recovery Services vault. To support the lowest possible RPO, Site Recovery takes two different types of snapshots when replicating your VM:

- **Crash-consistent**: Taken every 5 minutes. Represents all the data on the disk at that moment in time

- **App-consistent**: Crash consistent snapshots of the disks, plus an in-memory snapshot of the VM every 60 minutes

When you create your first Recovery Services vault and enable replication on a VM, a **replication policy** is created. The replication policy allows you to define how long crash-consistent snapshots, known as recovery points, are kept. The options are between 0 (none) and 72 hours.

The policy also allows you to modify the default crash-consistent snapshot from the default 1 hour to up to 12 hours.

Site Recovery also supports on-premises VMs as well as VMs in Azure. This provides you with a full DR site in Azure to protect against your own data center suffering an outage.

Site Recovery is the actual underlying mechanism used by Azure Migrate, which we covered in *Chapter 10, Migrating Workloads to Azure.*

Site Recovery can perform a failover automatically for you if your primary region goes offline, or you can manually failover services. Finally, you can also run DR drills, which will fully test a failover without disrupting your running workload.

With either drills or full DR failovers, you can group your VMs into workload groups called recovery plans.

Understanding recovery plans

Using recovery plans allows you to have far greater control over what is failed over and when. Using this mechanism, you can have more direct control over the timing of failovers for individual services.

Typically, you would group applications into a recovery plan; for example, if you have a web application consisting of a VM frontend and SQL backend, you will group the frontend and SQL server into a recovery plan to ensure they always fail over together.

Next, you can define the order of failover for individual services within that plan. Again, with the web application and SQL server example, you would want to ensure that the SQL server is moved first, followed by the frontend application. The following screenshot shows an example recovery plan in the Azure portal:

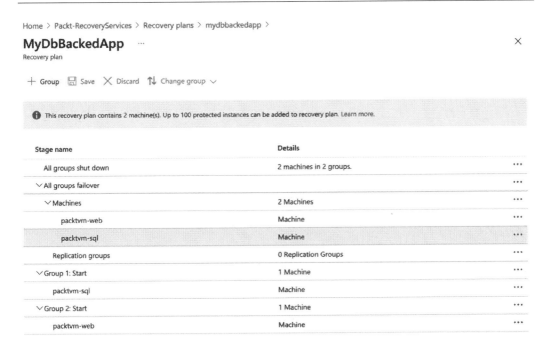

Figure 16.3 – Recovery plan example

Grouping services into plans also allows you to manage DR scenarios from the point of view of individual criticality. If you have many different systems, chances are some will be more important than others, or at least need to be brought online quicker. By grouping systems, you can bring each one online in a specific order, and thus prioritize critical systems.

Azure Backup and Azure Site Recovery provide scalable solutions for a wide variety of business requirements; however, they are predominantly designed for **Infrastructure as a Service (IaaS)** workloads such as VMs and file shares.

> **Note**
>
> For a complete walkthrough of using Azure Recovery Service vaults, see *Implementing Microsoft Azure Architect Technologies: AZ-303 Exam Prep and Beyond: A guide to preparing for the AZ-303 Microsoft Azure Architect Technologies certification exam* by Packt Publishing.

Many **Platform as a Service (PaaS)** services, such as Azure SQL and Cosmos DB, also provide backup services, but these are managed within the service itself, as we shall investigate next.

Planning for database backups

In the previous section, we looked at using Azure Backup to create backup and restore policies for VMs, including SQL on VMs.

One of the core offerings of Azure is Azure SQL, a managed database offering with complete flexibility and scalability. However, the Azure Backup solution we looked at for VMs and SQL on VMs is not the same backup solution we use for Azure SQL Database or Azure SQL Managed Instance.

Understanding Azure SQL backups

As managed services, backups are part of the platform, and by default, databases have full backups taken every week, differential backups every 12-24 hours, and transaction log backups every 5-10 minutes. Backups are also retained for 7 days – this means that as soon as you create an Azure SQL database or Azure SQL managed instance, your data is protected so that you can restore data from any point up to 7 days with recovery points every 5-10 minutes.

Backups, by default, are also geo-redundant. This allows you to restore a database to your primary region's paired region for the same timeframe, thus protecting you against regional outages. Backups also cover you against database deletion, so even if you accidentally delete a database, you can still restore it within the configured retention period.

For some organizations, 7 days retention may not be suitable – some solutions may need to keep longer-term copies for historical or compliance reasons. For this reason, you can increase the retention periods, and how long you need to keep databases for will determine whether you will use **Point-in-Time-Restore (PITR)** or **Long-Term Retention (LTR)**.

PITR is the standard backups that are taken as part of normal operational processes and can be configured to be retained for up to 35 days.

If you need longer-term backups, you can optionally configure LTR to separate store weekly, monthly, or yearly backups. Each type of backup is stored separately in blob storage, and each type can have its own retention. For example, you could keep weekly backups for 4 weeks, monthly backups for 12 months, and yearly backups for up to 10 years.

The following screenshot shows an example of the preceding retention configuration:

Configure policies   ✕

SQL server

Point-in-time-restore

Specify how long you want to keep your point-in-time backups. Learn more

How long would you like PITR backups to be kept? ⓘ

━━━━━━━━━━━━━━━━━━━━━━━━━━━○ | 35 | Days

Long-term retention

Specify how long you want to keep your long-term retention backups. You may choose to keep yearly backups for up to 10 years. Learn more

Weekly LTR Backups

Keep weekly backups for:

| 4 | | Week(s)   ⌄ |

Monthly LTR Backups

Keep the first backup of each month for:

| 12 | | Month(s)   ⌄ |

Yearly LTR Backups

Keep an annual backup for:

| 10 | | Year(s)   ⌄ |

Which weekly backup of the year would you like to keep?

| Week 1   ⌄ |

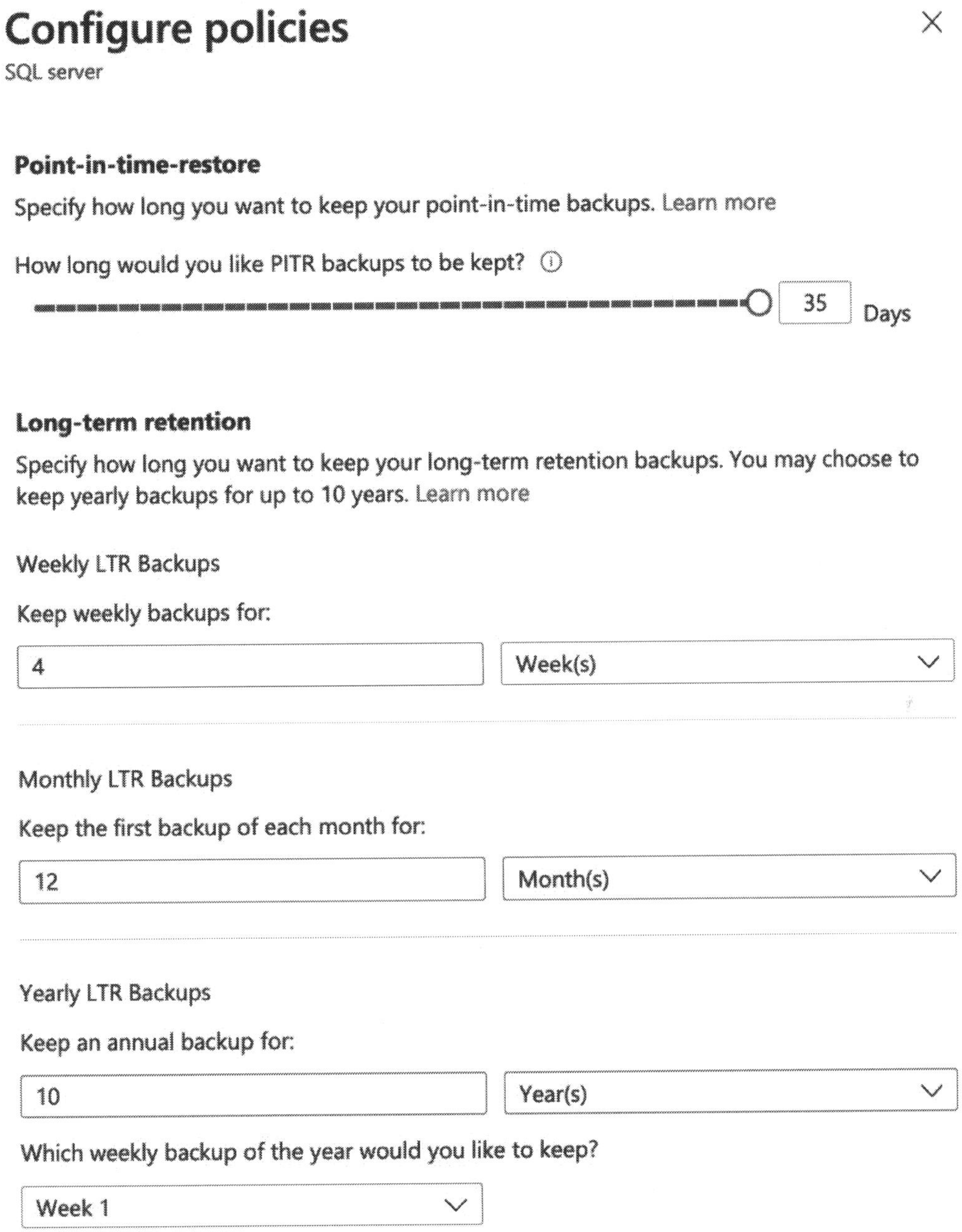

Figure 16.4 – Example SQL database retention configuration

Backup retention policies are configured on **SQL Server** in the **Backups** view, and individual policies are configured for each database. If a database is deleted it can therefore be restored from the **Backups** or **Deleted databases** view of SQL Server as the database will no longer appear in the normal **SQL Databases** view in the Azure portal.

Azure's other core database offering, Cosmos DB, has similar options for backups, but as you would expect, is slightly different.

Understanding Cosmos DB backups

Azure Cosmos DB, as a managed service, also manages your backups, and by default provides a default level of frequency and retention.

Backups are managed through the **Backup & Restore** view of your Cosmos DB and are configured for the entire account. The options are relatively straightforward, as we can see in the following screenshot:

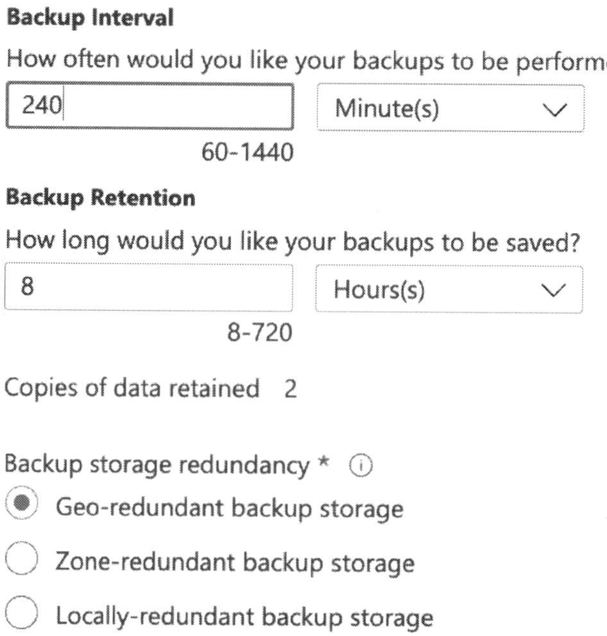

Backup Interval

How often would you like your backups to be performed?

| 240 | Minute(s) ∨ |

60–1440

Backup Retention

How long would you like your backups to be saved?

| 8 | Hours(s) ∨ |

8–720

Copies of data retained   2

Backup storage redundancy * ⓘ

◉ Geo-redundant backup storage

◯ Zone-redundant backup storage

◯ Locally-redundant backup storage

Figure 16.5 – Cosmos DB backup options

As you can see from the preceding screenshot, we can configure how often a backup is performed – every 60 to 1,440 minutes (or 1 to 24 hours) – and how long backups are stored for – 8 to 720 hours (or 1 to 30 days).

You can also set the backup redundancy, again choosing between **Geo-redundant backup storage**, **Zone-redundant backup storage**, or **Locally-redundant backup storage**.

An important aspect of the Cosmos DB backup and restore process is that unlike backups taken by Azure Backup or Azure SQL backups, you cannot directly restore those backups yourself. Instead, when a restore is required you must raise an incident support ticket through the Azure portal requesting a restore.

> **Important Note**
>
> You should advise Azure support within 8 hours of a restore requirement and increase the backup retention to at least 7 days to ensure your backup is retained long enough for the support team to enact the restore. Because backups will still be in operation (unless you have deleted the entire account), failure to increase the retention rate could result in the restore point you need being overwritten.

You can restore either the entire account, a database, a container, or even specific items within the container. When restoring an account that has been deleted, the new account will have the same name as the original account. For all other scenarios, restores will be performed against a new account named `<orginal_account_name>-restored1`.

If you need more control over your data, you could keep an up-to-date copy of your account in another account. Using the built-in triggers, you can use Azure Data Factory or the Cosmos DB change feed, which is a persistent record of changes, with an Azure function to continually copy data to storage or another account.

Before we finish with Cosmos DB backups, it is worth noting a new preview (at the time of writing) feature called **Continuous Backup**, which provides PITR capabilities. Because the feature is in preview, it may not be covered in the AZ-304 exam at the moment; however, this is subject to change.

In the final section of this chapter, we will look at data archiving. Although not strictly a backup mechanism, it is worth understanding the options for the long-term storage of data and how this can affect your overall backup strategy.

Understanding the data archiving options

Many organizations have a requirement to hold some data for longer periods of time. This may be for compliance reasons or simply for long-term record retention.

Although backup solutions do offer long-term retention options, for archival purposes Azure Storage offers a specific archiving tier. We covered the storage tiers in *Chapter 9, Exploring Storage Solutions*, but to recap, you can configure a storage account as **Hot**, **Cool**, or **Archive**:

- **Hot** is used for data that is accessed frequently – this is what you would normally choose for a day-to-day storage solution.

- **Cool** is for data that is accessed infrequently. It is lower-cost than the **Hot** tier, but it has slightly lower availability.

- **Archive** storage is design for data that will be kept long-term, but that will be rarely, if ever, accessed once written to. Archive storage is the cheapest option for storage; however, there are costs for reading data from it.

When creating a storage account, you set the *default* access tier, but you can only choose between hot and cool. After creation, an individual blob can then have its properties modified to move to another tier, including **Archive**.

> **Important Note**
> Only blob storage and **General Purpose v2 (GPv2)** storage accounts support tiering, and Microsoft recommends using GPv2 over blob accounts as they offer more features for a similar cost.

An important consideration for Archive-tier storage is that it is offline storage. This means once data is set as to be in the Archive tier, it is considered offline. This has the effect that the data can no longer be directly read or modified; if you do need to access the data, you must first rehydrate it.

When rehydrating data, you can either change the blob tier back to hot or cool, or you can copy the data to a hot or cool tier. Note that this process can take hours to complete. You can set a rehydrate priority on a blob by setting `x-ms-rehydrate-priority` when changing the blob tier back to hot or cool, or copying it.

Standard priority is the lowest cost but has an **service-level agreement (SLA)** of 15 hours, whereas **High priority** can be performed in under an hour but is more expensive. However, that timeline is not under SLA; all that is guaranteed is the operation will have priority over a standard request.

Although you can manually change the tiering of a blob, this might not always be practical, unless you know the data must be archived as soon as you write it.

Sometimes you may only want to archive data if it hasn't been accessed for a period of time. In these scenarios, you can set up a life cycle management rule to automatically move data.

You can create multiple rules in a storage account's life cycle management blade, and for each rule, you can define how many days since a blob has been modified and whether to move it to a Cool or Archive tier, or even delete the file.

The following screenshot shows a simple rule that moves data to the Archive tier if it has not been modified for 90 days:

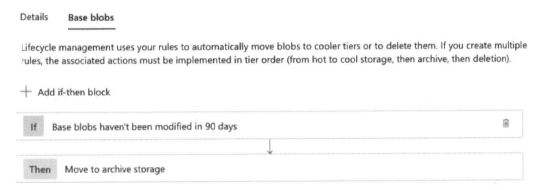

Figure 16.6 – Example life cycle management rule

By building multiple rules, you can set up complex workflows. For example, you could create multiple rules that move data to the Cool tier after 30 days, then to the Archive tier after 90 days, and then to finally delete the data after a year.

The ability to delete data after a set period can be crucial as many countries have strict rules on how long personal data can be kept for.

Through a combination of a well-defined backup solution and archiving policy, you can ensure your applications make the best use of storage based on costs and access requirements.

Summary

In this chapter, we looked at how an organization's DR requirements can differ and how the different Azure Backup mechanisms can be used to achieve varying levels of RTO, RPO, and data retention requirements.

We looked at how Azure Backup provides a scalable solution for backing up standard VMs as well as SQL on VMs, PostgreSQL on VMs, and SAP HANA on VMs.

Next, we looked at native database backup solutions and saw how Azure SQL and Azure Cosmos DB automatically perform backups for you, but how you can tweak them to your own requirements.

Finally, we looked at data archiving solutions and how we can automate the movement of data between the Hot, Cool, and Archive tiers, or even delete it through the use of life cycle management rules, which are a core feature of storage accounts.

In the next chapter, we continue our operations theme by looking at how we can automate the deployment of services using Azure DevOps.

Exam scenario

MegaCorp Inc. hosts an application that stores and manages customer calls in Azure.

The system comprises a web application running on a VM, with an Azure SQL database for the customer records. The records themselves are updated regularly.

As an internal application, the system is not considered critical, and it has been built in a single Azure region. In the event of an entire region failure, management would like to be able to fail over to a paired region; a downtime of 24 hours would be acceptable, but any data loss needs to minimal.

The management team would like to ensure database backups are taken and kept every month and retained for a year in case they ever need to examine historical data that could have been overwritten.

The VM does not contain any data, just the web application, and therefore only changes as new versions are rolled out.

Design a solution that will allow the business to recover in the event of an entire region outage.

Further reading

For more information on the topics covered in this chapter, you can refer to the following links:

- Azure Backup: `https://docs.microsoft.com/en-us/azure/backup/`

- Azure Site Recovery services: `https://docs.microsoft.com/en-us/azure/site-recovery/`

- Azure SQL backup: `https://docs.microsoft.com/en-us/azure/azure-sql/database/automated-backups-overview`

- Azure Cosmos DB backup: `https://docs.microsoft.com/en-us/azure/cosmos-db/online-backup-and-restore`

- Storage Access tiers: `https://docs.microsoft.com/en-gb/azure/storage/blobs/storage-blob-storage-tiers`

17

Scripted Deployments and DevOps Automation

In *Chapter 16, Developing Business Continuity*, we looked at how to ensure our solutions have adequate backups in the event that the unexpected happens.

In this chapter, we continue the operational theme, looking at how we can deploy components into Azure, specifically using scripts, templates, and automation tools.

We will begin by exploring what options are available and then start to investigate in more detail how Azure exposes a series of REST APIs. We will then continue looking at using the APIs via command-line tools and **Azure Resource Manager** (**ARM**) templates.

Finally, we will look at how to automate deployments using ARM templates and Azure DevOps, along with a brief overview of agile DevOps processes.

We will specifically explore the following topics:

- Exploring provisioning options
- Looking at the Azure RESTful API
- Choosing between PowerShell and Azure CLI
- Understanding ARM templates
- Looking at Azure DevOps

Technical requirements

This chapter will use the Azure portal (`https://portal.azure.com`) and the Azure DevOps portal (`https://dev.azure.com`) for examples.

Exploring provisioning options

When building solutions in Azure, the most obvious, and arguably easiest option, is to use the Azure portal.

Although this is great for the quick exploration of components, for learning, or even basic setup, using a manual hands-on approach is difficult to replicate with guaranteed consistency.

What we mean by this is the fact that any manual approach that involves a user clicking buttons or entering information cannot be easily repeated in a way that prevents mistakes from happening. In a traditional on-premises environment, solution builds might be verbosely documented so that other engineers can build the system by following step-by-step instructions.

The major problem with this, aside from the time it takes to write the documentation, is the fact that whoever is following the instructions could very easily enter some information incorrectly, misclick a button, or even miss entire steps.

This can be overcome by opting for a scripted environment. Using scripts, we can attempt to write in code the steps required to build and configure software, and with the advent of virtualization, we can even automate infrastructure in the same way.

Another aspect to consider is how solutions are built, especially when adhering to agile practices. We spoke briefly about waterfall and agile management practices at the very start of this book in *Chapter 1, Architecture for the Cloud*, and again in *Chapter 2, Principles of Modern Architecture*, when we spoke about architecting for DevOps.

One of the core tenets of agile development is that we should build small iterations of a solution with regular but incremental deployments. In the same fashion, we may often be called upon to build the supporting infrastructure in the same way.

Manually rebuilding or adding to the infrastructure using the Azure portal simply would not scale and, as already mentioned, is too error prone. Infrastructure therefore needs to be deployed using automation in order to ensure consistency.

All components in Azure can therefore be defined using scripts, and when architecting solutions, we must take into consideration how components will be deployed, as this may have a direct impact on the solution itself.

When deploying components, aside from the portal, we have a number of options, including these:

- Azure REST APIs
- PowerShell
- The Azure **Command-Line Interface (CLI)**
- ARM templates
- DevOps pipelines

We will explore each in more detail as we progress through this chapter.

Looking at the Azure REST API

The first option we will consider is the Azure REST API. All actions on Azure resources are managed through ARM, and this is exposed by a set of APIs. When we perform actions in the Azure portal, we are actually making HTTP calls to the REST APIs.

> **Information Note**
>
> **Representational State Transfer (REST)** is an architectural pattern that exposes data using a defined set of standards in a text-based format using stateless protocols – that is, information between calls (the state) is not expected to be maintained. A web service that implements this pattern is said to be RESTful.

Other management options such as PowerShell, CLI, and DevOps also just wrap calls to the APIs in a more friendly way; however, you can interact with those APIs directly, as we can see in the following diagram:

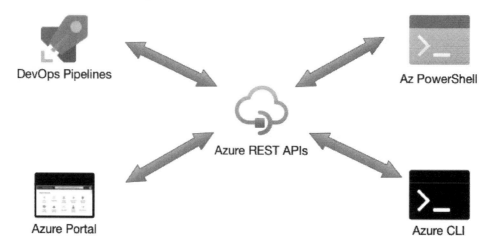

Figure 17.1 – REST APIs are used by other services

Any call to the API must use the following URI and format:

```
https://management.azure.com/<resource-path>?<query-string>
```

The resource path determines the resource or resource collection we want to work on and may involve multiple segments. Often, this includes stating the subscription and resource group where any particular resource may reside. For example, to create a virtual machine we could make the following PUT request:

```
https://management.azure.com/subscriptions/<subscriptionId>/
resourceGroups/<resourceGroupName>/providers/Microsoft.
Compute/virtualMachines/<vmName>
```

The query string is optional but can be used to provide additional information such as the API version or resource selection criteria.

Because the REST APIs allow complete access to the Azure platform, every request must include an access token in the request header. We obtain the access code by first making a call to `https://login.microsoftonline.com/<tenant>/oauth2/v2.0`.

How this is performed depends on many factors, which are included in the type of authorization flow you or the application making the calls uses. These flows are beyond the scope of this book; however, the important point to understand is that any calls to the Azure REST APIs must include an access token.

Using the REST APIs, we can directly interact with the Azure platform or we can build our own apps that use those calls to perform set functions. For example, we could build an application that allows users to perform specific tasks such as stopping and starting VMs without going via the Azure portal.

When automating deployments, we would usually use existing tools such as PowerShell or the Azure CLI, which we will cover next.

Choosing between PowerShell and the Azure CLI

When we start to consider automating the deployment and management of resources in Azure, the first option would be using the command line, and here we then have two further options: **PowerShell** and the **Azure CLI**.

PowerShell and the CLI are very similar: they both run from a command prompt, they both allow access to the Azure platform, and the commands are also very similar.

Traditionally, PowerShell was only available on Windows computers; however, in recent years, PowerShell has been made available on macOS and Linux platforms. PowerShell has a much broader use than Azure and can be used on Windows platforms to manage and script many processes and Windows management functions.

PowerShell is also extensible: you can build functions, classes, scripts, and modules in a similar fashion to development languages. It is a separate module, called the **Az PowerShell** module, that enables Azure functionality.

> **Information Note**
>
> The current Az PowerShell module is a replacement for an older **AzureRM** module that was originally built to provide the same level of functionality. AzureRM has since been deprecated and you should remove AzureRM before you install Az PowerShell if you had previously installed AzureRM.

The Azure CLI is a standalone set of commands, which means that you do not need PowerShell. The Azure CLI is available for Windows, macOS, and Linux environments.

Because both options are available cross-platform, the choice of one over the other is largely a personal choice; however, the Azure CLI is a single install on macOS and Linux, whereas Az PowerShell requires PowerShell to be installed first.

Both options can also be used in Azure Cloud Shell, which is an interactive browser-based tool available in the Azure portal.

When using PowerShell or the Azure CLI through Cloud Shell, you are already authenticated; however, when using the tools from your own computer, you must first authenticate. Remember from the previous section that the Azure REST APIs required a client access token, and because command-line tools essentially wrap calls to those APIs, you must log in to obtain the token.

We shall see next how similar the two options are by showing some example commands.

Signing in to Azure

The first step in using either tool is to authenticate against Azure:

- PowerShell:

```
connect-AzAccount
```

- Azure CLI:

```
az login
```

Depending on your OS and command line choice, the sign in process is slightly different; however, once authenticated, a list of subscriptions you have access to will be returned.

Selecting a subscription

If you have access to multiple subscriptions, you will need to select which one to use:

- PowerShell:

```
Select-AzureSubscription -SubscriptionName "<subscription name>"
```

- Azure CLI:

```
az account set -subscription "<subscription name>"
```

Once set, we can now perform actions.

Listing resource groups

The following examples simply list all resource groups in your selected subscription:

- PowerShell:

```
get-AzResourceGroup
```

- Azure CLI:

```
az group list
```

Both commands will return a list of resource groups.

> **Information Note**
>
> A full list of Azure CLI commands can be found here: `https://docs.microsoft.com/en-us/cli/azure/reference-index?view=azure-cli-latest`.
>
> A full list of Az PowerShell commands can be found here: `https://docs.microsoft.com/en-us/powershell/azure/?view=azps-5.8.0`.

Through PowerShell or the Azure CLI, you can perform any task, from obtaining information to creating, managing, and deleting resources.

One of the great benefits of either option is that you can perform actions on multiple resources by building logic-based routines. For example, if you wanted to build 100 VMs, you could write a script that would loop 100 times, automatically creating each VM.

The main drawback to scripting is that scripts can become quite complex, especially when deploying resources built from many different components; for example, VMs are actually built with additional components such as disks and network interface cards. Both PowerShell and the Azure CLI can be used with another core feature of Azure: the ability to create JSON-based templates for resources, as we will examine next.

Understanding ARM templates

Just as other tools are simply wrappers for the Azure REST APIs, everything that is built in Azure is defined as an ARM template. Whether you create a service through the Azure portal, PowerShell, REST APIs, or the CLI, ultimately that service is described within an ARM template.

An ARM template is a JSON-based text file and is broken down into the following sections:

- A header containing `$schema`, `contentVersion`, and `metadata`: As an evolving platform, Microsoft is continually adding new components and adding new capabilities to existing components. For this reason, an ARM template contains information that states the schema and version.

- parameters: ARM templates can be built to be re-usable by allowing you to define and pass in parameters. These are then added either as a separate parameters file, as command-line arguments, or, when deploying a template within the Azure portal, a parameters form.

- variables: The variables section enables you to define expressions that can be used throughout the rest of the template. For example, they can be used to generate names or other values.

- functions: There are a number of different built-in functions that can be used, or you can define your own in the functions section. This is useful for building complex logic that needs to be re-used elsewhere.

- resources: The resources section contains the details of the component you wish to deploy and allows you to set the different configuration elements. Each configuration setting can either be hardcoded, used as a supplied parameter, or a computed variable.

- outputs: This is useful for chaining multiple templates together. For example, you can capture the Id value of the component you have created in one template and pass that to another.

Microsoft also provides a catalog of quickstart templates on GitHub at https://github.com/Azure/azure-quickstart-templates.

An example template that creates a storage account can be found in the preceding repository under 101-storage-account-create:

```
{
    "$schema": "https://schema.management.azure.com/
schemas/2019-04-01/deploymentTemplate.json#",
    "contentVersion": "1.0.0.0",
    "parameters": {
        "storageAccountType": {
            "type": "string",
            "defaultValue": "Standard_LRS",
            "allowedValues": [
                "Standard_LRS",
                "Standard_GRS",
                "Standard_ZRS",
                "Premium_LRS"
            ],
```

```json
      "metadata": {
        "description": "Storage Account type"
      }
    },
    "location": {
      "type": "string",
      "defaultValue": "[resourceGroup().location]",
      "metadata": {
        "description": "Location for all resources."
      }
    }
  },
  "variables": {
    "storageAccountName": "[concat('store',
uniquestring(resourceGroup().id))]"
  },
  "resources": [
    {
      "type": "Microsoft.Storage/storageAccounts",
      "apiVersion": "2019-06-01",
      "name": "[variables('storageAccountName')]",
      "location": "[parameters('location')]",
      "sku": {
        "name": "[parameters('storageAccountType')]"
      },
      "kind": "StorageV2",
      "properties": {}
    }
  ],
  "outputs": {
    "storageAccountName": {
      "type": "string",
      "value": "[variables('storageAccountName')]"
    }
  }
}
```

Templates can contain individual components, as in the preceding example, or they can contain multiple components. ARM templates for defining VMs, for example, contain resource definitions for the VM itself, network interfaces, storage accounts, and virtual networks.

In complex templates such as a VM, resources can state whether they have a dependency on others within the template. Again, in the VM example, there is a requirement for an Azure **Virtual Network (VNET)** to exist. By stating the VNET as a dependency, the platform will ensure this is created before the VM.

You can also link templates, calling one template from within another. This is known as nested templates and allows you to decompose your deployments into individual components but still maintain a cohesive deployment.

Using functions, you can create logic within your templates to automatically generate values based on provided inputs. A common example is the `concat` function, which is used to combine two strings.

For example, in the preceding ARM template example for creating a storage account, we generate the storage account name using the text `store` followed by a GUID:

```
"variables": {
    "storageAccountName": "[concat('store',
uniquestring(resourceGroup().id))]"
},
```

Further complexity can be added using conditional statements using the following format:

```
"condition": "[equals(parameters('<someparameter>'),'
<somevaluetotestfor>')]"
```

For example, you can test for the value of a specific parameter and perform different actions depending on what is passed through, as in the following ARM template snippet.

By using logic and functions, you can create complex templates that can be dynamically re-used across many different use cases.

Templates can be used in a variety of ways to deploy resources. You can use ARM templates with PowerShell or the CLI to create resources instead of defining configurations as parameters.

You can also upload templates to the Azure portal when creating services. This enables you to create components with pre-agreed configuration elements, which in turns allows you to better control consistency. For example, if you always want your storage account to use the `StorageV2` kind, enable data lake hierarchies, and use geo-redundancy, you can define all these elements in your custom ARM template and always use that template instead of the standard portal wizard.

As well as writing your own from scratch, or using a start template from the Microsoft GitHub repository, you can also export the template for an existing deployment. This is great because it allows you to build the component through the Azure portal's GUI but then save those configuration elements for future use.

The following screenshot shows an example of exporting a template in the portal:

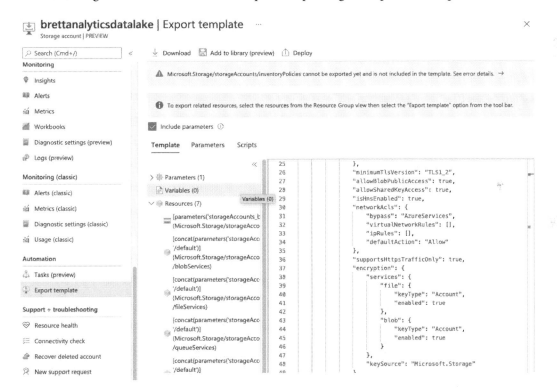

Figure 17.2 – Export a template from an existing component

The template can either be downloaded as a JSON document or added to a library in Azure. In *Figure 17.2*, you can see an **Add to library** button.

Once saved, either as a file or within the Azure library, you can then either create a component in the Azure portal as a template deployment or perform a deployment from the library. The following screenshot shows an example deployment initiated from a custom template:

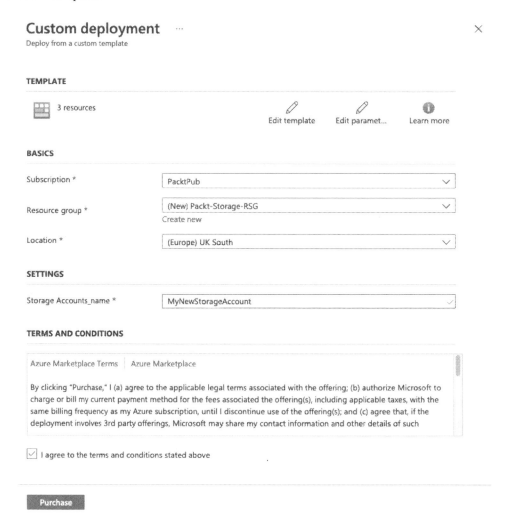

Figure 17.3 – Example deployment from a custom template

In the previous section, *Choosing between PowerShell or Azure CLI*, we said that ARM templates can be used with PowerShell or the Azure CLI to more easily deploy resources.

Using the `New-AzDeployment` (PowerShell) or `az deployment group create` (CLI) commands, we can reference an ARM template and a separate `parameters` file.

Again, these can be combined in complex scripts, performed ad hoc, or used in Azure Cloud Shell.

Using scripts and ARM templates provides a powerful tool to deploy, manage, and align our resources in Azure. However, once we combine the ability to define resources in code with the ability to automate deployments, we can gain complete control over our solutions and ensure consistency across both projects and environments.

In the final section of this chapter, we will therefore look at Azure DevOps, which provides these capabilities and more.

Looking at Azure DevOps

Throughout this chapter, we have been looking at how we can encode infrastructure in `script` files and ARM templates that then allow us to automate deployments using those artifacts. This process is often referred to as **Infrastructure as Code (IaC)** and fits well with agile-based delivery mechanisms as it provides the ability to build solutions iteratively.

Another related discipline is immutable infrastructure, which dictates that no changes should be made to existing infrastructure. When changes are required, the amendments should be made to the code that describes the system, and the existing infrastructure should then be completely destroyed and then re-deployed using the update code. This not only enforces the use of IaC but it also ensures that any changes are always encoded.

If, therefore, we are building out systems using code, we can start to utilize software development tools and technologies. Together, the tools and processes we employ are called DevOps, which is a combination of development and operations.

There are a number of DevOps toolsets available in the marketplace, and Microsoft has their own, known as Azure DevOps.

> **Information note**
>
> Technically Microsoft has two DevOps platforms: Azure DevOps and more recently GitHub, which they acquired in 2018. Whereas GitHub is often used by open source developers who wish to freely distribute code, Azure DevOps is more often used by teams working on private projects, although, of course, it is never quite that straightforward as both platforms offer free and paid tiers and public and private projects.

Azure DevOps brings together a whole range of the following developer tools into one integrated platform:

- **Azure Boards**: Helps plan and track team workloads through a suite of agile and Scrum management tools such as backlog tracking and Kanban boards.

- **Azure Repos**: Offers source control of code using Git repositories or **Team Foundation Version Control** (**TFVC**).

- **Azure Pipelines**: Automated build and release integration with Azure and many other vendors to manage and control builds and deployments.

- **Azure Test Plans**: Tracking and management of tests against your solution.

- **Azure Artifacts**: Share pre-compiled code packages or libraries such as NuGet, Maven, and npm.

As we can see from this high-level list of tools, Azure DevOps provides a range of services to help manage the end-to-end development life cycles. From an architectural perspective, we are most concerned with the elements that might affect how we build our solution; therefore, we shall look at the two key elements around code storage and deployment, namely, Azure Repos and Azure Pipelines.

Azure Repos

Azure Repos allows you to control and manage code changes by enforcing versioning and tracking of changes across files. Code is stored in a repository and repositories use branches to provide an additional layer of management.

Each repository has at least one branch; by default, this is called the master branch. When a user wishes to work on the code within a branch, they clone that branch to their local computer and perform any changes they need. When changes are saved to the user's computer, they do not automatically reflect in the repository. Instead, the developer must commit those changes to the local copy on their computer. Finally, changes are pushed to the remote repo so that others can see them.

For a single developer, this helps you track all your changes as each amendment you make is tracked and can be compared against previous versions. So, you can also revert commits to older versions should you need to.

When multiple developers are working on the same code base, there is the potential for the same files to be updated. Therefore, the process is to first perform a pull of the remote repo where you pull down any changes before you issue your own push. When you perform a pull, if conflicts are detected between the remote code and yours, you will be prompted to perform a merge. The merge process can be automatic, manual, or a combination of the two depending on the client software you are using and the conflicts themselves.

Once a merge has been completed and any conflicts resolved, the updated code can then be pushed back to the remote repository so that other developers can then pull down your code.

Although all work could be performed on the default master branch, it is better to create new branches for each piece of work or sprint. Creating a new branch makes a copy of the source branch that is independent. One possible usage scenario for this way of working is to create a new branch for each new iteration or feature that is being worked on. Once all work is completed, verified, and tested, the branch can then be merged back with the source. In this way, you always keep a working *clean* copy of your code.

> **Important Note**
>
> In agile, a sprint is a timeboxed period during which work will be performed. The amount of time is the same for every sprint within a project, and each sprint should finish with the deployment of working code. In this way, solutions involve multiple smaller releases over the project as opposed to one final release at the end of the project.

Another extension to this way of working is for each individual developer to create their own branch for the piece of work they are performing and enforce the use of a pull request.

A pull request is used instead of performing a merge with the source branch and is used to ensure that another developer reviews your code before allowing it to be merged. This is a great way of ensuring quality in your code as it means a second person must validate your changes and potentially prevent any issues.

Azure DevOps provides a series of options to control what users can do to a branch. For example, the master branch can be locked to only allow specific users to commit to it. Developers then work on their own branches and perform a pull request. Again, specific people such as senior developers can be set as the approvers of a pull request, and once approved, the merge into the master branch takes place. In this way, we can protect the master branch and enforce the use of code reviews.

The following diagram shows how this end-to-end process flow can work:

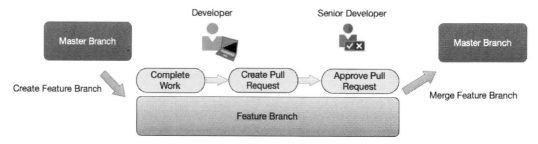

Figure 17.4 – DevOps branching process flow

With Azure Repos, you have a central storage repository for your ARM templates and scripts that tracks all your changes and provides tools for multiple DevOps engineers to work on them at the same time.

The next step of the process, once code has been built, is to build components with that code, which is where Azure Pipelines then helps.

Azure Pipelines

We can build and deploy components in Azure from ARM templates using PowerShell or the Azure CLI by using the `New-AzResourceGroupDeployment` or `az deployment group create` commands.

Azure Pipelines provides on-demand VM nodes with the necessary tooling installed to perform our deployments. In other words, rather than running the required PowerShell or Azure CLI scripts on our own computers, we can instead use the VMs provided by Azure Pipelines to run the code.

> **Information**
>
> Azure Pipelines allows you to implement **Continuous Integration and Continuous Deployment (CI/CD)** methodologies, or **CI/CD Pipelines**. CI/CD is a set of principles that DevOps or software development teams can use when building solutions. It states that changes should be made frequently and then validated by constantly redeploying those changes into an environment.

The VMs are specialist machines that are fully managed by Microsoft, which means you don't have direct access to them. Instead, you define what is run on them using the Azure DevOps portal. Through the portal, you can build pipelines using the classic method, whereby you can choose from a number of pre-built tasks such as building a library, deploying to a web app, and deploying from an ARM template. Or, you can use a YAML file to define what steps are to be taken.

The following screenshot shows an example pipeline that deploys a VM using the specific Azure deployment task that allows us to define an ARM template. The template itself is read directly from our Azure Repo:

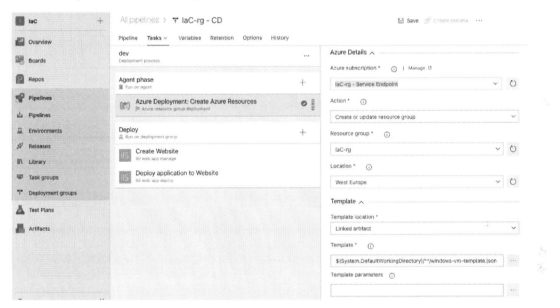

Figure 17.5 – Example of a classic pipeline

A YAML file is a JSON text document that can also define a series of steps you might want to perform as part of a deployment. When creating a pipeline, you are always asked whether to use YAML or the classic method. The following screenshot shows the same set of tasks as those we can see in *Figure 17.5*, but this time as a YAML file:

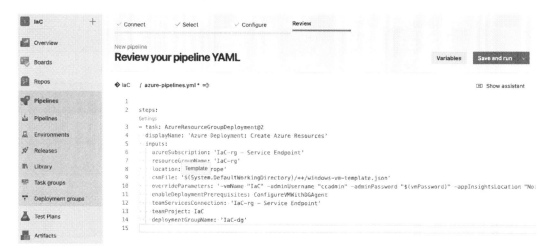

Figure 17.6 – Example of a YAML deployment

The choice between using YAML or the classic editor is largely down to personal preference and skillset. However, one of the great benefits of using YAML is that it is portable; that is, you can store the YAML file with your code, and therefore it is easier to share, manage, and include within your version control.

Finally, using Azure Pipelines, you can deploy to multiple environments. For example, in the following screenshot, we are deploying to a development environment followed by a production environment:

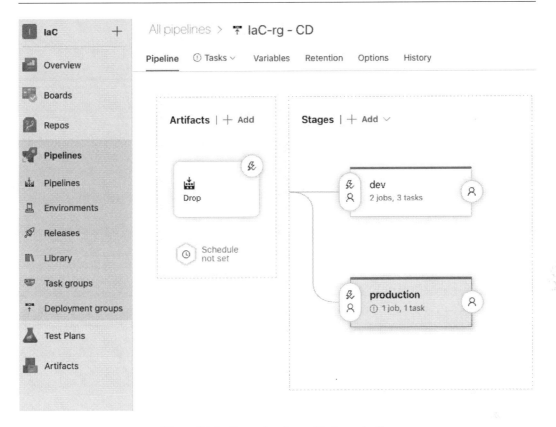

Figure 17.6 – Example of a multi-stage pipeline

The release to each environment can be individually controlled with different triggers and approvals. For example, a trigger can be set on the dev stage so that as soon as the code in the default master branch of your repository is updated, it will automatically deploy those changes. However, the production stage can have an additional approval required before it is deployed, for example, by ensuring a test team manager has validated the development deployment.

Azure Artifacts

In software development, it is common to want to share code or even pre-built components that execute specific tasks. For example, if a developer has built a function that performs a complex calculation, you may wish to share that with other developers as an **artifact** so that they can re-use it.

This is different from sharing code within a Git repository. The code in a repository can be easily modified by the developer consuming it and then the updates are sent back to the repository – in other words, they allow collaborative coding.

Artifacts may be compiled or obfuscated so that the original code cannot be easily updated, and they are designed to be used as is. Because of this, artifacts will be versioned, and any changes will be distributed as a new version.

Azure Artifacts provides a place to store your artifacts so that they can be easily shared with your teams. As part of the DevOps platform, they can be fully integrated into your build pipelines – for example, you could set up a pipeline to automatically build, version, and publish your artifact whenever a code change is made.

This section has been a high-level view of Azure DevOps and in particular how we can use Azure Repos and Azure Pipelines to manage and automate deployments from code. Azure DevOps and agile development practices are a big subject that is covered in detail in the book *Azure DevOps Explained*, by Sjoukje Zaal, published by Packt.

From an architectural perspective, understanding the process flow of code management and automated releases can be used in our overall solution designs. For example, when considering backup and disaster recovery scenarios, an automated pipeline that deploys your infrastructure components could form part of that strategy.

Summary

In this chapter, we have seen how everything in Azure can be managed by a series of REST APIs and how these are protected using your Azure account.

We saw how we integrate directly with these APIs or via command-line tools such as Azure PowerShell or the Azure CLI. We also looked at how we can use command-line tools and the Azure portal to automate and standardize deployments with ARM templates, which allow us to set specific configurations.

Finally, we looked at using Azure DevOps to manage and version control code and perform automated, repeatable deployments.

This chapter finishes our look at operations and monitoring. In *Chapter 18, Engaging with Real-World Customers*, we take our architectures beyond the exam to look at customer considerations, cost optimizations, and what types of challenges we face when dealing with large enterprises.

Exam scenario

MegaCorp Inc. is building a new platform in Azure for customers to view details of their own accounts. The solution will be built over time with regular releases and updates; therefore, the management team wishes to embrace agile development methodologies.

The project team will consist of two teams of developers with five developers in each team, and work will be assigned to each team at the start of every two-week sprint.

The project lead is concerned about developers overwriting each other's code or causing other conflicts. They also want to ensure that there is always a working copy of the core code base at any one time.

Each team has a senior developer who must review any code changes prior to a release. Because the deployment mechanism will change regularly as the solution grows, they also need a way to track and manage changes made to it as well.

Advise on how these requirements can be met as part of the solution design.

Further reading

Refer to the following links for more information on topics covered:

- PowerShell: `https://docs.microsoft.com/en-us/powershell/azure/?view=azps-5.8.0`

- The Azure CLI: `https://docs.microsoft.com/en-us/cli/azure/reference-index?view=azure-cli-latest`

- ARM templates: `https://azure.microsoft.com/en-gb/resources/templates/`

- Azure DevOps: `https://docs.microsoft.com/en-gb/azure/devops/user-guide/what-is-azure-devops?view=azure-devops`

Section 6: Beyond the Exam

The final section wraps up and discusses real-world scenarios and considerations, especially when working with complex, large organizations.

The daily role of an architect involves far more than what is covered on the official exam syllabus, and this section covers the best practices you need to stand out.

The following chapters will be covered under this section:

- *Chapter 18, Engaging with Real-World Customers*
- *Chapter 19, Enterprise Design Considerations*

18
Engaging with Real-World Customers

In the last chapter, we completed the *logging and monitoring* topic, and the part of the book that covers the *AZ-304 exam* requirements.

In this chapter, we'll look beyond specific design considerations and look at more general working practices in cloud architecture. What we cover in this and the next chapter will not be included in the *AZ-304 exam*, instead, we'll look at how we work with customers to understand their requirements and provide some example questions to help capture them.

We will also look at some tips on how to record and keep track of our responses as well as how we should respond to feedback as we work through projects.

We will be covering the following areas:

- Working with customers
- Exploring common goals
- Mapping requirements
- Getting feedback

Working with customers

All solutions start with a set of requirements, usually business leads. After all, every solution is built to address a need, and this is often in response to either a new process, to address an inefficient process, or to provide some form of service.

A solution architect is often involved, if not leading, the requirements gathering process, and without a full understanding of the underlying business needs, we cannot complete a successful project.

There are several ways we can gather the information we need, but simply sitting down and interviewing stakeholders is probably the most direct.

Who are my stakeholders?

A stakeholder is a member of the business who has a vested interest in the solution being built. Usually, we start with the person or team who requested, or is at least sponsoring, the new service. However, if your remit extends to an application interface, we should also reach out to who will eventually become the end users, after all, the solution needs to be user-friendly otherwise it will fail. In fact, the scope that you must consider will largely drive who you need to communicate with.

Another example may be a data analysis environment. In this case, involving the data scientists who will be using the platform is crucial as they will have insights into the tools they use and how they are configured.

You also need to consider supporting teams, from security and monitoring to finance and technical support.

The security and monitoring teams will have very specific requirements in regards to the type of metrics they will need access to and how they will access them. Finance teams may need involvement to understand both any budget constraints and how the day-to-day operations will be paid for.

The technical support teams may similarly have existing toolsets and alerting mechanisms that must be interfaced with.

Often, we simply look for the most obvious stakeholders, but as we can see, there are far more people involved than we might at first consider. Once we have a list of people to speak to about the proposed solution, we need to ensure we can ascertain their requirements in an accurate way, which is often more difficult than it sounds.

Gathering requirements

There are many examples of projects that have overrun budgets and timeframes, and quite often this is because of a lack of, or at least understanding of, requirements.

The choice of an agile delivery method over a waterfall approach is sometimes driven by the fact that it is difficult for customers to know what they want until they see it. However, even with an agile project, we need to help stakeholders articulate their requirements in a way that can be well understood and agreed upon.

The first step in this process is to simply listen to what is being asked. It is very easy for an architect who already has an intimate knowledge of a particular domain to think of the solution before they fully understand what is required. For example, if we know the project is to build a data-driven application, we may start from the assumption that this means an n-tier solution built from web apps and API apps.

This is a dangerous supposition; the business parlance may not align with our own understanding of the terminology. However, by ensuring we talk through the entire end-to-end requirements we can build a much better picture, and we may find that what we assumed was needed was not in fact correct.

Agreeing on the language used can be quite an important step, and in fact, part of the job of an architect may be to translate business talk into techie jargon and vice versa as we are often the go-between for different teams.

Even when we are speaking the same language, it can be difficult to articulate what we desire. Or, to put it another way, what the customer asks for is not always what they want.

A common problem is that a simple misunderstanding, or incorrect presumption, can lead to project delays or even failure as depicted here:

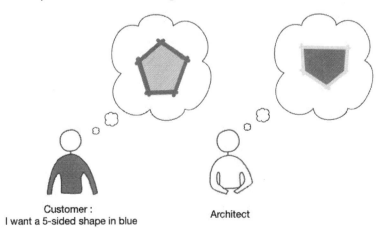

Customer :
I want a 5-sided shape in blue

Architect

Figure 18.1 – What the customer asks for versus what is understood

However, there are ways around this problem. First, we should ask open-ended questions that cannot be answered with simple yes or no answers. We should also ask questions in business terms rather than technical terms.

For example, the question *does the solution need to be resilient?* can be interpreted in many ways, and what you consider resilient may not be what the stakeholder considers resilient.

Instead, we should ask *what resiliency does the solution require?* This will incite a far more detailed response and offer the business a better opportunity to explain what their view is.

Another method of ensuring we have understood a requirement is to repeat it back to the customer in your own words. Repeating what you understand in your own words helps you both see the problem from different points of view. Often this can create further dialog as you explore the problem and any potential solution.

Always keep in mind that your stakeholder may or may not understand the available technologies. As part of the conversation, we should explore the different options and explain the art of the possible. Your stakeholder may now know that a particular technology exists that could make a particular process possible, especially with the growing tools around AI and big data analytics.

It is easy for stakeholders to fall into old ways of working and simply believe that moving to the cloud means using the same tools in a different place. For example, traditional data analysis tools involved filesystems, SQL databases, and spreadsheets. When moving to the cloud, you must opt to simply lift and shift but to truly leverage the power available to us we need to explore new ways of working using tooling such as **Cosmos DB**, **Data Lake Storage**, **Azure Databricks**, and **Azure Data Factory**.

With this in mind, we need to be careful that stakeholders provide requirements, and not attempt to dictate the solution. Again, in the previous data analytics example, a stakeholder may state their requirements as a SQL Server instance and a VM running Excel. We need to tease out what they are trying to achieve and suggest alternative, more modern approaches.

We often need to capture information around common areas, which we will look at next.

Exploring common goals

Microsoft Azure advises following what is known as the **Well-Architected Framework**, which covers the five key pillars that need to be considered when designing solutions.

Following these areas is a great way to ensure that your design has captured the main points and provide a starting point for your requirements gathering. As a refresher, the five pillars are the following:

- Costs
- Operations
- Performance
- Reliability
- Security

The questions you ask can and should be grouped into each of these areas, and we will look at some example questions for each area along with why they are important. We shall start with costs.

Understanding costs

We need to know how much a solution will cost to build, as well as how much it will cost to run. New solutions are often built as part of a project, and that project will have a defined number of resources in terms of people and technology. Once completed, a solution will have running costs, especially in the cloud where services are paid for by usage.

To be successful, we therefore need to understand what those costs are. If you spend more than has been allocated to the project, then you will be unable to finish. Likewise, if the running costs are more than has been budgeted for, then the business will not want to use it.

In many ways, the questions we need to ask are quite straightforward:

- How much budget and resources are available?
- What are the maximum or target running costs?

If a solution is designed to make money for the business, such as an e-commerce site or end user tool, then the running costs need to be less than the revenue being earned. One of the core features of the cloud is that you can easily start small and scale up. Therefore, the answers to these questions may need to accommodate increasing costs as the solution is utilized more so that the running costs always stay within the revenue.

Costs can also come from the next pillar: operations.

Understanding operational requirements

Operational requirements can cover many areas, from deployment to monitoring.

Sometimes a solution is built and then left unchanged. Modern development principles and operational methodologies dictate a continual release cycle as new features are continually added.

We must also constantly monitor the application for performance and reliability. This might require new tooling to be created as part of the solution or we may integrate existing processes and systems.

Operational excellence is therefore about ensuring that our solution is stable and performing well, taking into consideration multiple releases and updates as well as varying or even unpredictable usage patterns.

Of course, every solution will differ and as operations are closely related to costs, it is important we understand the requirements.

We therefore need to ask questions such as the following:

- What monitoring and management tools do you need to integrate?

- Who needs to be alerted to problems and how?

- What is your release cycle? Do you deploy to development and test systems first?

- Who signs off new releases?

As well as being aligned with costs, operations are also closely aligned with reliability and performance.

Understanding performance requirements

Performance is not just your solution's ability to respond in a timely manner, but its ability to change in response to varying levels of demand.

Cloud solutions provide the ability to scale out and up dynamically, but this of course comes at a cost. If demand is directly related to generating revenue, then we may want our application to scale without any bounds.

Conversely, if your solution is a business support function, or if usage patterns are well known, we may want to constrain resources.

For example, a subscription-based tool that end users must sign up to could scale indefinitely because as more users sign up, more resources are required to support the growing userbase. Conversely, a payroll system will have a known demand, and we might instead scale down at weekends and evenings or scale up at the end of the month.

We should therefore ask questions such as the following:

- What are the solution's usage patterns?
- What are the boundaries within which we must perform?

If a solution does not scale in line with demand, it will perform much slower, however, in extreme cases, it could even cause failure. We must therefore also understand reliability requirements.

Understanding reliability requirements

Reliability is your solution's ability to withstand outages, and from a business perspective, we need to know what impact downtime has.

An internal application that does not perform a critical or time-sensitive function can withstand being offline longer in the event of an issue. However, an external revenue-generating application will result in the loss of income if it is unavailable and therefore will most likely need to be more resilient.

Increasing resilience often means increasing costs, especially if you need to duplicate components in other regions to protect against regional loss. The increased costs need to be weighed against the potential loss of revenue. For example, you may decide that a small loss of income is less than the cost of a potential outage, at least up to a point.

Finally, the solution may offer external customers **Service-Level Agreements (SLAs)**, with penalties to be paid should they be breached. Internal systems may offer operational-level agreements.

As we can see, it is not a simple question of does your application need to be resilient? We also need to understand the levels of durability that are required.

These are some example questions we could ask:

- Do you have to adhere to any SLAs or **Operational-Level Agreements (OLAs)**? If so, what are they?
- What would be the financial cost of an outage?

Once we understand how resistant to an outage our solution must be, the final area to consider is security.

Understanding security requirements

Security generally impacts all levels of your solution, and we often need to include specialist security teams in our conversations to understand organizational-wide security requirements.

Business owners may also have their own views on security, especially if the solution is for another customer with specific security demands of their own.

Organizational requirements will usually be defined as a set of principles and policies, such as requiring all data to be encrypted, or for traffic to be internal only.

When building solutions for other parties, we may also need to consider additional levels such as who has access to data and how it can be transferred between systems.

Finally, many countries have their own restrictions and compliance rules around handling data, protecting it, and how long it can be kept.

Some example questions we may need to ask the business are as follows:

- Are there any specific data-handling requirements?
- Are there any rules around data retention periods?
- Are there any data residency requirements (such as, which countries data can reside or be processed in)?

The example questions are just a few examples, and although we align them with specific areas, in fact, many might span multiple concerns.

Over time you should build a standard set of questions that can then be added to or tweaked as each project demands. Once we have our business requirements, we can then start to map them to technical options.

Mapping requirements

It may seem obvious, but we need to ensure requirements are recorded and referred to during the projects life cycle. Especially with agile projects, requirements can change through the project, and any such decisions need to be logged and updated along with the reasons why they were changed.

There are specialist tools available to help do this, however, a simple spreadsheet or document and a central, easily accessible location is sometimes all that is needed. Other options could include **Microsoft Teams**, **Microsoft SharePoint**, or **Azure DevOps**. The point is that we don't need expensive, specialized, architecture toolsets; we just need a log.

For each requirement, we should log who it came from, any reasoning behind decisions, and what technology choices have been made. The following is an example of something I often use:

Category	Architecture requirement	Business requirement	Implementation specifications	Justification and notes
Costs	What are the maximum or target run costs?	Costs need to be minimal but scale with usage.	Consumption-based functions. Serverless SQL.	The application will start as a proof of concept and need to keep costs down. However, as we move into production, we need to be able to rapidly scale in line with demand.
Operations	Who needs to be alerted to problems and how?	The service operations team needs to be informed of outages via email.	Azure Monitor/alerts.	The existing support team will be alerted via email initially, with a view to an integrated approach in a later phase.
Security	Are there any data residency requirements?	Data must stay within the US.	Use the West US and East US regions.	As a US-based application managing sensitive data, we need to ensure it is not replicated to regions outside the US.

Other information you may wish to capture includes risks, assumptions, and dependencies. However, the key point is that we should log the requirements and reasoning behind them so that we continually refer to them as our design progresses. We can also refer to our original decisions for future iterations or if we encounter issues later.

As we progress through a project, we will no doubt be questioned and challenged on our designs, or even need to alter them in response to changing business needs. How we respond to this feedback can help ensure a project is successful.

Getting feedback

Agile projects are run with continual feedback built in. At the end of each period of work, known as a **sprint**, the customer is given a chance to see what has been built and feed back on what works and what doesn't. The project team also has an opportunity to receive feedback as part of a lesson-learned activity, whereby all the people working on the project can discuss what worked and what didn't and adjust accordingly for the next sprint.

Feedback is incredibly important to the success of a solution as the end goal is to create a solution that addresses the original business need and is usable. History is full of projects that failed simply because the resultant system was too difficult to use.

It can be challenging to accept feedback, but our role as architects is to help steer the business, and this is a two-way process of listening and adjusting.

For longer-running projects, business needs can change through the project. This is an inevitable consequence when solutions are large and complex, however, if our solution is flexible enough from the outset, we should be able to respond appropriately.

Cloud technologies are built with this type of flexibility in mind.

There are often many ways to achieve an outcome, for example, when a solution calls for a database, we can use **Azure SQL Database**, **Azure SQL Managed Instance**, or **SQL running on a VM**. We may start with Azure SQL Database, but as we start to build and test, Azure SQL Managed Instance may start to become more appropriate. Our solution designs must therefore be able to adapt in response to these challenges and changing requirements.

Another aspect of agile projects is that releases are iterative, each release building on the previous one, adding more functionality as we go. Again, as new features are added, we may need to adjust the components we use, either by adding additional services or changing existing ones.

We therefore need to be able to respond to feedback in a positive manner – any request to change or adapt is an opportunity to make our solution even better. By continually building on what we have learned throughout a project, and even across projects, we can bring value to the business as needed.

Summary

In this chapter, we have started to look beyond the *AZ-304 exam* requirements, moving away from technological choices, to look more at our working practices.

The success or failure of any project often comes down to how we engage with our customers. The closer we work with and understand their requirements, the better equipped we are to build our solutions.

We have looked at who we need to work with, who our stakeholders are, and highlighted one of the biggest challenges of capturing requirements: being able to correctly understand what is being asked for.

We have seen some common examples of questions we need to ask for each of the five main pillars of architecture: *costs*, *operations*, *performance*, *reliability*, and *security*. We have also seen some ideas on how we can record our decisions and why this is important.

Finally, we looked at the importance of responding positively to feedback and challenges, and why, ultimately, this helps us design better solutions.

In the final chapter, we continue beyond the exam theme, looking at some of the specific problems we may face as architects, and how we can address them.

Further reading

- Azure Well-Architected Framework – `https://docs.microsoft.com/en-us/azure/architecture/framework/`

- Azure Well-Architected Review – `https://docs.microsoft.com/en-us/assessments/?mode=pre-assessment&id=azure-architecture-reviewS`

19
Enterprise Design Considerations

In the previous chapter, we began looking at Azure design from an everyday working perspective, looking at examples of how to engage with customers, and then gather, map, and document requirements.

In this final chapter, we complete the *beyond the exam* theme by looking at what specific considerations we need to make when designing enterprise architectures.

First, we will examine two types of organization – the large-scale enterprise versus the small start-up, and how the size, age, and internal structure of a company can have an impact on our designs.

We'll then investigate some strategies for ensuring that we get the best value from cloud solutions by looking at cost optimization techniques.

We will then explore what Azure landing zones are, and how they can help us manage the Azure platform in enterprise systems that involve multiple subscriptions and individual solutions.

Finally, we will finish off the chapter, and the book, by looking at how we might build the platform over time.

Therefore, throughout this chapter, we will explore the following topics:

- Understanding your customer
- Optimizing costs
- Creating landing zones
- Building with continual iteration

Understanding your customer

Each organization can be very different, not just in terms of goals, but also the levels of risk, security, and resilience they are prepared to accept.

To highlight such differences, it is helpful to compare two very different types of company – a well-established, multi-national corporation with thousands of employees around the world, versus a newly formed start-up, with just a handful of staff.

Looking at process differences

A multi-national company will have existing processes and ways of working that have been built up over many years. The IT department will more than likely follow industry patterns such as the **Information Technology Infrastructure Library** (**ITIL**), which is itself a framework and set of practices for **Information Technology System Management** (**ITSM**), which defines how an organization manages their IT services. In other words, larger companies generally have a set of processes that everyone must follow for managing the companies' IT infrastructure, including implementing new services.

In addition, more staff means greater specialization for employees. Separate teams of experts will be responsible for managing specific systems, such as networking, servers, storage, security, and software development. The cloud is yet another, relatively newer addition, to the many IT departments that may exist.

How each team interoperates will be part of the IT process map. If the server team needs to build and connect some new servers, they will have to engage with the network and security teams and hand off responsibility for each area.

A small start-up will not have these well-defined processes; they will most likely be starting from a blank canvas. As a new company, they will be able to choose and adapt from a range of newer methodologies. The IT experts will most likely wear many hats – a single engineer or team could be responsible for the entire IT stack, from hardware to software and everything in between.

The larger company, in comparison to the smaller start-up, will therefore take much longer to implement new solutions as there will be a lot of coordination between teams. A new project could take months, if not years, to implement, not necessarily because of the time it takes to order and configure new systems, but because of the auditable trail of approvals that will be needed at each stage.

For example, before any new system can be built, it might go through a process of high-level design and approval by an enterprise architecture team, who will ensure that the new functionality sits in the overall IT strategy. Next, a low-level architecture will be produced and again signed off to ensure that the correct level of detail is documented, along with security and support processes. The actual build could then be handed to several implementation teams before a rigorous round of testing.

This lengthy process is there to protect the organization from wasting resources and reducing the possibility of failure, as well as implementing a system that aligns to a corporate strategy.

A smaller, more nimble company, will most likely build fast, fail fast, and iterate over many cycles when building systems. Smaller, close-knit teams can try new technologies and react much quicker to changing requirements. The overall IT strategy will most likely be much simpler and well known, which again helps everybody understand the end goal.

Smaller, younger organizations will often have IT at the core of their operations and product offering, and every member of staff will understand those technologies. For larger organizations, IT will just be one department of many, and again each department will be specialized and only have peripheral knowledge of the others.

When designing architectures, we need to consider the processes a company employs, as it will directly impact not only the complexity of any deployment but the time it takes to navigate the governance processes.

Although there is a wider movement for bigger companies to start moving toward agile ways of working, they will still be constrained in part by governance and security requirements, which we will look at next.

Understanding governance, risk, and security

A small company will be largely unencumbered by some governance requirements and will only need to worry about more general practices such as data protection and employment laws.

Larger companies, especially those that are publicly listed, or involved in highly regulated areas such as finance, will have very explicit rules that they must adhere to. In addition, some customers, such as government and public sector clients, will have additional needs that must be met to undertake work for them.

These governance and security requirements will impact the security reliability measures your design might need to include, as well as introduce additional tests and checks that may need to be performed.

Another field we must be aware of is risk. This is often tied closely with security and governance; however, the larger the company, and the more established, the more at risk they are.

For example, a new company that has started to provide a particular service will have very little risk in terms of how they may be impacted by a security breach. Many countries' data protection laws will fine a company for a data leak based on turnover – the bigger the turnover, the greater the fine.

> **Information**
>
> UNCTAD provides links to many countries' specific laws on data protection and other global reports: `https://unctad.org/page/data-protection-and-privacy-legislation-worldwide`.

Reputational risk is also a large factor. For an established company, any security breach can greatly damage their reputation, which in turn can result in huge financial losses as other customers lose faith in their services. A start-up company has no reputation, although it could be argued that they are, of course, trying to build one.

Finally, long-established companies have greater visibility and are therefore more likely to be targeted. Again, the smaller start-up, which is yet to make moves into the marketplace, is relatively unknown and therefore less likely to be targeted – at least not for financial gains.

As with processes, security and governance increase the complexity of your design, or at the very least will often result in more scrutiny by the relevant approvers.

This is not to say that a design can be any less secure for a smaller start-up, rather that the multi-national company will have far more checks and balances in place that can increase the amount and detail of documentation.

In the next section, we will examine a topic that needs to be considered for any size of company – keeping an eye on costs.

Optimizing costs

Cloud solutions can be built with incredible flexibility around the resources they consume. We can create systems that dynamically respond to usage so that they scale automatically as needed. Serverless options also allow for solutions that cost near zero when not being used. By way of an example, services such as Azure functions are billed per execution – if there's no execution, there is no cost.

This flexibility, however, leads to a problem with cost management – how do you define how much a service will cost? In a traditional on-premises architecture, projects will normally be costed based on the hardware and software licenses that need to be purchased. Whether the system is used a little or a lot, the costs will be the same.

Business leaders will often want to know how much a service will cost to run so that they can decide whether it is worth the expenditure. However, how can we state what a solution will cost until we can see how much it will be utilized?

We can start based on an estimate. We can estimate the number of users we expect to use the platform and we can create cost projections based on expected usage over time. But often, this will only be a best guess.

Therefore, any new solution needs to be monitored for resource and cost usage, especially in the first few months of operation. Some components can be purchased per execution – that is, serverless, or **Functions as a Service (FaaS)**, or they can be provisioned using a service plan where you define an amount of CPU and RAM.

FaaS is great for more dynamic use of resources, allowing you to start very small and automatically expand as required. However, as your solution scales, there is sometimes a tipping point whereby opting for a provisioned service results in a more predictable and efficient cost.

By monitoring usage and costs, we can then feed back into the solution design and change either the component or the pricing model as we see fit.

As we saw in *Chapter 15, Designing for Logging and Monitoring*, Azure includes the Azure Advisor service, which will make recommendations on some services such as VM sizes.

When calculating costs for a solution, we need a way to group the components. We have several ways to achieve this – we can group resources into resource groups, we can tag resources with a cost center, or we could group solutions into their own subscription, creating a new subscription per system. However, when building solutions in their own subscription, we need a way to ensure that each subscription contains all the necessary security, monitoring, and reporting mechanisms – often called a landing zone, which we will examine next.

Creating landing zones

Using subscriptions is a useful way of segregating duties and application workloads. However, if you wish to use that model, you need to consider how this affects your security and governance posture.

For example, you may wish to ensure that all network traffic is routed through a central firewall, or to centralize logging and monitoring. We therefore need to ensure that any new subscription is set up correctly and in line with your overall design strategy.

Defining a landing zone methodology is concerned with leveraging the various Azure components and tools to create consistency and compliance across all your subscriptions in an automated fashion. The latter point is crucial – ideally, your patterns should be implemented automatically with as little manual intervention as possible.

When designing a landing zone, you must keep in mind that it needs to be scalable – changing how landing zone patterns work later can be time-consuming and costly. They should also be modular, which helps add additional features and functionality later or change how you'll implement some services.

You must consider many different areas when designing a landing zone, including the following:

- Identity
- Network topology
- Governance requirements
- Disaster recovery and backup
- Maintenance operations
- Monitoring and logging

Your requirements for each will depend on your choice of technologies and implementation options, and of course, as all organizations are different, no one solution will be the same.

For each area, we can examine some of the considerations.

Identity

How your users are authorized and authenticated is often one of the first considerations. Will you use a single Active Directory for all users? Will you have multiple directories for different environments? Will you combine internal users and external clients using guest accounts or separate them? For example, Azure offers B2B and B2C integrations that allow you to connect users in other Azure tenants (B2B) or users using different identity providers, such as Facebook and Google (B2C). We cover the different options in *Chapter 3, Understanding User Authentication*.

Network topology

Will your solutions all be externally facing only? Or is there a need to integrate with an on-premises network?

Companies born in the cloud often expose services directly to the internet using native options, especially if all those services are client-facing. Established organizations may have a desire to integrate with existing traffic control and protection measures, such as utilizing existing firewalls, or perhaps a hybrid approach where Azure traffic leverages native Azure firewalls and you wish to route all traffic through such a device.

Governance

Many organizations have strict policies on auditing and enforcing specific security models. Will these policies be implemented in each subscription, and if so, how can we control it and ensure that those policies are adhered to?

Disaster recovery and backup

What will your backup strategy look like from a point of view of control and monitoring? Does each application have responsibility for ensuring adequate backups are taken, and each solution defines its own disaster recovery solution? Or will you design a central strategy and ensure that it is followed? As services such as Azure Backup are charged according to the amount of storage used, you need to decide who will be responsible for costs.

For example, will you use a central backup strategy with costs picked up by the operations teams? Or will you opt for a decentralized model whereby each solution is paid for, and backups managed by, the individual service owner?

Monitoring and operations

Do you use existing monitoring tools such as Microsoft's **Service Center Operations Manager (SCOM)**? Or will you leverage existing tools? Will all your components log to a central log analytics workspace, or will you decentralize logging and have each service owner be responsible? How will this affect security monitoring?

Ultimately, many areas come down to a choice between centralization or de-centralization. This affects costs as well as operational responsibility. For example, having a centralized log analytics workspace means costs and operations are also centralized.

We also need to consider how we configure each element to utilize our chosen strategy – for example, if we want all components to log diagnostics to a central log analytics workspace, we can create policies that will perform a `deployIfNotExists` action whenever the resource is created.

The following diagram shows one such example architecture that considers all these ideas in a single, high-level blueprint:

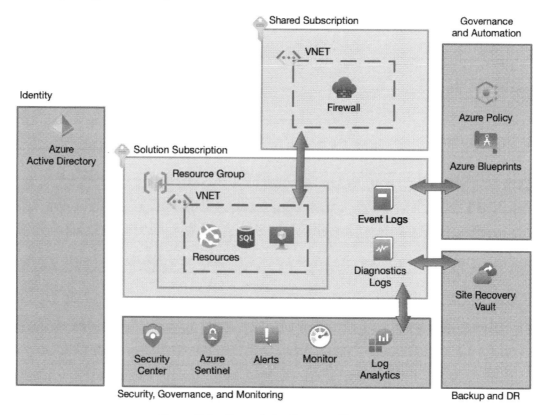

Figure 19.1 – Example landing zone blueprint

The final point to consider is whether you will define and build your landing zone strategy before any deployments are allowed, or whether you will build up your overall solution over time, which we will consider next.

Building with continual iteration

Building cloud solutions can be a complex process, especially when trying to build for large enterprises. One option when first developing your cloud adoption is to fully define and build your management tooling upfront; however, this can take some time and delay your ability to realize the cost benefits.

Another approach is to build a core baseline of services – decide what is most important and must be implemented before you can begin your cloud journey. This is a **minimal viable product** (**MVP**) and defines the absolute bare minimum solution.

From there, you can build upon that solution, adding new services or improving existing ones as you develop your cloud offering. Agile methodologies can help here and are ideally suited to building cloud solutions due to the modular nature of Azure's components.

Once you have a baseline environment, you can iteratively define, design, and build your platform. Each iteration will increase security, develop your governance, bring reliability to your solutions, and increase maturity.

Summary

This chapter completes the *beyond the exam* topic, and the book. Whereas most of the book has focused on the skills needed to pass the AZ-304 exam, these final two chapters have been a more general look at design considerations required to create and deliver successful designs for Azure-based solutions.

Each organization is very different, and we began the chapter by exploring the differences between two extreme examples – a multi-national corporation with existing systems and governance processes, versus a newly formed start-up. Each type of organization has its own challenges and opportunities, and so we explored some of the more common examples.

Next, we learned how cost management is a critical aspect of running any solution in the cloud, especially when building dynamic systems that respond and scale to usage, rather than more traditional infrastructure whose costs are fixed.

We have seen how Azure landing zones can impact our overall designs and looked at different areas we need to consider to ensure consistency, security, and compliance on our platforms.

Finally, we discussed how an iterative approach to building out our environments can help us get up and running quicker and start realizing the benefits of cloud-based solutions.

Unlike many of the other exams, the AZ-304 exam is about the choice of technology as opposed to how to implement each technology (which is covered by the AZ-303 exam). Therefore, throughout this book, we have looked at the various design choices we must make when building and architecting solutions in Azure.

We have covered the full spectrum of components in Azure, from authentication, authorization, and security, to platform governance, scalability choices, and how to architect highly available solutions.

Infrastructure as a Service (IaaS), **Platform as a Service (PaaS)**, and **Functions as a Service (FaaS)**, and serverless options have all been discussed and their relative strengths and weaknesses highlighted.

As well as looking at each individual technology, we have seen examples of how they can be used to address different requirements.

To help prepare you for the AZ-304 exam, and architecture work in general, I would encourage you to use the examples in this book as a basis for addressing common business needs.

Further reading

Refer to the following links for more information on the topics covered in this chapter:

- *Azure landing zones*: https://docs.microsoft.com/en-us/azure/cloud-adoption-framework/ready/landing-zone/

- *Cloud Adoption Framework (CAF)*: https://docs.microsoft.com/en-us/azure/cloud-adoption-framework/

- *Azure Sample Architectures*: https://docs.microsoft.com/en-us/azure/architecture/browse/

Mock Exam

1. The business needs to be able to keep a close eye on costs and each subscription has a separate owner and budget. Which of the following options can you leverage to help prevent overspend on subscriptions?

   A) Create a cost alert on your Azure tenant to email you whenever a budget of $100 is met. You can then email the subscription owner to keep them on budget.

   B) Create a weekly report that identifies current costs and email it out to all owners.

   C) On each subscription, set an individual monthly budget and an alert that will notify the owner when 80% of the budget is reached.

   D) On each subscription, set a monthly budget and shut down their services when the limit is reached.

2. You need to ensure that you capture activities that occur on the management plane of your Azure subscriptions, and those activities need to be held for 180 days and be easily queried. How can you achieve this?

   A) Create a logic app that scans for changes and then writes them to a storage account. Ensure the storage account is set to the archive tier.

   B) Configure your subscriptions to send diagnostics logs to a Log Analytics workspace. Configure the workspace with 180 days' retention.

   C) Configure your subscriptions to send diagnostics logs to a storage account.

   D) No action is required because Azure automatically captures and stores activities for 180 days.

3. You need to monitor a newly deployed VM and be alerted by sending an email to the admin group if the CPU exceeds 100% for sustained periods. How can you best achieve this?

A) Create an action group with the email address(es) of your administrators. Create an alert to trigger the action group when CPU usage hits 100%.

B) Create an alert to trigger a logic app that sends an email to your administrators when CPU usage hits 100%.

C) Create a VM scaling event when CPU usage hits 100%. As part of the scaling action, trigger an email to be sent to the administrators.

D) Configure the VM management agent to send an email when CPU usage reaches 100%.

4. Your organization wishes to implement **Multi-Factor Authentication (MFA)**, but only in specific scenarios, such as when it is suspected that their account has been compromised. Choose the best option to accommodate this.

A) Ensure security defaults are activated and enforce MFA for everybody.

B) Ensure security defaults are activated and enforce MFA for everybody in the "suspected" **Active Directory (AD)** group.

C) Purchase a P1 AD license for every user in your organization who you wish to protected with Conditional Access. Then define a policy that only enforces MFA for specific signals.

D) Purchase a P2 AD license for the administrators in your organization and enable Conditional Access. Then define a policy that only enforces MFA for specific signals.

5. You are extending your existing Microsoft AD-backed systems into the cloud. You need to ensure that if any connectivity is lost between Azure and your on-premises network, users can still connect. How might you achieve this?

A) Enable password writeback. This will ensure that users can always log on securely.

B) Use AD Pass-through Authentication to ensure that users are always authenticated against a live copy of AD.

C) Enable Seamless **Single Sign-On (SSO)** as this will ensure users are always authenticated without interruption.

D) Enable password hash synchronization. Because a hash of the user's password is stored within Azure, any loss of connectivity means users can still authenticate.

6. You run an Azure tenant that manages multiple subscriptions across a complex organization that is divided by geographic regions and departments. You need to plan a strategy for assigning owner-level access to each IT department in each region, and contributor-level access for the head of department in each region. What option might you choose to achieve this?

   A) Create a management group structure for each region and assign contributor-level access to each department level.

   B) Create a management group structure for each country and department, and then assign owner-level access for each country's IT department at the country level, and contributor-level access to each department level.

   C) Create a management group structure for each country and department, and then assign owner-level access to each department level.

   D) Create a management group structure for each department and assign owner-level access to each department level.

7. To tighten your security controls on the Azure platform, you want to only provide elevated access to users as and when they need it. How might you go about implementing this?

   A) Purchase a P2 license for each authorizing user. Activate **Privileged Identity Management (PIM)**. In the Active Directory management blade, edit the role you wish to control and mark the relevant users as eligible for that role.

   B) Purchase a P2 license for each user who needs to use a privileged role. Activate PIM. In the Active Directory management blade, edit the role you wish to control and mark the relevant users as eligible for that role.

   C) Purchase a P2 license for each authorizing user. Activate PIM. In the Active Directory management blade, edit the role you wish to control and assign users as members of that role.

   D) Purchase a P2 license for each user who needs to use a privileged role. Activate PIM. In the Active Directory management blade, edit the role you wish to control and assign users as members of that role.

8. As part of your Azure platform, you need to ensure every resource group is created with a `CostCenter` tag, and that every resource in that group also applies that tag. How can you ensure tags are enforced at the resource group level and automatically applied at the resource level?

    A) Create an Azure policy with a `DeployIfNotExists` setting to automatically apply a default `CostCenter` tag when creating resources.

    B) Create an Azure policy with a `DeployIfNotExists` setting to automatically apply a default `CostCenter` tag when creating resource groups.

    C) Create an Azure policy with a `Deny` setting to prevent resources being created without a `CostCenter` tag.

    D) Create an Azure policy with a `Deny` setting to prevent resource groups being created without a `CostCenter` tag, and another policy with a `DeployIfNotExists` setting to automatically apply the same tag to each resource in that resource group.

9. Your application development team needs to provide secure credentials as part of their application. Ideally, the developers will not know what those credentials are. What technologies can you suggest to achieve this?

    A) Store dummy credentials in a `web.config` file. Update the settings as part of a deployment pipeline.

    B) Store dummy credentials in a `web.config` file. Update the settings in the Web App settings blade in the Azure portal.

    C) Store the actual credentials in a Key Vault secret and have the developers build the code to pull credentials from the Key Vault.

    D) Store dummy credentials in a Key Vault secret and have the developers build the code to pull credentials from the key vault. Update the settings as part of a deployment pipeline.

10. To further tighten security an application owner wants to restrict access to secrets within Azure Key Vault so that a Web App can seamlessly access it without needing to be provided with an access key for the vault. How might you achieve this?

    A) Create an access policy on the Key Vault that allows secrets read access to the Web App. Modify the Web App code to pull the secret from the Key Vault without the need to authenticate.

B) Configure the Web App to use a system-assigned identity. Create an access policy on the Key Vault that allows secrets read access to the Web App. Modify the Web App code to pull the secret from the Key Vault without the need to authenticate.

C) Configure the Web App to use a user-assigned identity. Create an access policy on the Key Vault that allows secrets read access to the Web App. Modify the Web App code to pull the secret from the Key Vault without the need to authenticate.

D) Configure the Web App to use a system-assigned identity. Create an access policy on the Key Vault that allows secrets read access to the Web App. Modify the Web App code to authenticate against the Key Vault using **AzureServiceTokenProvider**.

11. You have developed an ASP.NET application that runs on a Web App within Azure. You need to provide secure access to the application for internal users, as well as for external users of other organizations who already use Azure or Office 365. How could you achieve this?

A) Register your Web App with Azure AD. Invite external users to your AD as guest users and then grant access.

B) Register your Web App with Azure AD. Configure your application to allow users with external email addresses.

C) Register your Web App with Azure AD. Create a B2C tenant. Grant access to users using their external email addresses.

D) Register your Web App with Azure AD. Configure your application to use the Google **Identity Provider (IdP)**.

12. You have several applications that use SQL databases. Each application has different usage patterns and therefore requires more performance from the database at different times of the day or week. Choose a database strategy that makes the most efficient use of resources.

A) Create individual databases for each application and size the databases according to peak usage.

B) Create individual databases for each application and place them in an elastic pool.

C) Create individual databases and resize them to fit usage patterns.

D) Create a single database that can accommodate all applications and set the size according to peak demand.

13. You have an application that outputs raw data to CSV files every evening. You have a separate database that amalgamates the raw data for reporting. Choose a solution that will automatically ingest that data into the database.

   A) Configure the application to output the data to a Data Analytics storage account. Use Azure Data Factory to create a data pipeline that imports the data from the data lake and stores it in a SQL database. Set a trigger on the pipeline to activate whenever new data is uploaded.

   B) Re-write the application to output the data to the SQL database.

   C) Configure the application to output the data to a Data Analytics storage account. Build a custom Azure Functions app that monitors for new files and uploads them to the SQL database.

   D) Configure the application to output the data to a Data Analytics storage account. Use Azure Databricks to create a data pipeline that imports the data from the data lake and stores it in a SQL database.

   E) Create a single database that can accommodate all applications and set the size according to peak demand.

14. You have an application that generates customer contracts. Contracts are only valid for 12 months, however, they must be retained for legal reasons for 7 years, but then they must be deleted. Choose an efficient archiving mechanism for those contracts.

   A) Store the contracts in a GP V2 storage account set to the archive tier.

   B) Store the contracts in a GP V2 storage account set to the cool tier.

   C) Store the contracts in a GP V2 storage account set to the hot tier. Create a life cycle policy that moves files older than 12 months from the hot tier to the archive tier. Create another life cycle policy to delete documents that are older than 7 years.

   D) Store the contracts in a GP V2 storage account set to the hot tier. Create a life cycle policy that moves files older than 12 months from the hot tier to the cool tier. Create another life cycle policy to delete documents that are older than 7 years.

15. You need to design a backup solution for a business-critical application that runs on VMs. The business owner has specified a **Recovery Point Objective (RPO)** of 30 minutes and a **Recovery Time Objective (RTO)** of 4 hours. Which of the following options would best suit these requirements?

    A) Use Azure Backup. Create a daily backup job and set the retention period to 31 days. Ensure cross-region recovery is enabled.

    B) Use Azure Backup. Create a daily backup job and set the retention period to 7 days. Ensure backups use a GRS-enabled storage account.

    C) Use Azure Backup with disk snapshots. Create a daily backup job and set the retention period to 7 days. Create an automation account to take snapshots every hour. Ensure cross-region recovery is enabled.

    D) Use Azure Site Recovery to replicate data between two regions.

16. You need to store data for your application and that data must be highly available so that if a region fails you can still read the data in it. Which options would be the most cost efficient?

    A) Configure your storage account with RA-GRS.

    B) Configure your storage account with GRS.

    C) Configure your storage account with ZRS.

    D) Configure your storage account with LRS.

17. You have a business-critical web app that uses a SQL database. Currently, the application and database only exist in a single region, however, the business wishes to extend the solution across an additional region for both resiliency and to increase performance in the other region. How might you extend the existing application's database to accommodate the new business requirements?

    A) Set up a new Azure SQL Database server in the paired region with geo-replication on the database. Configure each web app to one of the SQL server endpoints.

    B) Set up a new Azure SQL Database server in the paired region with geo-replication on the database. Create a failover group across the two servers. Configure each web app to one of the SQL server endpoints.

    C) Set up a new Azure SQL Database server in the paired region with geo-replication on the database. Create a failover group across the two servers. Configure your web app to use the read/write listener endpoint.

D) Set up a new Azure SQL Database server in the paired region with geo-replication on the database. Create a failover group across the two servers. Configure your web app to use the read-only listener endpoint.

18. Your application development team has built a new ASP.NET web application that they want to host in Azure. Usage will be variable with high and low usage peaks through the day, however, this is unpredictable. Choose an efficient solution to ensure performance at minimal cost.

A) Configure the web app with autoscaling enabled. Set the scale rule to add more instances at specific times of the day.

B) Configure the web app with autoscaling enabled. Create a scale rule to add more instances when the average CPU usage is at or above 80% for more than 10 minutes. Create another scale rule to remove an instance if CPU usage is less than 30% for more than 10 minutes.

C) Configure the web app with autoscaling enabled. Create a scale rule to add more instances when the average CPU usage is 80% for more than 10 minutes.

D) Create a high-spec App Service plan that can accommodate the peak usage.

19. You have a Web App that connects to an Azure SQL database. The database needs to be locked down to only allow traffic from the Web App. How might you achieve this?

A) Create your Web App with an internal IP address. Open the SQL server's firewall to allow access from that IP address.

B) Create a Web App and make note of its public IP. Open the SQL server's firewall to allow access from that IP address.

C) Create a Web App and enable VNET integration. In the SQL server's firewall blade, allow access from the VNET/subnet that the Web App is connected to.

D) Create a Web App and enable VNET integration. Open the SQL server's firewall and set **Allow Azure services and resources to access this server** to **Yes**.

20. Your company wants to ensure that all traffic into and out of your Azure solutions goes through a firewall. What option might be the most efficient way of achieving this?

A) Create an Azure Firewall instance in each subscription. Create a routing table in each subscription to route traffic through it.

B) Create an Azure Firewall instance in each subscription. Create a network security group that only allows traffic through the firewall.

C) Create an Azure Firewall instance in a central subscription. Peer the VNET that contains the firewall to all other VNETs in your solutions in a hub-and-spoke model. Create a network security group that only allows traffic through the firewall.

D) Create an Azure Firewall instance in a central subscription. Peer the VNET that contains the firewall to all other VNETs in your solutions in a hub-and-spoke model. Create routing tables in each subscription to route traffic through the peered VNET.

21. You have an Azure SQL database in a subscription and a VPN from your on-premises network into Azure. You need to allow access to the Azure SQL database from your corporate LAN to the database. How might you achieve this?

A) Connect the Azure SQL database to the VPN gateway subnet, which will route traffic through.

B) Create a Private Link IP and attach it to the SQL database. This will provide an internally routable IP address.

C) In the Azure SQL database's firewall blade, create a rule that allows traffic from your internal IP ranges.

D) In the Azure SQL database's firewall blade, create a rule that allows traffic from your internal network's public IP ranges.

22. You have four VMs in a solution that run as a web farm. You wish to assign a public IP address to that web farm; how can you achieve this?

A) Create an external load balancer with a public IP address. Set the VMs as backend targets.

B) Create an internal load balancer. Create a public IP address and assign it to the load balancer. Set the VMs as backend targets.

C) Create a public IP address and assign it to all four VMs.

D) Create all four VMs with public IP addresses, and set up round-robin DNS with your DNS provider.

23. You have developed a series of individually hosted web APIs that you want to expose internally to your other systems. You need a solution to help manage and secure your endpoints. The solution must scale across regions and support a lot of traffic. How might you achieve this?

A) Create an API gateway on the Developer tier and enable VNET integration.

B) Create an API gateway on the Standard tier and enable VNET integration.

C) Create an API gateway on the Premium tier and enable VNET integration.

D) Create an API gateway on the Consumption tier and enable VNET integration.

24. You are building a new order processing solution in Azure using a queuing mechanism. You need to be able to route messages to different regions (US and Europe). Messages must be processed in order. Which option would be the most efficient?

A) Create an Azure service bus. Create Azure functions in each region that subscribe to Service Bus topics filtered for messages bound for that region.

B) Create an Azure service bus. Create Azure functions in each region that subscribe to all service bus topics.

C) Create an Azure storage queue. Create Azure functions in each region that pull messages from the queue.

D) Create an Azure storage queue. Create Azure functions in each region that pull filtered messages bound for that region.

25. You are building a new database application that handles very sensitive **Personally Identifiable Information (PII)** data. The business wants to ensure that high levels of encryption are used, and they also need to have control over any encryption keys. What options can you employ?

A) Data on Azure SQL Database is encrypted at rest and no further configuration is required.

B) Activate **Transparent Data Encryption (TDE)** on the database. Configure the application's connection string with `Encrypt=True`.

C) Activate TDE on the database. Configure TDE to use customer-managed keys and store those keys in Azure Key Vault. Configure the application's connection string with `Encrypt=True`.

D) Activate TDE on the database. Configure TDE to use customer-managed keys and store those keys in Azure Key Vault. You do not need to modify application connection strings as connections to SQL databases are always encrypted.

Mock Answers

1. C) On each subscription, set an individual monthly budget and an alert that will notify the owner when 80% of the budget is reached.

    Cost alerts and budgets are a great way to alert owners when they are nearing set thresholds so that they can decide how to proceed.

2. B) Configure your subscriptions to send diagnostics logs to a Log Analytics workspace. Configure the workspace with 180-days retention.

    The Azure activities are only retained for 90 days. You could also send logs to a storage account; however, using a Log Analytics workspace enables full querying with the Kusto query language.

3. A) Create an action group with the email address(es) of your administrators. Create an alert to trigger the action group when the CPU hits 100%.

    Although you could technically have an alert trigger a logic app, the built-in functionality of using action groups would be the simplest option.

4. C) Purchase a P1 AD license for every user in your organization who you wish to be protected with Conditional Access. Then define a policy that only enforces MFA for specific signals.

    Conditional Access enables you to define specific triggers, such as IP location or users deemed at risk, and then implement additional layers of security such as MFA. You need a license for every user who you with to protect with a policy.

5. D) Enable **Password Hash Synchronization**. Because a hash of a hash of the user's password is stored within Azure, any loss of connectivity means users can still authenticate RBAC and management groups.

    Password Hash Synchronization stores the password in the cloud and therefore always uses those details when authenticating users. This can be used with AD Pass-through Authentication as well, which authenticates users to the on-premises databases but also provides a fallback option if there are connectivity issues.

6. B) Create a management group structure for each country then department and assign owner-level access for each country's IT department to the country level, and Contributor-level access to the department level.

    Using management groups, you can define hierarchical levels of access; however, as each level of access flows down, you need to ensure you set the lowest level of access at the lowest tiers.

7. B) Purchase a P2 license for each user who needs to use a privileged role. Activate **Privileged Identity Management** (**PIM**). In the Active Directory management blade, edit the role you wish to control and mark the relevant users as **Eligible** for that role.

    Using PIM, you need P2 licenses for approvers and users marked as eligible for that role.

8. D) Create an Azure policy with a `Deny` setting to prevent resources groups from being created without a `CostCenter` tag, and another policy with a `DeployIfNotExists` setting to automatically apply the same tag to each resource with that resource group.

    Azure policies can be used with tags to either enforce them or inherit them as required.

9. C) Store the actual credentials in a Key Vault secret and have the developers build the code to pull credentials from the key vault.

    Azure Key Vault enables you to store and manage access to your keys and secrets. In this way, secure information such as credentials can be stored and developers pull those credentials as part of their code. In this way, they never see the actual secrets used.

10. D) Configure the web app to use a system-assigned identity. Create an access policy on the key vault that allows read access to secrets to the web app. Modify the web app code to authenticate against the key vault using `AzureServiceTokenProvider`.

    Managed identities allow you to authenticate against services without the need to provide a username and password; however, your application code must be built to use the service.

11. A) Register your web app with Azure Active Directory. Invite external users to your Active Directory as guest users and then grant access.

    Inviting users as guest users using B2B integration is the simplest and easiest option for users who already have user accounts with Microsoft Azure or Office 365.

12. B) Create individual databases for each application and place them in an elastic pool.

    Elastic pools are great for dynamically sharing resources between databases.

13. A) Configure the application to output the data to a Data Lake Analytic storage account. Use Azure Data Factory to create a data pipeline that imports the data from the data lake and stores it in a SQL database. Set a trigger on the pipeline to activate whenever new data is uploaded.

    Although the other options are technically possible, Azure Data Factory is the quickest and easiest way to create automated data flows.

14. C) Store the contracts in a GP V2 storage account set to a hot tier. Create a life cycle policy that moves files older than 12 months from the hot tier to the archive tier. Create another life cycle policy to delete documents that are older than 7 years.

    The archive tier is the cheapest option for long-term storage.

15. D) Use Azure Site Recovery to replicate data between two regions.

    When you need to always have an up-to-date copy of your application and data, Azure Site Recovery is the best solution as it continually replicates data to a pair region and failover is relatively fast.

16. A) Configure your storage account with RA-GRS.

    Although GRS would also provide high availability across regions, RA-GRS would be more cost-efficient given that you only need to be able to read data in the paired region.

17. C) Set up a new Azure SQL Database server in the paired region with geo-replication on the database. Create a failover group across the two servers. Configure your web app to use the read/write listener endpoint.

    Using geo-replication on its own will provide a copy of your database in the secondary region; however, if the primary fails, an automatic failover does not occur. Therefore, you also need to set up a failover group. Configuring your services to use the read/write listener will ensure that if a failover does occur, services will automatically be sent to the health node.

18. B) Configure the web app with auto scaling enabled. Create a scale rule to add more instances when the average CPU usage is 80% for more than 10 minutes. Create another scale rule to remove an instance if CPU usage is less than 30% for more than 10 minutes.

    Auto scaling on web apps is a great way to be efficient with costs but ensure performance as demand increases. Scaling based on CPU enables you to perform this scaling as demand increases or reduce as demand decreases.

19. C) Create a web app and enable VNET integration. Open the SQL database's firewall to allow access from the VNET/subnet that the web app is connected to.

    This is called a service endpoint, and creates a direct, internal connection between the web app and the SQL database.

20. D) Create an Azure firewall in a central subscription. Peer the VNET that contains the firewall to all other VNETs in your solutions in a hub and spoke model. Create routing tables in each subscription to route traffic through it.

    The most efficient way to utilize an Azure firewall, from a cost and management perspective, is to create a hub and spoke model and control the flow of traffic using custom route tables.

21. B) Create a Private Link IP and attach it to the SQL database. This will provide an internally routable IP address.

    The Private Link IP allows you to connect to your SQL database on ranges addressable by your internal network and therefore route traffic over a VPN or ExpressRoute connection.

22. A) Create an external load balancer with a public IP address. Set the VMs as backend targets.

    You can create internal or external load balancers that can be configured to balance traffic between backend targets. External load balancers are specifically external connectivity.

23. C) Create an API gateway on the premium tier, enable VNET integration.

    The developer, basic, standard, and consumption tiers do not support multi-region deployments or VNET integration. The premium tier is the only option when you need multi-region deployments or VNET integration.

24. A) Create an Azure service bus. Create Azure functions in each region that subscribe to service bus topics filtered for messages bound for that region.

Azure Storage queues don't guarantee the order of messages. Azure Service Bus messages can use filters when other services subscribe to them.

25. D) Activate TDE on the database. Configure TDE to use customer-managed keys and store those keys in an Azure key vault. You do not need to modify application connection strings as connections to SQL databases are always encrypted.

Using customer-managed keys is the preferred method when using TDE, especially for secure applications. When connecting to databases in Azure, `Encrypt=True` is ignored and connections always use encryption.

Assessments

Chapter 3

We should consider which technologies to use for performing authentication. Because the customer needs a resilient system that would not be affected by communications outages, PHS would be a good choice because it does not require an always-on connection between the two environments.

For two-factor authentication, we should enable MFA but with a defined IP range for Mega Corp's networks to prevent prompts when signing in from an office. We would also enable Seamless SSO to remove any credential prompts when accessing Azure apps from these locations.

This example scenario highlights how you can use the different authentication tools in Azure to meet different requirements; however, the presented solution is only one possible option.

Chapter 4

Management groups are a great way of granting roles to users in a hierarchical manner that fits a company's geographical or divisional structure. In this scenario, the Global Administrator role would be set at the root tenant-level; however, for each region, a nominated administrator account could be set as Owner that only applied to a geographic management group.

Further service line groups could then be set within each country where the Owner Azure Role could be set on nominated IT Champions. The structure would look as follows:

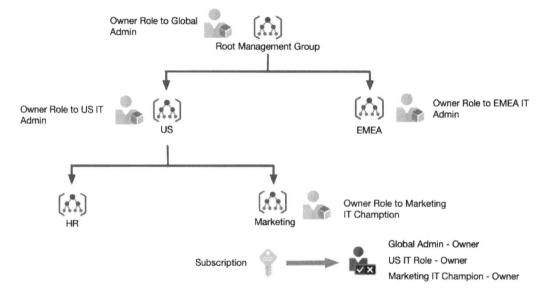

Example RBAC hierarchy

To apply the least privileged principle, AD Manager roles (such as User Administrator) would be assigned to users as an eligible role, with the IT Champion set as the approver. Yearly access reviews would also be applied to these roles.

Create risk policies that deny access should a score of high be met, and a separate policy to force a password change on medium and above.

Finally, to support these actions, P2 Licenses would be required for the administrative roles.

Chapter 5

Azure policies are the best way to ensure resources are configured as you need. The use of virtual machine guest policies, in particular, can help govern the operating system's configuration.

To support this, all virtual machines must have the guest extension installed and the following built-in guest policies applied at the relevant management group:

- Windows machines should meet requirements for Windows Firewall Properties
- Audit Windows machines that are not joined to the specified domain

The policy compliance dashboard can be used to report on non-compliant resources.

To enforce tagging, create a tagging initiative with the following built-in policies:

- Require a tag on resource groups
- Inherit a tag from the resource group if missing

Finally, to enforce the VNet, network security group, and storage account on every subscription, create an Azure blueprint with the VNet and network security group added, and a separate blueprint for the storage account.

Assign the VNet/network security group blueprint to the relevant management group and ensure the lock assignment is set to **Read Only**.

Assign the blueprint to the relevant management group and ensure the lock assignment is set to **Do Not Delete**.

Chapter 6

The example scenario can be broken down into three main requirements:

- **Protection of connection strings**

  To protect connection strings, we can use a key vault to store the connection strings as secrets. We can then use a user-assigned managed identity on any web or API app that needs the connection string, along with an access policy that allows that identity to read the secret. The apps themselves will need to be written with this in mind by using the appropriate NuGet packages.

- **Customer-provided keys for storage encryption**

  Generate and store a key in a key vault. Configure the storage account to use that key as a customer-managed key instead of the Microsoft-managed key.

- **An authentication mechanism that supports N-tier and distributed systems**

  Create an app registration for your app and enable ID tokens. On each of the apps, configure them to use Microsoft Active Directory in the authentication/ authorization blade and choose the app registration you created. Set the action to take when the request is not authenticated to log in with Azure Active Directory.

Chapter 7

There are many different options available for build services in Azure; however, we can focus on a few key elements from the requirements:

- This is a new application.

- The use of smaller services rather than a monolithic application.

- The development team is used to building websites with .NET but would like to start using containers.

- The HR team wishes to be able to amend components.

Building the solution as smaller services rather than a single monolithic solution, and the fact that this is an entirely new system, means we can use more modern components. Therefore, we don't need to worry about compatibility. This would suggest either Web Apps or Azure Functions.

However, as the development team wants to move towards containerization but is more used to building traditional .NET websites, Web Apps for containers might be a good solution.

Much of the solution is based on a document approval workflow. Therefore, a workflow creation tool such as Logic Apps may be a good suggestion. However, the HR department needs to be able to change workflows, meaning Power Automate could be better suited, with the development team creating the required plugins where necessary.

Chapter 8

One potential solution to the MegaCorp Inc. requirements would be to use an ExpressRoute connection into Azure as this helps provide a stable but resilient connection.

To control internet traffic from solutions built in Azure, Azure Firewall could be built on a central VNET that all other VNETs will be peered to. That VNET can also contain the ExpressRoute's gateway VNET. In other words, a hub-spoke model will be used.

Each peered VNET will have two custom routes set up. One route will send traffic for on-premises IP ranges to the ExpressRoute gateway subnet and the other route will send other traffic to the central firewall's IP address.

NSGs will be set to allow outbound HTTPS and HTTP traffic to the firewall VNET and standard ports for DNS resolution to on-premises DNS servers. VNETs will be set up to use on-premises DNS servers as the primary servers with the Azure DNS (`168.63.129.16`) as the secondary.

Chapter 9

First, you must consider which storage solutions are best suited to the different types of data. An Azure SQL database seems like the right choice for the day-to-day interactive data, but the generated PDF quotes would be better stored in an Azure Storage account.

As transactions will not be high, a GPv2 account set as a Hot access tier would offer adequate performance, with documents stored in blob containers. ZRS should be enabled on the storage account to protect against a zone failure.

A second storage account set as an Archive access tier should also be created to store quotes older than 6 months. The main storage account will have a life cycle management set up to move documents that have not been accessed for 6 months to the archive account. LRS will be sufficient for this storage account.

Chapter 10

One of the first points to consider when planning any migration are the business drivers, and in this case, the main requirement is that you must be able to migrate workloads in a short space of time with a hard deadline. Therefore, opting for a lift-and-shift approach is possibly the safest route.

As there are many inter-dependencies between systems, the as-is architecture needs to be fully understood. Using Azure Migrate, combined with business owners' discussions and collating existing documentation, will help in this task.

Enabling the Service Map feature of an Azure Log Analytics workspace will involve some work upfront to install the necessary agents on VMs. However, the end report will provide greater clarity on interdependent services and substantially reduce risk when the migration occurs.

The **DMA** tool will also help you understand any potential problems of moving databases, which will help you define the database migration strategy.

Finally, once the migration is complete, regularly check Azure Advisor to ensure the new platform runs optimally.

Chapter 11

There are many components to consider when designing the solution for MegaCorp. However, the key points to address are as follows:

- The customer-facing website will be hosted centrally.

- Updates must be validated before going live to ensure there is no disruption.

- Serverless options should be used where possible to keep costs low but with the ability to scale.

- APIs and microservices are desired patterns.

- A message queuing system that enables messages to be routed to different backend systems for local processing is required.

With these in mind, the following solution could be a good fit.

Use Azure app services for the frontend user interface and use deployment slots to test updates against live backend systems before go-live.

Use Azure app services to build APIs and use an API gateway to control and manage access to them. As serverless options are desired, use the Consumption plan for the API gateway.

When orders are placed, an API will write a message to Azure Service Bus, configured to use topics and subscriptions. Backend Azure functions can be used, hosted in the US, Europe, and India; each will subscribe to a topic with filtering applied, so they only collect orders for their region. The following diagram provides a high-level conceptual view:

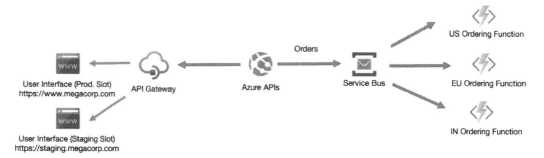

MegaCorp potential solution

Chapter 12

The first question to answer when designing a database solution is: What type of database do we need—SQL or NoSQL? The requirements state that the data will be highly relational, meaning it will be built from multiple tables that are linked, and that the integrity of that data is essential. This scenario makes Azure SQL Database and Azure SQL Managed Instance the best choice.

The next requirement is to keep costs low initially but be able to scale up as the platform grows. Azure SQL Database, using the Hyperscale tier, is the best option here as data and processing are separate and individually scalable. As growth will be controlled and managed by the team, dynamic scaling, such as that provided by the Serverless tier, is not required.

Finally, the Hyperscale tier supports creating multiple read-only replicas. A read-only replica can therefore be used for the reporting side of the solution, which will remove any potential performance impact on the primary read/write database, which will be used by the e-commerce website.

Chapter 13

The first aspect to consider for a data analytics solution is where data will be imported from. The sales data is already being stored in a database that can be interrogated directly. The marketing data is being stored as CSV files, and therefore ADLS Gen2 would make an excellent choice for holding these files.

Next, Azure Data Factory can ingest and combine the data into a single output, which can then be stored back in the ADLS.

Finally, Azure Databricks could be the best option for modeling and analyzing the data using optimized Spark clusters. Azure Databricks also supports the latest version of Spark.

The following diagram shows what this might look like:

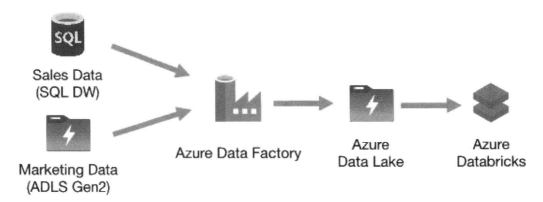

Example data pipeline using multiple technologies

Chapter 14

The first step to consider in this scenario is that the application code needs to run on traditional VMs. Presently, there are only two VMs that are overloaded at busy periods but underutilized at quiet periods. VM scale sets would be an ideal choice because the application can be built using an image and then configured to scale in and out, adding and removing nodes in response to demand.

Next, to provide the best performance in each country, the application could be duplicated in different Azure regions, for example, East US, East Asia, and West Europe.

As the development team has already confirmed, they could migrate the application to Cosmos DB; this would be a great move as Cosmos DB can be globally distributed with multi-region writes. Therefore, replicas of the database could be created in each of the Azure regions with read/write capabilities. This would ensure there is as little latency as possible for customers in each region.

As a local view of stock levels and processing is more important than a global reporting view, the **eventual consistency model** would be best. It ensures maximum performance on the local replica while still ensuring all replicas are kept in sync for reporting.

Chapter 15

The first consideration in our monitoring solution is which additional products, over and above the basic monitoring and logging, we will use. The ability to monitor for threats can be achieved using Azure Defender; however, if we want to be able to better respond to these threats, especially in an automated fashion, we require an advanced SIEM such as Azure Sentinel.

Azure Sentinel requires a Log Analytics workspace for capturing logs and metrics, and therefore the next step is to decide how we would structure this. For example, do we use a single workspace or multiple workspaces?

As security and overall health monitoring are managed by a single team, the best option would be to use a single workspace. However, as each division is responsible for their own solutions, we should additionally send the logs they need to their own individual workspaces as well. This can be configured on each Azure component.

Finally, to help control costs on proof-of-concept systems, we should implement budgets and alerts on those subscriptions to limit and monitor spend.

Chapter 16

The first requirement to consider is the **Recovery Time Objective (RTO)**, which in this case is 24 hours. This provides adequate time to perform a restore of a VM using Azure Backup.

Next, we must consider how to ensure the **Recovery Point Object (RPO)** is met – in this scenario, this is stated as minimal; however, as the data that changes most regularly is in an Azure SQL database, the standard SQL backup mechanism would meet our needs as transaction log backups are taken every 5-10 minutes.

Finally, monthly long-term backup retention should be configured on the SQL backups to keep each monthly backup for a 12-month period.

Chapter 17

As part of the overall solution, you could leverage Azure DevOps tooling as this is built specifically for development teams and aligns to agile and Scrum practices.

All code will be stored in a central repository for the project. A master branch will always contain fully working and tested code, and at the start of each sprint, two branches will be created for each team.

As developers work on tasks, they will create their own separate branch for their work, and once finished, they will create a pull request to have their individual code merged into the sprint branch. The senior developer on each team will review each pull request from the junior team members and approve as required, which will trigger a merge into the sprint branch.

At the end of the sprint, the individual sprint branches will be tested, validated, and then merged into the master branch prior to deployment.

The pipeline deployment will be built as YAML files as this allows the pipeline configuration and steps to be stored in code along with the main code base and therefore gives the benefit of code tracking and management features in Azure Repos.

Packt.com

Subscribe to our online digital library for full access to over 7,000 books and videos, as well as industry leading tools to help you plan your personal development and advance your career. For more information, please visit our website.

Why subscribe?

- Spend less time learning and more time coding with practical eBooks and Videos from over 4,000 industry professionals

- Improve your learning with Skill Plans built especially for you

- Get a free eBook or video every month

- Fully searchable for easy access to vital information

- Copy and paste, print, and bookmark content

Did you know that Packt offers eBook versions of every book published, with PDF and ePub files available? You can upgrade to the eBook version at packt.com and as a print book customer, you are entitled to a discount on the eBook copy. Get in touch with us at customercare@packtpub.com for more details.

At www.packt.com, you can also read a collection of free technical articles, sign up for a range of free newsletters, and receive exclusive discounts and offers on Packt books and eBooks.

Other Books You May Enjoy

If you enjoyed this book, you may be interested in these other books by Packt:

Implementing Microsoft Azure Architect Technologies: AZ-303 Exam Prep and Beyond – Second Edition

Brett Hargreaves and Sjoukje Zaal

ISBN: 978-1-80056-857-0

- Manage Azure subscriptions and resources
- Ensure governance and compliance with policies, roles, and blueprints
- Build, migrate, and protect servers in Azure
- Configure, monitor, and troubleshoot virtual networks
- Manage Azure AD and implement multi-factor authentication

- Configure hybrid integration with Azure AD Connect
- Find out how you can monitor costs, performance, and security
- Develop solutions that use Cosmos DB and Azure SQL Database

Azure for Architects – Third Edition

Ritesh Modi, Jack Lee, and Rithin Skaria

ISBN: 978-1-83921-586-5

- Understand the components of the Azure cloud platform
- Use cloud design patterns
- Use enterprise security guidelines for your Azure deployment
- Design and implement serverless and integration solutions
- Build efficient data solutions on Azure
- Understand container services on Azure

Packt is searching for authors like you

If you're interested in becoming an author for Packt, please visit `authors.packtpub.com` and apply today. We have worked with thousands of developers and tech professionals, just like you, to help them share their insight with the global tech community. You can make a general application, apply for a specific hot topic that we are recruiting an author for, or submit your own idea.

Leave a review - let other readers know what you think

Please share your thoughts on this book with others by leaving a review on the site that you bought it from. If you purchased the book from Amazon, please leave us an honest review on this book's Amazon page. This is vital so that other potential readers can see and use your unbiased opinion to make purchasing decisions, we can understand what our customers think about our products, and our authors can see your feedback on the title that they have worked with Packt to create. It will only take a few minutes of your time, but is valuable to other potential customers, our authors, and Packt. Thank you!

Index

M

N

Printed in Great Britain
by Amazon